AGRARIAN CHANGE AND IMPERFECT PROPERTY

RURAL HISTORY IN EUROPE 15

THE SERIES RURAL HISTORY IN EUROPE

The countryside forms a complex and evolving universe. Clearly, it exhibits both inertia and ruptures, but it would be an illusion to contrast a contemporary rural world in rapid transformation with a traditional rural world of frozen landscapes, petrified societies, immobile economies and lethargic political contexts. Even if rural societies have been overthrown, rural landscapes have been profoundly transformed and the intervention of the State has considerably strengthened the regulation of production and trade, history must of necessity be considered as the main explanatory factor for our time.

The rural world can also only be fully understood if it is viewed in a manner which transcends national boundaries and if the discrepancies which can best be observed by adopting a broad view are taken into account. The aim must be to create a dialogue between researchers which goes beyond national frontiers, crosses chronological barriers and breaks disciplinary boundaries.

The main objective of the 'Rural History in Europe' collection is thus to provide keys to unlock the changes experienced by present-day European rural societies in the light of their historical experience. It will produce the necessary historical knowledge to make it possible for all to conceptualise the future of European country-dwellers as they face problems of the kind historians have always grappled with in examining societies of the past. How can the changes taking place in present-day Europe be understood without taking into account a past which is still very present, and which determines both structures and behaviour?

The volumes will be published after a peer-review process for each paper, supported by the editorial board, the authors and the editors of each book. In order to ask the relevant questions about the future of the peasantries and rural spaces in transformation, the volumes of this collection will deal with the longue durée and will present either research in progress or a synthesis on a regional or national scale. The outcome of this procedure will be a series giving a detailed overview of historical developments in Europe as a whole.

Agrarian Change and Imperfect Property

Emphyteusis in Europe (16th to 19th centuries)

Edited by

ROSA CONGOST & PABLO F. LUNA

BREPOLS

This publication came into existence thanks to the funding of the Spanish Ministry for Science and Innovation (Ministerio de Ciencia e Innovación) through research projects HAR2011-25077 and HAR2014-54891-P, the Government of Catalonia through ICREA Academy Program and the GDR (Groupe de Recherches of the CNRS) 2912, Histoire des Campagnes Européennes.

We are grateful to Judith Le Goff, Julie Marfany and Elizabeth Comuzzi, who edited the English versions of the papers.

Cover: Catherine Wernette, *Vignes en Languedoc-Roussillon*, 2011

© D/2018/0095/156
ISBN 978-2-503-57923-8
e-ISBN 978-2-503-57924-5
DOI 10.1484/M.RURHE-EB.5.114897
ISSN 2032-6084
eISSN 2566-0063

Printed in the EU on acid free paper.

Contents

List of Contributors

Efi Argyrou	Open University of Greece Greece
Michela Barbot	École normale supérieure de Cachan France
Gérard Béaur	CNRS & EHESS, Paris France
Michel Boehler	Université de Strasbourg France
Fabrice Boudjaaba	CNRS, Paris France
Benedita Camara	Universidade da Madeira Portugal
Giorgio Chittolini	Università degli Studi di Milano Italy
Rosa Congost	Universitat de Girona Spain
Llorenç Ferrer-Alòs	Universitat de Barcelona Spain
Pere Gifre	Universitat de Girona Spain
Gabriel Jover Avellà	Universitat de Girona Spain
Sevasti Lazari	Open University of Greece Greece
Pablo F. Luna	Sorbonne Universités & CRH, Paris France
Belén Moreno Claverías	Universidad Autónoma de Madrid Spain
Antònia Morey Tous	Universitat de les Illes Balears Spain
Pegerto Saavedra	Universidade de Santiago de Compostela Spain
Enric Saguer	Universitat de Girona Spain
Eleftheria Zei	University of Crete Greece

List of Figures

List of Tables

GÉRARD BÉAUR, ROSA CONGOST,
PABLO F. LUNA

1. Emphyteusis: A Practical Question?

Emphyteusis: what's in a name? It has been many years since this question was first asked in an article by the historian of Spanish law Bartolomé Clavero (1986)[1]. Nonetheless, it is likely that many historians, including historians of agrarian Europe, do not know exactly what it means. Even historians who are familiar with the term may react in different ways to the appearance of an entire volume dedicated to this issue, although some specialists have already attempted this in the field of urban history (Faron & Hubert, 1995). The present book focuses on emphyteusis in the early modern period. This allows us not only to emphasise the historical roots of this form of property rights by going back to the ancient and medieval origins of many of the contracts studied, but also their relevance for the present day[2]. Moreover, this study highlights the different stakes held by various social actors in their particular contexts, contexts in which the memory of past dispossessions and hopes of future appropriation may be very much alive.

To focus on emphyteusis is to draw attention to one of the possible contractual forms by which agrarian structures and systems of cultivation were transformed. Although historians have devoted considerable attention to short-term contracts as a means of extracting value from the land, they have been less forthcoming on long-term contracts, except during periods of reconstruction or expansion, such as the Middle Ages and the beginning of the modern era. The emergence of tenant farming and its uses have been the subject of much debate, as has the persistence or the supposedly archaic character of sharecropping and all types of contract involving shares of the harvest. By contrast, much less has been said about of the uses, advantages and disadvantages of long-term contracts, as if emphyteusis were a survivor or an eccentricity left over from an earlier period. This interpretation can no longer be maintained.

Thus, though it concerns a form of contract widely seen as atypical, in a distant past, this study has wide implications for the present. It is the outcome of an international workshop organised in Girona by a French and Spanish committee, within the framework of the GDR 2912 of the CNRS and the

1 The article title translates literally as 'Emphyteusis, what's in a name?'.

2 For the legal debate on emphyteusis, see also Clavero (1986), Meynal (1908) and Piret (1937).

Agrarian Change and Imperfect Property, ed. by Rosa Congost and Pablo F. Luna, Rural History in Europe, 15 (Turnhout, 2018), 11-38

DOI 10.1484/M.RURHE-EB.5.116116

Centre de Recerca d'Història Rural of the University of Girona. We were able to review the nature of emphyteusis and the complicated relationship between this and other forms of contract, especially leases and sales, while still taking into account the variety of existing practices (Béaur, Arnoux & Varet-Vitu, 2003). In preparing this volume, we also tried to reflect upon the questions that are important to understand emphyteusis: the reasons why its actors considered it to be a success, the reasons for conflict that it might generate, and finally its role in the development of the agrarian economy.

I. Trying to define emphyteusis

I.1 Historical and contemporary perspectives on emphyteusis

Much of the historiography on emphyteusis regards the practice in a negative light. For a long time, emphyteusis was classed as a feudal, medieval and backward remnant and considered an obstacle to the development of perfect property rights and hence economic progress. After the emergence and success of the idea of absolute property rights emphyteusis has shared in the opprobrium inflicted upon all forms of divided property rights. This was not always the dominant view, however (Congost, 2003; Luna, 2006). English commentators of the eighteenth century frequently used the contract as a means of contrasting Roman and common law. We find opposing points of view among British travellers in Spain. Arthur Young, despite spending only three weeks in Catalonia (in July 1787), did not approve of the smallholdings that he saw everywhere, and was vexed by the tangible material progress achieved by such holdings and by the Catalan region as a whole[3]. In contrast, Joseph Townsend, during his travels through Spain at the end of the eighteenth century, praised the effects of emphyteusis in Catalonia:

> To the power retained by them of making emfiteutic contracts, has with reason been attributed the cultivation of such waste lands as are most susceptible to tillage, and the constant increase of population. Industry has been promoted, new families have been called into existence, and many, rescued from poverty and wretchedness, are now maintained in comfortable affluence (Townsend, 1792: 332).

Nearer to our own time, Salvatore Jannelli also took a positive view of emphyteutic contracts and showed how this sort of contract had benefits for the land in the Kingdom of the Two Sicilies. He sees emphyteusis as a better choice, by comparison with the rigidity of ownership; it allowed land to circulate and be worked in an economic way, while limiting its use

---

3 See Luna (2012). For an overview of Young's travels and the relationship between the eighteenth-century Enlightenment and agriculture, see Jones (2016).

for speculative purposes. Thus emphyteusis provided a rent to the owner without depriving him of his land and also gave the emphyteutic tenant a long-term right over the land he worked. The two protagonists, the owner and the emphyteutic tenant, both profited from it, as did who knows how many other actors (Janelli, 1945; 11, 13).

Similar reflections can be found in a work considered to be one of the classics of European legal history, Henry Sumner Maine's 1864 work *Ancient Law*: 'the Emphyteusis, if we may so interpret the allusions to it in the *Corpus Juris*, became a favourite and beneficial modification of property; and it may be conjectured that wherever free farmers existed, it was this tenure which regulated their interest in the land (Maine, 1864)'. Some years later, 1883, the same author, closely following the arguments of Henry Doniol (Doniol, 1876), posed the following question on the origins of the French Revolution: 'Why did the Manor in its decay produce such different results in England and France? Why did its transformation end in one country in a revolution which is an epoch of history? Why, in another, in a somewhat inconvenient form of landed property?' In his response to these questions, Mayne assigned emphyteusis – here translated as copyhold – a central role: 'If I were to say the first French Revolution took place because a great part of the soil of France was held on Copyhold Tenure, the statement would doubtless sound like a paradox'[4].

Maine considered the position of the French peasant to be of great importance: 'But the French peasant holding by servile tenure, never compared himself with the farmers of the domain land of the nobles, who were a very special class, the *metayers*, not only hiring their land from the lord, but having it stocked by him. The peasant compared his lot with that of the nobles themselves, and bitterly chafed at the contrast'. Another English thinker, Edmund Burke, writing at the time of the French Revolution, had developed a similar idea: 'The leaders teach the people to abhor and reject all feudality as barbarism of tyranny, and then they tell them afterwards how much of that barbarous tyranny they are to bear with patience' (Burke, 1993: 223).

In 1843, Pépin-Lehalleur's history of emphyteusis presented the contract as a perpetual form of *censive*, typical of countries with written law codes before the French Revolution (Pépin-Lehalleur, 1843: 310). This author, like the French thinker Jean-Baptiste-Victor Proudhon, placed great importance on the law of 29 December 1790 (Proudhon, 1839: 320):

---

4 See MAINE, 1883 s.v. 'copyhold tenure' in David HEY (ed.), 1996: 'A form of customary tenure by which a tenant held a copy of the entry in the rolls of the manorial court baron which recorded his or her possession of a holding on agreed terms… Copyhold was abolished in 1922'. VENN (1933: 92) also equates emphyteusis with copyhold in his reflections on Italy: 'while referring to Italy it may be appropriate to mention that emphytéusis, or the granting of leases in perpetuity, or for very lengthy periods, is still practised. This is really copyhold'. See SCRIVEN (1896) and TURNER & BECKETT (1998), WILLIAMS (1901).

> In the past, emphyteutic leases were established in perpetuity, above all in the transfer of the dominium utile, which the tenants acquired in this way; but now, ever since the law of 29 December 1790, it is forbidden in France to draw up emphyteutic leases for a time longer than ninety-nine years. On this point, it is worth noting that the law only sets a term to the emphyteusis, without otherwise changing its character, and the nature of all its conditions except that of length and the inherent results of this abridgement, must still be defined according to the principles of the ancient law.

Outside France, we find the same identification of emphyteusis with censives at a much later date as, for example, in this extract from the Belgian economist Émile de Laveleye in 1874:

> Emphyteusis became a very common mode of tenure. The owner conceded to the farmer the hereditary enjoyment of a property against the payment of a canon, or annual due, and a fine to be paid if the property was transmitted. In emphyteusis and colonat or share-cropping, the double ownership typical of censive tenure can be seen; the suzerain retained dominium directum with the dues appertaining to it, while the farmer had the hereditary enjoyment (Laveleye, 1874: 115).

This author takes a particularly positive view of the possibilities of applying this contract in what were new countries at the time when he was writing: 'this is what Australia and the United States could do in the future, if they were to cede their land in emphyteusis, instead of selling it, as they do at the present' (Laveleye, 1874: 363).

I.2 Divided property and long-term contracts

The literature on emphyteusis and similar contracts does not fill many shelves and, with few exceptions, none of it is recent. Despite this, there are a certain number of works that show fairly precisely what emphyteutic practices looked like.

Thus we know, first, that it was a form of agrarian contract, of Ancient Greek origin, characterised by a split in property rights into two types which, under Roman law, came to be known as dominium directum and dominium utile (Meynal, 1908; Piret, 1937; Vilar, 1962; Feenstra, 1974; AAVV, 1986; Béaur and Chevet, 2013). According to nineteenth-century jurists, the Romans also distinguished three sorts of emphyteusis, according to the type of property concerned: public, ecclesiastical or individual. It seems that towns entrusted their property to individuals under a temporary or perpetual title, the rent being used for communal expenses (Dominici, 1845: 4).

The owner of the dominium directum was prepared (almost certainly less painfully than we might imagine nowadays) to separate out the use-rights to his property in order to transfer these to another (who held more than just the usufruct), so that the latter could 'exploit' it, in the economic sense or, more precisely, realise its value: the use of the word 'exploit' did not initially refer to planting e.g. with vines, as it did in Ancient Greece and would come to do later. In doing this, the original owner transferred the use-rights, retaining only the dominium directum or formal possession, which usually took the concrete form of an annual rent and/or the regular exercise of certain rights, for the duration of the contract. The transfer of the actual land surface was accompanied, however, by subtle distinctions between the ownership of the land and that of any buildings upon it, between the ownership of any plants and that of the land, between the use of land and the collection of fees, and so forth, not, for the moment, to mention the difference between ownership of the surface and ownership of land beneath it (foundations and basements) – a distinction often introduced at a later date by state or public authorities. There could also be subtle differences over whether or not the cultivator was obliged to plant certain crops or build certain types of edifice.

The content and titles of the different chapters in this book illustrate the difficulty of discussing one single type of emphyteusis, not just because practices varied across regions, but also because they could vary over time within the same region. It is therefore vital to clarify which contracts we have considered to be emphyteutic, particularly since we know that agrarian contracts take very different forms in lease, land, credit and labour markets (Béaur, 2003). For this reason, some emphyteutic contracts look much like sales, and others like leases, but in both cases, as has been mentioned, what defines emphyteusis is above all the existence, when the contract was signed, of shared rights in the same land.

Thus if emphyteusis is considered as a type of agrarian contract, it should be noted that it gave the holder the ability to dispose of the property. Emphyteutic contracts allowed the holder of the dominium utile to sell 'his' property and bequeath it as an inheritance. This aspect sets emphyteusis apart from other types of leasehold contracts, such as farming and share-cropping contracts, and is explained by the fact that these latter did not make a distinction between dominium directum and dominium utile. In the light of this, we may wonder about the effect of emphyteusis on the circulation of land and immovable property. How far and under what conditions did the payment due to the owner restrict, or, in Béaur's contrarian view, activate, the market?

The second characteristic of emphyteusis is the long-term nature of the contract. In most cases emphyteusis is defined as a perpetual or indefinite contract. This point is an important one, and this volume considers the different forms a perpetual contract could take. After the Revolution, contracts in France were no longer perpetual. Gerard Béaur recalls that the definition of emphyteusis enshrined in the French Civil Code referred to long-term contracts of between 18 and 99 years and no longer to perpetual ones which had been common during the Ancien Régime. For the revolutionaries, perpetual contracts were suspected of being carriers of a despised feudalism. Indeed, there were similarities between emphyteusis and other seigneurial contracts, such as the *bail à cens* and there was some confusion between the two, particularly in southern France, as has already been mentioned. In Boehler's studies of early modern Alsace, the emphyteutic contracts known here as *erblehn* and *hoflehn* were usually indefinite, and in practice could be considered perpetual. Of a similar nature were the Greek emphyteusis studied by Zei and by Efi Argyrou and Sevasti Lazari and the Italian *livelli* studied by Giorgio Chittolini and Michela Barbot.

Some long-term contracts could be considered perpetual in practice. This kind of situation could arise, for example, whenever a tenant, on quitting the land, had the right to claim for improvements made during his tenure. This right had no small influence on how both parties perceived the contract and is key to understanding many of the debates that arose concerning the need to acknowledge, in reality and in law, the many different ways that tenants could be said to have improved the land. As a result, this right to claim for improvements could open up a never-ending succession of conflicts. By contrast, when contracts were formally described as perpetual, the length of the contract could still be affected by the ease or otherwise with which certain penalties could be applied, such as the right to evict a tenant for non-payment of rent.

Also perpetual are the forms of emphyteusis described here for Catalonia by Rosa Congost, Pere Gifre and Enric Saguer and for Majorca by Gabriel Jover and Antonia Morey, chapters which introduce the rise of new forms of emphyteutic contracts in the eighteenth and nineteenth centuries. In the north of the Iberian peninsula, by contrast, the length of the *foros*, as emphyteutic contracts were known, was measured in lives, first of the tenants, then of kings, as Pegerto Saavedra and Pablo F. Luna show in their chapters on Galicia and Asturias respectively. The length of the specific form of contract known as the *rabassa morta*, again, a Catalan contract, studied here by Llorenç Ferrer and Belén Moreno, was determined by the life of the vines. Finally, in the case of the *colonia* contract in Madeira, studied by Benedicta Camara, it was the upholding of compensation for improvements that in turn supported the claim that such contracts were emphyteutic and, by extension, perpetual. This type of contract was very similar to the Breton *domaine congéable* which distinguished clearly between *superfices* and *edifices* and gave the owner the right to evict the tenant at any moment, as Gérard Béaur has stressed. In this case the contract made no mention of the transfer of use-rights but recognised the notion of improvements by the tenant, improvements which only applied, however, to specific types of property considered his own (plants and buildings), but not to the land itself (Sée, 1906; Jarnoux, 2013).

I.3 The central role of emphyteusis in the history of agrarian contracts

The aim of this work, therefore, is to show that emphyteusis has played a central role throughout history, and especially in the early modern period, in the organisation of rural and urban space in certain regions and that, contrary to popular belief, it continues to have an notable impact on property rights, albeit a subtle and often hidden effect. It may be argued, for example, that much land in London is held by emphyteutic lease, as are plots and gardens in southern France, garages, petrol stations and other buildings in Paris, the land and basements of convents and monasteries in Lima, or the old market of Parián in Mexico City[5]. In France, emphyteusis has recently been seriously envisaged as the most efficient way to return and restore the land expropriated to build the airport at Notre-Dame des Landes, near Nantes. Emphyteutic contracts are also found in Asia: the Japanese Civil Code recognises this type of contract (Hatoyama, 1902) and emphyteusis features in current projects of agrarian reform in China (Guo-ping He, Hou-qing Luo, 2016). Emphyteusis also exists in many African countries, both in former French and in former English colonies (Rubin and Cotran, 1970). Not all these contracts are described as emphyteutic, but they all share the characteristic of divided property rights common to long-term contracts, even now.

It is also clear that many European states passed laws regarding emphyteusis and similar forms of contract, reflecting what we might describe, at the end of the nineteenth century and at the beginning of the twentieth century, as the 'social function' of property rights, or what are termed in the USA 'a bundle of rights' (Congost and Santos, 2010; Congost, Gelman and Santos, 2016)[6]. Finally, in more recent times, the rush to seize land (land-grabbing in Africa, Asia and Latin America, but also in Eastern Europe) has opened up new territories to forms of emphyteusis. Many African states, for example, use a legal form of emphyteusis in order to lease out lands, but without the usual clauses – for example without sharecropping, entry fines, the obligation to improve the land or to build upon it; without a right to a fine if the land is sold, and without right of repurchase. These states abandon thousands of hectares, along with their inhabitants, their forests, their rivers, their animals and their customary rights, in return for derisory rents, for leases lasting up to 99 years, underbidding each other to the greater benefit of monopolists, not all of whom are Westerners by any means[7].

---

5 See, among others, Avila (2015); García Ruiz (2015); Luna (2014, 2017a).

6 Emphyteusis is not uncommon in this period, which falls outside the time frame we have set ourselves in this volume. Indeed, there was a flurry of works on the subject at this time: in France (Primois, 1904, Pugnière, 1904) after the law of 25 June 1902, on *Erbpacht* in Germany (Mitteis, 1901) and also on English copyholders (Scriven, 1896, Williams, 1901).

7 The activity of the Korean firm Daewoo in Madagascar in 2007-2008 is only the most visible example of numerous similar investments across Mali, Cameroon, Uganda, Ethiopia, Tanzania, and so on. Without exception, the price paid for such contracts has been derisory or non-existent – in the cases when contracts have actually been signed. Prices per hectare, when they have been set, have been very low; there have been instances of land concession bearing no fixed price or even no price at all. Local actors have been, and still are, excluded from the negotiation of these contracts (Luna, 2016).

Indeed, the need to analyse emphyteutic practices in the early modern period stems in part from the recognition that doing so may help explain the continuation of these practices up to the present day. In the first place, it is clear that liberal reforms did not put a stop to emphyteusis in many countries (Cárdenas, 2002; Saint-Joseph, 1956; Congost, 2000). Moreover, in some of the new states that emerged in nineteenth-century Latin America during the 'liberal revolutions' after 1825 and especially after 1850, emphyteusis became a particularly useful means for the transfer of 'national property', that is, property recovered from Spanish rule (notably Jesuit or Crown property), and also religious and lay property confiscated during the wars of independence from Spain (Teruel, 2015, Barsky and Gelman, 2009). Emphyteusis proved to be an elegant means of rewarding loyalty during the war, of creating new networks of patronage and of continuing to deprive indigenous communities of their property (Fandos and Teruel, 2012).

II. The practice of emphyteusis

II.1 The versatility of emphyteusis

A brief overview of the chapters in this volume also demonstrates that the combination of the two factors we are insisting upon – divided property rights and long-term contracts – had important repercussions on both the old feudal structures and on the emergence of new social groups. Important as it is to date the origins of emphyteutic contracts, it is even more important to analyse the changing social dynamics that resulted from them. These changes could lead to situations in which the holders of dominium utile achieved full property rights – for example, by converting emphyteutic contracts into fixed-term rents – or the reverse, the recognition of full property rights for the tenants, regardless of the clauses in the original contracts.

Both kinds of process are studied in this volume. Under certain conditions, the holders of dominium directum sought changes, often dedicating themselves wholeheartedly to the task. One example is the monasteries and convents of northern and central Spain, in Asturias and Galicia, though Pegerto Saavedra shows that this happened earlier in Galicia than in the 'Spanish Siberia' of Asturias described by Pablo F. Luna. Their researches show that these lords tried first to suppress the perpetual nature of old emphyteutic contracts, then, later, to establish a fixed term in order to combat the tactics of the peasants, whose contracts for three lives displayed a suspicious longevity, with tenants 'living' longer than average life expectancy would suggest. Finally, the lords sought wherever possible to replace emphyteusis with fixed-term leases. Similar cases can be found elsewhere of holders of dominium directum (or the equivalent) who tried to break emphyteutic contracts and replace them with either fixed-term rental agreements or sharecropping arrangements, usually increasing their share of the crop or the rent from the land. This was what happened, to varying degrees, in Catalonia from the mid-eighteenth century. There were also some cases where the reverse happened, in that lords sought to convert fixed-term rents to emphyteutic contracts. In the Milanese region studied by Michela Barbot, the choice between emphyteusis and leasing varied according to the demographic, economic and financial context. Inflation could be an incentive towards leasehold, with a preference for short-term contracts but equally, the deflation of the 1630s, in the area around Milan, drove a shift from fixed-term rents to emphyteutic contracts. The interest of the holder of dominium directum, in this case the *Duomo* of Milan, was in regaining stable and regular income, finding a means to maintain the purchasing power of its rents.

As mentioned, however, the history of emphyteusis also provides plenty of examples in which the tenants became first *de facto* and then *de jure* full property owners of the lands they held. Such a development seems less surprising when we remember that the perpetual or long-term nature of the contract placed the tenant in an advantageous position, as many chapters in this book argue. How was it, though, that some tenants were able, at a given moment, to act as full property owners? Gabriel Jover and Antonia Morey describe the shift from *feudal* to *common* emphyteusis in Majorca. Elefthéria Zei also sees these centuries as witnessing 'the formation of local elites in the complex and divided world of the modern Eastern Mediterranean'. Boehler describes the shift in the seventeenth and eighteenth centuries from a 'Roman' to a 'Germanic' emphyteusis, in the shift from *erblehn* to *hoflehn* based in part on the adoption of the maxim 'no lord without title'. In this respect, the judicial context in which emphyteusis took shape and developed needs examination. Although the mediaeval concept of property rights as emanations of objects makes it possible to understand the notion of divided property, the relation of emphyteusis to Roman law through Roman emphyteusis is unclear (Boehler, 2014), particularly as Roman, unlike mediaeval, law recognised the right to individual private ownership, without separation of *dominia* (Dominici, 1845: 10), just as the Napoleonic Code did.

The evolution of contracts in one direction or another can be explained, as in the previous section, by important economic changes, but also as a result of the strategies of the actors involved. It is striking that tenants often refused to acquit the redemption payments attached to contracts. Without lingering here over the detail on the ruses employed by crafty Sicilian *contadini* and their wily Alsatian counterparts, we should note that several papers have insisted that peasants themselves chose emphyteusis and preferred this form of contract over others. This preference showed up not just in response to the owners of dominium directum, but also in the peasants' frequent practice of sub-letting their own use-rights to other tenants, despite any and all laws to the contrary.

As its use became more intense and more widespread, emphyteusis became part of many regions' social fabric. This process is described by Eleftheria Zei for the Cyclades, where emphyteusis not only facilitated the rise of a group of nouveau riche tenants, holders of vineyards, and their insertion into the elites of the islands, but also allowed the peasantry and native populations to assert themselves against a nobility of Venetian origin. These new elites sought to follow in the footsteps of earlier tenants, who had also enriched themselves. A similar process is described for Majorca by Antonia Morey and Gabriel Jover. They show that the traditional rentier oligarchy, formed through *fideicomiso* (a form of *mayorgazo* or entail, designed to prevent the break-up of estates), was ready time and time again to transfer use-rights to tenants, either to overcome financial difficulties, or to exploit new areas of land and to expand the agricultural frontier. This strategy of transferring use-rights took on a different meaning in the nineteenth century, however, when the Spanish law dissolving entail forced this oligarchy to break up estates and sell them (Bodinier, Congost & Luna, 2009). The landowners chose then to transfer their use-rights via emphyteusis as a means of maintaining some form of ownership with dominium directum.

In both Majorca and in Catalonia, as described by Rosa Congost, Pere Gifre and Enric Saguer, the spread of emphyteusis and sub-emphyteusis has shaped early modern and contemporary agrarian history. Certain features stand out. First, emphyteusis allowed not only well-off landowners to enrich themselves still further, but also allowed access to land for other groups, such as well-off peasant families, or, in a word, people who were not part of the traditional rentier aristocracy. In Catalonia, it was the *pagesia de mas* who were the driving force behind trends in emphyteusis, both imposing the contract on the holders of dominium directum and, later, eventually acting as a brake upon its rapid expansion. Thanks to a different balance of forces, the *rabassa morta* contract in the Girona region established perpetual use-rights (effectively full property rights), whereas in central Catalonia, it came more closely to resemble a sharecropping contract.

In this context, it is easy to understand, as Rosa Congost has shown in previous works, why Catalan tenants were uninterested in the liberal reforms of the nineteenth century which proposed, within the framework of Spanish disentailment laws, the redemption of emphyteusis, that is, the purchase of dominium directum by the tenants (Congost, 1999, 2007). Why re-purchase a property of which they were, in effect, full owners, with quasi-perfect property rights?

Michela Barbot asks similar questions about the law of 1864, in the Milan region, which allowed the *livellari* in theory to purchase the dominium directum of the land for which they held dominium utile and to gain full title. Few took up the offer. Did Milanese *livellari* thus have no desire to become full owners? Was it because they already considered themselves owners of the rights which were offered to them for purchase? Did they share the reaction of those French peasants who, encouraged by the Revolution to rid themselves of the feudal dues with which their lands (held by emphyteutic contract) were supposedly burdened, refused to take up the offer to purchase back their lands (Béaur, 2000 and 2008)? Or the reaction of certain *censitaires* who were also in no hurry to wipe out the (light) dues they owed to their Québécois seigneurs

(Grenier, 2012)? It is also worth noting that the history of English copyhold seems to have followed a similar pattern until it was abolished in 1922 (Venn, 1933; Turner & Beckett, 1998).

To answer such questions, we need to go beyond issues of motivation, the balance of forces, and the uncertainty regarding economic circumstances, important though all these factors may be, and consider the issue of the institutional price of full property, as fixed in each specific place and time by the so-called liberal state and the social groups that controlled both the structures and the circumstances of power. This price reflected not just the quantity fixed for repayment, but also the differing socio-economic circumstances surrounding access to full property rights, such as the availability of credit, the terms of payment, any delays that were imposed, and so on.

II.2 The flexibility of emphyteusis

If we return, however, to the work of Bartolomé Clavero cited earlier, we find that this author defined emphyteusis according to three specific rights known in Spanish as *pena de comiso (confiscation)*, *laudemio (laudemium)* and *tanteo* or *fadiga* (preferential right to purchase). In Italy this right was termed *retratto* and corresponded to the right held by the owner of dominium directum to buy back full ownership of his property at a reduced price. It appears, for example, in the *Codice Civile per gli Stati di Parma, Piacenza e Guastalla* (1820)[8].

All three refer to the relationship between the owners of the dominium directum and the holders of dominium utile and are closely linked. *Confiscation* is the right to evict the owner of the dominium utile for non-payment of any rent. *Laudemium* refers to the right of the owner of dominium directum to charge a sum every time the use-rights change hands, usually a percentage, varying from place to place, of the sum agreed upon for the sale or lease of these rights. *Laudemium* was closely related to *fadiga*, which gave the owner of the dominium directum the first option to purchase back the use-rights of property at the price for which the owner of the dominium utile was prepared to sell them. However, both the history of emphyteusis during the early modern period and legal theory reveal that, even if we limit our study only to those contracts specifically described as emphyteutic, these three rights did not always coincide. For example, where the sub-letting of emphyteutic rights appears to have been practised, this was not usually accompanied by the payment of *laudemium*.

---

8 Thus Article 418 states 'If the emphyteutic tenant wishes to dispose of the dominium utile by a contract inter vivos, he must give priority to the holder of the dominium directum and offer it to him at the same price. He must inform him and wait two months for his decision…' [*Volendo l'enfieuta alienare per atto tra vivi il dominio utile, é tenuto di preferire il padrone diretto ad ugual prezzo. Deve perciò interpellarlo, ed attenderne per due mesi la deliberazione …*].

In principle, land held by emphyteusis could be confiscated in case of non-payment of rent during two or three years. The tenant could be evicted and, in this regard, emphyteusis gave the landlord more room to manoeuvre than the French *bail à cens*, since with this latter contract, recovery of property was more difficult. In practice, however, eviction was often difficult to carry out, in part because it was heavily dependent on the value of any improvements made by the tenant and the latter's capacity for negotiation. In France, after the Revolution, it was a subject for judicial debate how far temporary emphyteusis was subject to this so-called *commise*. Writers drew on Roman law to argue that *commise* had not been observed by common law in the majority of ancien régime emphyteutic contracts (Pépin-Lehalleur, 1843: 310). As for *fadiga*, there are few examples of this right operating in practice. Instead, it seems to have been a very 'efficient' and, in some ways, very modern means by which fraud in the payment of *laudemium* could be avoided. By contrast, the practice of resisting the termination of leases, like the so-called *mauvais gré*, harked back to a form of informal emphyteusis (Debouvry, 1899). This kind of practice allowed a tenant to prolong his contract indefinitely. The contract thus became tacitly if confusingly a long-term contract which could therefore become emphyteutic.

We consider as emphyteutic all those practices which, regardless of how they may be described in their local contexts, share two features, as mentioned: perpetual or long-term duration, which in practice, could become perpetual, and a division of property rights. Until now, this perpetuity has led the association in the historiography of emphyteusis with immobility and stagnation. Because of an excessively rigid and institutional approach to property rights, the flexibility and thus the possibility for change offered by the second characteristic have tended to go unnoticed.

Nonetheless, the different cases studied in this book demonstrate, often unintentionally, this flexibility. They also demonstrate the value of not restricting our analysis to those contracts that were formally described as emphyteutic. Several chapters describe contracts that were not described as emphyteutic or given similar labels, such the *livello* in Italy or *foro* in Spain, but which nevertheless had features of emphyteusis. Gérard Béaur presents a map showing the different forms of contract in France which include, under different labels, clauses which can in fact be regarded as essentially emphyteutic. These are to be found across France, from the *albergement* in Dauphiné and Savoie to the *baux à rente foncière* in the jurisdiction of the Coutume de Paris to the *abenevis* of the Forez or the *baillettes* of the Poitou. Fabrice Boudjaaba discusses the Norman *fieffe* in the region of Vernon; it was an emphyteutic contract which in principle applied only to land with buildings, but which in reality could be applied to all types of property. Although it was a contract which suited both parties, it did not survive the Napoleonic Civil Code and declined after 1810. Likewise, Jean-Michel Boehler has studied the Alsatian *hoflehn*, which resembled a denaturalisation or usurpation and shows how peasant trickery could make short-term contracts take on the appearance of emphyteusis. In this way, they were able to enlarge their holdings, at the expense of both lay and ecclesiastical lords, lords who were weakened by the Thirty Years War and never able to recuperate their landholdings, especially once the Revolution confirmed the usurpers.

Michela Barbot argues that emphyteusis in the strict sense was essentially an urban contract, since it established a distinction between land and buildings, whereas *livello* fits with the broader sense of emphyteusis used in this study, and indeed, has been described as emphyteusis in other parts of Italy, as in the chapter by Chittolini. Gérard Béaur has shown that in Meaux too, emphyteusis was used mainly for houses and not for land. Emphyteusis was thus a way of getting buildings built, and a tool for urbanisation. The cession of land on a long-term basis and for a minimal return was an acceptable exchange for the effort required to put up a building.

This diversity of terminology, as it emerges from the study of different countries, also hides challenges to the emphyteutic contract and to the way in which it was applied. From this aspect, the method of calculation and amount of the dues can be of prime importance. For example, according to an Italian observer of the first half of the nineteenth century, the *livelli* contracts in force in the Valtelline region were only so in name and duration, as the total dues were so high that in his view they should be considered purely as long-term and indeed hereditary leases[9].

II.3 The recurring renewal of an old practice

Emphyteusis thus should not be seen as a universal tool, nor as a practice that always held equal importance at any point in time. It varied considerably, and not just as a function of differences in geography, climate, demography or socio-economic conditions. Although these factors are essential to understanding why this form of contract was chosen over another, we must remember that the decision depended above all on the aims of the parties and the balance of forces between them. For example, in the case of Meaux presented by Gérard Béaur, the great majority of emphyteutic contracts involved institutions, especially ecclesiastical institutions. There are legal and financial, that is, fiscal, reasons behind this choice of contract. It is clear that emphyteusis was particularly well suited to owners for whom longevity, even eternity, was guaranteed. No one was in a better position than the religious orders to take advantage of contracts that bound the entire community for the long term, as demonstrated by taking on the attempt at a public debt (Boureau, 2006). Religious orders were not the only ones to adopt this type

9 According to this observer, the dues paid to the owner were generally more than half, sometimes even two-thirds, of the total production of the land (Balardini, 1834: 166). It seems that during the first half of the nineteenth century, with the rise in wine prices, the owners took advantage of the renewal of emphyteutic contracts to increase their dues.

of contract. Again, in eighteenth-century France, lords also came to cede land on *baux à cens*, and thus perpetually, or through emphyteusis, for the very long term. In other cases, as in Catalonia, it was not the nobles who let land in such a fashion; rather rich peasants, themselves emphyteutic tenants, let out numerous small plots on emphyteutic leases. In fact, the clauses in the contract were very diverse, and often arose unexpectedly in particular circumstances, thus giving the contract its essential quality, that of being able to adapt to the needs of the moment. Such adaptability in part explains the contract's success.

Emphyteutic contracts thus responded to different strategies on the part of the two interested parties, and led to a wide range of reactions, both individual and collective, some of which could call into question the very nature of the contract. All of this we already knew, more or less, before the workshop in Girona, or thought we knew it. The participants were not slow to remind us of this, but they also went much further in opening up new perspectives.

Given that the contracts defined as emphyteutic that are covered in this volume were created at different times, it is unlikely that they were the outcome of the same strategies and reasons. It is this historical awareness that allows us to view these contracts by the early modern period in terms of 'path dependency', in that the continuation of older forms of emphyteusis reveals a degree of institutional longevity. At the same time, however, a historical perspective reveals that this apparently 'old' institutional form was capable of a surprising degree of adaptability and flexibility in the face of new opportunities during the early modern period and especially during the profound transformations of the eighteenth century[10]. That is, the types of emphyteusis to be found in early modern Europe, the period with which almost all the chapters in this volume are concerned, cannot be properly understood without reference to earlier periods, but they owed their particular form to the broad agrarian transformations of this period. One of the works that has done the most to illustrate this co-existence of old and new aspects of emphyteusis within a single region is that of Pierre Vilar for Catalonia (Vilar, 1962). It is no accident that the two chapters in this volume which deal with Catalonia, and also the one on Majorca, reiterate this idea.

The Catalan example, however, in which early modern forms of emphyteusis retained their feudal and medieval origins alongside newer aspects, was not matched everywhere. An interesting contrast is central Italy, where, as Chittolini shows, with more attention to the medieval period than in any other chapter, the contract already had features that could not be described as 'seigneurial'. By contrast, the seigneurial nature of emphyteusis clearly persisted in the early modern documents for the Greek islands. At the other extreme, the forms of exchange and transfer around the *fieffe* studied by Boudjaaba show no traces of a feudal nature.

---

10 For a critique of the way some new institutional authors have abused the concept of 'path dependency', see Congost, Gelman & Santos (2016: 185-191).

Once we recognise that old and new forms of emphyteusis could co-exist, we need to be aware that the line between the different forms is not always clear in the sources. Moreover, when it is, this clarity can be an indicator of important social change. This is how Boehler views the shift from *erblen* to *hoflehn* in Alsace. In France, the seigneurial origins of the contract imply a nominal distinction between *bail à cens* and *bail à rente*, but they can be confused. Often, the identity of those transferring land can be misleading, as the authors of some of the chapters on Spain remind us. While Asturian and Galician monasteries did usually have feudal origins, many Galician and Majorcan nobles were originally tenants, the first to obtain use-rights from a much older nobility. Where written law provided a terminology to distinguish between emphyteusis and sub-emphyteusis, it could still be the case, as Congost, Gifre and Saguer show, that the first emphyteutic tenants ended up presenting themselves as the direct land owners.

In general, by the early modern period, those transferring land, although they might be descended from feudal lords, no longer made use of the more visible feudal tropes, such as acts of homage and forms of servitude. We are thus confronted with a form of contract stripped of its seigneurial trappings, and it is this form that came to dominate in the minds of those who used it. In these new circumstances, as Boudjaaba reminds us, the life cycle could play an important role in the choice of emphyteusis by household heads, regardless of socio-economic status, so long as they had the desire and the means to become landholders.

What, then, compelled owners and cultivators to seek to take on or refuse emphyteusis? We have to be very careful in ascribing strategies to the two sides, given that what we often see are contracts that were drawn up at different times and that were in force for some duration. To begin with, the strategies that determined the main clauses of the contract can only be analysed in the context in which they were drawn up. In this way, the nature of the annual rent most probably reflects the specific interests at play in the particular context in which the conditions were set out. The rent could take the form of a fixed sum, in cash or in kind, or a portion of the harvest to be handed over to the owner of the dominium directum. However, this decision could have unforeseen consequences for future generations. A money rent which might, at the time of its stipulation, have been an important sum, could be rendered insignificant by inflation, thus strengthening the position of the tenant. The terms of the rent could have been fixed to take into account the enormous initial effort required to clear and plant a wooded area, but, again, future generations might benefit hugely from the work invested by their ancestors.

The diffusion of emphyteutic contracts owed much to the state and to demographic trends. Demographic contexts could also influence a set of initial conditions imposed by contracts, which could then have different social outcomes in the future. It could be that the cultivator had no other way to get access to the land he needed to make a living, or that the owner saw a chance to extract through emphyteusis rents from land which hitherto had hardly been worth claiming as his own. Emphyteusis has been used by both civil and ecclesiastical lords to populate deserted lands and to fix populations upon the land, usually in contexts of demographic decline, following wars, plagues and other epidemics, or as part of the process of reconquest. We might think, therefore, that the pressures of dynamic population trends would reduce the importance of emphyteusis for future contracts and call into question past contracts. As the next section will argue, however, this was not always the case.

At this point, we must keep in mind the flexible nature of emphyteutic contracts, a flexibility seen in the multiple functions that emphyteusis acquired, depending on the situations in which it was used. These contracts could be a tool for keeping people on the land at a time when population was sparse and hands in short supply[11]. But they could also be a means for absentee landlords to ensure a fixed and regular rent. Or, as in the Italian case, a strategy employed by the small landowners, who offered their own land to the Church in exchange for protection against appropriation by feudal overlords, or in search of the privileges and immunities enjoyed by ecclesiastical property[12]. In this last case, it seems that the dynamics of divided ownership arose both from the cession of dominium utile and from the cession of dominium directum. The historical trend in either direction seem to have arisen from changes in the economic and political situation that remain to be evaluated.

III Emphyteusis, Agrarian growth and rural conflict

III.1 Stagnation or economic growth?

Up to now we have insisted on the point that, while adapting to circumstances of time and place, emphyteutic contracts have still retained certain features which distinguish them clearly from other forms of contract. These could include the obligation to improve the land received, especially if it took the form of uncultivated land or land to be cleared and cultivated, to be planted or, in urban contexts, to be built upon. In these contexts, emphyteusis, far from being a strange choice, could be the best option for all, given that otherwise the land in question would have required a huge investment before it could be rented out. We know, for example, from the work of Pierre Vilar, that in Catalonia, emphyteutic contracts, often really sub-emphyteutic contracts and particularly *rabassa morta* contracts, promoted by the established holders of use-rights, were the driving force behind the agrarian transformation of the

11 It was by means of these hereditary rental contracts that the Walser populations colonised the highlands of the Alpine arc (Mazza, 2014: 57-126) and it was by emphyteutic contracts that reconstruction in Alsace was organised and farmers attracted after the wars of the seventeenth century (Boehler, 1994: 84).

12 See the *Dizionario Storico del Diretto Italiano ed Europeo* (on-line edition).

eighteenth century (Vilar, 1962). They drove the extension of the cultivated land surface in some areas, the intensification of irrigation systems in others, and especially the expansion of viticulture. In Spain, it was those regions where emphyteusis was particularly active that witnessed the greatest economic and demographic growth over the eighteenth century (Llopis, 2002).

The idea that this contract could be a force for economic growth stands in contrast to the stagnation traditionally associated with it in the literature. We can see it in very different historical schools. For example, in 1976, Robert Brenner, in a famous article, not only started from the superiority of English development, based on the emergence of an early agrarian capitalism in the great farms, but related this process to the disappearance of 'customary tenants'. In his words, in England, unlike France, 'many former customary peasant holdings removed from the "customary sector" and added to the "leasehold sector"' (Brenner, 1976: 47). It is perhaps significant that in the Spanish edition of the article, customary tenant was translated by *enfiteuta*.

Recent work (Béaur et al., 2013, Congost and Santos 2010, Gelman, 2005, 2009, Congost, Gelman & Santos, 2016) has questioned the theories of the new institutionalists regarding a close link between 'secure property rights' and agricultural growth. The emergence of 'perfect', absolute property did not live up to its promises. It has not been demonstrated anywhere that absolute property rights were a prerequisite for ensuring the agricultural development of a region or country (Béaur and Chevet, 2013; 2017). From this perspective, emphyteusis has been vindicated as a useful means for realising the value of land (Congost, 2013). Giorgio Chittolini shows that in central and northern Italy the economic, commercial and demographic flourishing of cities and their *contados* (those between 1,000 and 3,000 km^2) from the late Middle Ages to the early modern period was accomplished without much recourse to emphyteusis. Instead, success came from the commercial division of land, achieved mainly through leasing. Nonetheless, many historians have shown the flexibility that emphyteutic contracts could offer, particularly in contexts where there was a shortage of capital or of cash (Normandy, the Greek islands or Majorca). There is also the specific case of the Cyclades, described by Eleftéria Zei, where emphyteusis was almost obligatory in order to invest in land, with an entry fee that only came into effect if the contract was broken. The reason for such apparent leniency lay in the concern to compensate the cultivator for work invested in the property he received, or indeed any task carried out by him, or again to pay off a longstanding debt, previously contracted with the holder of dominium directum. Here we are dealing with a somewhat tortuous yet revealing way of accessing land.

It seems that there are various illustrative cases, yet the question of whether emphyteusis hindered or promoted economic growth remains largely open. In those cases where emphyteusis was clearly associated with crops such as vines, the mere extension of such crops could be regarded as a form of agrarian growth based upon specialisation, an alternative to the classic model of agricultural revolution proposed for England. The *colonia* in Madeira, the Catalan *rabassa morta* and some of the emphyteutic contracts found in the Greek islands were all associated from the start with viticulture as a form of improving the land. Given that viticulture was the driver of agrarian change in many regions of southern Europe, this association casts emphyteusis in a positive light, since the obligation in the contract to improve the land was here specifically framed in terms of planting vines. Nonetheless, such an obligation, though it appears intrinsic to the contract, was not a constant in all emphyteutic agreements.

Emphyteusis also played an important role, though, in some grain-growing regions, as in northern Spain. Pegerto Saavedra has shown that the rents in kind obtained by Galician monasteries held up and even rose over the second half of the eighteenth century and at the start of the nineteenth. Such an achievement was possible even though the royal decree that confirmed the use-rights of tenants in Galicia and Asturias remained in force. Examining the trend in rents and leases of the monastery of San Pelayo in Asturias, Pablo F. Luna has observed a significant rise in the income of this Benedictine house over the second half of the eighteenth century, despite the protection offered to tenants by this law. Convents and monasteries were still able to benefit because of their active commercial involvement and their ability to profit from changing prices by demanding rent payments in the kinds of grain that were most profitable at the moment.

Without pushing the argument too far, and leaving aside for the moment the question of cause and effect, it is none the less possible at least to argue that emphyteusis has accompanied certain forms of agricultural growth and commercial wealth. This claim is borne out by several of the studies in this volume. In this regard, far from being an obstacle to agricultural process, as is so often said, emphyteusis could be a valuable means of promoting it. Yet one might also point to various bottlenecks caused at certain points by the limits of available production techniques and by diminishing returns, or by population trends, or by land shortages and rising prices. Though it would be excessive to blame such bottlenecks on emphyteusis, the contract could have been seen by landowners as a restriction on their ability to increase their income. Was it actually an unsurmountable barrier to such an increase for civil and ecclesiastical landowners? Answering this question requires further research. The contributions to this volume can suggest some partial answers, but only some indications. The field remains wide open for an investigation into the relationships between emphyteusis, investment, production, economic circumstances and land rents. Neo-institutionalists and others have been guilty of turning emphyteusis into a bogeyman, or the evil goblin of medieval forests. It should not be assumed without proof that divided property rights were necessarily an obstacle to economic growth.

III.2 The nature of the conflicts resulting from emphyteutic practices

New institutional historians have placed great emphasis on violence and have absorbed conflicts into transaction costs (North, Wallis & Weingast, 2009). Within a multi-faceted view of property rights, however, violence can mean many things. For example, in the two extreme scenarios we have set out for the evolution of emphyteusis towards either fixed-term rents or full property for tenants, we often find a reaction on the part of either an older tenantry or an older seigneurial class, often collectively organised, who did not accept the new state of affairs. Indeed, there is a long-standing consensus, not just among neo-institutional economists, that all forms of divided property, such as emphyteusis, were a source of conflict, giving rise to judicial tactics, legal suits and constant social instability.

Nevertheless, it is worth asking whether it was the nature of the contract itself that caused such instability. It is tempting to argue that it was when legal contracts were partially or totally broken that conflicts arose. The Majorcan and Galician cases suggest that emphyteusis was capable of lending itself to the latter situation, of tending towards illegality in certain situations. Might it become a right that the poorest claimed as a weapon against the exactions of the rich, a recourse to a kind of moral economy?

Many papers have examined, to a greater or lesser extent, the social conflicts surrounding emphyteusis, without necessarily attributing such conflicts to this type of contract. The Spanish cases, Galicia, Asturias, Majorca and Catalonia, have all shown the reaction of peasant emphyteutic tenants to the attempts (sometimes successful) by lords to question the emphyteutic basis of contracts and to change the terms. Pegerto Saavedra has described how Galician monasteries and convents were quick to realise that they were losing their property rights (despite holding dominium directum) in the face of two different trends. On the one hand, the Galician *hidalgos*, the original aristocratic tenants, began to include the ecclesiastical properties to which they held only the use-rights, with those properties of their own that were subject to entail. On the other hand, lower down the social scale, the sub-tenants of these *hidalgos* were in turn dividing and subletting their lands in order to give parcels to their children or to sell or exchange plots. In Galicia, in Asturias and in part of Leon, emphyteutic tenants had been confirmed in the possession of their use-rights by a law of Charles III dating from 1763, and by other later laws and measures (Luna, 2017), precisely in order to prevent the holders of dominium directum from carrying out a series of tenant evictions as soon as circumstances appeared favourable to the landlords. In Catalonia it is likely that widespread, yet unequal, enrichment pushed the peasantry to question the legality of emphyteusis, and to denature or allow to degenerate a form of contract from which they had previously benefitted. In their attempt to (amongst other things) get to the heart of the dispute over the origins of emphyteusis, and in seeking out the first documented instances of a *rabassa morta* contract, Llorenç Ferrer Alòs and Belén Moreno remind us when and how the attraction of emphyteusis started to decline. The region of Girona offers an interesting counterpoint, as Congost, Gifre and Saguer show: here the *rabassa morta* contract developed, at the end of the eighteenth century, into a form of perpetual emphyteusis. As such, it represented a form of empowerment, the result of negotiation, for the *rabassaires*.

In mid-nineteenth century Madeira, the defenders of the *colonos* – some of them at any rate – tried to change this contract into an emphyteutic one. The vague impulses in this direction, however, were overcome by the complexities of the Portuguese Civil Code, wrangling between owners and tenants, all in a context of increasing international demand, which in turn intensified the need for technical improvements and increased capital investment.

The fact that emphyteusis was often a tool for bringing unproductive land into cultivation draws attention to another type of social conflict, this time related to common rights and property. Some authors have recalled that often, particularly in cases where land was to be cultivated for the first time, emphyteusis was a good choice not only for those who sought access to land but those ceding it, especially if it was a case of extracting rents from land where no one could be the sole cultivator and thus private property rights were likely to be doubtful or open to challenge. Antonia Morey and Gabriel Jover describe different situations in which the Majorcan peasantry sought to exert pressure on the holders of dominium directum. The peasants did so particularly during the seventeenth and eighteenth centuries, when the old debt-plagued Majorcan aristocracy ceded land via emphyteusis, but they took advantage of other circumstances when emphyteusis was on the rise and when it was suddenly halted. They exerted pressure above all by illegally clearing and cultivating lands other than those transferred, by taking back and occupying former common lands which had previously been usurped by the nobility and by refusing to pay rents and by 'stealing' wood, nuts and fruit from the woodland.

Similarly, Congost, Gifre and Saguer have highlighted the use of emphyteusis in the eighteenth century as a means to reinforce property rights by privatising common lands. Here, the leaders of this process were the owners of use-rights, the substantial peasantry (*pagesos de mas*), who managed to replace the holders of dominium directum, while at the same time tightening up the contracts of their new sub-tenants. During the Venetian domination of the Ionian Islands, the control of common lands by emphyteutic tenants was a key element in the consolidating of this group's elite status. Here the forms of property held in emphyteusis and the forms of collective rights (usage rights), that were also founded on divided ownership, seem to have shared something in common. For this reason, it seems appropriate to ask whether the geographic pattern of surviving emphyteusis coincides with that of the remaining common land.

In sum, the key question here is the alternative uses to which the contract could be put, depending upon circumstances, and depending upon the degree to which different landholders feared the dispossession of their rights. The shift from emphyteusis to leasehold and vice versa could be a solution proposed or imposed by those who held dominium directum, but it could equally suit the demands, forced or voluntary, of the tenants. This was the case in certain rural and urban contexts in Lombardy. Elefhtéria Zei also mentions the peasant movements in the Cyclades, where established peasants sought new emphyteutic transfers, but agrarian labourers also made demands against the established tenantry. For Zei and also for Argyrou and Lazari, feudal structures did not hinder, indeed, they encouraged, the appearance of new local elites, that is, a powerful middle class.

Emphyteutic tenants or whatever we want to call them were at a clear advantage whenever conflict was focused on whether particular contracts should be defined as emphyteutic or not. Such was the case in the eighteenth century for the Asturian and Galician *foros* studied by Pablo F. Luna and Pegerto Saavedra, or the Catalan *rabassa morta* analysed by Llorenç Ferrer and Belén Moreno. The courts decided in favour of the tenants (*foreros*) in the first instance and in favour of those transferring the land in the second, but it is interesting to note that these authors all agree that the judicial decisions in both cases benefited an intermediate group between the older feudal lords and the lowest ranks of the peasantry. The *rabassaires* continued to defend the emphyteutic nature of the contract until the Second Republic (Giralt, 1965). Similarly, in nineteenth-century Madeira, the jurists debated whether or not contracts should be defined as emphyteutic, in the knowledge that this was the preferred option of those who cultivated the land.

This was so during the historical period during which the liberal model began to wipe out divided ownership in favour of individual and indivisible private property. The texts clearly show the factors that made leaseholders reluctant to take on the full ownership of their property and demonstrate the capacity of emphyteusis for survival. The Italian example shows it was ineffective, in the years after Italian unification, to promote enfranchisement from the *livelli* by encouraging individuals to invest in state bonds, because the leaseholders lacked sufficient savings to do so (Lorenzetti, 2013). A few years earlier, in Lombardy, the attempts to privatize communal property failed because individuals were unable to pay for the full ownership of these lands – with the paradoxical outcome that communities signed emphyteutic contracts transferring the possession and management of these lands to individual leaseholders in return for payment in kind (Jacini, 1857: 167).

IV. Conclusion. Emphyteusis and the debates over property rights.

Emphyteusis is naturally concerned with practical questions, since it relates above all to the use of land or buildings. Practical questions do not mean, however, that we cannot draw conclusions at a more theoretical level. The study of emphyteusis goes beyond a survey of landholding, in that emphyteusis was shaped by particular legal frameworks, but had the ability to adapt to circumstances with remarkable flexibility. Nevertheless, since emphyteusis existed within given time-frames, within which it mobilised labour, it had lasting impacts, positive and negative, upon the mentality of both the tenant and the owner of dominium directum. Emphyteusis without doubt shaped people's ideas and brought with it changing perceptions and self-awareness. This question needs to be borne in mind, and future research should aim at identifying sources that would allow it to be addressed. This may prove to be one of the more striking differences between emphyteusis and other forms of tenure (leasehold, transfer of usufruct, mortgage and the like) even if in specific contexts emphyteusis may take on the appearance of these forms.

To return to the beginning: it is the combination of long-term duration (or perpetuity) and the division of property rights in the same contract that has been responsible for initiating important social changes in particular settings. The length of the contract implies not just hereditary status, but that such social change can appear long after the original contract was signed. Such was the case of many of the tenants featured in the chapters here, who, despite their original descent from feudal serfs, had come to represent a powerful class by the seventeenth and eighteenth centuries. How we interpret these social changes depends not only upon the characteristics of the original contracts, but also on our own ability to remain flexible in our thinking about property rights, rights which, by definition, were divided in these contracts.

For this reason, we have also sought in this introduction to emphasise the importance of social actors, both those responsible for the early contracts, and those who instigated changes in emphyteutic practices during the early modern period. We have also laid weight upon the conflicts surrounding these practices in this same period. Once again, we are confronted by two possible ways of observing and interpreting emphyteusis. The idea of 'path dependency' may help us to notice, understand and interpret elements of continuity, but it is not sufficient for understanding and interpreting the elements of change behind the choice of action in any given moment. Among these elements of change we would emphasise the emergence of new social groups and, what is crucial for our purposes, the emergence of new social conflicts. It is evident that, by the eighteenth century, society was no longer divided neatly into feudal lords and peasants and thus tenants were no longer simply 'victims' of feudalism. In many of these chapters, emphyteutic tenants appear as the new middle classes and even new elites who on occasion exercised power, sometimes, in fact, because of emphyteutic contracts, over new 'victims'.

In addition, our focus on social groups, both older and emerging, has allowed us to identify the presence of the most disadvantaged rural strata in the social conflicts around emphyteusis. Even if these poorer and landless peasants did not play a leading or always visible role in the protests often started by the more powerful tenants against the owners of the dominium directum, they nevertheless managed to keep hold of the land they cultivated, to hang on to the fruits of their labour and that of previous generations, and to consolidate their family holdings (Luna, 2017b). The sources often allow us to detect such defensive action. In some cases, such as Catalonia, the humblest peasants, in their position as sub-tenants, were able to benefit from the arguments of richer tenants to challenge their rents.

The key to interpreting these social transformations, we argue, lies in how one approaches the analysis of contracts and property rights. Emphyteusis is a particularly interesting case because the division of property rights inherent to the contract obliges the historian to 'problematise' the study of landed property. The existence of different interest groups and the different strategies of the various social actors, requires an open and multi-faceted approach to property rights. Some of us would argue that such an approach is always necessary, but here its potential is clearly evident. Reaching this conclusion, however, has meant setting aside many preconceived notions of emphyteusis, notions which get in the way of recognising the flexibility and adaptability of the contract, instead of dismissing it out of hand as unchanging. The regional focus adopted in this book has helped with this aim. The variety of economic effects evident here – growth in some regions, stagnation in others – and also social effects – the rise of new middle classes in some regions and greater social polarisation in others – makes it clear that the simple existence of emphyteusis is not enough to explain these different outcomes. The main contribution of this work is thus not to prove that emphyteusis led – or did not lead – to economic growth or to social change, but to emphasise that recognising the flexibility and adaptability of this contract, whatever we choose to call it, requires a more complex, and thus more than usually effective, analysis of the evolution of property rights and groups within society.

Bibliography

AAVV, *Emfiteusis i censos agraris a l'Estat espanyol* (1986), *Estudis d'Historia Agraria*, núm. 7.

Avila Quijas, Omar (2014), *El ayuntamiento de Antigua Guatemala y la administración de sus ejidos. De la enfiteusis a la propiedad privada, 1818-1885*, México, El Colegio de México, Centro de Estudios Históricos.

Azcárate, Gumersindo de (1879-1883), *Ensayo sobre la historia del derecho de propiedad y su estado actual en Europa*, 3 vols Madrid, Imprenta de la Revista de la Legislación.

Balardini, Lodovico (1834), 'Notizie agrarie intorno alla provincia di Sondrio (Valtellina)', in *Agricoltura. Scoperte e invenzioni nel Regno Lonbardo-Veneto*, fasc. ott.-nov.-dic.

Barsky, Osvaldo & Gelman, Jorge (2009), *Historia del agro argentino. Desde la conquista hasta comienzos del siglo XXI*, Buenos Aires, Ed. Sudamericana.

Béaur, Gérard, (2000), *Histoire agraire de la France au XVIII*[e] *siècle. Inerties et changements dans les campagnes françaises à la fin de l'époque moderne (jusqu'en 1815)*, Paris, SEDES.

Béaur, Gérard, (2003), 'Contrats d'exploitation et systèmes de contrats sous l'Ancien Régime', in Gérard Béaur, Mathieu Arnoux et Anne Varet-Vitu (dir.), *Exploiter la terre. Les contrats agraires de l'Antiquité à nos jours*, Rennes, Association d'Histoire des Sociétés Rurales, Bibliothèque d'Histoire Rurale, vol. 7, p. 35-44.

Béaur, Gérard, (2008), 'Révolution et redistribution des richesses dans les campagnes: mythe ou réalité?', *Annales historiques de la révolution française*, numéro spécial *Articuler les temps composés de l'économie*, n° 352, avril-juin, p. 209-239.

Béaur, Gérard, Arnoux, Mathieu & Varet-Vitu, Anne (eds) (2003), *Exploiter la terre. Les contrats agraires de l'Antiquité à nos jours*, Rennes, Association d'Histoire des Sociétés Rurales, Bibliothèque d'Histoire Rurale, vol. 7.

Béaur, Gérard, Schofield, Phillipp, Chevet, Jean-Michel & Pérez-Picazo, Maria-Teresa (eds) (2013), *Property rights, land markets and economic growth in the european countryside (13th-20th centuries)*, Turnhout, Brepols, Rural History in Europe, 1.

Béaur, Gérard & Chevet, Jean-Michel (2013), 'Institutional change and agricultural growth', in Gérard Béaur, Phillipp Schofield, Jean-Michel Chevet, Maria-Teresa Pérez-Picazo (eds), *Property rights, land markets and economic growth in the european countryside (13th-20th centuries)*, Turnhout, Brepols, Rural History in Europe, 1, p. 19-68.

Béaur, Gérard & Chevet, Jean-Michel (2013), 'Droits de propriété et croissance. L'émergence de la propriété "parfaite" et l'ouverture du marché foncier, moteurs de la croissance agricole ?', *Histoire et Sociétés Rurales*, 2017, 48, p. 49-92.

Bodinier, Bernard, Congost, Rosa & Luna, Pablo F. (eds) (2009), *De la Iglesia al Estado. Las desamortizaciónes de bienes eclesiásticos en Francia, España y America Latina*, Zaragoza, Prensas Universitaria de Zaragoza – Sociedad Española de Historia Agraria (SEHA), 7.

Boehler, Jean-Michel (1994), *Une Société rurale en milieu rhénan : la paysannerie de la plaine d'Alsace (1648-1789)*, Strasbourg, Presses Universitaires de Strasbourg.

Boehler, Jean-Michel (2014), 'L'Art d'être propriétaire sans l'être tout en l'étant', *Revue d'Alsace*, 140, p. 79-96.

Borsari, Luigi (1850), *Il contratto d'enfiteusi*, Ferrara.

Brenner, Robert (1976), 'Agrarian Class Structure and Economic Development in Pre-Industrial Europe', *Past & Present*, 70, p. 30-75.

Boureau, Alain (2006), 'Le Monastère médiéval, laboratoire de la dette publique?', in Jean Andreau, Gérard Béaur & Jean-Yves Grenier (dir.), *La dette publique dans l'histoire*, Paris, Comité pour l'Histoire Economique et Financière de la France, p. 21-33.

Burke, Edmund (1993 [London, 1790]), *Reflections on the Revolution in France and on the Proceedings in certain societies in London relative to that event*, ed. and intro. L.G.Mitchell, Oxford.

Cárdenas, Francisco de (2002 [1873-1875]), *Ensayo sobre la historia de la propiedad territorial en España*, Madrid, Imprenta de J. Noguera, 2 vols [reprod. facsímil, Pamplona, Analecta, 2 vols].

CLAVERO, Bartolomé (1986), 'Enfiteusis, ¿qué hay en un nombre?', *Anuario de Historia del Derecho*, LVI, p. 467-519.

CONGOST, Rosa (1999), 'Terres de masos, terres de censos. La complicada fi dels drets senyorials a la regió de Girona', Rosa CONGOST & Lluís TO (eds), *Homes, masos, historia. La Catalunya del nord-est (segles XI-XX)*, Barcelona, Publicacions de l'Abadia de Montserrat, p. 409-450.

CONGOST, Rosa (2000), 'Sagrada propiedad imperfecta. Otra visión de la revolución liberal española', *Historia Agraria*, 20, p. 61-93.

CONGOST, Rosa (2003), 'Property Rights and Historical Analysis. What Rights? What History', *Past & Present*, 181, p. 73-106.

CONGOST, Rosa (2007), *Tierra, Leyes, Historia. Estudios sobre 'la gran obra de la propiedad'*, Barcelona, Crítica.

CONGOST, Rosa (2013), 'The social dynamics of agricultural growth. The example of Catalan emphyteusis in the eighteenth century', in Gérard BÉAUR, Phillipp SCHOFIELD, Jean-Michel CHEVET, Maria-Teresa PÉREZ-PICAZO (eds), *Property rights, land markets and economic growth in the European Countryside (13th-20th Centuries)*, Turnhout, Brepols, Rural History in Europe 1, p. 439-454.

CONGOST, Rosa and Rui SANTOS (2010), 'From formal institutions to the social contexts of property', in Rosa CONGOST and Rui SANTOS (eds), *Contexts of Property in Europe. The Social Embeddedness of Property Rights in Land in Historical Perspective*, Turnhout, Brepols, Rural History in Europe 5, p. 13-36.

CONGOST, Rosa, GELMAN, Jorge & SANTOS, Rui (2016), 'Property rights in land. Institutions, social appropiations, and socio-economic outcomes', in Rosa CONGOST, Jorge GELMAN & Rui SANTOS (eds), *Property Rights in Land. Issues in social, economic and global history*, Routledge, London and New York, p. 177-204.

DEBOUVRY, François (1899), *Étude juridique sur le « mauvais gré »*, Lille.

DOMINICI, Zaccaria (1845), *Trattato dell'enfiteusi*, Palermo.

DONIOL, Henry (1876), *La Révolution française et la féodalité*, Paris, Guillaumin et Cie et André Sagnier.

FANDOS, Cecilia & TERUEL, Ana (2012), '¿Cómo quitarles esas tierras en un día después de 200 años de posesión? Enfiteusis, legislación y práctica en la Quebrada de Humahuaca (Argentina)', Bulletin de l'Institut Français d'Etudes Andines, 41 (2), Lima, (https://bifea.revues.org/597).

FARON, Olivier & HUBERT, Etienne (1995), *Le Sol et l'immeuble. Les formes dissociées de propriété immobilière dans les villes de France et d'Italie (XIIe-XIXe siècle)*, Roma, École Française de Rome.

FEENSTRA, Robert C. (1974), 'Les Origines du dominium utile chez les glossateurs', *Fata Iuris Romani, Études d'histoire du Droit*, Leiden, Presse Universitaire.

FERGUSON, William Dwyer & Vance, Andrew (1851), *The Tenure and Improvement of Land in Ireland, considered with Reference to the Relation of Landlords and Tenants and Tenant Right*, Dublin.

GARCÍA RUIZ, Luis (2015), 'Demandas sociales y propiedad imperfecta en Veracruz: el impulso a la enfiteusis (1760-1811)', Secuencia, 93, p. 29-49.

GARSONNET, Eugène (1879), *Histoire des locations perpétuelles et des baux à longue durée*, Paris, Larose.

GARRIDO, Samuel (2013), 'Improve and Sit: The Surrendering of Land at Rents Below Marginal Product in Nineteenth-Century Valencia, Spain', in Christopher HANES, Susan WOLCOTT (ed.), *Research in Economic History*, Volume 29, p. 97-144.

GELMAN, Jorge (2005), 'Derechos de propiedad, crecimiento económico y desigualdad en la región pampeana, siglos XVIII y XIX', Historia Agraria, 37, p. 467-488.

GIRALT, Emili (1965), 'El conflicto "rabassaire" y la cuestión agraria en Cataluña', *Revista de Trabajo*, 7, p. 51-72.

GRENIER, Benoît (2012), *Brève histoire du régime seigneurial*, Montréal, Boréal.

HATOYAMA, Kazno (1902), *The Civil Code of Japan compared with the French Civil Code*, 11 Yale L.J. 6-8, 296-393, 345-370, 403-419.

HE, Guo-ping, LUO, Hou-qing (2016), 'The Drawbacks and reforms of China's current rural land System: an analysis based on contract, property rights and resource allocation', *Review of innovation and competitiveness*, Vol. 2, Issc 1.

HEY, David (ed.) (1996), *The Oxford Companion to Local and Family History*, Oxford.

JACINI Stefano (1857), *La proprietà fondiaria e le popolazioni agricole in Lombardia. Studi economici*, Milano-Verona.

JANELLI, Salvatore (1945), *Dell'enfiteusi. Commento al Tit. IX L. III della prima parte del Codice Civile per lo regno delle Due Sicilie*, Palermo, Dalla Stamperia di Francesco Lao.

JARNOUX, Philippe (2013), 'Manorial rules, land market and agricultural change in early modern Brittany', in Gérard BÉAUR, Phillipp SCHOFIELD, Jean-Michel CHEVET & Maria-Teresa PÉREZ-PICAZO (eds), *Property rights, land markets and economic growth in the European Countryside (13th-20th Centuries)*, Turnhout, Brepols, Rural History in Europe, 1, p. 425-438.

JONES, Peter (2016), *Agricultural Enlightenment. Knowledge, Technology, and Nature, 1750-1840*, Oxford, Oxford University Press.

LAVELEYE, Emile de (1874), *De la propriété et de ses formes primitives*, París, Librairie Germer Baillière.

LLOPIS, Enrique (2012), *El legado del Antiguo Régimen en España*, Barcelona, Crítica.

LORENZETTI, Luigi, 'Property relations, socio-economic change and the state: the Valtellina in the nineteenth century', in Gérard BÉAUR, Jean-Michel CHEVET, Maria Teresa PÉREZ-PICAZO, Phillipp SCHOFIELD (eds) (2013), *Property Rights, Land Markets and Economic Growth in the European Countryside (13th-20th centuries)*, Turnhout, Brepols, Rural History in Europe, 1, p. 179-194.

LUNA, Pablo F. (2006), *La Reforma de la sociedad y la defensa de los derechos del propietario, según G.M. de Jovellanos, a finales del Antiguo Régimen*, Oviedo, Real Instituto de Estudios Asturianos.

LUNA, Pablo F. (2012), 'La Catalogne de Ponz, de Young et de Zamora: l'utopie agropastorale et du travail, dans le dernier tiers du XVIIIe siècle', *e-Spania*, 14 [en ligne]: https://e-spania.revues.org/21936#ftn48.

LUNA, Pablo F. (2013), 'Property, Dominium, and the Hispanic enlightenment on both sides of the Atlantic in the second half of the eighteenth century', in Gérard BÉAUR, Phillipp SCHOFIELD, Jean-Michel CHEVET & Maria-Teresa PÉREZ-PICAZO (eds), *Property Rights, Land Markets and Economic Growth in the European Countryside (13th-20th centuries)*, Turnhout, Brepols, Rural History in Europe, 1, p. 87-104.

LUNA, Pablo F. (2014), 'Production et approvisionnement: Le Tumulto de 1692 à México', *Communication ESSHC*, Vienne, *Sesion: Rhythm and evolution of staple food markets in Europe (1650-1950)*, manuscript.

LUNA, Pablo F. (2016), 'Le landgrabbing: Une « contre-réforme » agraire ?', *Revue d'histoire moderne et contemporaine*, 63 (4), Paris, p. 157-182.

LUNA, Pablo F. (2017a), *El tránsito de la Buenamuerte por Lima. Auge y declive de una orden religiosa azucarera, siglos XVIII y XIX*, Madrid, Francfort, Ibeoramericana-Vervuert.

LUNA, Pablo F. (2017b), 'Terre et droit dans le Nord-Ouest de l'Espagne : Entre le manifeste légal et la raison naturelle', in Pablo F. LUNA & Niccolo MIGNEMI (dir.), *Prédateurs et résistants. Appropriation et réappropriation de la terre et des ressources naturelles (16e–20e siècles)*, Paris, Ed. Syllepse, p. 89-117.

MAINE, Henry Sumner (1864), *Ancient Law*, London, Toronto and New York, 1917.

MAINE, Henry Sumner (1883), *Dissertations on Early Law and Custom Chiefly Selected from Lectures Delivered at Oxford*, B.R. Publishing Corporation.

MAZZA, Mauro (2014), 'Itinerari di ricerca sugli assetti fondiari collettivi: dal (micro) caso del Walser alla (macro-) prospettiva della comparazione giuridica intersistemica (e interculturale)', in Matteo COSULICH & Giancarlo ROLLA (dir.), *Il riconoscimento dei diritti storici negli ordinamenti costituzionali*, Quaderni della facoltà di giurisprudenza, vol. 4, Trento.

MEYNAL, Eduard (1908), 'Notes sur la formation de la théorie du domaine divisé (domaine direct et domaine utile) du XIIe au XIVe siècle dans les Romanistes. Étude de dogmatique juridique', *Mélanges Fitting*, II, Montpelier.

MITTEIS, Ludwig, *Zur Geschichte der Erbpacht in Alterthum*, Leipzig, 1901.

NORTH, Douglas C., WALLIS, John Joseph & WEINGAST, Barry Robert (eds) (2009), *Violence and Social Orders: A Conceptual Framework for Interpreting Recorded Human History*, Cambridge, Cambridge University Press.

PÉPIN-LEHALLEUR, Émile (1843), *Histoire de l'Emphitéose en droit romain et en droit français*, Paris.

PIRET, Armand (1937), *La rencontre chez Pothier des conceptions romaine et féodale de la propriété foncière*, Sirey, Paris.

PRACHE, Laurent (1882), *Étude sur la condition juridique et économique des fermiers*, L. Larose et Forcel, Paris.

PRIMOIS, Pierre (1904), *Du Bail emphytéotique d'après la loi du 25 juin 1902*, Caen (thèse).

PROUDHON, Jean-Baptiste-Pierre (1839), *Traité du domaine de propriété*, t. II.

PUGNIÈRE, Roger (1904), *Du Bail emphitéotique*, A. Rousseau, Paris.

Reports Respecting the Tenure of Land in the Several Countries of Europe (1869-1870), Parliamentary Papers.

RUBIN, Neville & COTRAN, Eugen (ed.) (1970), *Annual survey of African Law*, vol. 1, 1967, IV, XXVI, London, Frank Cass and Co, Ltd.

SAINT-JOSEPH, Anthoine de (1856), *Concordance entre les Codes civils étrangers et le Code Napoléon*, 4 vols Paris.

SANTOS, Rui & SERRÂO, José Vicente (2013), 'Property rights, social appropiations and economic outcomes: Agrarian contracts in southern Portugal in the late 18th century', in Gérard BÉAUR, Phillipp SCHOFIELD, Jean-Michel CHEVET & Maria-Teresa PÉREZ-PICAZO (eds), *Property Rights, Land Markets and Economic Growth in the European Countryside (13th-20th Centuries)*, Turnhout, Brepols, Rural History in Europe 1, p. 475-494.

SCRIVEN, John (1896), *A Teatrise on the Law of Copyholder*, London, A. Brown.

SÉE, Henri (1906), *Les Classes rurales en Bretagne du XVIe siècle à la Révolution*, Paris, V. Giard et E. Brière.

SIMPSON, Alfred William Brian, *An Introduction to the History of the Land Law*, Oxford, 1961.

TERUEL, Ana (2015), 'Propriété collective et propriété privée des terres au Nord de l'Argentine et au Sud de la Bolivie (XIXe et XXe siècles)', *Histoire(s) de l'Amérique latine*, 15, Paris, (http://hisal.org/?journal=revue&page=article&op=view&path%5B%5D=teruel2015&path%5B%5D=229).

TOWNSEND, Joseph (1792), *A Journey through Spain in the Years 1786 and 1791*, 3 vols London.

TURNER, Michael and BECKETT, John (1998), 'The lingering survival of ancient tenures in English agriculture in the 19th century', in Clara Eugenia NÚÑEZ (ed.), *Land, Labour and Tenure: The Institutional Arrangements of Conflict and Co-operation in Comparative Perspective*, Proceedings of the Twelfth International Economic History Congress, Madrid, 1998.

VENN, John Archibald (1933), *The Foundations of Agricultural Economics together with an Economic History of British Agriculture during and after the Great War*, Cambridge.

VILAR, Pierre (1962), *La Catalogne dans l'Espagne moderne.* Recherches *sur les fondements économiques des structures nationales*, Paris, S.E.V.P.E.N.

WILLIAMS, Joshua (1901), *Principes of the Law of Real Property*, 19 ed., London.

GIORGIO CHITTOLINI

2. Some Points on Emphyteusis in Central-Northern Italy between the End of the Middle Ages and the Early Modern Age

I regard the aim of this book as to examine a widespread contractual device, the emphyteusis, in a broad perspective, not limited to the juridical aspects, in order to understand the economic and social dynamics it engages with: development of agricultural settlements, putting wasteland under plough, amelioration of production and of productivity, etc. I should first of all make clear two arguments of my contribution:

- what type of emphyteusis I refer to, what were its functional qualities, the *substantia contractus*, as the jurists would say, beyond its diverse denominations (§ I);
- what geographic and economic context it belongs to, within the form it took on in the central and late centuries of the Middle Ages (§ II).

In the subsequent paragraphs I will then examine the characteristics of the emphyteutic contract in the Modern Age, seeking to assess the extent of the lands held under emphyteusis, and their role in the agricultural economy (§ III, 1 e 2).

I. What do we intend by emphyteusis?

Verbum emphyteusis est equivocum, wrote the French jurist Dumolin. We may in fact easily notice the variety of definitions and meanings this term takes on in the broad scope of common law vocabulary, and in the additional intricacies of local variants and uses (Clavero, 1986: 473)[1].

Even in the sources from Italy, both medieval and modern – in notarial deeds, in chancery documents, and even in juridical literature – we are presented with a variety of definitions: emphyteusis, *livelli*, perpetual or *ad longum tempus* contracts, *precariae*, *ficta*, *investiturae ad fictum*, etc.

---

1 This author suitably distinguishes between the general meaning of the term 'emphyteusis' in the common Latin language of European law culture, which ruled up to eighteenth century, and the more differentiate and particular meanings it assumes in vernacular and local juridical languages.

Agrarian Change and Imperfect Property, ed. by Rosa CONGOST and Pablo F. LUNA, Rural History in Europe, 15 (Turnhout, 2018), 39-51

DOI 10.1484/M.RURHE-EB.5.116117

Nonetheless many of these contracts, albeit under different names, do not differ one from the other in the *substantia*, moreover they share the same *animus*, the same function; they enact often very similar contractual relations, and overall correspond to the model I will below expound. At times, on the contrary, we do come across contracts all likewise defined as 'emphyteutic', or leases, in the customary practice, that nonetheless display dissimilar qualities. In the case of emphyteusis, for example, the jurists felt the need to distinguish between an 'improper emphyteusis' (in those instances in which, notwithstanding the definition, it is rather closer to a rent contract, the *location-conductio of roman law*, with a high rent fee, or not merely a sum of acknowledgement) from an ameliorative emphyteusis, etc.

This is a well known situation, and the law scholars who sought to define the different types of contract were well aware of the issue since the twelfth and thirteenth-XIII centuries[2].

Within this variety of denominations, aggravated itself by the variety in local uses[3], the contemporary lexicon doesn't make it easy to set out distinctions, and it is thus up to the historian to point out and delimit the subject of his enquiry, from among the different formal typologies and the various definitions. I thus intend to refer to a type of contract – most often defined as emphyteusis, yet also going by other names (for example also *livello* in the Lombard and Venetian regions) – which is characterised, within a practical linguistic homologation accepted also by the jurists, in both individual as well as collective grants, by the following elements:

- long-term extent (twenty or thirty years, lifetime, or *perpetuum*): under all circumstances *ad longum tempus*;
- low rent, as compared to the rents drawn for plots of land of equal extent and quality (either because the fee is deliberatively incongruous, or because it is intended to rise with the increase of production in the granted plots, and above all, if it is drawn in coin, because of the devaluation of the currency itself).
- the tenant had very broad rights over the land, to the point of actually detaining the so called dominium utile ('useful' right of ownership);[4] frequently since the first issuing of the entrusting, in other cases they strengthened over time, precisely because of the perpetuity of the lease and because of the slight rent – and eventual further devaluation of it. Jurists often consider the

2 Ranieri from Perugia, in his *Ars notaria* (2, I) introducing the issue of emhyteusis, notices that *variatur enim secundum condictiones et nomina que sortitur, alias enim … remanet hic contractus in suum nomen generale, ac appellatur vulgo emphyteosis vel emponema, alias precaria, alias libellus, alias canoon alias census … secundum varia idiomata terrarum, quare, ut opinor, nullam credo fore inter eos differentiam assignandam, nisi dumtaxat in sono vocis* (Grossi, 1966: 493).

3 On the different features of these contracts, variously settled by *consuetudines* and local custom, see Giorgetti, 1974: 97-103.

4 The owner retaining the *directum dominium*. The two terms were taken from the law of action, which knew that an action was *directa* and another was *utilis* (Feenstra, 1974: 215-259).

lessor's rights of dominium directum no longer as a dominium, but rather a simple *jus in re aliena* (which might be hold over lands belonging to another) (Borsari, 1850; Cariota Ferrara, 1950: 29-126; Grossi, 1963: 237-262).

By virtue of these elements the emphyteusis is set apart from the more commonplace land tenant contracts, abiding to the model of Roman law *locatio-conductio*: short-term contracts with an equitable rent, with no immediate, or subsequent, restrictions to the owner's rights. In case of contracts established with the direct cultivators, the contract lasts one, two, or three years; they have more expensive *canons*, in coin or kind, or either they are sharecropping contracts (the owner getting a portion of what the peasant tenant harvested, often 'a mezzadria' (*métayage*), or *ad tertium*. Even in cases of extensive plots of land leased to non-cultivators (e.g. hundreds of hectares transferred to a tenant who takes care of the plot himself, or by sub-contracts), the contracts applied are leases or contracts of 'large rent' ('grande affitto') slightly longer (yet no more than nine years), and with high rents, proportional to the actual yields of the land.

Another feature distinguishing of northern-central Italy is the fact that, in the late Middle Ages and Early Modern period, emphyteutic contracts lacked all of the feudal or seigniorial elements that in other countries often appear bound to or muddled with the emphyteutic contract[5]. Clauses on land amelioration that distinguished classical emphytheusis are not imposed except in unusual cases. Moreover emphyteutic contracts, as we will discuss further, are chiefly used for extensive ecclesiastical proprieties.

II. The Economic Context of Northern-Central Italy in the Central and Late Middle Ages

These features lead to my second argument: the issue of the geographic and economic context, within which the use of these contracts must be set, and which I wish to deal with here.

---

5 'In Italy sooner that anywhere feudalism was rapidly transformed from a political (and military) into an economic (or civil)institution, embracing by the eleventh century both aristocratic and rustic or ministerial vassals, noble and inferior form forms of service (*servitium militare, rusticum*), and eventually, also tenure (*feudum militare* or *rectum et gentile, feudum condizionale*). Among the upper classes particularly, beginning perhaps with occupants of ecclesiastical lands, the fief was corrupted early by contamination or joint holding with traditional leasehold contracts (emphyteusis, libellus) into a further species of perpetual tenure or *dominium* (when not converted to outright alod, *allodium*): divisible, alienable, with mainly negative obbligations, and commonly free of homage, fealty, and even service (*sine fidelitate, sine servicio*)' (Jones, 1997: 113-114). On the great and deep transformations of the agrarian régime in these centuries see Cherubini (1967: 65-67). On the lasting interlacing and connections between feudal and seignorial components of emphyteutic contracts in other European countries, see Clavero (1986).

This context appears to some extent to depart from the one implicitly delineated by our book's editors' introductive considerations in speaking of the emphyteusis as interesting estates of wasteland, or improductive land, mountainous areas, marshlands, or borderlands; and in considering the lessees overall as the direct farmers, at times even subject to seigniorial or feudal rights.

The context I am here taking into consideration is the so-called 'Italy of the cities': it is that area of northern-central Italy running from the sub-alpine zone abutting the Alps, down along the peninsula unto southern Tuscany and the southern Marche: it is an area distinguished by an intense urban expansion, during the central centuries of the Middle Ages, and by a political-territorial system centred on strong city-states (each constituted by a city and its territory, the 'contado', covering about 1.000-2.550/3.000 Km^2, in the regions of the plain of the river Po valley and in Tuscany). It is not only a question of the great number of inhabitants, but of the economic and political influence which these centers could exert on large territories. This structure of city-states, notwithstanding the political, institutional and administrative changes during the Renaissance (with the formation of regional states) holds up until the early centuries of the Modern Age, as the underlying structure of the territorial and administrative organisation (Chittolini, 2010: 287-241).

The pervasive presence of cities confers a unique tone to the economic life of these regions[6]. They are marked –since the Roman Age and notwithstanding the fallbacks of the early Middle Ages – by a widespread and diffused land occupation, and by a tight network of settlements. The urban expansion of the eleventh to

6 To the sole purpose of providing an example to assess the degree of urbanisation in Italy, we may consider the figures relative to the number of cities with a population over 10.000 inhabitants in Italy and in Europe, about the year 1500, according to (De Vries, 1984: 28, 36) (to that data we may also add, as an example, the extension of the areas taken into consideration by De Vries, and the assessment he provides for the total population within those areas):

Number of cities, urban population, total population (*c.* 1500)

	Number of cities	Urban population	Total pop. in millions
Scandinavia	1	13.000	1,5
England, Scotland, Wales	6	93.000	4,4
Netherlands	11	150.000	0,9
Belgium	12	295.000	1,4
Germany, Austria, Bohemia, Switz.	27	445.000	16,2
France	32	688.000	16,4
Italy	44	1.303.000	10,5
Nothern Italy	*21*	*638.000*	
Central Italy	*9*	*287.000*	
Southern Italy	14	377.000	
Spain, Portugal	21	444. 000	7,8
Europa	154	3.441.000	61,6

thirteenth centuries, the formation of the great communes in the cities, and then and city-states, brought on a powerful impulse to the growth of agrarian economy, and bound the organisation of farming in the countryside areas to their respective cities: the countryside is impressed with dynamic stimuli coming from the urban ambient, even though it must then accept heavy conditioning by it.

We thus reckon a redistribution of agrarian property, bearing a strong increase of property in the hands of townsmen, earlier and in greater measure than in other areas of Europe: property of the *cives*, of urban corporations, or urban ecclesiastical corporations (which often means city clergy). On the contrary, the presence of territorial nobility is strongly reduced, both in its rights of jurisdiction, as well in regard to its landed estates. Agriculture is soon directed in favour of the market (the populous city market and the great markets held throughout the territory), and the organisation of agriculture is made functional to that scope: the large estates, that had once been ecclesiastical or noble, become fractioned by the spread of plots and holdings (measuring between a few, and up to tens of, hectares). Land occupation by the townsmen is more substantial in the city ground itself, the same ones that, with the city's growth, would later become urban ground (Faron & Hubert, 1995), in the vicinity of the city, where the fragmentation of the estates is also more pronounced; yet it also pushes into farther areas, where plots, vineyards, meadows can be owned and tended by the citizens, within the safe boundaries of the *contado* and fiscally protected by the city laws: a situation which also extended in the early modern period. Agrarian contracts concerned with the cultivation and trade of produce were preponderantly introduced from the age of the communes: short-term contracts, often with rent in kind. Towns were anxious to secure the cheapest possible food supplies for their inhabitants, and to draw to the urban market the surplus production of the neighbourhood.

In this context a contract such as the emphyteusis (long-term, not inclined to changes in crop types or in rent fees, hardly adaptable to a briskly fluctuating and vigorously growing market) has an ever dwindling diffusion. In the high Middle Ages it had enjoyed a widespread diffusion, on the large possessions of ecclesiastical and noble land, as well as on smaller plots, and in areas near the city; between the twelfth and thirteenth centuries it rapidly falls into disuse, as it became ever less appealing for the estate owners. Emphyteutic concessions or 'livelli' tended somewhat to continue and survive in the marginal regions

---

I also recall the data on the total population in Italy and Spain at the end of the sixteenth century (it is noteworthy that the population density in Italy is very high even if refers only to the northern-central area here taken into consideration).

	Surface in km²	population (in millions)	density
Spain	500.000	8,200	16,4
Castile	378.000	6,910	18,2
Italy	300.000	12,500	41,7

rather to lessen: in the extensive alpine area, where the enjoyment of the land is strongly subject to environmental conditions (Andenna, 2004: 255), or along the lower course of the Po (areas with unregulated water systems, subject to floods and river-routes, thus with major hindrances to the organisation of agriculture); or furthermore along the coasts of the northern-Adriatic, in danger of turning into swampland; or in the grazing region of Maremma.

III. The Modern Age: the extent of lands on emphyteusis

In the Modern Age the lands held by emphyteusis are more limited than the those transferred by other kinds of contracts, or directly cultivated by the farmers: the productive organisation of most of the territory, and furthermore of the best part of it, is defined rather by allodial property, owned in absolute property by citizens, patrician or merchants (or partly owned through ecclesiastical tenures) and marked by the strong and comprehensive influence of the urban economy. In the large land farms the predominant contract forms were 'large-scale rent', handed over to middlemen, or middlemen / entrepreneurs such as *gros fermiers* or yeomen; in the management of small plots, rent or sharecropping contracts are very common, especially of *mezzadria*: short-term contracts, with equitable and often high rents, in coin or in kind. Property held by farmers, whereby the owners directly cultivate the land, is much more uncommon and limited.

It is not at all a simple task to assemble an overall picture of the diffusion and extent of 'emphyteutic' lands: of those lands over which stands the superior right of an 'owner of dominium directum' (to whom a form of census is conferred), and nonetheless the holder of the 'dominium utile' (the lessee of the emphyteusis) has unlimited right to the land's enjoyment. In the cadastral surveys, produced in the various Italian states during the sixteenth to eighteenth centuries, these plots are often registered together with those held in full property, with which they in fact tend to be confused, and the holders of dominium utile are likened to owners with full property rights to all the purposes of tax duties. The registrations were nonetheless careful to mark the presence of burdens (such as the emphyteutic rents, in fact) pending over the plots of land, and by these figures we may thus purport some assessments.

We may estimate the ratio of emphyteutic lands in the state of Milan in the eigteenth century at 9% of the extent of all property (corresponding to 8% of the whole value); in the Venetian terra-firma, 'beyond the Mincio river' this ratio stands at between 4% and 12%. In most cases, as already in the previous centuries, the 'enfiteusi' and 'livelli' are gathered in mountainous areas or, less often, in the low marshlands of the plain[7].

---

7 See Beltrami (1961: 145 and maps n.n. last and second last); Romani (1957: 91-103); Carera (1986: 39, 42). On other situations see for instance Vaini (1973).

IV. The economic and social role of the emphyteutic contract

The emphyteutic contract holds an even smaller role in the system of agricultural production:[8] this is because only rarely – exceptionally – did this contract itself concern the direct cultivators on the land, but rather more often both the parts of the emphyteutic contract belonged to the elevated classes of society, clergy or nobility.

In most cases the landlord/lessor was an ecclesiastical corporation. These contracts traced back to a remote past, even centuries earlier. The intention of the ecclesiastical corporation – a church, a monastery, a bishop – rather than to create an actual agrarian contract, had been to transfer part of their rights over the land to a person of eminence or social standing: noble families, or families of the urban patriciate. In this way the ecclesiastical corporation could in any case ensure itself with a form of revenue, though often disproportionate to the land's productivity, from landed assets or immovable properties that it wasn't able, or didn't wish to, administer directly: direct management would have required commitment, expenses, advance-payments, and strong investments. In spite of losses over greater revenues, this course of action sought to provide reputed tenants, who would be willing to take full charge of the farm: essentially to be *fideles et utiles emphyteutae*. Certainly another motive that contributed to the choice of this contract was the wish to establish favourable social, and broadly political, ties with those classes: these were 'necessary generosities' on behalf of the church, in order to ensure those classes' benevolence, and were often set out by pre-existing ties of kinship or rank; 'necessary generosities' in order to safeguard their relationship with the laymen in a long-term perspective, beyond any circumstantial advantages, on the basis of the broad network of interests within which the employment of ecclesiastical lands had fallen since the early Middle Ages (Morris, 2008: 327-344; Duby, 1973: 63-66, 68-69, and Rosenwein, 1989)[9]. These contracts usually required a slight rent, usually in coin (and in this case destined to devalue over time); they were of long-term (20 years, one or two generations, lifelong, or *in perpetuum*); they included the prospect of descendable transmission (with some limitations for women), and furthermore alienation of the useful rights of ownership, with the consent of the lessor.

In these cases however the emphyteusis risked turning into a form of alienation. The leased lands went to be part of the patrimony of the emphyteuta:

---

8 Such as was said, in the *longue durée* history of agrarian contracts, in the centuries between the central Middle Ages and the Early Modern period, the enmphiteusis 'si collocava progressivamente fuori della storia viva dei rapporti agrari… ' (Giorgetti, 1974: 97-103).

9 These authors mark out the multiple meanings taken on by the donations, the sales and transactions related to it, as elements of a much more complex system of rapports, not merely economic but furthermore 'social' in a broad sense; and he points out the importance of the *relationship* that the use of land established.

as lands subject to canons, to *passive leses*, yet administered and enjoyed in complete freedom of right (and by these attributes the contracts started being registered in the inventories and account books of the leaseholding families). On the contrary, in the inventories and account books of the landowning ecclesiastical corporations, they pass to being registered only as monetary revenue, under the entries *censi*, *livelli attivi* or the such, bearing an ever lower value.

These contracts lasted decades, or often whole centuries, and their continuity was endangered only in relatively rare situations. Nonpayment of the rent wasn't prejudicial to the rights of the emphyteuta, nor did it necessarily imply rescission of the contract: forms of penalties and time-deferred payments were accepted. In order for these contracts to be annulled, 'rescinded', for the emphiteusis to be extinguished, a necessary condition was, for example, the interruption of the male line of descent (when the right to female succession wasn't recognised), or else the alienation of the useful rights of ownership *irrequisitio dominio*. Long-lasting litigations aroused in these cases, which could carry on for decades or centuries, and generated recurring judicial procedures, with much production of a bulky documentation, voluminous judicial acts ('atti in causa'); the parties summoned important jurists, who in turn wrote extensive and reputed *consilia*; the law courts, civil and ecclesiastical, pronounced sentences, and yet again appeals were interposed, and so forth, for generations.

When the landoning ecclesiastical corporation wished to recover actual possession over the land – re-joining the dominium directum they did hold with the dominium utile that had been transferred to the lessee – complications were not at all few. The opportunities to attempt these claims were rare; the procedures were long and expensive; moreover the jurists' appraisements and the courts' sentences were often favourable to the emphyteutas.

It must be said that the cases in which the ecclesiastical corporations stubbornly pursued their claims were actually infrequent. In the Age of Reformation, mainly at the end of the sixteenth century, there were unyielding 'reforming' prelates, bent onto recovering their churches' rights, such as Carlo Borromeo in Milan, or some of the combative regular orders (Brambilla, 1984: 395-450, 1987: 71-114 and Landi, 1996: 28 ss.), yet these uncompromising stances became more uncommon in the following decades and centuries, when the predominant effort was in achieving peaceful cohabitation between the churchmen and the dominant classes, a relationship that wasn't to be jeopardised by overzealous prelates. The problem of the modes of employment of ecclesiastical assets was but one aspect of the more complex and structured system of relations between church and society. This state of affairs of overall concord, albeit marked by frequent if petty disputes, carried on essentially for all of the Ancien Régime: a situation in which nobles and clergy shared rights and revenues over the lands, the former enjoying the dominium utile, and the latter the dominium directum[10]. This was like re-drawing a sort of ancient manner of joint property, a coexistence of reciprocally non-excluding rights, in a long-term perspective, and with the primary aim of upkeeping the goods and together stable relations (Chittolini, 2000: 11-34; 2008: 11-31), maintaining a form of balance that could yet be modified in favour of the landowner/lessor or of the lessee, in accordance with the different compulsions coming from the changes in the economic conditions, the social and political circumstances, from the rise of new approaches to the administration of the Church's patrimony.

This also explains why a good number of emphyteutic contracts continue to be written even in the sixteenth, seventeenth and eighteenth centuries, in spite of the limited income that would come to the churches, and in spite of the risk of losing that property to the lessees, as in fact substantiated by long time experience.

V. Final thoughts

The emphyteusis contract, in this way, in these forms, and according to these features, cannot be considered as an actual agrarian contract. The burden of organising the administration of the land fell into the lessee's competence (as, on the other hand, did most of the earnings go to him), and very rarely did he recur to emphyteusis. Emphteusis and 'livelli' were rather a 'play of interchange' among the ruling classes of the society, laymen and clergymen. Nevertheless the overall tendency had been towards the consolidation of full right of ownership in the hands of the laymen, even before the laws of eversion of ecclesiastical property, in the second half of the eighteenth century.

Uncommon were those cases in which the contracts of emphyteusis concerned the direct cultivators. This did occur, as mentioned above, in mountainous areas, pastures or forests, with slower productive cycles; and in hilly regions where the agrarian economy was less advanced; and in a few areas of the low plains where the emphyteuta had to take charge of weighty expenditures to preserve the land from the rivers. Many 'emhyteutas' were thus small lessees with their families, who had perhaps lived onto those lands since long ago. When renewing those contracts, or by their extension to new farmers, the rapports that had long ago, been established between churches (and nobles) on the one hand, and their lands and their cultivators on the other, were kept ongoing; it didn't seem correct or convenient to modify

10 *Ut unico fere patrimonio sociati, indivisa charitate iungeremur* encouraged a jurisconsult in Ferrara, remarking the need for concord between clergy and aristocracies on the basis of common temporal interests, according to the principles of the ideology that was to order the economy of ecclesiastical institutions; a concord that stood as the condition for the common and beneficial functioning of the two orders to the advantage of the whole collectivity (Pigantii, 1694: 48-78).

those relationships, and maintaining them preserved a form of social stability that wasn't to be perturbed (and that could in itself turn out to be a factor of long-to-mid-term upkeep and increase of productivity). Many cases have been evidenced in the Venetian area, where the contract often took on the name of *livelli* (and were called *livelli al modo antiquo*; the rents were 'moderate', or undeniably cheap, yet not merely a token of acknowledgment, to the point of configuring an *improper emphyteusis* (Varanini, 1987: 122-125; Lamaro Sartori, 1987: 209 ss, 220, 241-242)[11]. Even in this region nonetheless, particulary during the eighteenth century, the predominant trend that emerged was towards rejoining the two rights into full ownership, which could be managed efficiently according to the requirements of the market. In these cases it was mostly the large ecclesiastical corporations that took profit, although not without a trail of (sometimes violent) disputes with the cultivators (Stella, 1980: 171-193; Fasulo, 1980: 113-149)[12].

Instances in which the emphyteutas achieved full rights of ownership were quite exceptional. This occurred mostly when the original emphyteutic leases from the ecclesiastical corporations had been of collective quality, as was the case of the so called *agrarian participations* in the region of Emilia, in the low plain of the Po river valley along the waterway. The communities that had been so invested had taken charge of defending the lands from the waters for centuries, building embankments and canals, preserving cultivability, by sustaining burdensome expenses and commitments:[13] thus they matured full rights of ownership over the years. The same process took place *de facto*, if not *de iure*, among many alpine and mountainous communities, in which the superior right of an ecclesiastical corporation functioned in preserving through the centuries the locals' beneficial enjoyment of the goods from external threats and dangers (Della Misericordia, 2006).

---

11 The great diffusion of these contracts in this area was stressed by a jurist of Verona in the second half of the fifteenth century: *Maior pars omnium possessionum territorii nostri is 'a livello': non enim est in tota Italia una civitas magis livellata quam sit nostra* (Cepolla, in Varanini (1982: 198). See also Fassina, 1985: 87-100 and Pizzati, 1994: 96-97, 118.

12 The full disposability of the land, obtained to the prejudice of the peasants, made it possible to introduce managing innovations (Stella, 1980: 177-176; Landi, 1996, 1999: 269-279). On the peasants' reaction and on the 'rustics furor' produced by these innovations, see: cfr. J.Cauacius [Jacques Cujas], *Opera omnia in decem tomos distribuita…* (M. Aloysii Mutio, 1722, t. 3, in nota 18 p. 176, s.; Fassina, 1984: 147-154).

13 See the essays in Fregni, 1992, especially Cazzola, 1992: 294: the common feature, among the variety of the specific forms of participations, consisted in the fact that 'only a long-lasting and intensive collective effort could have made the lands productive'.

Bibliography

ANDENNA, Giancarlo (2004), 'Le grandi abbazie dell'Italia settentrionale', in Giorgio PICASSO & Mauro TAGLIABUE (eds), *Il monachesimo italiano nel secolo della grande crisi*, Cesena, p. 223-264.

BELTRAMI, Daniele (1961), *La penetrazione economica dei veneziani in Terraferma. Forze di lavoro e proprietà fondiaria nelle campagne venete dei secoli XVII e XVIII*, Venezia-Roma.

BRAMBILLA, Elena (1984), 'Per una storia materiale delle istituzioni ecclesiastiche', in *Società e storia*, VII, nr. 24, p. 395-450.

BRAMBILLA, Elena (1987), 'Politica, chiesa, e comunità locale in Lombardia: l'abbazia di Civate nella prima età moderna (1500-1700)', in *Nuova Rivista storica*, LXXI (1987), p. 71-114.

BORSARI, Luigi (1850), *Il contratto di enfiteusi*, Ferrara.

CARERA, A. (1986), 'Agricoltura e regime fondiario: la proprietà ecclesiastica della terra nelle aree di collina, altopiano e pianura dello stato di Milano del primo Settecento', in S. ZANINELLI (ed.) *La proprietà fondiaria in Lombardia dal catasto teresiano all'età napoleonica*, Milano, p. 3-92.

CARIOTA FERRARA, Luigi (1950), *L'enfiteusi*, Torino.

CHERUBINI, Giovanni (1967), *Qualche considerazione sulle campagne dell'Italia centro-settentrionale tra l'XI e il XV secolo. In margine alle ricerche di Elio Conti*, in *Rivista Storica italiana* LXXIX.

CHERUBINI, Giovanni (1974), *Signori, contadini, borghesi. Ricerche sulla società italiana del basso Medioevo*, Firenze, p. 51-119.

CHITTOLINI, Giorgio (2010), 'Urban population, urban territories, small towns: some problems of the history of urbanisation in northern and central Italy', in P. HOPPENBROUWERS, A. JANSE & R. STEIN (eds), *Power and persuasion. Essays in the art o State Building in honour of W. P. Blockmans*, Turnhout, p. 287-341.

CHITTOLINI, Giorgio (2000), 'Alcune note sulle "enfiteusi ecclesiastiche" ferraresi', in L. ANTONIELLI, C. CAPRA, M. INFELISE (eds), *Per Marino Berengo. Studi degli allievi*, Milano 2000, p. 11-34.

CHITTOLINI, Giorgio (2008), 'Appunti su alcune bolle pontificie a favore degli "amfitiotici" nello Stato della Chiesa (secoli XIV-XVII), in Con la ragione e con il cuore', in M. MERIGGI, S. LEVATI, *Studi dedicati a Carlo Capra*, Milano, Franco Angeli, p. 11-31.

CLAVERO, Bartolomé (1986), 'Enfiteusis. ¿Qué hay en un nombre?', in *Anuario de historia del derecho español*, LVI, p. 467-519.

CAZZOLA, Franco (1992), *Tra conflitto e solidarietà: considerazioni sull'esperienza storica delle partecipanze agrarie nell'Emilia*, in Euride FREGNI, *Terre e comunità nell'Italia padana. Il caso delle partecipanze agrarie emiliane: da beni comuni a beni collettivi, Cheiron*, 8 (1990-1991), 14-15, Mantova, p. 293-307.

DE VRIES, Jan (1984), *European Urbanisation, 1500-1800*, London.

Della Misericordia, Massimio (2006), *Divenire comunità. Comuni reali, poteri locali, identità sociali e territoriali in Valtellina e nella montagna lombarda nel tardo medioevo*, Milano.

Duby, Georges (1973), *Guerriers et paysans. VIIe-XIIe siècle, premier essor de l'économie européenne*, Editions Gallimard, Bibliothèque des Histoires.

Fasulo, Franco (1980), 'Livelli e livellari del monastero di Praglia tra '400 e '500. Primi risultati di una ricerca, in *San Benedetto e otto secoli (XII-XIX) di vita monastica nel Padovano*, Padova, p. 113-149.

Fassina, Michele (1984), '*"Astrenzer i contadini e lasciar stare il monastero". Le disavventure della proprietà di un ente ecclesiastico in una comunità contadina nel XVI secolo'*, *Annali Veneti. Società Cultura Istituzioni*, 1, p. 147-154.

Fassina, Michele (1985), *Le chase sparpanade. Marcon secoli XVI-XVIII*, Marcon.

Faron, Olivier & Hubert, Étienne (dir.) (1995), *Le sol et l'immeuble. Les formes dissociées de propriété immobilière dans les villes de France et d'Italie (XII*[e]*-XIX*[e] *siècle)*, Roma, École française de Rome, 206.

Feenstra, Robert (1974), *Les origines du* dominium utile *chez les glossateurs*, in *Fata iuris Romani*, Leiden.

Fregni, Euride (ed.) (1992), *Terre e comunità nell'Italia Padana. Il caso delle Partecipanze agrarie emiliane: da beni comuni a beni collettivi*, Mantova, *Cheiron*, 8 (1990-1991), 14-15.

Giorgetti, Giorgio (1974), *Contadini e proprietari nell'Italia moderna. Rapporti di produzione e contratti agrari dal secolo XVI a oggi*, Torino, Einaudi.

Grossi, Paolo (1963), *Locatio ad longum tempus. Locazione e diritti reali di godimento nella problematica del diritto comune*, Napoli.

Grossi, Paolo (1966), 'Problematica strutturale dei contratti agrari nella esperienza giuridica dell'alto medioevo, in Agricoltura e mondo rurale in occidente nell'alto Medioevo', in *Settimane di studio del Centro italiano di Studi sull'alto medioevo, XIII, 22-28 aprile 1965*, Spoleto, p. 487-530.

Jones, Philip (1997), *The Italian City State. From Commune to Signoria*, Oxford.

Lanaro Sartori, Paola (1987), 'Reddito agrario e controllo fiscale nel cinquecento: la Valpolicella e Verona', in Gian Maria Varanini (ed.), *La Valpolicella nella prima età moderna (1500-1630)*, Verona, p. 205-245.

Landi, Fiorenzo (1996), *Il paradiso dei monaci. Accumulazione e dissoluzione dei patrimoni del clero regolare in età moderna*, Roma.

Landi, Fiorenzo (1999), 'The Great Estates of the Regular Male Clergy: Distinctive Characteristics of a Managerial and Accounting System', in Fiorenzo Landi (ed.), *Accumulation and Dissolution of Large Estates of the Regular Clergy in Early Modern Europe*. Rimini: Guaraldi, p. 269-279.

Morris, Rosemary. (2008), 'The Problems of Property', in Thomas F. X. Noble & Julia M. H. Smith *Christianity Early Medieval Christianities, c. 600–c. 1100*, vol. III, Cambridge, p. 327-344.

Pigantii, Herculis (1694), *Ad Statuta Ferrariae Lucubrationes in quibus quaestiones, quae passim in foro emergunt, explicantur*, 2 tomi, Ferrariae 1694, t. II.

Pizzati, Anna (1994), *Conegliano. Una 'quasi città' e il suo territorio nel secolo XVI*, Treviso.

Romani, Mario (1957), *L'agricoltura in Lombardia dal periodo delle riforme al 1859. Struttura, organizzazione sociale e tecnica*, Milano, Vita e pensiero Rosenwein, Barbara H. (1989), *To Be the Neighbour of Saint Peter. The Social Meaning of Cluny's Property, 909-1049*, Cornell University Press, Ithaca, New York, U.S.A.

Simoncelli, Vincenzo (1922), *Della enfiteusi*, Napoli e Torino.

Stella, Aldo (1980), 'Bonifiche benedettine e precapitalismo veneto tra Cinque e Seicento', in *San Benedetto e otto secoli (XII-XIX) di vita monastica nel Padovano*, Padova, p. 171-193.

Vaini, Mario (1973), *La distribuzione della proprietà terriera e la società mantovana dal 1785 al 1845. I, Il catasto teresiano e la società mantovana nell'età delle riforme*, Milano.

Varanini, Gian Maria (ed.) (1987), 'Problemi di storia economica e sociale della Valpolicella', in Gian Maria Varanini (ed.), *La Valpolicella nella prima età moderna (1500-1630)*, Verona, p. 47-154.

Varanini, Gian Maria (ed.) (1982), *Le campagne veronesi del 400 fra tradizione e innovazione, in Uomini e civiltà agraria in territorio veronese (secoli IX-XVIII)*, a cura di G.Borelli, Verona, Banca Popolare di Verona, 1982, I.

MICHELA BARBOT

3. What the *Dominia* Could Do

Enfiteusi *and Other Forms of Divided Property Rights in Lombardy from the Fourteenth to the Twentieth Centuries*

I. Introduction

In January 1896, one of the largest landowners of Northern Italy, the Congregation of Lay Institutions (*Congregazione dei Luoghi Pii Elemosinieri della Lombardia*) rented *a livello* to a textile merchant a shop located in the *Carrobbio di Porta Ticinese*[1], one of the most commercial neighbourhoods of Milan[2]. About a year and a half later, in the village of Crenna, near Varese, the same Congregation authorized the tenant Marco Bossi to continue occupying an estate of 28 acres where his family had been *enfiteuta* for four generations[3].

Before explaining the legal and economic meaning of these two contractual devices – the *livello* and the *enfiteusi* – let us take a few steps back. In 1804, under French rule, Lombardy officially adopted the Napoleonic Code (Cavanna, 2000 and 2001). Even without eliminating other forms of ownership, this legal code imposed private, absolute, abstract and exclusive property as the main form of property right legally possible (Grossi, 1981; Halpérin, 2003). Sixty years later, in 1864, the Italian government passed a national law encouraging the reunification in the hands of a single subject of all the property rights previously shared and divided among several individuals or institutions[4]. The lawmakers intended these two reforms to open the way for the triumph of an ownership culture centred on individual rights, at the expense of the other two major property regimes that had existed in Europe since medieval times: collective rights (Commons) and divided rights (also called Dominia, from the Latin *dominium*: Grossi, 1992).

Both the Commons and the Dominia gave priority to effective possession over formal deeds (Grossi, 1996 and 2006). But unlike the Commons, in which ownership was – and still is (Ostrom, 2000) – collective and shared by the

1 Archivio Centrale Lemosiniero (hereafter ACL), Patrimonio Attivo, Livelli, B. 161-194.

2 On the commercial area of *Carrobbio di Porta Ticinese*, see S. D'Amico (1994).

3 ACL, Patrimonio Attivo, Case e Poderi, Cart. 67, f. 1105: Ufficio Tecnico (1897-1898), October 18th, 1897.

4 This law – the longest in Italian history – was abolished only in 2008 (Mobili & Rogari, 2008).

Agrarian Change and Imperfect Property, ed. by Rosa Congost and Pablo F. Luna, Rural History in Europe, 15 (Turnhout, 2018), 53-73

DOI 10.1484/M.RURHE-EB.5.116118

members of a group or a community, the medieval and early modern Dominia sharply separated property right into two levels, a dominium directum and an a dominium utile, both of which could be attributed to different individuals or institutions. The specificity of the Dominia regime, in fact, was that it allowed an infinite division and sub-division of the usage and direct rights[5]. Both of them could be entirely or partially sold, subleased or conveyed from a generation to another. These characteristics, in turn, made this system very different from the full, abstract and individual ownership imposed by the Napoleonic Code, which is based on the exclusivity and indivisibility of proprietors' rights (Halpérin, 2008).

I.1. The Dominia system in search of a history

The legal imposition of private and full property at the expense of collective ownership has been extensively treated in Italy and elsewhere[6]. In recent decades, in fact, the Commons have been at the centre of many attempts to understand what their disappearance meant for the European Industrial Revolution (Allen, 1992; Neeson, 1993; Clark, 1998; De Moor, Shaw-Taylor & Warde, 2002; Démelas, Vivier, 2003; Béaur, 2006)[7]. The debate on the so-called 'Tragedy of the Commons' (Hardin, 1968) and the emergence of the New Institutional Economics paradigm (North and Thomas, 1973; North, 1990) have both attracted further interest in this area of research. In their classic formulation, both of these frameworks share the basic idea that, in general, private, exclusive and individual property rights, by reducing conflicts and minimizing transaction costs (Coase, 1960), are the most rational, certain and efficient form of legal ownership (North, 1981)[8].

Within the New Institutional paradigm, a recent body of studies has challenged this thesis, showing that the Commons, under certain local conditions, could also be perfectly efficient (Ostrom, 1990 and 2005). However, these theoretical insights have not been brought to bear on the system of the Dominia. In most cases, in fact, the contractual devices associated with this

---

5 It should be noted, however, that in some cases the difference between Commons and Dominia could be complicated because ending the Commons system could sometimes give rise to Dominia contracts. This was, for example, the effect of the law of 16 June 1839, in which the government of Lombardy-Venetia compelled municipalities to sell or lease uncultivated land in order to make it useful and productive. This law favoured the enforcement of the Dominia system wherever the farmers did not have the resources to buy the freehold of the land.

6 On the Italian case, see Fregni (1990-1991); Alfani & Rao (2011).

7 For an anthropological analysis of these processes, see also the classic work of Macfarlane (1978).

8 More specifically, in the classical New Institutional Economics perspective, collective ownership could be explained in terms of efficiency as it can cope with imperfections or 'failures' of the market system: in this sense, the neo-institutional interpretation integrates and expands the analytical framework of neoclassical economics (Stanziani, 2011: 215).

legal regime have been treated as if they belonged to the same institutional family as collective ownership, without any attention to the differences between them.

Moreover, the few extant studies of the Dominia have focused much more on rural than on urban spaces[9]. The contrasting geographic focus of these studies can be explained in several ways. One of the most important of these is a bias – reinforced by some highly influential traditional theories (Sombart 1902; Weber 1966) – towards the belief that the city, as the epicentre and the engine of Western modernization, was where private property and proprietary individualism were affirmed in their earliest and most absolute form. Following this bias, many scholars have interpreted the gradual triumph of the full private property system in Western societies as the outcome of the cities' early escape from feudal constraints, in contrast to a rural world that remained inexorably backward, archaic and immobile.

Despite the widespread diffusion of this theory, the equivalence between the city and private property has recently been questioned by a series of works showing that, for a long time and even until quite recently, European cities have been the realm of lease and divided property in their many forms[10]. So even leaving aside the *a priori* assumption of modernity, empirical evidence casts doubt on the hypothesis that private ownership arrived earlier in urban than in rural spaces. In this perspective, Lombardy represents an interesting case study. Since medieval times, the Po Valley has been subjected to a process of agrarian individualism (Romani, 1957; Bevilacqua, 1989) which challenges the idea that an urban world integrated in a capitalistic full property system co-existed with a rural space crushed under the weight of feudal and pre-capitalistic institutions.

I.2. The Dominia system in Lombardy

This investigation addresses the historical case of Lombardy in detail, focusing on the long-run process by which local inhabitants transformed themselves into full owners after being *domini utilis* and *domini directi* for several centuries.

To analyse the Dominia in both rural and urban Lombardy we have used a set of primary sources collected in an ongoing and wider investigation into rights over land, real estate and water resources in the ancient Duchy of Milan (*Ducato di Milano*), and more particularly within the jurisdiction of the capital

---

9 On rural Europe, see the recent and exhaustive work by Béaur, Arnoux & Varet-Vitu (2003). Among the few studies dealing with the urban world, see Béaur (1994); Faron & Hubert (1995).

10 In Italy and France, for instance, between the sixteenth and eighteenth centuries the percentage of full owners of their residence ranged from 4-5% (in Venice, Milan and Turin) and 20% (in Florence and Paris): Roche (1982); D'Amico (1994); Curto (1995); Levi (2000); Benfante (2003).

and its county (*Contado*)[11]. These data consist of 4,916 notarial deeds, 457 appraisals and estimates, and 821 legal reports on property conflicts dating from medieval times to the mid-twentieth century. These documents are stored in the two major regional landowners' archives: the aforementioned Congregation of Lay Institutions, which provided assistance and charity to the regional population (Bascapé, 2001), and the Factory of the Dome (*Fabbrica del Duomo*), which was responsible for building and maintaining the Cathedral of Milan (Braunstein, 1990; Barbot, 2009). To analyse these historical data, we have combined three main analytical techniques:[12] a case study methodology, a comparison with other Northern Italian areas, and a moderate recourse to measurement and quantification[13]. From a narrative point of view, our paper is organized as follows: the second section discusses the most common contractual forms of divided ownership in Lombardy between the fifteenth and the mid-twentieth centuries, setting forth the socio-economic implications of the *enfiteusi* and *livello* in relation to the rental forms associated with the full ownership system. The third section empirically discusses the applicability of the neo-institutional thesis about the greater efficiency and certainty of private and full property rights[14] by analysing property conflicts in Milan and its region from the fourteenth to the twentieth centuries. the fourth section, finally, shows some general implications of our analysis and offers some final hypothesis.

II. Overlapping Rights

As some studies have shown (Brewer & Staves, 1996; Grossi, 2006), although the logics of the Dominia were almost the same throughout continental Europe,

---

11 From 1535 to 1713, the Duchy of Milan – roughly corresponding to the current region of Lombardy – was part of Charles V's empire, and at his abdication (1555) it passed under the control of the Spanish monarchy. During this period, Milan lost political autonomy in foreign affairs, although it maintained its own legal and administrative structures. The Duchy was organized in provinces that had large autonomy in the matters of economic policies, taxation, public order and roads. Because of their long tradition of autonomy, the central government did not exert strong control over the provinces. Under the Utrecht Treaty of 1713, Milan passed to the Austrian monarchy. In the 1760s Vienna, under Maria Teresa, showed a strong desire to strengthen its royal authority and to discipline local powers. This process ended in 1790, and in 1861 the Duchy of Milan became a part of the Italian state: Chittolini (1994).

12 On the fruitful possibility of combining qualitative and quantitative methods, see Tilly (2004).

13 As we have already demonstrated (Barbot, 2008a), the divided forms of property in Lombardy's rural and urban spaces were so overlapping and inextricably linked to each other (and to the full property-rights systems), as to make any purely statistical or macro-analytical technique largely useless and historically inappropriate.

14 For a critical discussion of this thesis and its historical implications, see Congost (2003), Ogilvie (2007) and Congost & Santos (2010); Béaur, Schofield, Chevet & Pérez Picazo (2013).

their contractual forms were deeply influenced by local practices and customs. Within the area of Lombardy, three major rental forms of land and real estate were in use since medieval times: the *enfiteusi*, the *livello* and the *fitto semplice*.

Both the *enfiteusi* and the *livello* belonged to the divided property system, although the forms of dissociation they produced were different. The *enfiteusi*, one of the oldest contracts existing in Italy (Cencetti, 1939), created a physical separation between the land property and the buildings constructed on it (Vaccari, 1965; Scaffardi, 1981). Conversely, the *livello* gave rise to an abstract dissociation between the right to use the leased good – attributed to the dominus utile – and the right to collect the rents on it – attributed to the dominus directus (Corazzol, 1979 and 1986; Faccini, 1988; Barbot, 2008a and 2008b). Beyond their differences, both these contracts gave to the tenant the same status of 'almost owner' (*quasi proprietario*), with the legal obligation to pay taxes on the property and maintain or improve it for the entire duration of the contract. In medieval times, the duty of improvement often coincided with the obligation to build at one's own expense on an empty lot. This allowed many direct proprietors – mostly religious and lay institutions – to create new towns or to promote the repopulation of those abandoned without any cost to themselves (Hubert, 1992). In consideration of these duties, the tenants and their families were usually given the opportunity to occupy the building or the land for a long time – often for several generations – to customize these goods according to their needs, and to pay the direct owner an annual rent generally 'frozen' at very low levels (Fregna, 1990). This rent, in fact, did not have a primarily economic function, but was mainly intended to give legal recognition to the hierarchy of all the existing property rights (Chauvard, 2003).

Unlike the *enfiteusi* and the *livelli*, the *fitti semplici* (also called *pigioni* by notaries) belonged entirely to the legal sphere of full ownership. Then, the property rights were neither shared nor divided (Grossi, 1992), and the tenant was forced to leave no trace of his use of the good. At the same time, all the maintenance costs were borne by the full owner, who often failed to accomplish these duties punctually (Gauthiez, 1995; Barbot, 2010). The length of these contracts was usually between three and five years, and this circumstance allowed the full owner to increase the rent more often than in the *enfiteusi* and *livelli* contracts (Barbot, 2008a: 93-96).

In the Duchy of Milan, these three forms of lease involved also different spaces and goods (Table 3.1).

Although *enfiteusi*, and even more, *livelli*, were more common in the suburbs of Milan and in its *Contado*, that is, where most of the biggest buildings, vacant lots and farms were to be found (Scaramellini, Zoia, 2006), the *pigione* was mostly used to rent shops, flats and small rooms located within the city centre (Barbot, 2008a). It should be noted, however, that this distinction blurs important differences, since all of these contracts could easily coexist within the same building or even the same room. That was the case, for example, of a building located on the central Cathedral Square (*Piazza del Duomo*), consisting of four shops on the ground floor, five apartments on the first floor

Table 3.1. The most frequent rental contracts in the Duchy of Milan (16th-18th centuries)

	Enfiteusi	*Livello*	*Fitto semplice* or *pigione*
Type of ownership dissociation	Between land and buildings	Between the usage right and the right to collect rents	No dissociation: full and private property regime
Length	99 years, often perpetual	more than nine years, often perpetual	Between six months and nine years
Sublease	Possible	Possible	Possible
Objects	Vacant lots; houses to be rebuilt	Large residential buildings, often with gardens; lands in the *Contado*	Individual apartments, rooms, workshops
Geographical location	Suburbs and *Contado*	Anywhere, but more in the *Contado* than the city centre	Anywhere, but more in city centre than in the *Contado*
Rent	Low but stable	low but stable	High and instable
Forms of payment	Nature	Nature	Money
Maintenance duties	Tenant	Tenant	Owner
Property tax payment	Tenant	Tenant	Owner

Sources. 4,916 notarial deeds, from the Archivio Centrale Lemosiniero (ACL) and the Archivio della Veneranda Fabbrica del Duomo di Milano (AVFD).

and 11 rooms in the attic. A notarial deed dated 1615 shows the impressive variety of contracts by which the building was rented: the shops were subject to 11 *livelli*, two *sub-livelli* and three *pigioni*; the five apartments were occupied by five *livellari*, and the top floor rooms were inhabited by seven *sub-livellari* and four *pigionanti*[15]. Two centuries later, a similar legal overlap still predominated. According to an accounting register dated 1720, for instance, 77 per cent of the 292 buildings belonging to the Factory of the Dome were still entangled in several rental forms (*pigioni, livelli, sub-pigioni*, and *sub-livelli*)[16].

15 AVFD, Cart. 198.

16 AVFD, Nota delle case, e botteghe, possessioni, livelli et altro della Ven. Fabbrica del Duomo, 1720, Cart. 436, f. 3.

II.1. The enfiteusi contract and its absorption by the livello from the late seventeenth century on

Despite the long coexistence of these various rental forms, in early-modern Lombardy the *pigione* gradually triumphed at the expense of the other contracts, and in particular of the *enfiteusi*, which were used less and less from the late seventeenth century on. Among the 4,916 lease contracts analysed, in fact, only 2% corresponded to *enfiteusi* in its purest version (i.e. a physical dissociation between lands and buildings). The archives of the Factory of the Dome between the sixteenth and eighteenth centuries record only two of such contracts, both related to properties outside of Milan. In the first act, dated 1593, the Factory gave the monks of *San Dionigi* 40 perches of land in the city suburbs (the so called *Corpi Santi*) in *enfiteusi*, with the obligation to build their convent and pay an annual rent in kind[17]. The second contract, signed in 1638 in the peripheral area of *Porta Tosa*, relates to a building partially burned during the 1630 plague, which the tenants agreed to rebuild within 25 years[18]. A similar strategy was also employed by the Congregation of Lay Institutions, which used these contracts only to rent a few ruined properties located in suburban or rural areas.

This use of the *enfiteusi* can be partially explained by a comparison with Venice and Rome, two cities of the same size as Milan (Beloch 1994). In the case of Venice, the works of Elisabeth Crouzet-Pavan (1992), Jean-Francois Chauvard (2005) and Federica Masè (2006) have largely demonstrated that the *enfiteusi* disappeared completely in the late fifteenth century. The only exception to this trend was the Jewish *ghetto*, which for political reasons remained subject until the end of the Old Regime to the legal system of *casacà*. This was a property system very similar to the *enfiteusi*, since it dissociated the direct property of urban land, reserved to the Christian citizens, from the use of the *ghetto*'s buildings, granted to the Jewish local community (Boerio, 1856; Concina, Camerino & Calabi, 1991).

In contrast to Venice, the case of Rome was completely different. According to Renata Ago's study (1998), in the seventeenth century about a third of the real estate was still subject to the *enfiteusi* regime.

The striking difference between Venice and Rome may be explained both by the spatial morphology and the real estate structure of these two cities. In early modern times, the Venetian urban space was completely built up and could not be further expanded because of its natural constraints. To a very large extent, the basic elements of the urban morphology that we can observe today already existed in the later Middle Ages. In addition, the real estate ownership was considerably fragmented and there were almost no large landowners (Crouzet-Pavan, 1992; Chauvard, 2005). By contrast, early

17 AVFD, *Case in Milano*, Cart. 231, f. 107.

18 AVFD, Cart. 276, *Provvidenze generali*, 1638.

modern Rome was dotted by many vacant lots and marked by a considerable concentration of real estate in the hands of large organizations, especially religious ones (Vaquero Piñeiro, 1999). These two features made the *enfiteusi* very advantageous in Rome, because it allowed the big owners to build on empty spaces and maintain their properties at reasonable costs.

These two different urban examples are very useful for understanding the intermediate case of Milan. From a geographical point of view, its city centre was very dense and populous and closely resembled the Venetian area. But like Rome, the Milanese suburbs contained plenty of open space. This dual morphology explains why the *enfiteusi* were more widespread in the suburbs than in the urban centre. At the same time, as land was increasingly put under cultivation and urban spaces filled up with buildings, the rationale for this contract gradually disappeared.

The opposite happened to the *livelli*. Archival sources show that they completely replaced *enfiteusi* from the late seventeenth century, when notaries began to use the term *enfiteusi* as a perfect synonym of *livello*. The widespread use of *livelli* did not diminish even with the national law of 1864, encouraging the reunification and consolidation of the Dominia of lay and religious institutions in the hands of a single institution or private subject. In fact, this law did not really become operational until the first half of the twentieth century (Barbot, 2013a). Several factors explain this long delay. First of all, despite the legal opportunity created by the 1864 law, only a minority of Lombardy's *domini utilis* and *directi* proved to be really eager to become full owners. The most frequent situation was the opposite: after a long-term process of fragmentation and breakdown of property rights, they were inevitably forced to change their legal condition. As time went by, all the disposals, leases, subleases and hereditary divisions carried out on single fractions of dissociated rights actually made impossible to manage the Dominia. The case of *Verrua Siccomario*, an estate of the Congregation of Lay Institutions located in the heart of the Po Valley, is emblematic of this trend: in the late nineteenth century, the property rights of this estate were shared by more than 280 different 'almost' and direct owners[19], and only a judicial sale was able to end this intricate situation. In many other cases, the actors intentionally decided to create new dissociations rather then apply the full property system. As we have seen, even in 1896, over thirty years after the 1864 law, the Congregation of Lay Institutions chose to rent by perpetual *livello* a shop located in one of the most commercial areas of Milan, while refusing to pay the improvements due to the 'almost owners'. This contract, which expired in 1925, is far from the only example to be found in the archives[20].

19 ACL, Patrimonio Attivo, Livelli, Cart. 176, f. 3612, 3917.

20 Many examples are available in ACL, Livelli (1450-1914): Cart. 161-194.

II.2. Explaining the livelli's long life: the example of the seventeenth-century crisis

To better understand the reasons why the *livelli* lasted so long, even in the heart of one of the urban epicentres of the Italian Industrial Revolution (Bigatti, 2000), we must take a step back and focus on the seventeenth century recession.

As is well known, early-modern Milan – like many other Italian cities – knew a sustained growth from the 1540s to the 1620s, followed by a recession whose peak coincided with the 1630 plague, which deprived the city of 58% of its inhabitants (Sella, 1959 and 1979). These changes had many effects for the urban rental market. Because of their short duration, the *fitti semplici* suffered the most from the crisis. Already in 1625, at the first signs of the recession, 84% of the short-term rents collected by the Factory of the Dome had fallen by between 6 and 23% compared to five years before[21]. Given this situation, the Factory and other urban owners decided to shorten the *pigioni* from five years to three years so as to push rents back up again. But despite this measure, rental fees declined until the end of the 1650s, and only when the crisis was over did the *pigioni* become predominant once again (Barbot, 2008a: 151-152).

The case of the *livelli* was completely different, because the immobilization of rents in these long-term contracts served to hedge against their downturn. In the 1630s and 1640s, many owners decided to convert the *pigioni* into *livelli*, which provided a generally lower income, but more stable and secure. Such changes were made with the double aim of stabilizing rents and maintaining the urban buildings in good condition. After the 1630 shock, in fact, many properties leased by *pigione* deteriorated within a few months after being physically abandoned (Barbot, 2010). This did not happen to the *livelli*, usually associated with a greater residential stability (Barbot, 2006). In this case, the regular upkeep carried out by the tenants had the positive effect of preserving many buildings that undoubtedly would not have survived for long without maintenance.

The two parallel stories of the *casa alle Quattro Marie* and of the *casa al Prestino delle Scanze*, both located on the Cathedral Square, demonstrate this phenomenon very well. The first property, rented *a pigione*, was a big estate of 19 apartments and shops built in 1610. During the 1630 crisis, this building was abandoned by many of its inhabitants and fell into ruins much more quickly than the *casa al Prestino delle Scanze*, built two centuries before[22]. Between the sixteenth and seventeenth centuries, this old building underwent two major legal changes. Previously rented by a ten-year *livello* that was renewed several times, it was rented *a pigione* in 1593 after a period of economic growth, and then was returned to *livello* in 1653 (Barbot, 2008a: 149-151).

---

21 During the peak of 1629-1631, this fall become even more dramatic, with reductions from between 16 and 63% compared to the previous five years: BARBOT (2008a: 143-158).

22 The appraisals and estimates made on these two buildings by the Factory of the Dome's architects are available in AVFD, Cart. 236, 237, 247, 248, 258, 259, 273.

Table 3.2. Monthly rents on the *casa alle Quattro Marie*'s (in *Lire imperiali milanesi*), 1610-1649

Flats	1	2	3	4	5	6	7	8	9	10	11	12	13	14	15	16	17	18	19
1610	615	1700	1000	1050	850	700	690	500	550	580	800	480	610	500	540	450	500	410	700
1615	750	1730	1035	1064	875	710	720	575	570	595	850	505	640	520	565	502	525	450	750
1620	810	1750	1050	1149	700	1210	1100	843	1000	955	850	605	960	893	650	640	530	700	892
1625	750	2000	900	980	649	1300	800	700	700	725	800	436	650	515	500	500	480	540	910
1631	350	V	600	650	450	950	534	475	V	440	540	180	V	320	V	V	300	V	465
1632	V								V				370		V	V		V	
1633	475	1365							V						305	V		355	
1634			660	700	500	950	540		460	450	620	265		340		410	330	370	480
1635								510					400						
1636	600														313				
1637	600		700	750	550	950	575		480	500	625	300		350		370	350	392	510
1638		1400						510					410						
1640				830	V	V	525		500	550	660	305		370	320	V	360	405	525
1641	600		705		V	V										V			
1643		1415		900	620	1025	860	530	545	750	662		430	370	V	370	400	405	530
1644			750												V				
1646				730	640	880	705	540	580		675	305	435	390	V		400	405	540
1647	600	1420	750							V					400				
1649				750	600	800	610	450	550	V	690	332	400	420	410	380	410	405	550

Sources. AVFD, Cart. 236, 237, 238, 247, 248. [V = vacant flat]

Table 3.3. The casa al prestino delle Scanze's monthly rents (in Lire imperiali milanesi), 1610-1649

Year	Monthly Rent
1610	310
1615	320
1620	340
1625	300
1631	225
1634	175
1637	180
1640	180
1643	265
1646	265
1649	270

Sources: AVFD, Cart. 247.

This last choice had two positive effects: during the seventeenth-century crisis, the rent of the *casa al Prestino delle Scanze* remained more stable than that of the *casa alle Quattro Marie* (Tables 3.2 and 3.3); at the same time, the upkeep carried out regularly by the *dominus utilis* preserved this large house from ruin or collapse[23].

III. Divided rights, contentious rights?

Although the *livelli* could be economically advantageous, especially in times of crisis, during the nineteenth century the full property regime gradually replaced them not only in the regulations, but also in contractual practice. As we have seen, one of the most popular explanations of this phenomenon, developed by the theories of New Institutional Economics, assumes that private property gradually triumphed in contractual practices because it reduced the transactions costs and the uncertainty associated with the other legal systems. In the case of the Dominia, this uncertainty would have been caused by three major factors: a weak certification of the contracts belonging to this legal regime, the fragmentation of property rights, and a near-absence of public institutions capable of protecting these rights[24]. According to this thesis, in early modern Europe these three factors multiplied property conflicts,

23 This is widely confirmed by an architectural expertise dated 1710, which shows the good condition of the *casa al Prestino* despite its great age: AVFD, Cart. 247.

24 On the lack of public protection of property rights in early modern Europe, see North (1981).

making their resolution both expensive and time-consuming (Rosenthal, 1992). This, in turn, made economic transactions more difficult and weakened the entrepreneurialship of economic actors, preventing economic growth.

Although the neo-institutional interpretation is very widespread, it is far from sufficiently tested[25]. In the case of Lombardy, we have tried to verify this hypothesis by two main tests: an analysis of the conflicts over land and houses belonging to the Factory of the Dome between the sixteenth and eighteenth centuries, and an examination of the judicial disputes over water resources of the Congregation of Lay Institutions from 1386 to 1953.

III.1. Land and Houses

Our first test was to analyse a set of 257 conflicts over land and houses of the Factory of the Dome in two different areas: the city of Milan and the rural fief of Volpedo, in an outlying part of Lombardy, near Piedmont. 49.3% of these 257 conflicts involved properties leased in full ownership, while 50.7% involved properties rented by *livello*. The lack of certification and protection accounted for only a very few of these conflicts[26]. Most of them dependend in fact on four other causes: (1) the infringement of a specific legal status (as owner, virtual owner, tenant, or heir); (2) the non-fulfilment of one or more clauses of a contract of *fitto semplice* or *livello*; (3) the violation of the physical boundaries between two properties; (4) confiscations, seizures and expropriations made by the local and central authorities[27]. In the case of assets managed through the Dominia system, property rights were so split that the conflicts generally involved a large number of actors. This phenomenon made the coordination very difficult, but, at the same time, it often generated new economic opportunities. Even in the case of perpetual contracts, in fact, conflicts could act as agents of change, driving the economic actors to define, clarify, negotiate and bargain all the rights at stake (Barbot, 2008a and 2008b).

Moreover, it is important to note that the conflicts brought different claims according to the objects and places concretely involved. Within the city walls of Milan, disputes over the houses and shops of the factory of the Dome often had serious implications for the dynamics of social inclusion. Gaining (or losing) a right on the main living and working space, in fact, meant taking a decisive step towards a more (or less) integration into the urban community (Barbot, 2013b). On the other hand, in the countryside, as the conflicts took place over an asset – land – with very strong jurisdictional implications, they

---

25 Also in this case, rural spaces have been analysed much more than the cities. On the French case, see Rosenthal, 1990 and 1992.

26 In early-modern Lombardy, in fact, a large range of oral and written proofs were available to establish both divided and full property of lands and houses (Barbot, 2011).

27 On these procedures, see Barbot, Lorenzetti & Mocarelli (2012).

were more often related to the distribution of political power within the local community (Barbot, 2011).

Ultimately, these two opposite case studies show that we cannot state that divided property rights generated, in absolute terms, more litigation than the full private rights. Much more than the legal form of these rights, it was the asset actually involved in the disputes that could make the real difference.

III.2. Water resources

The second test we made is based on the analysis of 564 lawsuits (*atti in causa*) over 191 irrigation canals belonging to the Congregation of Lombardy's Lay Institutions between 1376 and 1953. These water resources were managed partly under the Dominia and partly under the regime of full property. In order to understand whether the imposition of private property in the nineteenth century acted as a pacifying factor, we have taken the year in which the Napoleonic Code was brought into Lombardy, in 1804, as the turning-point, splitting the analysis of all the conflicts into the two periods 1376-1804 and 1805-1953[28].

Figure 3.1 groups the starting dates of these disputes by ten-year segments. It shows that the period with most conflicts ran through the 1860s and 1870s, across the turning point marked by the introduction of the 1864 law. This law, therefore, not only had no immediate impact, but was even followed by an increase in disputes over irrigation rights.

Along with this first result, many other elements reinforce the idea that the nineteenth century was a rather contentious period. After 1804, the average duration of conflicts fell by only three years in relation to the previous period, while the average number of disputes per year more than doubled (Table 3.4), reaching their peaks in the 1860s and 1870s (Figure 3.2).

The 564 disputes involved almost equally irrigation rights granted under the regime of divided property (51.2 per cent) and those under the full property regime (48.8 per cent). In both cases, the most frequent reason for litigation was the imprecise definition of water rights (Table 3.5)[29].

It is also interesting to note that, both before and after the introduction of the Napoleonic Code, the area affected by the largest number of disputes was the Po Valley (Barbot, 2013a), i.e. the area of Lombardy's capitalist agriculture *par excellence*, where private property had triumphed more rapidly than elsewhere (Romani, 1957; Giorgetti, 1974).

Among the reasons of litigation (Figure 3.3), the disputes generated by undefined property rights were mostly concentrated in the period before 1804. This seems to indicate that the nineteenth century's institutional changes finally provided a better way to clarify water rights. Nevertheless, this change took place erratically over a very long time. Even in the middle of the

28 We have fully analysed these data in Barbot 2013a.
29 This was the pretext for the longest conflict of all (184 years).

Figure 3.1. Starting dates of conflicts, broken down by decade

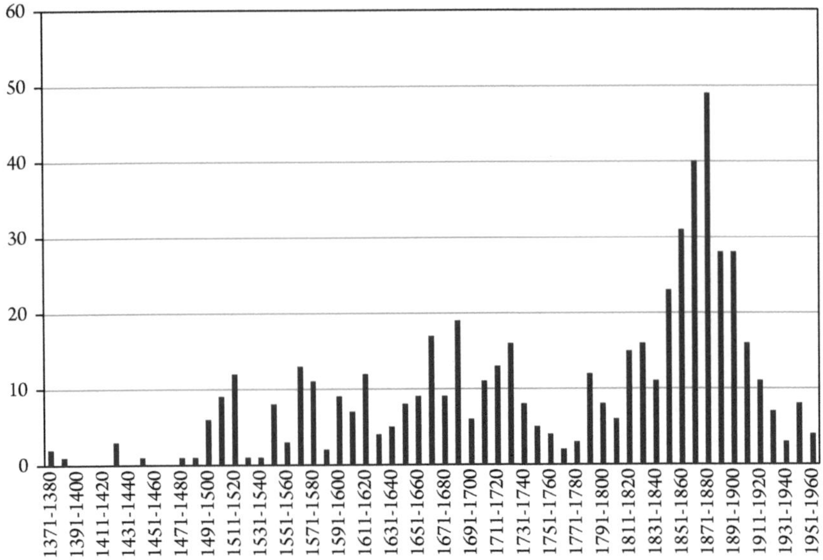

Sources:ACL, Fondi Acque, Poderi, Livelli

Table 3.4. Length and number of conflicts, 1376-1953 (average per year)

	1376-1953	1376-1804	1805-1953
Average length (years)	13,9	15,8	12,4
Average number of conflicts underway each year	16,8	11,9	27,3

Sources: ACL, Fondi Acque, Poderi, Livelli

Figure 3.2. Average number of conflicts per year, 1492-1953

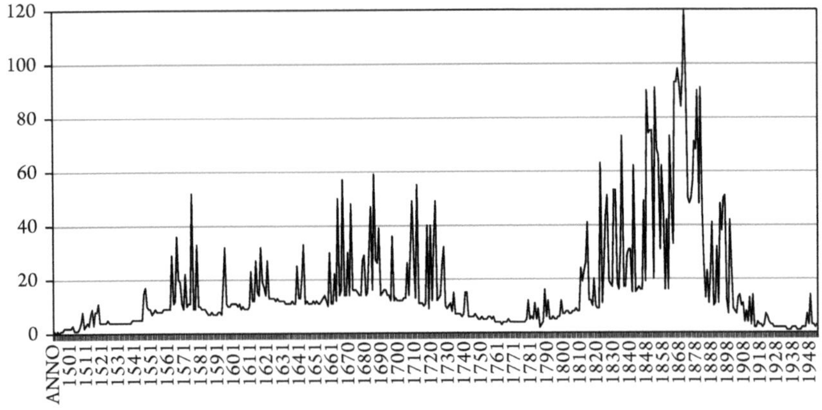

Sources: ACL, Fondi Acque, Poderi, Livelli (The period 1376-1491 has been not considered because of the shortage of conflicts)

Table 3.5. Reasons and length of conflicts (1376-1953)

Reasons	% of conflicts	Average duration (in years)	Maximum duration (in years)
Property rights definition	24.6	18.1	184 (from 1503)
Damages and abuses	20.3	10.2	171 (from 1508)
Unauthorized withdrawals	16.7	13.5	67 (from 1852)
Maintenance costs' allocation	14.5	22.8	179 (from 1607)
Competing uses of water	9.2	10.9	159 (from 1519)
Unauthorized deviations	6.4	7.6	23 (from 1886)
Expropriations	1.8	6.1	39 (from 1883)
Rent payment	1.4	12.3	38 (from 1849)
Other reasons	5.1	-	-

Sources: ACL, Fondi Acque, Poderi, Livelli

Figure 3.3. Number of disputes by cause (pre and post 1804)

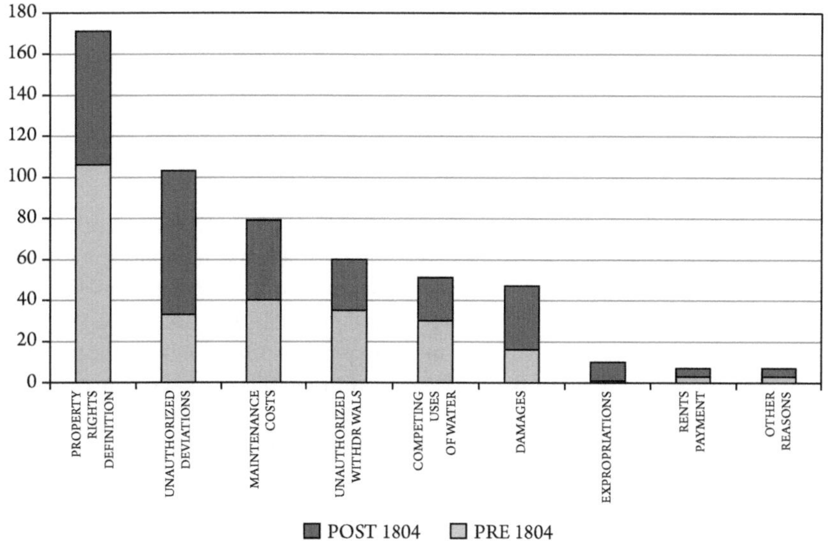

Sources: ACL, Fondi Acque, Poderi, Livelli

twentieth century, in fact, it is possible to find in the archives many conflicts harking back to undefined irrigation and water rights (Barbot, 2013a). During the twentieth century, however, many of the old disputes finally ended, and conflicts over irrigation rights really diminished (Figure 3.2).

IV. Why did the Dominia disappear from Lombardy's contractual practices?

In concluding this analysis, we would briefly return to our two main research questions: why did the system of Dominia survive for more than seven centuries? And why, at the same time, was it replaced by private property, not only in regulations but also in economic practices?

Several examples have shown that Dominia were not always systematically less profitable than the full private ownership. In times of crisis, the immobilization of rents in these long-term contracts could shield against cyclical fluctuations. Furthermore, the economic benefits of Dominia resided mainly in the possibility of laying on tenants the two big burdens of maintenance costs and property taxes. In addition, as it provided the opportunity to trade simultaneously both the goods and the rights on them, the divided property system created a larger market than the one we have today, which is restricted almost exclusively to the exchange of full ownership. Finally, in its long coexistence with private property, the Dominia also had the advantage of allowing hybrid and flexible forms for managing real estate. As the choices of Lombard landowners show very well, these two legal systems were often used strategically, either separately or together. Ultimately, the hypothesis that the divided property regime was inefficient is backed by no strong empirical confirmation, at least in our case study. The explanation of the gradual triumph of private property in Lombardy must therefore be sought elsewhere. But where?

A possible interpretation may perhaps be found in the language used by the archival sources. In Lombardy's notarial vocabulary, the main form of lease under the full ownership system was defined as *fitto semplice*: it may be that the reason for its success has to be found precisely in its *simplicity*. We have seen, in fact, that the divided property regime tended to multiply the number of holders of any single asset. Over the centuries, this multiplication certainly produced many conflicts, but, above all, it generated an increasing lack – if not a total impossibility – of coordination between the economic actors. From this point of view, at least in the case of Lombardy, the end of the nineteenth century became a point of no return: after several decades of dissociations of the property rights over land and water resources, many 'almost' and direct owners – often in spite of their own intentions – turned themselves into full owners so as not to succumb to the weight of contractual stratifications that had become too pronounced, and therefore totally unmanageable.

Bibliography

AGO, Renata (1998), Economia barocca. Mercato e istituzioni nella Roma del '600, Roma, Donzelli.

ALLEN, Robert (1992), *Enclosure and the Yeoman. The Agricultural Development of the South Midlands, 1450-1850*, Oxford, Oxford University Press.

ALFANI, Guido & RAO, Riccardo (eds) (2011), *La gestione delle risorse collettive. Italia settentrionale, secoli XII-XVIII*, Milano, Franco Angeli.

BARBOT, Michela (2006), 'Aria di famiglia. Rapporti di parentela e relazioni di familiarità nello scambio immobiliare a Milano fra XVI e XVII secolo', *Cheiron. Materiali e strumenti di aggiornamento storiografico*, 3, p. 285-302.

BARBOT, Michela (2008a), *Le architetture della vita quotidiana. Pratiche abitative e scambi immobiliari a Milano in età moderna*, Venezia, Marsilio.

BARBOT, Michela (2008b), 'Per una storia economica della proprietà dissociata. Efficacia e scomparsa di un altro modo di possedere', *Materiali per una storia della cultura giuridica*, 1, p. 33-62.

BARBOT, Michela (2009), 'Una Fabbrica imprenditrice? L'azione imprenditoriale degli uomini della Fabbrica del Duomo di Milano fra Età moderna e contemporanea', in F. AMATORI & A. COLLI (eds), *Imprenditorialità e sviluppo economico. Il caso italiano (sec. XIII-XIX)*, Milano, Egea, p. 377-384.

BARBOT, Michela (2010), 'Quand les droits charpentent les espaces. Formes architecturales et formes de la propriété à Milan entre XVIe et XVIIIe siècle', in R. CARVAIS, A. GUILLERME, V. NÈGRE & J. SAKAROVITCH (eds), *Édifice et artifice. Histoires constructives. Actes du premier congrès francophone d'histoire de la construction*, Paris, Picard, p. 1089-1098.

BARBOT, Michela (2012), 'Incertitude ou pluralité? Les conflits sur les droits fonciers et immobiliers dans la Lombardie d'Ancien Régime', in Julien DUBOULOZ & Alice INGOLD, (eds), *Faire la preuve de la propriété : droits et savoirs en Méditerranée (Antiquité-Temps modernes)*, Roma, École Française de Rome, p. 275-301.

BARBOT, Michela (2013a), 'Non tutti i conflitti vengono per nuocere. Usi, diritti e litigi sui canali lombardi fra XV e XX secolo (prime indagini)', in Luca MOCARELLI (ed.), *Quando manca il pane. Origini e cause della scarsità delle risorse alimentari in età moderna e contemporanea*, Bologna, Il Mulino, p. 35-56.

BARBOT, Michela (2013b), 'La résidence comme appartenance. Les catégories spatiales et juridiques de l'inclusion sociale dans les villes italiennes sous l'Ancien Régime', *Histoire Urbaine* [forthcoming].

BARBOT, Michela, LORENZETTI, Luigi & MOCARELLI, Luca (eds) (2012), *Property Rights and Their Violations. Expropriations and Confiscations, 16th-20th Centuries*, Berne, Peter Lang.

BASCAPÉ, Marco (ed.) (2001), *Il tesoro dei poveri. Il patrimonio artistico delle Istituzioni pubbliche di assistenza e beneficienza (ex Eca) di Milano*, Milano, Silvana Ed.

BÉAUR, Gérard (1994), *L'immobilier et la Révolution. Marché de la pierre et mutations urbaines 1770-1810*, Paris, Armand Colin.

BÉAUR, Gérard (2006), 'En un débat douteux. Les communaux, quels enjeux dans la France des XVIIIe-XIXe siècles', *Revue d'Histoire Moderne et Contemporaine*, 53-51, p. 89-114.

BÉAUR, Gérard, ARNOUX, Mathieu & VARET-VITU, Anne (eds) (2003), *Exploiter la terre. Les contrats agraires de l'Antiquité à nos jours*, Rennes, Association d'Histoire des Sociétés Rurales, Bibliothèque d'Histoire Rurale, vol. 7.

BÉAUR, Gérard, SCHOFIELD, Phillipp R., CHEVET, Jean-Michel & PÉREZ PICAZO, Maria Teresa (eds) (2013), *Property Rights, Land Markets, and Economic Growth in the European Countryside (13th-20th Centuries)*, Turnhout, Brepols, Rural History in Europe 1.

BELOCH, Karl Julius (1994), *Storia della popolazione italiana*, Firenze, Le lettere [original edition 1937-1961].

BENFANTE, Filippo (2003), 'Le proprietà urbane di Santa Maria Nuova (Firenze, XVI-XVIII secolo)', *Quaderni Storici*, 113, p. 325-344.

BEVILACQUA, Piero (1989), *Storia dell'agricoltura italiana in età contemporanea*, Venezia, Marsilio.

BIGATTI, Giorgio (2000), *La città operosa. Milano nell'Ottocento*, Milano, Franco Angeli.

BOERIO, Giuseppe (1856), *Dizionario del dialetto veneziano*, Venezia, Andrea Santini.

BRAUNSTEIN, Philippe (1990), 'Il cantiere del Duomo di Milano alla fine del XIV secolo: lo spazio, gli uomini e l'opera', in J.-C. MAIRE VIGUEUR & A. PARRAVICINI BAGLIANI (eds), *Ars et Ratio. Dalla torre di Babele al ponte di Rialto*, Palermo, Sellerio, p. 147-164.

BREWER, John & STAVES Susan (eds) (1996), *Early Modern Conceptions of Property Rights*, New York, Routledge.

CAVANNA, Adriano (2000), 'Influenze francesi e continuità di aperture europee nella cultura giuridica dell'Italia dell'Ottocento', in *Studi di Storia del diritto*, III, Milan, Giuffrè, p. 719 ff.

CAVANNA, Adriano (2001), 'Mito e destini del Code Napoléon in Italia', *Europa e diritto privato*, 1, p. 85-129.

CENCETTI, Giorgio (1939), *Il contratto di enfiteusi nella dottrina dei Glossatori e dei Commentatori*, Bologna, Cuppini.

CHAUVARD, Jean-François (2003), 'Rendita, diritto e morale. Proprietari e inquilini in Età moderna', *Quaderni Storici*, 113, p. 305-323.

CHAUVARD, Jean-François (2005), *La circulation des biens à Venise. Stratégies patrimoniales et marché immobilier (1600-1750)*, Roma, École Française de Rome.

CHITTOLINI, Giorgio (1994), 'Cities, "City-States", and Regional States in North-Central Italy', in C. TILLY & W. BLOCKMANS (eds), *Cities and the Rise of the State in Europe, A.D. 1000 to 1800*, Oxford, Westview Press, p. 28-43.

CLARK, Gregory (1998), 'Commons Sense: Common Property Rights, Efficiency, and Institutional Change', *Journal of Economic History*, 58, p. 73-102.

Coase, Robert (1960), 'The Problem of Social Cost', *Journal of Law and Economics*, 3, p. 1-44.

Concina, Ennio, Camerino, Ugo & Calabi, Donatella (eds) (1991), *La Città degli Ebrei. Il Ghetto di Venezia: architettura e urbanistica*, Venezia, Marsilio.

Congost, Rosa (2003), 'Property Rights and Historical Analysis: What Rights? What History?', *Past & Present*, 181, p. 74-106.

Congost, Rosa & Santos, Rui (eds) (2010), *Contexts of Property in Europe. The Social Embeddedness of Property Rights in Land in Historical Perspective*, Turnhout, Brepols, Rural History in Europe, 5.

Corazzol, Gianluigi (1979), *Fitti e livelli a grano. Una forma di credito rurale nel Veneto del '500*, Milano, Franco Angeli.

Corazzol, Gianluigi (1986), *Livelli stipulati a Venezia nel 1591. Studio storico*, Pisa, Giardini.

Crouzet-Pavan, Élisabeth (1992), *Sopra le acque salse. Espace, pouvoir et société à Venise à la fin du Moyen Âge*, Roma, École française de Rome.

Curto, Renato (1995), 'Da un'idea convenzionale di valore al valore rendimento: estimi e significati della proprietà urbana tra '700 e '800 a Torino', *Storia Urbana*, 71, p. 67-87.

D'Amico, Stefano (1994), *Le contrade e la città. Sistema produttivo e spazio urbano a Milano fra Cinque e Seicento*, Milano, Franco Angeli.

Démelas, Marie-Danielle & Vivier, Nadine (eds) (2003), *Les propriétés collectives face aux attaques libérales (1750-1914). Europe occidentale et Amérique latine*, Rennes, Presses Universitaires de Rennes.

De Moor, Martine, Shaw-Taylor, Leigh & Warde, Paul (eds) (2002), *The Management of Common Land in North West Europe, c. 1500-1850*, Turnhout, Brepols, CORN 8.

Faccini, Luigi (1988), *La Lombardia fra Seicento e Settecento. Riconversione economica e mutamenti sociali*, Milano, Franco Angeli.

Faron, Olivier & Hubert, Étienne (eds) (1995), *Le sol et l'immeuble: les formes dissociées de propriété immobilière dans les villes de France et d'Italie*, Roma, École Française de Rome.

Fregna, Roberto (1990), *La pietrificazione del denaro. Studi sulla proprietà urbana tra XV e XVII secolo*, Bologna, Clueb.

Fregni, Euride (ed.) (1990-1991), 'Terre e comunità dell'Italia padana. Il caso delle Partecipanze Agrarie Emiliane: da beni comuni a beni collettivi', *Cheiron*, 8 (1990-1991), p. 14-15.

Gauthiez, Bernard (1995), 'La forme des immeubles et le statut juridique des terrains: l'exemple de Rouen du XIIIe au XVIIIe siècle', in Olivier Faron & Étienne Hubert (eds), *Le sol et l'immeuble: les formes dissociées de propriété immobilière dans les villes de France et d'Italie*, Roma, École française de Rome, p. 267-299.

Giorgetti, Giorgio (1974), *Contadini e proprietari nell'Italia moderna. Rapporti di produzione e contratti agrari dal secolo XVI a oggi*, Torino, Einaudi.

Grossi, Paolo (1981), *An Alternative to Private Property: Collective Property in the Juridical Consciousness of the Nineteenth Century*, Chicago, University of Chicago Press.

Grossi, Paolo (1992), *Il dominio e le cose: percezioni medievali e moderne dei diritti reali*, Milano, Giuffrè.

Grossi, Paolo (1996), *L'ordine giuridico medievale*, Roma-Bari, Laterza.

Grossi, Paolo (2006), *La proprietà e le proprietà nell'officina dello storico*, Napoli, Editoriale Scientifica.

Halpérin, Jean-Louis (2003), *Le code civil*, Paris, Dalloz.

Halpérin, Jean-Louis (2008), *Histoire du droit des biens*, Paris, Economica.

Hardin, Garrett (1968), 'The Tragedy of the Commons', *Science*, 162, p. 1243-1248.

Hubert, Étienne (1992), *Espace urbain et habitat à Rome du xe siècle à la fin du xiiie siècle*, Roma, École française de Rome.

Levi, Giovanni (2000), 'Note conclusive', in P. Lanaro, P. Marini & G. M. Varanini (eds), *Edilizia privata nella Verona rinascimentale*, Milano, Electa, p. 404-405.

Macfarlane, Alan (1978), *The Origins of English Individualism: The Family, Property and Social Transition*, Oxford, Blackwell.

Masè, Federica (2006), *Patrimoines immobiliers ecclésiastiques dans la Venise médiévale (xie-xve siècles). Une lecture de la ville*, Roma, École française de Rome.

Mobili, Marco & Rogari, Marco (2008), 'Ecco le prime 3.574 leggi che il Governo vuole abrogare', *Il Sole 24 ore*, 6, 25 june 2008.

Neeson, Jeanette M. (1993), *Commoners. Common Right, Enclosure and Social Change in England, 1700-1820*, Cambridge, Cambridge University Press.

North, Douglass C. (1981), *Structure and Change in Economic History*, London, Norton.

North, Douglass C. (1990), *Institutions, Institutional Change and Economic Performance*, Cambridge, Cambridge University Press.

North, Douglass C. & Thomas Robert Paul (1973), *The Rise of the Western World*, Cambridge, Cambridge University Press.

Ogilvie, Sheilagh (2007), '"Whatever Is, Is Right"? Economic Institutions in Pre-industrial Europe', *Economic History Review*, 60, 4, p. 649-684.

Ostrom, Elinor (1990), *Governing the Commons. The Evolution of Institutions for Collective Action*, Cambridge, Cambridge University Press.

Ostrom, Elinor (2000), 'Private and Common Property Rights', in B. Bouckaert & G. De Geest (eds), *Encyclopedia of Law and Economics*, vol. ii. *Civil Law and Economics*, Cheltenham, Edward Elgar, p. 332-379.

Ostrom, Elinor (2005), *Understanding Institutional Diversity*, Princeton, Princeton University Press.

Roche, Daniel (1982), *Le peuple de Paris. Essai sur la culture populaire au xviiie siècle*, Paris, Aubier.

Romani, Mario (1957), *L'agricoltura in Lombardia dal periodo delle riforme al 1859. Struttura, organizzazione sociale e tecnica*, Milano, Vita e pensiero.

Rosenthal, Jean-Laurent (1990), 'The Development of Irrigation in Provence 1700-1860. The French Revolution and Economic Growth', *Journal of Economic History*, 50, p. 615-637.

ROSENTHAL, Jean-Laurent (1992), *The Fruits of Revolution: Property Rights, Litigation and French Agriculture, 1700-1860*, Cambridge, Cambridge University Press.

SCAFFARDI, Gian Paolo (1981), *Studi sull'enfiteusi*, Milano, Giuffrè.

SCARAMELLINI, Guglielmo & ZOIA, Diego (eds) (2006), *Economia e società in Valtellina e Contadi nell'Età Moderna*, 2 vols Collana storica, n. 12, Sondrio: Fondazione Gruppo Credito Valtellinese.

SELLA, Domenico (1959), 'Premesse demografiche ai censimengti austriaci', in *Storia di Milano*, Milano, Istituto per l'Enciclopedia Italiana Treccani, vol. XII, p. 459-478.

SELLA, Domenico (1979), *Crisis and Continuity. The Economy of Spanish Lombardy in the Seventeenth Century*, Cambridge, Mass., Harvard University Press.

SOMBART Werner (1902), *Der moderne Kapitalismus*, Leipzig, Duncker & Humblot.

STANZIANI, Alessandro (2011), 'Comparaison réciproque et histoire. Quelques propositions à partir du cas russe', in Jean-Paul Zúñiga (ed.), *Pratiques du transnational*, Paris, Bibliothèque du CRH, p. 209-230.

TILLY, Charles (2004), 'Observations of Social Processes and their Formal Representations', *Sociological Theory*, 22, p. 595-602.

VACCARI, Paolo (1965), 'Enfiteusi (storia)', in *Enciclopedia del diritto*, XIV, Milano, Giuffrè, p. 915-920.

VAQUERO PIÑEIRO, Manuel (1999), *La renta y las casas. El patrimonio inmobiliario de Santiago de los espanoles de Roma entre los siglos XV y XVII*, Roma, L'Erma di Bretschneider.

WEBER, Max (1966 [1921]), *The City*, New York, The Free Press.

GÉRARD BÉAUR

4. The Many Faces of Emphyteusis in France

An Overview, with a Case Study from the Meaux Region (1600-1800)

Emphyteusis is a very unobtrusive kind of contract which has not aroused much interest from French rural historians; this is true of both the Old Regime and more recent periods. Hitherto, only urban forms of emphyteusis have attracted the attention of researchers (Faron & Hubert, 1995). However, papers on property rights given at two conferences in 2005 and 2006, at Thonon and Gregynog, have shown how frequently this type of contract occurred in the countryside (Béaur, Schofield, Chevet & Pérez-Picazo, 2013) Strangely, however, these contributions concerned only Mediterranean countries (Spain, Portugal and Italy), while, even though it was an important type of imperfect property in northwest Europe, the papers on that area mostly ignored it (Congost, 2013; Santos & Serrâo, 2013).

Emphyteutic leasing has traditionally been on the black list of all varieties of divided ownership on the grounds that it hindered agricultural progress[1]. It is therefore not surprising that researchers from countries reputed to be in the vanguard of the Agricultural Revolution only rarely encountered this type of contract, particularly if they were not looking for it. The difficulty is that all the contributions on regions in southern Europe rejected the commonly-accepted belief that emphyteusis was a handicap before the Revolution brought in perfect ownership[2]. Quite the opposite: those authors praised its flexibility and effectiveness in turning land to account. It is also significant that emphyteusis did not disappear with the Old Regime and that it is even used in contemporary societies, as can be seen from the large part it plays in the 'land-grabbing' currently going on (Luna & Mignemi, 2017), as well as in the ways urban land is allocated.

---

1 'Emphyteusis is alienation of ownership to the person of the lessee for the period of the concession, while the lessor retains the direct ownership'. 'It is a long term lease of a (heritage) in order to cultivate and improve it; or of a plot in order to build on it, or of a house in order to rebuild it; in return for a modest sum paid every year by the lessee: and also, usually, for a certain amount payable by the lessee at the time of the contract' (D'Agar, 1805: 129-130).

2 See papers in Béaur, Schofield, Chevet & Perez-Picazo (2013).

Agrarian Change and Imperfect Property, ed. by Rosa Congost and Pablo F. Luna, Rural History in Europe, 15 (Turnhout, 2018), 75-96

DOI 10.1484/M.RURHE-EB.5.116119

Can it be claimed that emphyteutic leasing was specific to the southern regions of Europe in the modern period but was little used outside them? It is very hard to answer this question in the light of our present knowledge, but we may at least ask whether there was something typically Mediterranean about the contract. What happens if we leave that setting and look elsewhere, particularly in a region of early large-scale capitalist agriculture, at a key period, the end of the Old Regime, when there was a break with the ownership system inherited from the feudal period (Béaur, 2005-2007)? What do we see if we examine a 'neutral' space, neither completely free from some types of superimposed rights, nor completely bogged down in the horrors of imperfect ownership? What was the situation in a country like France and, to give more point to the comparison, in the Brie region, around the city of Meaux and close to the booming Paris market? This paper is an attempt to suggest some answers to these two questions.

In order to do this we need to look at the nature and conditions of the contract, to understand why its status as a legal underpinning of imperfect ownership seemed to condemn it, and then to compare these theoretical ideas to the real place it occupied in pre-Revolutionary France, to the actual forms it took and the use that lessors and lessees, landowners and farmers, made of it. For this, we have worked on two different scales, using data from two enquiries, one national and one from a micro-region. For the 'macro' scale, we used a sample of information from the land transfers recorded on the one hand in the registry of notarized acts (*Enregistrement*) during the last two decades of the eighteenth century in several dozen sites across France; for the 'micro' example, we examined a collection of post-mortem inventories for the region around Meaux during the seventeenth and eighteenth centuries[3].

I. A contract in disgrace

An emphyteutic lease was halfway between sale and renting (Garaud, 1958; Garsonnet, 1879). It was a long-term lease which gave the lessee the status of quasi-owner, for a temporary period, over the property thus occupied in return for a usually modest payment. Within this general framework emphyteusis could take several forms. This was because 'the legal definitions are often uncertain. Jurists are not all of the same opinion; on certain questions like emphyteusis, there are as many theories as there are authors. And the documents often reveal that things were even more complex in the real world' (Gallet, 1999: 101).

An emphyteutic lease could have a variable length: from 18 to 99 years, or even perpetual. It is therefore understandable that the line between it and an outright sale may seem tenuous. The Old Regime administration showed

3 The origin of these two samples is explained below.

how well it understood this when it set its registration taxes on leases of more than 18 or 27 years on the same level as those on land sales. By doing this, it not only deprived the emphyteutic contract of some of the fiscal advantages that could have been attached to it such as exemption from the obligation to pay the 'hundredth penny' (*centième denier*), a royal tax ranging upwards from 1 per cent to 1.5 per cent of the transaction[4], it also set a limit beyond which the transfer of possession ceased to be a simple, temporary deprivation of enjoyment and became a real appropriation; and it clearly set this type of lease apart from all other rental contracts. Subsequently, the Revolution forbade perpetual leases, but retained emphyteusis, though automatically restricting such leases by law to a maximum term of 99 years.

The payment was also variable. In principle it consisted of an annual due called the *canon*, of more or less token value. However, nothing prevented the lessor from demanding an additional entry right (*introge*), which could be substantial and more or less equivalent to the price of a sale. This was the case with the *abenevis* of Forez (Garnier, 1982: 96)[5]. Nor did anything prevent the owner from imposing a relatively high annual payment, equivalent to a normal rental payment.

The extent of rights conferred by this status was also variable. Sometimes the contract insisted on the lessee's real ownership, sometimes his entitlement was limited by forbidding him to run down the land or by requiring him to improve it[6], to such an extent that the meaning of the emphyteusis was distorted. Sometimes it was stressed that the emphyteusis was only a simple right to enjoyment like any other form of perpetual concession (Gallet, 1999: 110).

However, as a general rule, we may say that the property rights of land under an emphyteutic contract were divided between the lessor and the lessee, since the property returned to the lessor at the end of the period defined in the deed. Nevertheless, up until the end of the contract the lessee had most if not all the attributes of an owner: he could cede his rights and he could mortgage the land or rent it out. The only restriction was that he could not put an emphyteutic contract on land already held in emphyteusis. At the end of the defined period, in principle, there should have been no tacit renewal. In fact, though, the lessor could then choose either to renew the contract or to take the property back, to work it directly, to make another emphyteutic contract, or to lease it out in another way, in rental (*fermage*) or share-cropping (*métayage*) for example. The lessee also had a choice; he could ask for a renewal

---

4 Emphyteutic leases were also subject to dues relating to another formality: the *contrôle des actes*.

5 Though it was still used in the eighteenth century in its original sense of concession of access to water, in a larger sense the term *abenevis* denoted 'all concession made by a seigneur for any due' and particularly the *cens* (Garnier, 1982: 94).

6 'An emphyteutic contract is always made on condition that the lessee will improve the property he holds on a long-term lease. He may not deteriorate it or alter it in such a way that the value of it is diminished' (D'Agar, 1805).

of the contract or get the chance to stay on the land by signing some other type of contract. He could also decide to put an end to his activity on the parcel concerned. But in the meantime, he behaved like an owner.

Emphyteusis thus falls precisely into the category of that juxtaposition of rights, general but not universal, of several persons or institutions on the same land that was so stigmatised by the current of opinion in favour of perfect, absolute, ownership over property. Nowadays this criticism has been renewed by institutionalist historians (North, 1990; North & Thomas, 1980) and there is an abundant historical literature on the perverse effects of the numerous stake-holders, of the splitting of property rights between the individual landholder and the community, with its right of collective enjoyment, and of the co-existence of several possessors with specific rights over the same property (Congost, 2003). Divided ownership was suspected of slowing the circulation of property, accused of inducing routine habits and agricultural stagnation. It remained one of the symbols of a system of property rights that needed to be abolished (van Bavel & Hoppenbouwers, 2004) probably for ideological as much as economic reasons. Consider the criticisms directed by the Physiocrats or economists like Turgot against a system that handicapped the economy by maintaining multiple stake-holders, by imposing harmful extra burdens that put more pressure on producers, by discouraging competition between tenants (Quesnay, 1768; Turgot, 1766). Consider the violent attacks of Boncerf on the whole feudal system (Boncerf, 1776). It was chiefly the association of all types of divided ownership with feudalism that led to their being lumped together and condemned on the same grounds as seigneurial property rights (Gallet, 1999: 171-172).

It was thus understandable that in the case of emphyteusis the co-existence of two ownership rights on the same property seemed indefensible and that emphyteutic leases, like all other forms of imperfect ownership, were considered unjustified. It, too, contravened the sacrosanct principle of individualism on which the rise of capitalism was thought to be predicated. It hindered coordination between economic actors and obstructed the growth of the property market, which allowed the best farmers to be selected (van Bavel, 2008; Hoppenbrouwers & van Zanden, 2001). Enclosures and the Napoleonic Civil Code finally put an end to such harmful confusion and opened the way for the necessary clarification of property rights (Congost, 2003), since all the rights were now concentrated in one and the same person. Yet there is a paradox: those who drew up the Civil Code were well able to distinguish between the attribution of a perpetual right and the possibility of retaining the long-term lease. They abolished perpetual emphyteusis but not fixed-term emphyteusis.

But independent of considerations of law and political economy, which, after all, are matters of theory, a critical revision is underway, designed to rehabilitate this contract, once considered obsolete or at least unsuited to modern economies, by studying how it worked in practice. It has been shown that, far from obstructing the circulation of landed property or buildings because of the large number of stakeholders (van Bavel, 2008), it may be seen as an instrument for ensuring the fluidity of landholding and thus as a factor favouring the property market. Each co-owner was in fact able to negotiate that part of the rights he possessed and so able to find investors who might be interested in a fraction of the property, worth much less than the property as a whole (Béaur & Chevet, 2013).

Finally it has been noted that an emphyteutic lease was an effective way to develop uncultivated land or to experiment with speculative crops that could take several years to become profitable, such as vines, trees and the like. It was also a useful method for peasants without resources to cultivate collective land on an individual basis. We should remember that the word emphyteusis comes from the Greek and originally referred to the action of planting. The lessee took a lease for a modest payment on condition of improving the land, that is, of putting it under cultivation, with labour as his only contribution, unless of course the contract stipulated otherwise. Just as in an urban setting the lessee was often expected to parcel out the land conceded to him, in the same way in the countryside he had to turn to account, perhaps to plant, uncultivated property, which was initially without almost any value.

The holder of an emphyteutic lease had complete freedom to improve the property over and above the improvements he was obliged to make under the terms of the lease. He could construct whatever he thought necessary and maintain or demolish buildings as he chose. He could mortgage the property like any ordinary owner; he was free to lease it, but obviously not to concede it under another emphyteutic contract. He also could not sell it. If he no longer wished to exercise the right himself he could transfer it to someone who would continue to observe the conditions of the original lease and in particular, maintain the payments.

We can see how attractive an emphyteutic lease would have been for a peasant with no resources but his labour. All studies of the subject have emphasised this. On the other hand, the advantages for the lessor are less obvious. The lessor gave up a property belonging to him for a long term in return for a modest income, the value of which was further diminished if he failed to ask for an entry fee. But we can assume that over time it was worthwhile. Without investing any money, he obtained the improvement of property which would have been costly to develop. It was up to the lessee to work the land and keep up the buildings if necessary. The lessor was even freed from paying the taxes and dues on the land under this contract. He was guaranteed against everything. He could have the lessee evicted for not maintaining the property or not observing the conditions of the lease, damaging the property or failing to pay the rent. He was completely free to alienate the rights he held under the contract. At the end of the lease he could take back the property when he pleased, as the lessee had no automatic right to renewal: when the term expired the emphyteutic tenant became an occupant without any rights or title and had to leave the property unless he could get a new contract. At that point, the lessor benefited from the improvements with no obligation at all to recompense the lessee unless there was a clause to that effect in the contract. Conversely, the contract forbade the lessee from taking any action that would reduce the value of the property. The lessor could thus increase the value of his land without much expense.

II. A contract that was mostly ignored?

One might think that with conditions so advantageous to both parties, emphyteutic leases would be very common. However, this type of contract, at first sight, seems to have been rare in Old Regime France. Among all the land transfer acts concluded in the second half of the eighteenth century in the Beauce (at Maintenon and at Janville between 1761and 1790) there was no mention of emphyteutic leases (Béaur, 1984). In another region, the Livradois, in the Massif Central, the village of *ugerolles* saw almost no emphyteutic leases during the eighteenth and nineteenth centuries (Brunel, 1992). There is the same disappointing result in eighteenth-century Touraine, where, as Brigitte Maillard notes in her thesis, 'Emphyteutic or life leases were very rare'. She admits that there were exceptions for *prébendes* and *closeries* conceded for one 'canonical lifetime' (*vie canoniale*) and gives an example, the *métairie* of Chantemerle at Rouziers, which the Carmelites of Tours ceded for 99 years in 1779. In this specific case it was a renewal of an initial rent that had been set relatively high, 190 livres a year; and it was linked to a substantial increase of the amount paid when the lease was drawn up again; at 400 livres the rent had more than doubled, thereby keeping up more or less with the general trend in rents (Maillard, 1998: 152).

Why were there so few emphyteutic rents in these cases? One possible explanation is that emphyteusis, as we have seen above, met a specific need. It allowed the owner of badly cultivated or uncultivated lands to have them brought into cultivation, or planted over, or built on, without paying any money or doing any work, because that was the responsibility of the lessee. The payment was so small precisely because the lessee was bound to bring the land into cultivation and invest his labour in it. If it had been otherwise, the owner would have demanded higher rents. On the other hand, land that had been cleared for a long time and put under intensive cultivation was not suitable for such contracts. In these circumstances we can see that there could be limits of geography or timing to the use of emphyteutic leases. Regions that were very slow to be developed for profit, regions with large uncultivated areas, needed such an arrangement. Thus mountain zones were suitable for emphyteutic leasing, as were all areas with large spaces without crops. It is not surprising that Spanish historians have emphasised how useful emphyteusis was in making it possible to cultivate abandoned land, particularly for the very poor who could not make high payments but were able to take on the heavy work needed to improve it.

Regions undergoing a severe population decline were also suitable for emphyteusis. It is well known that the periods after the catastrophes caused by the Great Plague and Hundred Years War saw the use of long leases, for three lives, for 99 years, or even in perpetuity. The same story was true after the ravages of the Thirty Years War. In Alsace 'the eighteenth century, because of the need for reconstruction, was the great epoch of emphyteusis – *Erbbstand, Erbpacht, Erlehen, Erbzinsgut, zu einem ewigen Erbe* – which was considered as the alienation, explicit, official and perpetual, of a property that the farmer could transmit to his heirs under certain, very lenient, conditions' (Boehler, 1994: 547). It was normal that such contracts became progressively less frequent as more land was put under the plough, and it is just as understandable that emphyteusis tended to fade away as a contractual practice and remain only as a historical relic. Returning to the case of Alsace, Jean-Michel Boehler rightly observes that 'from 1750 onward, [emphyteusis] was increasingly resisted and more and more the object of either seigneurial repossession or peasant usurpation' (Boehler, 1994: 549). The lords tried to replace it with short-term leases, which were much more profitable, and the peasants attempted to assimilate it to pure and simple ownership.

Emphyteusis could thus evolve from a classic rental by usurpation. The insidious transformation of 'short-term lease into hereditary, indefinite, perpetual lease' (Boehler, 1994: 554), the steady slide through leases renewed over generations into tacit renewal, into 'land subject to the cens, ständiges Gülgut, Hoflehn or Erblehn' was never impossible[7]. Thus 'de facto emphyteusis' could take place, clandestinely, in spite of the lessors' resistance, and could result in a pure and simple takeover.

In other words, without any signed contract and merely by usurpation, a rental lease could be transformed into an emphyteutic lease and an emphyteutic lease could disappear and become full ownership. Conversely, under pressure from a seigneur, an emphyteutic lease could disappear and be replaced by a standard rental lease. This explains why, according to some jurists, a lease longer than nine years became emphyteutic. This definition reminds us how very porous were the boundaries between the two ways of leasing land, even when the fiscal administration, as we have seen, attempted to impose limits on long-term leases of 18, 27 or 30 years.

In Alsace during the eighteenth century emphyteusis lost its attraction after the reconstruction was completed, and this opened the way for full and complete appropriation. The lords no longer needed to settle peasants on deserted or undesirable land and the danger of appropriation by stealth emerged. In the Forez, also, the *abenevis* so generously conceded at the beginning of the early modern period tended to disappear or become padded with entry rights so large that the *greffiers* did not hesitate to describe them as *abenevis et vente*. 'In the seventeenth and eighteenth centuries the time was

7 See Boehler, in this volume.

long past when the vassal turned his demesne land to account by letting it out to a tenant for a *cens*… Emphyteutic leases were rare in the last two centuries of the Old Regime' (Garnier, 1982: 340-341). This statement is perhaps a bit too definite; it is clear that emphyteusis, just like the *bail a cens*, could still be a valued contract in some circumstances. Land clearing in response to demographic growth constituted one such situation, but clearing occurred less often now, as the general context had changed so much. However, just because emphyteusis was resorted to less frequently does not mean that old leases dating back to a more or less distant past were not still in force, even at the end of the eighteenth century, even in intensively cultivated areas.

III. A substitute or hidden contract: a national overview

These however are localised accounts. We have therefore tried to judge the importance of emphyteusis and the reasons for its apparent fading away by looking at the flow of land transfers at the national level through the contracts made in several significant land markets at the end of the Old Regime.

There are several collections of transactions available across France, compiled from the *centième denier* registers kept by the administration of the General Tax Farm (*Ferme Générale*) and then by the Public Domain Administration (*Administration des Domaines*). These institutions were responsible for recording all property transfer acts and collecting a levy on them. They are well known, mainly because of two reference works: a guide that makes it possible to understand the archives they have left us (Vilar-Berrogain, 1958) and a history of the way they operated (Massaloux, 1989). We know that, among other things, it was their responsibility to register (*insinuer*, in the administrative language of the time) all the transfers of immovable property, apart from direct successions. These administrations had roughly three thousand offices, where the employees were required to enter in the registers an abbreviated summary of all the acts subject to registration, and collect the taxes bearing on the transaction. This included all operations that involved a change in possession for a period longer than the normal rental term and thus appeared to signal a definitive transfer of ownership. There is an enormous quantity of data. We therefore took samples in different regions, by selecting one out of ten acts in about sixty randomly-selected offices from the whole of the territory under the Crown's control during the period 1770-1790. The striking thing that emerges from this data is that mentions of emphyteutic contracts during these two decades are mostly absent. Of course there are a few references here and there, but nothing that could be analysed and used to counter the idea that emphyteusis had become only a curiosity.

The expression 'emphyteusis' was used for different kinds of contracts. Jean Gallet (1999: 105) provides an eloquent list of them. Under the Old Regime emphyteusis for a term and perpetual emphyteusis were not exactly the same type of contract. Emphyteusis for a term was found more in the North of France and perpetual emphyteusis more in the South. Actually, in Northern France it was simply a long-term contract that was clearly distinguishable from the *bail à cens*, because the latter was always perpetual and generally included a range of obligations stemming from seigneurial overlordship[8]. There was a great temptation to fall back on the *bail à cens* in order to turn a property to account; this contract, though irrevocable, none the less conferred suzerainty over the property and also provided other financial and symbolic advantages. Even in the eighteenth century the convenient practice of attributing a tenure *à cens* to a peasant so that he could bring an unworked parcel of land under cultivation had not disappeared. Of course, the lord received only a more or less symbolic payment. However the essential thing was not the payment itself but the body of complementary rights from which he benefited, starting with the seigneurial transfer tax of the *lods et ventes*. Failing that, a very popular alternative for the person conceding the property was a *bail à rente*[9], which was also perpetual and in addition guaranteed a much more substantial revenue: experience shows that payments under *bail à rente* corresponded to a rent set at 5 per cent of the sale value of the property (Garsonnet, 1879: 420).

In southern France an emphyteutic lease was usually perpetual and was often confused with *bail à cens*, if it was a seigneurial concession, or with some variant of *bail à rente*, if it was non-seigneurial (Gallet, 1999: 111). The situation was so unclear that the clerk of the Domains administration sometimes showed his confusion by repeating the notary's terminology in summarizing the deed as a *bail à cens ou emphyteutique* particularly in the regions of Lyon or Grenoble[10]. In Forez 'the synonymy of the two designations is proved by the undifferentiated use made of them by lawyers (*practiciens*) and legal scholars (*jurisconsultes*)...' (Garnier, 1982: 95). After all, *bail à cens* was only a particular instance of perpetual emphyteutic contract which happened to be endowed with a seigneurial burden, usually involving obligations other than a regular annual payment. On the other hand, to make matters more complicated, the *bail à fief*, a real 'contract mill' (Aubin, 1989: 100) – and a snare for researchers – was confused with the *bail à cens* in the region around Bordeaux but could also just as easily bear on non-seigneurial property and be considered in the same category as the *bail à rente* or other forms of long-term lease. It then had no feudal or seigneurial aspects and could thus take the place of emphyteusis.

8 We should note, however, that the advantages conveyed by the seigneurial contracts were not enough to differentiate them from emphyteusis since there was a choice among a range of clauses that could just as well have been included in an emphyteutic contract.

9 *Bail à rente* was a contract by which the lessor ceded the property for a perpetual annual rent, while the lessee retained the possibility of selling it, that is, transmitting it to a third person who had to continue to pay the rent.

10 In the *centième denier* registers found in these offices in our nation-wide sample.

More frequent than the tenure *à cens*, the *bail à rente* could be found almost everywhere; it was an instrument of sale, an instrument of credit and an instrument of rental all rolled into one. When the lessee signed this contract, agreeing to pay a substantial due (more often than not more expensive than an ordinary rental) in perpetuity, he became the virtual possessor of the land, as in a typical emphyteusis. This contract was called a *bail perpétuel* in Provence, *bail à locatairerie* in Provence and around Toulouse and Bordeaux in the Southwest, *arrentment* in the West, *bail à fief* in the Bordeaux region (see above) and *bail à rente* nearly everywhere else (see Map 1). The lessee could sometimes free himself of the *rente* by paying an amount equivalent to twenty times the cost of the lease by an act of amortisation, but in most cases the lease was *irraquitable*, that is, nonredeemable, and it was this system that was ended by the Revolution at the same time as the *bail à cens*. However, there are some questions about the *bail à locatairerie* in the Toulouse region. The concession was made on condition of improving the property and paying a so-called *rente colloque*, which looked much the same as a simple emphyteutic contract, but also included other conditions that cast doubt on its status; in particular it was compulsory to renew the contract every 29 years (Gallet, 1999: 118; Bastier, 1975: 225-228) and the lessee was forbidden to cede the property without giving the lessor a chance to acquire it. Was this really an emphyteutic lease? It is not clear. It seems that this type of lease was a compromise between emphyteusis, *bail à cens* and *bail à rente*.

A distinctive feature of Normandy was the contract termed the *fieffe*, which has been thoroughly studied by Fabrice Boudjaaba (Boudjaaba, 2008). This had all the characteristics of a *bail à cens* or *bail à rente*, and it occurs almost as frequently in the notarial archives in some parts of the region as the regular, mutually agreed, sale (Béaur, 1992). It is almost identical to an emphyteutic contract, except that it clearly does not totally match the model Bardet established for Rouen: a contract with a low annual payment for the lessee to build a house, a purchase on credit for the lessee and an investment with an assured revenue for the lessor (Bardet, 1983: 178). However, in the case of Rouen, these were urban leases. There is another difference: here and there, in about one case out of four, there was a retrocession of the *fieffe* which put an end to the contract and which the administration considered to be an ownership transfer resembling that of a *fieffe* (Béaur, 1992).

Baux à rente and also *baux à cens*, were convenient alternatives to emphyteusis, particularly in northern areas, while in the South they tended to be confused with it to some extent. Both were widely used during the reconstruction after the Hundred Years War; this is why emphyteusisis is so hard to find in the North and why it is scarcely easier to locate in the South, at least under that name. This is what Map 1 suggests. There is a simple reason why emphyteutic contracts were less easy to find in the South: this was the long-lasting confusion with seigneurial-type leases, such as the *bail à cens* (Chenon, 1881: 50). However, the *bail à cens* was not the only contract that was a source of confusion, to such an extent that it was often difficult for the clerk (*greffier*) who registered the

Map 4.1. *Baux à rente* and equivalent acts

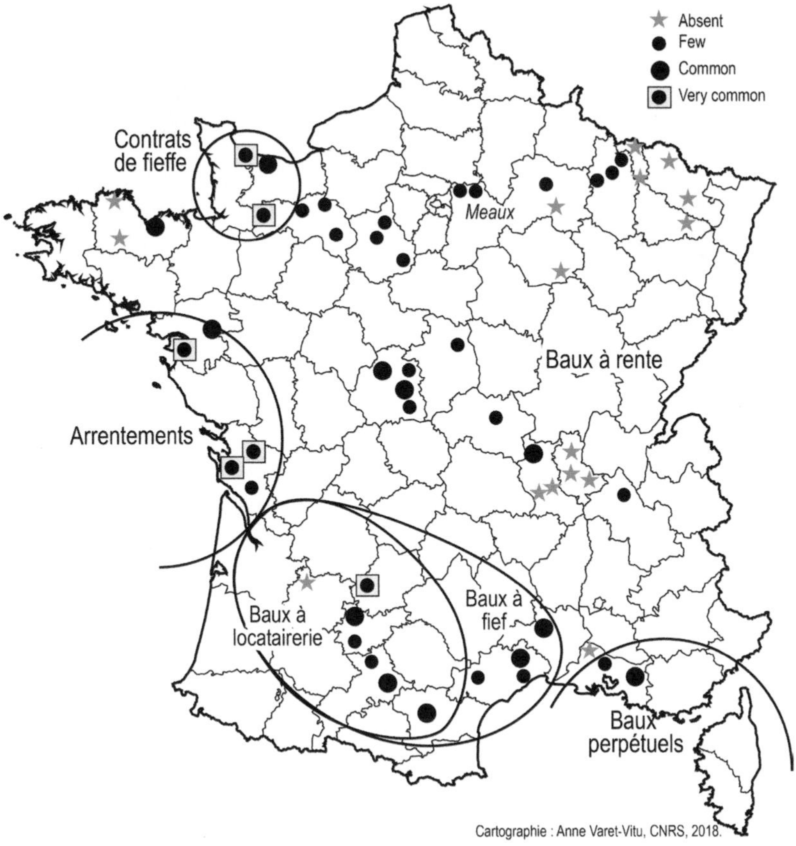

contract to distinguish between them. In other words, there were a great many contracts that resembled emphyteutic contracts and maintained some of their characteristics but differed in the methods of implementation. Emphyteutic leases were concealed by a complex terminology. The confusion could arise both from the use of different contracts with a similar content and from the dubious use of some contracts. Our sample on the national level allows us to show the geographical distribution of some of them in Map 1, while Map 2 illustrates the occurrence of various types of long-term concession, mostly intended to turn to account abandoned or uncultivated land, and retaining a strong seigneurial imprint (Béaur, 1991).

There were other types of contract, more or less widespread, all perpetual, which were really emphyteusis in all but name. The *abenevis* was omnipresent in Forez. It was at first used in contracts for water conveyance for irrigation and eventually spread into the contract system and came to refer to a wide range of land concessions. It was as much an emphyteutic lease as a *bail à*

Map 4.2. Types of emphyteusis with seigneurial characteristics

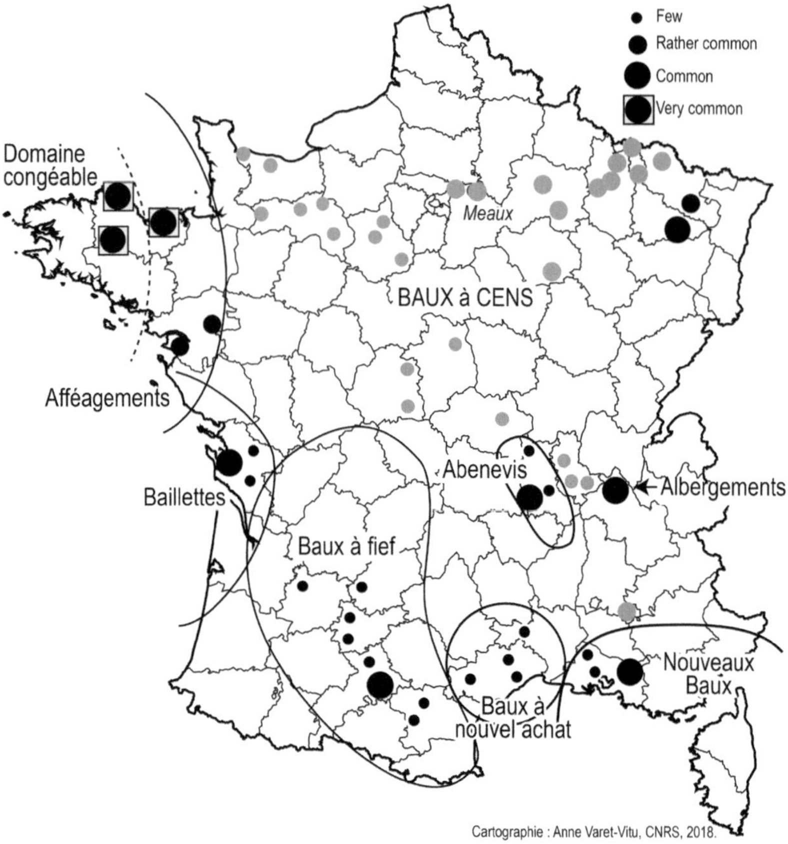

cens, requiring annual payment of a modest rent (Garnier, 1982: 94). The *baillettes* of Poitou and Aunis, which were feudal-type contracts for small properties, had similar characteristics. They could be prevalent in notarial archives in some places, for instance, around La Rochelle (Jousmet, 1999). Further south were the *baux à fief* in Aquitaine, previously mentioned, and the *nouvel baux* or *baux à nouvel achat* in Provence. Should *albergments* be included under this heading? They had a definite feudal characteristic, granted in return for the payment of fairly substantial dues, in a context which went far beyond that of pure emphyteusis, but, in practice, they were very close. They were very common in Dauphiné and could be found in the Kingdom of Savoy, where the implications were not exactly identical, but we have no registry office from Savoy in our sample (Chianea, 1968-1969). An even more doubtful case is that of Breton enfeoffments (*afféagements*), which allowed the seigneur or anyone holding the right to land, to enfeoff and clear wholesale, wooded or uncultivated land, or wipe out heathland in order to put it into

Table 4.1. Summary of types of emphyteutic leases

Designation	Location	Type of lease	Weight of dues
Abenevis	Forez	Feudal or non-feudal	Moderate
Afféagement	Brittany	Feudal	Moderate
Albergement	Dauphiné	Feudal	High
Arrentement	Poitou	Non-feudal	High
Bail à cens	Everywhere	Feudal	Moderate
Bail à fief	Bordelais	Feudal or non-feudal	Variable
Bail à locatairerie	Aquitaine	Non-feudal	High
Bail à nouvel achat	Provence	Non-feudal	Moderate
Bail perpétuel	Provence	Non-feudal	Moderate
Bail à rente	Everywhere	Non-feudal	High
Baillette	Saintonge	Feudal or non-feudal	Low
Fieffe	Normandy	Non-feudal	High or moderate

cultivation (Gallet, 1983: 398-405). In return for a low rent, a host of peasants were allotted a series of parcels on land previously left abandoned or, more frequently, considered as seigneurial, even though subject to the exercise of collective rights by the community. Although the concession had no formal link with an emphyteutic contract, it kept some of the same spirit. It should be noted that some of these contracts, all perpetual, could be granted in return for derisory rents (*baillettes, afféagements, abenevis*) but some (*albergements, baux à fief*) could also involve very heavy entry fees or specify payments in kind and thus deviate from the spirit of emphyteusis[11].

In order to clarify these distinctions we have drawn up a table listing the 'true' and 'false' emphyteutic contracts encountered in our exploration of the *centième denier* records.

IV. A contract rediscovered: post-mortem inventories in the Meaux region

Diversity in France has thus led us to make some key distinctions, which made it possible to locate emphyteutic contracts that were disguised by substitution or concealment, while emphyteusis in its pure form seems to have been strangely under-used by lessors and lessees. The preceding section has shown how emphyteusis was easily absorbed into the system of contracts but does not explain its astonishing absence even in areas where we might

11 On the other hand, *bail à domaine congéable*, based on an analogous, and complicated, principle, cannot really be treated as a form of emphyteusis; its legal term was normally nine years though in reality tenants stayed on much longer (Le Goff, 1989).

easily expect to find it. Unless we have just been incredibly unlucky in the choice of the sixty offices that make up our sample, we might simply say that that this kind of contract was no longer popular and corresponded to a type of agreement that had gone out of style in France by the end of the eighteenth century – all the more so in that France, broadly speaking, was fully under cultivation and land reclamation was no longer needed. But is this lack of visibility not mainly an illusion?

To get a better idea of the situation we tried stepping back from the end of the eighteenth century, not necessarily a particularly significant period, to look more closely at the local level over a longer period. Fortunately we have been able to use a collection of post-mortem inventories drawn up by several notaries in the Meaux region. The records concern the town of Meaux and the neighbouring parishes in the Brie (Baulant, 2006), just to the north-east of Paris, during the seventeenth and eighteenth centuries. There are 1,200 of these records, patiently and carefully collected and analysed by the historian Micheline Baulant[12]. They make it possible to measure, over the long-term, from 1590 to 1790, the evolution of the stock of properties held in emphyteusis, and not just the flow, as with the *centième denier*.

Some of these deeds mention papers left by the deceased and tell us what properties they had when they died. Of course, this only occurs in a minority of cases, particularly in cases from the seventeenth century; and even when the titles of properties are listed, we certainly cannot claim that the lists are exhaustive. Therefore the numbers cited in this article are minima only. Still, in these conditions, when 42 inventories refer to at least one property held on a long-term lease, which is more or less consistent with an emphyteusis, and 55 contracts of this type are recorded in all (several leases of this type can exist in the same inventory) it is quite significant. It is all the more remarkable in that it is harder to find documentation before the eighteenth century. It is very striking that out of the 42 cases, 25 come from the period between 1750 and 1790 (33 contracts out of a total of 55)[13]. In other words, at a time where the documentation is at its best, more than 10 per cent of the deceased held a property under a form that can be considered as emphyteutic. Moreover, this is in area where there was little uncultivated land and so it was not guaranteed that we should find such contracts.

---

12 We would like to express our most heartfelt thanks to Camille Baulant for making this collection available to researchers.

13 This does not necessarily mean that more properties were held in emphyteusis towards the end of the Old Regime than in the previous centuries. The difference is really due more to the varying abundance and quality of the documentation.

Table 4.2. Leases termed emphyteutic in the Brie inventories

Period	Number of inventories	Number of cases	Percentage of corpus
1600-1650	2	3	2
1651-1700	6	6	1.6
1701-1750	9	13	2.4
1751-1790	25	33	9.4

In fact, it is not quite so easy as this to argue that emphyteutic leases were frequent, since in the 42 inventories, only five make a specific reference to an emphyteutic lease (there are eight in all). The others refer to leases for 99 years, occasionally 96 years, often 'forever', or sometimes 'for life'. In other words, if we stick to only the terms used, emphyteutic leases were comparatively rare. However, if we go by what the contract actually said, they were quite common.

Table 4.3. Leases with emphyteutic characteristics in the Meaux region

Name	Number of inventories	Number of contracts
Emphyteusis	5	8
96 years	22	28
99 years	2	3
Forever	8	10
For life	1	1
Other	4	5

The evidence of these two tables suggests two corrections with what has been said.

First of all, we can certainly argue that leases considered as emphyteutic were bound to appear in our corpus of inventories with a delayed effect, since many years may have gone by between the date of the contract and the death of the lessee and, even more for the leases mentioned in the inventories of possessions; so these could even have been old contracts which were no longer in effect by the end of the Old Regime. But this is not the case. The statistics show that there was a continuous flow of recently-made contracts after 1750 and that the proportion of old contracts hardly varied at all from that observed before 1750.

Table 4.4. Age of emphyteutic contracts in the inventory

Age of contract	1600-1750	1751-1790
Under 10 years	3	7
Between 10 and 50 years	9	11
Over 50 years	3	4

So these were not contracts from a long distant past; this type of contract was still being made in the Brie at the end of the Old Regime. How can the apparent abundance of this type of contract be explained?

This is where a second point comes in. The emphyteusis, in the vast majority of cases, concerned houses, or sometimes gardens or plots of land in town, and much less frequently land or other properties (such as mills) in the countryside. It is also noticeable that after 1750, it became very rare for leases to apply to land in need of improvement. Emphyteusis was becoming a contract used for built-up land in towns and not for land that had to be put under cultivation. This explains why it became so rare in the countryside.

Table 4.5. Types of property held in emphyteusis

	1600-1750		1751-1790	
	No. of inventories	No. of leases	No. of inventories	No. of leases
Houses	10	12	18	22
Land, Vinyards	5	8	2	2
Plots, Gardens	0	0	3	5
Mill	0	0	1	2
Unknown	2	2	1	2

There is an extra point worth emphasising and which may, in retrospect, explain why we found so few emphyteuses in our corpus of sales from the *centième denier*. The lessors were usually institutions, more specifically religious institutions. Very few individuals used this type of lease and when they did they were usually heirs who were ceding a house, almost never a piece of land, for a long term. This is what Ferrière means when he asserts that the 'emphyteutic lease is more in use for the estates and properties of the church than for others' (Vismes & Ferrière, 1771)[14]. Why were religious institutions so eager to dispose of land in this fashion? There are many reasons and it is hard to choose between them.

One hypothesis, strongly supported by one of the referees of this article, would have it that religious communities wanted to evade the government's attempts to set limits to Church enrichment and to encourage the circulation of property. Ceding their property on long terms gave religious communities a way to avoid the many measures designed to enforce that policy, solemnly reiterated in an important edict issued in August 1749, though frequently

14 'Church properties may not be ceded for more than nine years because the beneficiaries are only enjoying the usufruct and leases longer than nine years are a form of alienation' (Vismes & Ferrière, 1771). 'However, church properties may be rented out on long term leases, either by *bail à cens* or in other ways, by observing the required formalities' (Vismes & Ferrière, 1771).

not applied[15]. Among its provisions, this piece of legislation required *gens de main-morte* – religious and other communities whose property was not subject to division upon the death of an owner – to obtain Letters Patent before acquiring land or accepting legacies of land. This was a long and awkward business which opened the transaction to scrutiny by royal courts and administrators. It also threatened religious communities, and other *gens de main-morte* who had acquired property since 1666 or in the last 30 years, with the obligation to give it back. In the circumstances, emphyteusis may have provided a clever way to obey the law without completely giving up property received by legacy or gift. So perhaps it was the obstacle created by the obligation to seek Letters Patent, and not the cost of the property transfer tax, which explains why there are so few emphyteutic contracts in the registers of the *centième denier, because otherwise their number should increase and not diminish.*

On the other hand, it could be claimed that emphyteusis provided a way around the strict regulations on alienation of church property. According to Ferrière, it 'could not be alienated without just cause and without the required formalities. The reason was that ecclesiastics were not just the simple administrators and usufructuaries of the property of their church' (Ferrière, 1754: 195). Thus, in order to validate the sale, it was necessary to obtain the decision of the local Chapter, the authorisation of the bishop or even of the Pope, of the patron, of the appropriate seigneurial court and finally, of the local royal judge! A cession by emphyteutic contract, for an annual payment and above all for a large entry fee (*pot de vin*) would have made it easier to cede a piece of land. It would also have ensured a regular payment and a chance, at least in theory, of recovering the property if things improved in the distant future. But perhaps *à son tour* this financial and legal logic is not the real one? Could it have been quite simply that the religious communities saw these long term contracts, which contained obligations to improve the property, as an economical and effective way of turning the properties to account for 'owners' who had all of eternity ahead of them?

A third factor should be taken into account at this point: the special circumstances of ecclesiastical institutions when they acted as landlords. Unlike individuals, religious communities did not die, and therefore could act in the long term. As a result they had no difficulty drawing up perennial leases. This was another example of the way they could take on enduring commitments, which has already been noted in relation to the debts they felt free to incur. This characteristic featured in Alain Boureau's claim that religious orders were at the origin of public debt (Boureau, 2006).

15 *Edit… concernant les établissemens et acquisitions des gens de main-morte* (Paris, 1749), BNF Gallica.

Table 4.6. The lessors of emphyteutic properties

Chapter	24
Hôtel Dieu	4
Chapel	3
Seminary	1
Curé	1
Abbé, convent	3
Vestry	3
Individuals	11
Other	3
Unknown	2

Should we then argue that the amounts involved were abnormal, occurring either in fake emphyteutic leases, made in the same way as a rental or a *bail à rente*, or concerning only sums so trivial as to have very little importance?

Neither of these theories is correct. If we break down the leases according to price we see that very few were concluded at a noticeably high price and conversely that it was also rare for the rent to be very small.

Table 4.7. Breakdown of rents by annual rent due for emphyteutic leases

Under 1 livre	5
From 1 to 10 livres	20
From 11 to 25 livres	12
Over 25 livres	14

There are a few cases of very low prices but on the whole, even though we lack comparisons, the amount of the lease would seem to be more or less equivalent to the market price. There are too few cases before 1700 for any change to be noticeable but it is clear that the lessors sold the property at a relatively high price; certainly not a ridiculously low one in any event. The highest price was paid for a mill ceded by the Chapter in 1755 for a term of 96 years in return for an annual payment of 256 livres. This was most definitely not a token rent but was fairly modest for this type of property, even though we do not know the yield of the mill or the quality of its product. It should also be noted that although the price might seem quite moderate there was also a substantial entry fee or *pot de vin* to complete the reckoning. For instance, the lease on the farm, set in 1761 at 80 livres a year 'forever', also required an additional cash payment of 950 livres. This was really a disguised sale combined with the payment of a perpetual rent that was stipulated in the lease.

Though some leases showed a desire to turn a property to account by conceding it for a long period before recovering it in an improved state later on, it was common for emphyteusis to act merely as a long term lease. In this it was not clearly distinguished from other long term, or even perpetual, land concessions. This no doubt contributed to the way these contracts blended in with all the other types of rental and sale that are regularly encountered in the notarial records.

Emphyteusis has an important place among the agrarian contracts allowing land to be turned to profit in the Old Regime (Béaur, Arnoux & Varet-Vitu, 2003). It filled specific needs and was found in different forms and under different names which often make it difficult to identify. In addition to the handicap of contracts which were not identified as such or contracts that supplemented it, other barriers prevented it from being used more often as a way of putting land under cultivation. As a result, other kinds of contract which had little to do with emphyteusis gradually filled the same functions with ease and became indistinguishable from it. As its initial purpose was to make it easier to plant vines, one might have expected that it would at least have been used to encourage the spread of vineyards, particularly during the 'planting craze' of the eighteenth century. However, this did not usually happen, as there were other, much more effective, methods of introducing vines, such as the *bail à complant* which reigned supreme in Saintonge and also around Nantes and in the Loire valley (Garsonnet, 1879: 227).

Emphyteusis, freed from its faded splendours might have regained strength, in the absence of rival forms of concession, and indeed there are a few examples from the nineteenth century, even in such a widely cultivated area as the Beauce. But emphyteusis did not take off again, as the priority given by the Revolution and the Code Civil to free and complete ownership made it unattractive, and the lengthening of the terms of leases and rents (*bail à ferme* and *bail à loyer*) made it less useful. The system of divided ownership was still distrusted, and it still retained feudal and archaic connotations; this explains why this contract was so uncommonly used. We have seen that emphyteutic leases were frequently tainted by feudalism, to the point where it is often hard to distinguish them from seigneurial forms of land concession. However Revolutionary legislation did not abolish emphyteutic leases, and in various forms, they retained the distinctive characteristics and functions that characterized them during the Old Regime.

Five important conclusions emerge from this research. Emphyteutic leases were much appreciated by religious communities for reasons which are not entirely clear but which were certainly not irrational. This form of alienation was frequently diverted from its initial function, becoming a long-term concession similar to other contracts so frequently found in notarial archives and which favour a deferred payment over a lasting, or perpetual, rent, whether small or not. They existed almost everywhere under various forms and methods but were more clearly identifiable in northern areas of France. They tended to proliferate in rural areas, where land needed to be brought into cultivation, and were less common in widely cleared and intensively cultivated areas. They were no doubt used even more as a method of letting urban lands and were often the typical form of concession used when towns were being built. Despite what its detractors say, they were a useful tool for turning the land to profit. They gave farmers who did not want to sink large capital sums into full and complete ownership, access to landed property; and they freed up the ground in towns[16], making it possible to expand built-up property there at reasonable cost.

Bibliography

AUBIN, Gérard (1989), *La Seigneurie en Bordelais d'après la pratique notariale (1715-1789)*, Rouen, Publications de l'Université de Rouen, n°149.

BARDET, Jean-Pierre (1983), *Rouen aux XVIIe et XVIIIe siècles : les mutations d'un espace social*, Paris, SEDES, 2 vols.

BASTIER, Jean (1975), *La Féodalité au siècle des Lumières dans la région de Toulouse vers 1670-1789)*, Paris, Bibl. nat., Commission d'histoire économique et sociale de la Révolution, 'Mémoires et Documents, XXX'.

VAN BAVEL, Bas J. P. (2008), 'The Organization and Rise of Land and Lease Markets in Northwestern Europe and Italy, *c.* 1000-1800', *Continuity and Change*, 23 (1), p. 13-53.

BAULANT, Micheline (2006), *Meaux et ses campagnes. Vivre et survivre dans le monde rural sous l'Ancien Régime*, in Gérard BÉAUR, Arlette SCHWEITZ & Anne VARET-VITU (eds), Rennes, Presses Universitaires de Rennes.

BÉAUR, Gérard (1984), *Le Marché foncier à la veille de la Révolution. Les mouvements de propriété beaucerons dans les régions de Maintenon et de Janville de 1761 à 1790*, Paris, Éd. EHESS.

BÉAUR, Gérard (1991), 'Le Marché foncier éclaté. Les modes de transmission du patrimoine sous l'Ancien Régime', *Annales ESC*, 1, p. 189-203.

BÉAUR, Gérard (1992), 'Le Fonctionnement du « marché-père» : la circulation des propriétés dans le bocage normand au XVIIIe siècle', in Rolande BONNAIN, Gérard BOUCHARD et Joseph GOY (eds), *Transmettre, hériter succéder. La reproduction familiale en milieu rural. France-Québec XVIIIe-XXe siècles*, EHESS-Presses Universitaires de Lyon , p. 77-87.

BÉAUR, Gérard (2005), 'Les Rapports de propriété en France sous l'Ancien Régime et dans la Révolution. Transmission et circulation de la terre dans les campagnes françaises du XVIe au XIXe siècle', in Nadine VIVIER (ed.), *Ruralité française et britannique, XIIIe-XXe siècles. Approches comparées*, Rennes, PUR, p. 187-200. Spanish transl.: 'Las relaciones de propiedad en Francia bajo el Antiguo Régimen y durante la Revolución. Transmisión y circulación de la tierra en el campo francés entre los siglos XVI y XIX', in Rosa CONGOST & José Miguel LANA (eds), *Campos cerrados, debates abiertos: análisis histórico*

16 We have not spent much time discussing this aspect as we have focused our work on rural areas. Examining the role of emphyteusis in the expansion of towns would have led us away from the main subject.

y propiedad de la tierra en Europa (siglos XVI-XIX), Universidad Pública de Navarra, 2007, p. 75-92.

BÉAUR, Gérard, ARNOUX, Mathieu & VARET-VITU, Anne (eds) (2003), *Exploiter la terre. Les contrats agraires de l'Antiquité à nos jours*, Rennes, Association d'Histoire des Sociétés Rurales, Bibliothèque d'Histoire Rurale, vol. 7.

BÉAUR, Gérard, SCHOFIELD, Phillipp R., CHEVET, Jean-Michel & PÉREZ-PICAZO Maria-Teresa (eds) (2013), *Property Rights, Land Markets and Economic Growth in the European Countryside (13th-20th centuries)*, Turnhout, Brepols, Rural History in Europe 1.

BÉAUR, Gérard & CHEVET, Jean-Michel (2013), 'Institutional change and agricultural growth', in Gérard BÉAUR, Phillipp R. SCHOFIELD, Jean-Michel CHEVET & Maria-Teresa PEREZ-PICAZO (eds), *Property Rights, Land Markets and Economic Growth in the European Countryside (13th-20th centuries)*, Turnhout, Brepols, Rural History in Europe 1, p. 19-68.

BOEHLER, Jean-Michel (1994), *Une Société rurale en milieu rhénan : la paysannerie de la plaine d'Alsace (1648-1789)*, Strasbourg, Presses Universitaires de Strasbourg.

BONCERF (1776), *Inconvénients des droits féodaux*, Paris.

BOUDJAABA, Fabrice (2008), *Des Paysans attachés à la terre? Familles, marchés et patrimoines dans la région de Vernon (1750-1830)*, Paris, Presses de l'Université de Paris-Sorbonne.

BOUREAU, Alain (2006), 'Le Monastère médieval, laboratoire de la dette publique?', in Jean ANDREAU, Gérard BÉAUR & Jean-Yves GRENIER, *La Dette publique dans l'histoire*, Paris, Comité pour l'Histoire Economique et Financière de la France, p. 23-31.

BRUNEL, Bernard (1992), *Le Vouloir vivre et la force des choses. Augerolles en Livradois-Forez du XVIIe au XIXe siècle*, Clermont-Ferrand, Université Blaise-Pascal, Institut d'études du Massif Central.

CHÉNON, Emile (1881), *Les Dénombrements de la propriété foncière en France avant et après la Révolution*, Paris.

CHIANEA, Gérard (1968-1969), *La Condition juridique des terres en Dauphiné au XVIIIe siècle, 1700-1789*, Grenoble-Paris.

CONGOST, Rosa (2003), 'Property Rights and Historical Analisis. What Rigths? What History?', *Past & Present*, 181, p. 73-106.

CONGOST, Rosa (2013), 'The social dynamics of agricultural growth. The example of Catalan emphyteusis in eighteenth century', in Gérard BÉAUR, Phillipp R. SCHOFIELD, Jean-Michel CHEVET & Maria-Teresa PEREZ-PICAZO (eds), *Property Rights, Land Markets and Economic Growth in the European Countryside (13th-20th centuries)*, Turnhout, Brepols, Rural History in Europe 1, p. 439-454.

D'AGAR, Charles (1805), *Le Nouveau Ferrière ou Dictionnairee de droit et de pratique, civil, commercial, criminel et judiciaire*, vol. 2.

DE FERRIÈRE, Claude-Joseph (1754), *Dictionnaire de droit et de pratique, contenant l'explication des termes de droit, d'ordonnances, de coutumes et de pratique.*

Faron, Olivier & Hubert, Etienne (1995), *Le Sol et l'immeuble. Les formes dissociées de propriété immobilière dans les villes de France et d'Italie (XIIe-XIXe siècle)*, Collection de l'Ecole Française de Rome, 206.

Gallet, Jean (1983), *La Seigneurie bretonne (1450-1680), l'exemple du Vannetais*, Paris, Publications de la Sorbonne.

Gallet, Jean (1999), *Seigneurs et paysans en France, 1600-1793*, Rennes, Editions Ouest-France.

Garaud, Marcel (1958), *Histoire générale du droit privé français. La Révolution et la propriété foncière*, Paris.

Garsonnet, Jean-Baptiste Eugène (1879), *Histoire des locations perpétuelles et des baux à longue durée*, Paris, Larose.

Garnier, Josette (1982), *Bourgeoisie et propriété immobilière en Forez aux XVIIe et XVIIIe siècles*, Centre d'Etudes Foréziennes.

Hoppenbrouwers, Peter & Van Zanden, Jan Luiten (eds) (2001), *Peasants into Farmers? The transformation of rural economy and society in the Low Countries (Middle Ages-19th century) in light of the Brenner debate*, Corn publication series 4, Turnhout, Brepols.

Imbert, Jean (1992), 'Les Gens de mainmorte et l'édit d'août 1749', *Cahiers des Annales de Normandie*, 24, p. 337-346.

Jousmet, Raymond (1999), *Paysans d'Aunis à la veille de la Révolution*, Saintes, Le Croît Vif.

Luna, Pablo & Mignemi, Niccolò (eds) (2017), *Prédateurs et résistants. Appropriation et réappropriation de la terre et des ressources naturelles (16e-20e siècles)*, Paris, Syllepse.

Maillard, Brigitte (1998), *Les Campagnes de Touraine au XVIIIe siècle. Structures agraires et économie rurale*, Rennes, Presses Universitaires de Rennes, 1998.

Massaloux, Jean-Paul (1989), *La Régie de l'Enregistrement et des Domaines aux XVIIIe et XIXe siècles : étude historique*, Genève, Librairie Droz.

North, Douglas (1990), *Institutions, Institutional Change and Economic Performance*, Cambridge, Cambridge University Press.

North, Douglas & Thomas, R. P. (1980), *L'Essor du monde occidental. Une nouvelle histoire économique*, Paris, Flammarion.

Quesnay (1768), *Physiocratie, ou constitution naturelle du gouvernement le plus avantageux au genre humain*.

Santos, Rui & Serrâo, José Vicente (2013), 'Property rights, social appropriations and economic outcomes: Agrarian contracts in southern Portugal in the late 18th century' in Gérard Béaur, Phillipp R. Schofield, Jean-Michel Chevet & Maria-Teresa Perez-Picazo (eds), *Property Rights, Land Markets and Economic Growth in the European Countryside (13th-20th centuries)*, Turnhout, Brepols, Rural History in Europe 1, p. 475-494.

Turgot, Anne Robert Jacques (1766), *Essai sur la formation et la distribution des richesses*.

Vilar-Berrogain, Gabrielle (1958), *Guide des recherches dans les fonds d'Enregistrement sous l'Ancien Régime*, Paris, Imprimerie nationale.

Vismes, François-Benoît de & Ferrière, Claude-Joseph de (1771), *La science parfaite des notaires, Ou le parfait notaire…*,. Paris, chez Durand

JEAN-MICHEL BOEHLER

5. *Erblehn* and *Hoflehn* in Germanic Lands

Disguised Forms of Ownership? The Alsatian Countryside in the Seventeenth and Eighteenth Centuries

Erblehn and *Hoflehn* are terms for types of Germanic emphyteutic tenure of indeterminate or, even unlimited, duration. To a French observer, unused to the situation in the Rhineland, the Alsatian plain seems a special case, but in fact it shares many of the characteristics of Baden, Wurtemberg and the Palatinate. The present study combines and compares information from four kinds of Sources.

1. jurisprudence: mainly essays and law theses defended at the University of Strasbourg during the eighteenth century
2. land enumerations and surveys of land (*terriers* and cadasters)
3. notarial documents, dealing with the land market and successions
4. judicial documents: lawsuits and trials

Since there was no official land registry in Alsace before the Revolution and the practices we are dealing with took place at the fringe of legality the existing documentation usually takes the form of studies written 'from below', on the level of the practices, reactions and sensibilities of the peasant world itself.

The statement that 'the Alsatian peasant was the owner of his land without being so while at the same time being so' is a rather free definition of emphyteutic practice, but corresponds to reality. The Alsatian countryside existed in a triple context:

- a spatial and land tenure context, that of the influence of Roman law. True, Roman Law always had to compromise with customary law: peasant owners, though not a majority, were solidly established and succeeded in maintaining their emphyteutic practices in the face of petty landed or territorial nobility by claiming that the property they cultivated was allodial;
- a peculiar set of economic circumstances, in which a succession of wars in the seventeenth century (the Thirty Years War and the campaigns of Louis XIV) was followed by a period of reconstruction, that encouraged voluntary or constrained concessions from the ground landlords and also usurpations by the peasants, and then by an era of relative prosperity in the eighteenth century that was favourable to a peasant policy of land acquisition in spite of attempts at a seigneurial reaction;

Agrarian Change and Imperfect Property, ed. by Rosa Congost and Pablo F. Luna, Rural History in Europe, 15 (Turnhout, 2018), 97-112

DOI 10.1484/M.RURHE-EB.5.116120

- finally, a social context, a permanent contest between lords and peasants, between those who owned and those who worked the land, which, with a little help from the Revolution, turned in favour of the latter group and in particular of the small group of comfortable peasants. These better-off people, unlike the small peasants, were able to offer guarantees for the good management of rented lands. Emphyteusis thus had a role to play in reinforcing social inequalities.

I. A particular land law context

Jurists tell us that Alsace was one of the northern areas marked by Roman Law, either from its origins or because they were re-imposed over time, although, as historians working from notarial archives have shown, it also took account of local usage based on very old customary law. Roman law was restored during the Carolingian renaissance, fell out of use from the eighth to the twelfth centuries, was rediscovered in the thirteenth century through the Church and jurists trained in Italian universities, and reached its apogee at the Renaissance (Thomann, 1983). It is thus considered to have gone beyond the borders of Middle Europe, 'Médioromanie' as it is sometimes called, travelling up the Rhine-Rhône corridor and spreading to a large part of the Holy Roman Empire, which was thought of as a continuation of the Roman Empire. When jurists refer to Romano-German Law they are being too hasty; legal historians, with a more nuanced approach (Dannhorn, 2003: 1-4, 173-192, 305-318) have shown that there was a transition in the seventeenth and eighteenth centuries from 'Roman' emphyteusis to 'German' emphyteusis[1] that involved much adaptation to local conditions and a genuine process of Germanisation. Whatever explanation is offered – was it adaptation, assimilation or autonomy? – this transition marks the emergence of the *deutsche Erbleihe*, an institution of Germanic law, and so of Alastian *Erblehn* or *Erhblehen*. The Alsatian version could be renewed by tacit agreement from one generation to another though theoretically the landlord needed to agree to the right of succession. This was a much longer term than that of an emphyteutic long-term lease (up to 99 years) and only expired when there no heir was left. As we shall see, this jurisdiction had the advantage of conferring a real sense of ownership and security since it worked in favour of the farmers.

The situation of Alsace, between France and the Empire (Boehler, 2005) at the meeting-point of two antinomic juridical entities[2], corresponds rather well to the simplistic opposition between the North and the South of France,

1 Dannhorn asserts that this transition was effected by Schilter, *Praxis Juri Romani* (1698).

2 In the German bibliography, see the classic works of AUBIN & ZORN (1971); FRANZ (1976); KELLENBENZ (1977); ABEL (1978); ENGELSING (1983); BOELCKE (1987); HENNING (1991); ACHILLES (1993).

with the province serving as an example of an 'in-between country' where two essential principles intersect (Boehler, 2000: 339-351):

- 'no land without a lord', which, in French law, in the context of tight seigneurial control, meant that there were large seigneurial domains that because of the engrossement of farms (*réunions des fermes*) were often placed under powerful general farmers, as in the Ile de France, as described by Jean Jacquart and Jean-Marc Moriceau. From the peasants' point of view, this meant that most of the land was held in copyhold, as *censive*, and little as freehold (*alleu*). In Alsace, however, with only a few exceptions, there was very little large seigneurial ownership, and there was hardly any structure of demesnes (*domaines*) or copyholds (*censes*) based on direct farming of the land (Boehler, 1994: 524-527).
- 'no lord without title' was the second principle: it held sway in Alsace as in all of the Rhine Valley and most of West Germany. In the context of *Grundherrschaft* (landholding lordship) the peasantry needed the protection of a landholding lord who was himself dependent on a territorial lord, the *Landesherr*. In Alsace, according to 'German custom', mentioned by successive Intendants and *avocats* of the *Conseil Souverain* in the eighteenth century, this situation, which gave a certain amount of liberty to the peasants, was reinforced by the scattered nature of seigneurial property and its fragmentation into a host of small tenures that could depend on several different owners. The lord thus was seen as the landlord of a few dozen hectares rather than a significant territorial ruler.

We have emphasised the institution of the seigneurie because emphyteusis existed in the context of privileged ownership, lay or ecclesiastic; it had little to do, as it was not immediately profitable, with the property that townspeople rented out to peasant farmers, mostly on short terms. However it would be wrong to oppose, in a simple-minded way, ownership and farming of land. Instead, we should go back to the notion of possession, which shifts the boundary between owning and not owning, and leads directly to the concept of emphyteusis. 'Possession' is quite close to *Volleigentum* or *allodium*, full and complete ownership, of which there are traces in notarial archives (*ledig und eigen*, *freies eigen*). From the thirteenth century on, but particularly in the sixteenth century, the jurists, strongly influenced by Roman law, and reasoning by analogy, tended to assimilate German emphyteusis to Roman emphyteusis and the lords, who were close to them, tended to take the same position. But those who worked the land, with little access to 'learned' law but well aware of their own interests, held on to *Erblehen*, which was familiar to them. We thus have two cultures that coexisted without necessarily understanding each other.

As good Cartesians we might be tempted to confine ourselves to the figures and work out some statistics. Unfortunately, averages are deceptive: between 30 and 60 per cent of surface area belonged to peasants, both in old France and in the Germanic areas, or, roughly speaking, half of the land;

the other half belonged to the classes privileged by birth or fortune. For Alsace the proportions were as follows: the nobles had 15 to 25 per cent, the urban bourgeoisie, only 5 to 10 per cent, and the religious institutions were particularly present, with 25 to 35 per cent (Boehler, 1994: 508-522). What is unusual about this? It is true that Alsace is closer to 60 per cent than to 30 per cent, more like Baehrel's Basse Provence (Baehrel, 1961), impregnated with Roman Law (60 to 80 per cent) than the Nord (30 to 40 per cent according to Georges Lefebvre (1924)) or the Brie (only 20 per cent, according to Mireaux (1958)). But, taking into account the sources used it is difficult to fix the extent of emphyteusis, which is hard to measure if only because of the uncertain vocabulary used, both for the surface area and the number of tillers of the soil. What is clear is that peasant ownership grew in eighteenth-century Alsace by a process of 'nibbling away' linked to the high yield of the land and increased grain prices. This growth, however, was nothing in comparison with the large transfers that took place when the *biens nationaux* were put up for sale in the Revolution.

What made this difference, though, was not the proportion of land held in "eminent" ownership dominium directum, or *Obereigentum*, in the Roman sense of the term, but that held in 'use' (*Nutzeigentum*), notions very present in feudal law; and this is where the concept of emphyteusis comes in. The line between the two was so tenuous that 'possession' through forms of lease that were very advantageous for tenants was almost the equivalent of 'ownership', but it was a disguised form of ownership over and above the 60 per cent of land in whole and complete ownership. This shows how complex and ambiguous the notion of ownership is, and how it cannot be captured in the context of an institution or a statistic. Though a large part of the land –at least half– did not belong to peasants, they made up for it by possession, ownership by 'usage', that was only a particularly advantageous type of tenure, linked to a presumption of allodial status in favour of the tenant, based on occupation rather than naked possession of the soil. In these conditions peasant appropriation, through a pseudo-rental, could well approach or exceed three-quarters of the area under cultivation (Boehler, 1994: 503-559, 597-600).

In legal terms, of course, the land in question belonged to the person who 'possessed' it in full ownership, not to the one who cultivated it. But in economic terms, it belonged to the one who 'held' it. The ideal situation would be to combine the "eminent" ownership dominium directum and the 'real' or 'use' ownership in the same person, which sometimes happened in Alsace. This distinction may seem shocking to those with a Cartesian mindset and categorical conceptions but it corresponds perfectly to the feudal notions of dominium directum and dominium utile. Although the official law disliked such imprecisions the peasant had no hesitation in disposing of another's property. There has been a great deal of discussion about the landowner-lord but what happened with the urban bourgeoisie, knowledgeable about the law, who might well share these judicial concepts with the peasant? In fact, the administrative and merchant elite, and even more so the artisans, preferred to collect *rentes fractionnées*[3] from short term leases, because these *Gülten* were more profitable, easier to negotiate and better adapted to economic developments as productive or occasional investments. Emphyteusis thus remained, in large part, something for lay and ecclesiastical lords.

II. The significant adaptation of modes of tenure to the economic situation

The *Erblehn* were extremely flexible, not only structurally but in relation to economic change. For exceptional situations there were exceptional solutions. After the seventeenth-century wars, at a time when there was abundant land waiting to be cultivated, but few men to take on the work, it was necessary to attract and keep potential farmers. At the time of the 'reconstruction', between 1680 and 1720, the situation was truly catastrophic. There was a depreciation of property values and land left uncultivated because of the shortage of both labour and livestock. There was disorder caused by unauthorized cultivation of land. There was an increase in 'unused' land (*terres caduques* or *terres vacantes*), former *Gültguter* where often neither the owner nor the farmer was known, land left unclaimed in any case; such land, by right of escheat, should logically have reverted to seigneurial land but had either been occupied without any legal proceedings or alienated without the authorisation of the legitimate proprietors. There was a shortage of potential settlers and of potential renters, and so on and so forth. All these constraints obliged the owners, faced as they were with a loss of income and unable to enforce their will, to loosen their grip (Boehler, 1994: 167-340). By freely-given or forced concessions, short-term leases, for 3, 6, 9, 12, or 18 years, were replaced by long-term leases, *longi temporis*, greater than 18 years according to jurists, and preferably by life leases (*Vitalleihe*), sometimes hereditary, sometimes of indeterminate length (*ständiges Gültgut*) which were termed *Erblehn* or *Erbpacht*, the prefix *Erb* alluding to their hereditary character. This was really an alienation, a type of lease-sale, that reflected the very generous conditions awarded at the period when the land was first brought into cultivation, the

3 The expression *rentes fractionnées* refers to the acquisition, mostly by the urban bourgeoisie, of scattered properties. Sometimes it happened by chance, as when peasants ran into debt or noble estates disintegrated; sometimes it occurred because of circumstances that could be turned to account, such as the rise in grain prices during the eighteenth century. These properties were still farmed by their former owners and produced rents (*Gült* with the meaning of rack-rents) or portions of rents, if the property came to be divided over the years; for a single buyer of land, this could amount to dozens, even hundreds of sacks of grain from various sources. This was sufficient to get control of the land by slowly building a landed estate. The next step for the purchasers, or their heirs, was to gather in these fractional rents, one at a time, by exchange or purchase, as Jean Vogt has demonstrated in his many local history articles. Emphyteusis provided a partial remedy for such dispersal of property.

'use' domain going to the person who cultivated the land, the eminent domain remaining in theory with the person who was the legitimate proprietor, and who, in fact, had no other choice. Could the latter sell the land? There were no interested buyers. Could he work it on his own account? There was not enough labour. The only possibility was to rent it out for a reasonable entry fee and a symbolic quitrent (*cens*).

But even though *Erblehn* was the formula best suited to an era of reconstruction, this does not mean that that it should be seen as solely a product of the early modern period; emphyteusis had existed since Gallo-Roman times and the Carolingian renaissance as a recognised legal contract under the name of *jus heriditarium* or *emphytenum perpetuum*. This authorised an explicit, official and perpetual alienation, resting, in principle, on an official document, the emphyteutic letter. This was the equivalent of what is known elsewhere as rental in perpetuity (*locatairie perpétuelle*) or perpetual settlement (*colonie perpétuelle*).

The conditions for such a rental were actually much easier than those for a simple farming lease (*bail à fermage*) (Boehler, 2005). There were three:

- an entry fee, *laudème* or *Ehrschatz*, a tax, paid as a mark of deference (*pro honore, Ehr, laudatio*) outside of the rental contract proper; on the part of the incoming tenant it meant recognition of another's ownership before becoming a right conferring enjoyment of the property;
- possibly a transfer fee, similar to *lods et ventes*, even though the property could not be divided;
- a small and fixed payment, transferrable and possibly subject to repurchase, called *Ernzins*, around one to two bushels (*boisseaux*) for each acre (*arpent*), that is, one half to one hectolitre per hectare; this was three to six times less than an ordinary rental lease. This payment was in the form of a token *cens* bearing on the land itself. It was not the same as a flexible rental contract based on the presumed product of the land and its yield, which amounted to around 10 to 15 per cent of a normal harvest, that is three bushels (*boisseaux*) to one *rézal* (= 6 bushels) per acre (*arpent*). This *cens* was termed either a *contrat de cens* or a *bail à rente*. There is a difficulty here because this *cens*, sometimes termed a 'reconstruction *cens*' or a 'clearance *cens*' by jurists, was occasionally hidden, not just under the term *Zins*, which was normal, but also as *Gült*, which also designated annual rent under a lease. Unlike rent, which was subject to renewal, the *cens* assured the enfeoffment and perpetual alienation of the eminent owner's property, even though it gradually lost its feudal basis. The underlying difficulty was how to know whether the *Gült* was a simple lease or an emphyteutic *cens* and the peasants, wily as foxes, willingly played on the ambiguity of the wording.

The owner had the right to take back possession of his property at will if the holder did not fulfil his obligations, by virtue of the right of *seizin*, which resembled the feudal right of *committimus*. This, in theory, introduced an element of insecurity, however small, into the legal emphyteusis, but everything depended, in the last resort, on the power of the owner. In any case it was a recognition of an ancient and imprescriptible "eminent" property dominium directum right, not subject to redemption, theoretically indivisible, by right of a sort of enfeoffment, a type of perpetual alienation in favour of the eminent owner; the latter was most often a lord-landlord, who was disposed to put some order in his affairs at the same time as he was obliged to make concessions to those who worked the land.

The situation changed during the eighteenth century, and the peasants, rather than sticking to the law and the legal value of concepts, preferred the flexible and fluid notions resulting from concrete situations and pragmatic solutions. In the eighteenth century (Boehler, 1994: 559-570), encouraged by the rise in prices and profits, they took advantage of either the absenteeism of the lord-landlord, more and more attracted by urban life, or the lord's ignorance of his own best interests, or his inability to gain respect for his rights at a time when seigneurial institutions were losing ground. The peasant profited from these weaknesses to get control of lands that were not legally his, but which were assimilated, not *de jure* but *de facto*, to peasant ownership, becoming a *Hoflehn* or a *bien censitique*. Unlike *Erblehn*, this was no longer alienation but a change in the nature of land leased out by ordinary rental and then annexed as farmstead to the *Hof*, literally the yard, that is, the peasant farm. Thus it became in fact a disguised form of ownership. From the prefix *Erb* to the prefix *Hof* peasant possession was consolidated and the indivisibility of the property was reinforced. Unlike *Erblehn* the farmer claimed full ownership, profiting from the flaws in the system and alert to certain traps which had to be avoided:

- when the original titles had been lost and there was no contract, there was prescription.
- when there was no renewal of a limited-term lease, accompanied with variable entry fees (*canons*), and thus incompatible with the emphyteutic *cens*, or even when there were no offers of a discharge or diminution, even if such offers were only for reason of bad weather of agricultural calamities (if more than a third of the crop was destroyed because of war or hail, but not including flooding or drought, where the risks were divided); these were proof of an ordinary rental lease given to the farmer. Silence was golden; whereas periodic renewal of the lease was a sign of an ordinary rental, in contradiction with the principle of emphyteusis, the absence of renewal, or the taking of a fixed payment, termed steel rent (*stählerne Gült*) suggested emphyteusis, in fact if not in law. In 1766 there occurred a violent dispute, followed by a trial that made legal history, about the possessions of the abbey of Pairis at Andolsheim, in the Colmar region. The farmer refused to accept a new lease of nine years:[4] were the lands in

4 Arch. dép. Haut-Rhin 2J 45 II/4. See Boehler (1994: 2266-2267, Annex 17).

question subject to an ordinary rental lease, as proved by changes in the amount of rent (as the abbey maintained) or did they count as *Hoflehn* (as the farmers argued) because there was no lease, only a tacit renewal? We do not know how the affair ended but we do know that evidence going back to 1577 (nearly two centuries!) was brought in to support the two opposed positions.
– finally, continuous possession in the same family from generation to generation went in the same direction and led to ownership with thirty-year prescription, for individuals, forty years for non-peasants.

Short, personal, rental leases were thus transformed, in time, into hereditary leases with no official contract, disconnected from the parcels of land supposedly bearing the rent and becoming proper farmsteads in the hands of a single owner, attached to the lands worked by peasant families. By guile or dishonesty the rent for land had changed into a seigneurial *cens*. Holding the land: the concept takes us back to divided property, split between the lessee and the lessor, and it is this division, not necessarily an opposition between the two, that the German economist Thaer refers to when he states that 'the land is the wife of the owner and the mistress of the tenant'! In any case, emphyteusis, imperfect property, certainly distinguished the soil as infrastructure from the product of the soil, which was part of the superstructure.

This amounts to a transfer of ownership from the lessor to the lessee; the expression *eigen und erbe* is revealing in this regard. The manoeuvre was subtle and all to the advantage of the lessee as the *Erbzins* was, in comparison with the rent (*fermage*) that should have been paid, a cut-price *cens*, invariable and hereditary. Moreover the tenant was not liable to expulsion as in the case of a legal emphyteusis, as there was no official right of retreat in a recognised contract. Finally, if he acquired the right to transmit to his heirs, by tacit renewal, along with the farm, a farmstead that could be neither divided nor shared, the farmer's dynasty was guaranteed continuity on the farm. The lands attached to the farmstead were an integral part of the farm and notarial acts mentioned them separately as they could not be shared or sublet, nor sold separately, while they could be alienated with the farm.

The truly original characteristic of Alsace was not legal emphyteusis, but *de facto* emphyteusis (Vogt, 1955, 1966, 1983), which put the farms in an extra-legal situation, or as the jurists put it, a state of acquisitive pre-emption. Does this mean that the lessor, faced with almost suicidal options, had no advantages to gain? By no means, for several overlapping and sometimes contradictory reasons:
– It should be realized that short leases led to subdivision of the farms rented and fragmentation of the parcels of land, which necessitated a system of *porterie* (*Trägerei*) for collecting rent. This was somewhat similar to the ancient *colonage*, a kind of emphyteusis on a large scale where the *porteurs* were chosen among the larger farmers. Emphyteuesis, on the other hand, brought, in addition to its status of perpetual colonage, a sort of protection

against fragmentation and made rent collection much easier as it avoided all the problems inherent in short-term leases; there was no need to fight with aggressive or wily peasants or to have to put up with frequent changes of farmers.

- Emphyteusis avoided the risk of exhausting the soil, since with short-term leases there was a danger that as the land was supposed to be given back it would be poorly cultivated and manured, particularly at the end of the lease; what was the point of putting manure on a field that would not be yours when it was most fertile? The contract might well state that the land had to be given back in the state in which it was received, properly drained and manured; these clauses were not always respected in short-term leases. Over the longer term, however, improvements were possible, and in themselves produced revenue in the form of *mélioration* or *Schaufelrecht* ('shovel rights' or 'ploughing rights'). This was a right of possession and devolution: in fact, at the moment of transmission (*Ackergang*) it was not so much the soil but the long-term improvements (*méliorations*) that were transferred, which shows that the farmer looked after what he considered to be 'his' land, even though, legally, it did not belong to him.
- Finally, we see that the emphyteutic *cens* was often paid by substantial peasants, carefully chosen as men of means and of good reputation. Continuity and security were guarantees that *fermages* would be regularly paid, even if these were not real *fermages*. This is what Chauffour l'Ainé and Reichstetter, barristers at the Conseil souverain d'Alsace, said in 1776: 'These properties are solid and permanent establishments which have for centuries made up the finest farmsteads… it is very profitable to have comfortable heads of families, who, by their work and economy found new generations and multiply them… The owner of the *rente* receives it from one person, one barn, one granary, the products delivered are of the same quality … Experience shows what a great difference there is between the rent delivered by one farmer and that collected in bits from a large number of debtors' and they added that it was most important 'to establish good *laboureurs* who could afford to pay the seigneurial dues'[5].

At the beginning of the nineteenth century, the agronomist Schwerz did not hesitate to attribute the flourishing state of agriculture in Alsace in the previous century to the use of emphyteusis, which he saw as the catalyst of agricultural progress and a real protection against land subdivision. In general, he thought it an important factor in the agrarian progress, particularly in the introduction of commercial plants. This latter point is, however, questionable (Schwerz, 1839: 23). In fact it is obvious that the immediate profitability of speculative crops such as hemp, tobacco and madder did not fit with the emphyteusis system, but rather with short-term and adjustable leases. There

5 Arch. dép. Haut-Rhin 18J 716 (Colmar 8/6/1789).

were two different ways of generating income; through long-term progress and through short-term profitability. Emphyteusis, tradition or modernity? That is the essential question.

The taking back of *Erbehn* by owners in the second half of the eighteenth century shows that this formula was not a panacea and also that there was not a linear progression over time of dominant modes of tenure. These sometimes brutal retaliations, with threats of expulsion and real cases of eviction, took place in the context of the successive 'seigneurial reactions' after 1750. This tactic was not as straightforward in relation to *de facto* emphyteusis, which was difficult to identify, as it was with legal emphyteusis which became an anachronism along with the conditions that had given birth to it. The rental contract (*Lehnungsbrief*) attributed a property (*Lehnacker, Lehngut, Gültgut*) to a named person to work the land for a limited period. This was a return to the traditional leases of 3, 6, 9, 12, 15, and 18 years maximum, hence the terms *Temporallehen* or *Stichlehn*, which expressed the double reality of 'temporary' or 'pin prick' leases, the result of multiple lettings.

This was because short-term leases had become more profitable than emphyteutic contracts. With 'land-hunger', with rising cereal prices (up 100 or 150 per cent in the eighteenth century), and thereby with the growth of profit and increase of ground rent, speculative leasing developed within the short-term rental system, by mutual agreement, and tended to become generalised and personalised. These developments were sometimes accompanied by a fortunate readjustment in grain price levels and of the conditions of supply and demand, as a result of changes in specie, which were really disguised price increases, of subdivision of plots or their auctioning to the highest bidder (the same thing happened with auctioning of tithes) in the hope of additional profits. These different techniques satisfied the lessors' desire for gain and allowed them to reap full benefit from the economic conditions. 'To grant an emphyteusis', said the lord of Landser at this period, 'is to alienate' [6] and thus those who worked the land became tenant farmers (*fermiers*) in the strict meaning of the term.

This was the response of the masters of the land, a counter-offensive against emphyteutic practices, of which the most illegal was to try, without a contract, to transform a simple rental lease into a long term indefinite lease until it became hereditary and passed on from one generation to another. *De facto* emphyteusis was now considered as usurpation following the change in the nature of the existing leases. On the other hand, the landlord-lord tried to recuperate property previously alienated legally or by mistake or negligence, and found himself confronted with forgetful peasants who refused to identify parcels, or former tenants who showed completely outdated authorisations for clearing land (*Stockbriefe*) as the equivalent of property titles (Boehler, 1998: 66-71).

---

6 Arch. dép. Haut-Rhin 1E 44/16 (1771-1777).

Did the French Revolution mean the end for emphyteusis? The revolutionary decrees of 1790, which concerned only emphyteutic agreements that had survived and escaped these attempts at recovery, officially abolished legal emphyteusis and made it open to purchase, like all perpetual *rentes*, at the rate of denier 20 or 25, that is, at 20 or 25 times the amount of a moderate and fixed emphyteutic *cens*, the purchase price being fixed as a function of the *cens* itself (that is in general at less than 4 or 5 per cent of the value of the land). The purchase was thus very advantageous for those who had formerly worked the land.

The abolition of perpetuity in principle only concerned legal emphyteusis, but it also posed a real problem to *de facto* emphyteusis. It allowed the peasants, with their old practices, long memories and penchant for cunning intrigue to pass off simple annual payments as ancient emphyteutic *cens*. The sale of National Property (*biens nationaux*) in the Revolution (Marx, 1974: 80-108; Vogt, 1989/1990) revived the old conundrum of the *terres caduques*: were they seigneurial properties alienated for a low price owing to circumstance, or were they lands that had purely and simply been usurped by the farmers?

These protests reached their peak when entire farmsteads belonging to religious institutions were sold off, perfectly legally. The peasants, however alleged that their ancestors had cultivated them with the sweat of their brow over many generations and considered themselves the legitimate owners – a flagrant confusion between 'ownership' and 'possession' – and denounced the 1790 decrees as a piece of robbery and a profound injustice. Jean Lienhart, the provost (*prévot*) of Wolfisheim, near Strasbourg, could not understand why, when the *biens nationaux* were put up for sale, he had to buy at a high price (7,350 *livres tournois* at auction) the 12 acres of land (about 2 or 3 hectares) he held on lease from the Convent of Sainte-Marguerite in Strasbourg, which his ancestors had worked for more than 30 years[7]. In this particular case the land was held in an ordinary lease, so it is easy to imagine the reactions of peasants when emphyteutic leases were involved. In the final analysis, the Revolution upheld the right of the lessee to the detriment of those of the lessor. But which lessee?

However, the survival of emphyteusis was assured because Revolutionary decrees were often misapplied or avoided, as with the Napoleonic Civil Code. Though emphyteusis officially disappeared it could easily be prolonged by unlimited, almost hereditary, simple leases. Until the twentieth century, the villages were dominated by one or two *laboureurs* who held sufficiently solid blocks of land to merit prestigious titles like *Thomasbüre* (farmers of the Protestant Saint Thomas Chapter of Strasbourg) or of *Spitalbüre* (farmers of the Hôpital des Bourgeois of Strasbourg).

7 Arch. dép. Haut-Rhin 2E 73/20 and AN Q2 135.

III. The actors: the balance of power and increasing inequality

In theory nothing prevented the *Erblehn*, which were supposed to be universal, from benefitting all social groups. But, with the development of the *Hoflehn* the balance of power between lessors and lessees, and within these groups, between big and small peasants, tended to become more extreme. Really, there was no such thing as 'the'typical Alsatian peasant and there were very different 'typical cases', depending on who was involved.

The choice between simple leasing and emphyteutic leasing was often imposed by peasants themselves, according to the greater or lesser ability of the landowner, most often the lay or ecclesiastical lord, to put up a resistance. There were thus 'strongholds', such as Kochersberg or the plain of Erstein, where the peasant offensive was particularly energetic: they appropriated rights, profiting from seigneurial weakness. However, not all peasants had the luxury of being able to transform land held on simple lease into emphyteusis, simply because this most often occurred with a farmstead dependent on one and the same owner and attached to a farm. And not just any farm; these farmsteads were reserved for a rural elite, with large ploughing capacity (*Rossbüre*, ploughmen with horses), with sufficient guarantees of solvency and collateral if necessary, whereas the vast majority of small farmers were liable to be poor payers. To give a short summary of Alsatian property structure: the more the ownership was split up, even 'dwarfed' as German historians say, and this fragmentation accompanied by subdivision of the land, the more rentals tended, in the second half of the eighteenth century, to be concentrated, since a minority of farmers monopolised almost all the landed property (Boehler, 1994: 600-614). The average surface area of a farm was between two and five hectares but the large (between 10 and 50) and the very large farms, by Alsatian standards (over 50 hectares) were held by *laboureurs* who, although they made up only a quarter or a third of all heads of households, had on average 10 to 30 hectares and controlled 40 to 60 per cent, even sometimes as much as 90 per cent, of the surface area under lease, particularly that under emphyteutic lease (Boehler, 1994: 508-522). It was these emphyteutic contracts that made such farms profitable, by a skilful compromise between ownership and leasing, enabling them to amortize the cost of the equipment and plough teams they used, and saved others from ruin. How many benefited from this? Perhaps 5 to 10 per cent of the heads of households, one or two farmers in a village? Emphyteusis is difficult to quantify, given the state of our sources and the fact that contracts only show part of the reality, both in terms of those benefiting from it and of the surface areas concerned.

The *Hof*, like the Mediterranean *domus*, had a deliberately vertical and linear concept of direct descent that meant that transmission of ancestral property, including emphyteutic property, fell not to the individual but to the collective entity that made up the family: 'preservation of families' is explicitly invoked in the Wurtemberg-Montbéliard domains in the 1770s (Boehler, 1994: 1241-1244). The family, however, was founded more on a linear descent from a common ancestor (*lignée*), than on lineage (*lignage*) relationships within the family, which meant that the system resulted in transmission to a single heir. This manifested a visceral attachment to the undivided ownership and frankly inegalitarian ideology, which was already present in the model of inheritance of the nobility, with complicity between the owner who wanted to find 'good *laboureurs*' and these *laboureurs* who formed the core of the peasant elite[8]. The topic of succession customs on large farms is outside our subject, but it is impossible to avoid making comparisons with the ancient institution of the stem family (*Stammgut*), which, at the time of the Nazi occupation, was renamed *Erbhof*.

We should not go so far, however, as to assert that the social differences between rich *laboureurs* and peasants on smallholdings created an opposition between emphyteutic lands, held by the first group, and lands let on rental for a fixed period, which were left to the second. The latter group were in no way excluded from emphyteotic leasing. The situation was not as rigid as it may appear as the poorer peasants, looking for protection in exchange for a rental, or as a result of a donation or bequest to a religious institution, could take part in the system. But they only received the 'crumbs', while the dispersal of a large farmstead could lead to a real redistribution of property to the benefit of an old peasant aristocracy, and thus reinforce inequalities. Inequality, resulting from concentration of rentals, thus reinforced fragmentation: it was the price to pay for 'emphyteutic appropriation'.

To conclude, *Erblehn* and *Hoflehn* seem, in spite of their specific characteristics, to be a variant of the classical emphyteusis. But emphyteusis was not only a legal or technical matter; it had a social content and revealed the patient and secretive struggle of the peasants for possession of the land that was crowned, rather than initiated, by the Revolution. It was part of the mechanism of the struggle that led the actors, on both sides, to change the very nature of the contract, from emphyteusis to leasing and vice-versa. It was not a simple usufruct since the formula bestowed the ownership with the possibility of transmitting and alienating it, often without the consent of the landlord, when it brought together eminent ownership and real ownership in the same person.

Studying emphyteusis thus leads us into the history of mentalities. The reflexes underlying it do not depend on learned legal jargon or more or less esoteric conceits but on concrete notions such as length of tenure, security and stability of possession, and the ability to transfer or alienate the whole property, with or without consent of the owner; that is why we need to look beyond the legal treatises. The peasants, with their consummate ability to muddy the issues, were owners while not completely owners – even though they really were.

8 Arch. dép. Haut-Rhin E 130 (receveur Rosé, 22/12/1777).

Sources

Archives départementales du Haut-Rhin et du Bas-Rhin; Archives Nationales.

Procès-verbal des séances de l'Assemblée provinciale d'Alsace (du 10 novembre au 10 décembre 1787), Strasbourg, 1788.

Considérations sur les droits particuliers et le véritable intérêt de la province d'Alsace, Strasbourg, 1789.

D'Agon de la Contrie, Louis Bernard Antoine (1825), *Ancien statutaire d'Alsace ou recueil des actes fournis en 1738-1739 par M. de Corberon… suivi d'une notice sur les Emphytéotes, les Colonges, les Locatairies perpétuelles, dites « Schauffelrecht », les Cens, Rentes et redevances foncières*, Colmar.

Koch, Christophe Guillaume (1797), *Traité sur la nature des biens ruraux dans les deux départements du Rhin*, Strasbourg.

Schilter, Johann (1698), *Praxis juris romani.*

Schwerz, Jean Népomucène (1816), *Beschreibung der Landwirtschaft im Nieder-Elsass*, Berlin 1816, (French translation, V. Rendu, Paris, 1839).

Thaer, Albert (1809-1810), *Grundsätze der rationellen Landwirtschaft*, Berlin, (French translation 1811-1815).

Bibliography

Abel, Wilhelm (1978), 'Geschichte der deutschen Landwirtschaft vom frühen Mittelalter bis zum 19. Jahrhundert', in Gunther Franz (ed.), *Deutsche Agrargeschichte, vol. 2*, Stuttgart, Eugen Ulmer.

Achilles, Walter (1993), *Deutsche Agrargeschichte im Zeitalter der Reformen und der Industrialisierung*, Stuttgart, Eugen Ulmer.

Aubin, Hermann & Zorn, Wolfgang (1971), *Handbuch der deutschen Wirtschafts- und Sozialgeschichte*, I, Stuttgart, Klett-Cotta.

Baehrel, René (1961), *Une Croissance: la Basse Provence rurale, de la fin du seizième siècle à 1789. Essai d'économie historique statistique*, Paris, SEVPEN [Paris, EHESS, 1988].

Boehler, Jean-Michel (1994), *Une Société rurale en milieu rhénan: la paysannerie de la plaine d'Alsace (1648-1789)*, Strasbourg, Presses Universitaires de Strasbourg.

Boehler, Jean-Michel (1998), 'Loups ou renards? Les paysans de la plaine d'Alsace entre violence et ruse (xviie-xviiie siècles). Contribution à l'histoire des mentalités en milieu rural', *Revue d'Alsace*, 124, p. 55-80.

Boehler, Jean-Michel (1999), 'De la reconstruction agraire à la mise en vente des Biens nationaux: possession de la terre, conjoncture agraire et rapports sociaux dans la plaine d'Alsace (xviie et xviiie siècles)', *Histoire, Economie et Société*, 4, p. 43-62.

Boehler, Jean-Michel (2000), 'L'Agriculture dans l'Europe médiane du xvie au xviiie siècle', in Annie Antoine, Jean-Michel Boehler, Francis Brumont (eds), *L'agriculture en Europe occidentale à l'époque moderne*, Paris, Belin, p. 257-409.

BOEHLER, Jean-Michel (2005), 'De la frontière au carrefour culturel: perception de l'identité de l'Alsace rurale aux XVIIe et XVIIIe siècles', in *Identités, appartenances, revendications identitaires, colloque international du Centre d'histoire sociale et culturelle de l'Occident*, Université de Paris X-Nanterre, 2003, Paris, p. 203-211.

BOEHLER, Jean-Michel (2010), 'Bail rural', in *Dictionnaire historique des institutions de l'Alsace*, 2, Strasbourg, p. 127-130.

BOELCKE, Willi A. (1987), *Wirtschaftsgeschichte Baden-Württenbergs von den Römern bis heute*, Stuttgart, Konrad Theiss.

DANNHORN, Wolfgang (2003), *Römische Emphyteuse und deutsche Erblehe. Ein Beitrag zur Entstehung der Wissenschaft vom deutschen Privatrecht in Forschungen zur deutschen Rechtsgeschichte*, 21, Köln-Weimar-Wien.

ENGELSING, Rolf (1983), *Sozial- und Wirtschaftsgeschichte Deutschlands, Göttingen*, Vandenhoeck & Ruprecht.

FRANZ, Günther (1976), 'Geschichte des deutschen Bauernstandes vom frühen Mittelalter bis zum 19. Jahrhundert', in Günther FRANZ (ed.), *Deutsche Agrargeschichte*, 4, Stuttgart, Eugen Ulmer.

HENNING, Friedrich Wilhelm (1991), 'Deutsche Wirtschafts- und Sozialgeschichte im Mittelalter und in der frühen Neuzeit', in Friedrich Wilhelm HENNING (ed.), *Handbuch der Wirtschafts-und Sozialgeschichte Deutschlands*, München-Wien-Zürich, F. Schöning.

HOFFMANN, Charles (1899-1906), *L'Alsace au XVIIIe siècle au point de vue historique juridique administratif, économique, intellectuel*, Colmar, 1, p. 199-261.

KELLENBENZ, Herrmann (1972), *Deutsche Wirtschaftsgeschichte*, Munich, C.H. Beck, 1, 1977.

LEFEBVRE, Georges (1924), *Les Paysans du Nord pendant la Révolution française*, Paris [Paris, A. Colin, 1972].

MARX, Roland (1974), *La Révolution et les classes sociales en Basse-Alsace. Structures agraires et vente des biens nationaux*, Paris, Bibliothèque Nationale.

MIREAUX, Emile (1958), *Une province française au temps du Grand Roi: la Brie*, Paris, Hachette.

THOMANN, Marcel (1983), 'Le droit rural à la Faculté de Droit de Strasbourg', in Jean-Michel BOEHLER, Dominique LERCH, Jean VOGT (eds), *Histoire de l'Alsace rurale*, Strasbourg, Istra, p. 271-277.

VOGT, Jean (1955), 'L'évolution du fermage au XVIIIe siècle (Alsace d'Outre-Forêt et Plaine du Palatinat)', in *80e Congrès national des Sociétés savantes*, Lille, Paris, 1955, p. 113-131.

VOGT, Jean (1983), 'Les problèmes de tenure', in Jean-Michel BOEHLER, Dominique LERCH, Jean VOGT (eds), *Histoire de l'Alsace rurale*, Strasbourg, Istra, 1983, p. 245-253.

VOGT, Jean (1966), 'Notes agraires rhénanes : emphytéose et fermage dans la région de Wissembourg à la fin du XVIIe siècle', *Revue géographique de l'Est*, 6, 1-2, p. 59-62.

VOGT, Jean (1989-1990), 'Propriété et tenure: les Biens nationaux à la lumière des pratiques foncières antérieures et postérieures', *Revue d'Alsace*, 116, p. 145-171.

Vogt, Jean (2015), *Moissons d'histoire (XVe-XIXe siècle). Jean Vogt : un demi-siècle de recherches sur l'histoire de la campagne alsacienne (1952-2015)*, Strasbourg, publ. Société savante d'Alsace, t. 86, p. 35-41 and 310-335.

FABRICE BOUDJAABA

6. Emphyteusis in Practice in Eighteenth-Century Normandy

Why Choose the Fieffe?

The changes in property rights brought about by the Revolution and the Napoleonic Civil Code were so great that it is not surprising that we occasionally find it difficult to understand subtleties of customary law, particularly certain kinds of ownership that existed under the old regime but dropped out of sight with the advent of 'inviolable and sacred' legal property rights[1]. The Civil Code recognized only one kind of property right: full and complete ownership. Ownership became 'the right to enjoy and dispose of things in the most absolute way';[2] distinctions between dominium utile and dominium directum for instance, disappeared (Ikni, 1980: 390-424).

In these conditions it was not surprising that the Code Civil had almost nothing to say about emphyteusis since it was a form of divided property that went against this principle. But, emphyteusis survived the Code. Nineteenth-century jurisprudence allowed it, it was officially recognized and regulated by the Act of 25 June 1902 and embedded in the Code Rural, which defined its nature and detailed its effects. An emphyteutic lease was a long-term lease (18 years minimum to 99 years maximum) which gave the lessee a real right to the property. This kind of lease applied only to immovable property, land and buildings, it was established by a notarized act and was made public in the land registry on the basis of a certified document. But it could not be extended by tacit agreement, and the document establishing the emphyteusis was subject only to the land registry tax (*taxe de publicité foncière*) and to the registry and transcription fees on farming leases or on long-term, limited leases, and not to the taxes on property transfers.

For all that, did emphyteusis have a clearly identified place in customary law, to the extent that the old regime allowed complex types of property rights? The answer is not so simple, as the case of Norman customary law shows. First, the word emphyteusis itself did not really have a place in Norman Custom; this arrangement did exist, but was termed *fieffe*. Even though the *fieffe* was very frequently used at the end of the old regime, this aspect of the Norman Customary Law was not clearly defined. Some authors saw it as a

1 Article 17 of the *Déclaration des droits de l'homme et du citoyen*.

2 Decree of 27 January 1804, art. 544 of the Code civil.

Agrarian Change and Imperfect Property, ed. by Rosa Congost and Pablo F. Luna, Rural History in Europe, 15 (Turnhout, 2018), 113-132

DOI 10.1484/M.RURHE-EB.5.116121

kind of sale while others considered it as type of long-term lease, because of its particular method of payment, which was by an annual rent.

The purpose here is not to give a complete account of the legal debate over the nature of this type of contract. In a way, both sides of the argument had a solid legal basis; the *fieffe* had aspects of both a sale and a lease. Legal history in its narrowest sense adds new difficulties to understanding the nature of the *fieffe* and refers back to old regime property law where the categories of customary law are not the same as ours. So it seems more profitable and enlightening to go beyond that approach and analyse what really took place.

To that end, this article, summarises the essential elements of the legal debate on the status of the *fieffe* and looks at the surviving *actes de fieffe* themselves for the region of Vernon between roughly 1750 and 1800, in the archives of the *Centième denier* and in notarial archives. The aim is to understand in what way the *fieffe* was peculiarly suited to the constraints of a rural, preindustrial society. Rather than trying to settle a debate on the legal nature of the *fieffe*, this is an attempt to learn more about this particular form of right by examining how the *fieffe* could be the preferred way to get ownership or manage possessions at certain points in the life cycle. In order to understand how the *fieffe* fitted into the management of inheritance it seems relevant to compare it to two of the most common types of land tenure; full and complete property obtained by outright purchase and simple rental using short and medium term leases.

I. Legal definitions of the *fieffe*: a very long-term rental or a type of sale?

The *fieffe* is a type of contract very close to that known in the Coutume de Paris as *bail à rente*. The jurist Houard (Houard, 1780-1782: 319-344), at the end of the eighteenth century, attributed a similar origin to these two contracts. According to him 'Roman perpetual emphyteuses [...] gave rise to *baux à rente* in the Coutume de Paris and to our *fieffe* contracts with non-redeemable rentes'. The *fieffant* ceded his property to the *fieffataire* in consideration of a fixed payment. This ground rent (*rente foncière*), generally non-redeemable, was to be paid by the 'lessee' in perpetuity. He engaged to maintain the property in good condition – without many details on what that involved – and could not be dislodged by what we might call the 'lessor' as long as he made the regular payments. The *fieffataire* could sell and transmit this property he 'held' in the same way as any other purchased property.

Houard devoted twenty-six pages to the *fieffe*, which shows how important that type of contract was in Norman law at the end of the old regime. But the length of the article also shows how difficult he found it to prove that it was really a perpetual lease and not a sale. In fact, the celebrated jurist wrote, 'the essential characteristics that distinguish emphyteusis [the category to which the *fieffe* belonged] from *baux à ferme* are the transfer and perpetuity of a kind of ownership; the characteristic which distinguishes it from a contract of sale is that the direct ownership remains with the seller'. Houard's article reflects the many different statuses given to the *fieffe* in the eighteenth century since he comes back several times to what differentiates it from a sale contract and, above all, because he answers those who see this type of contract as a type of sale and a real transfer of ownership[3]. Houard concludes 'The *fieffe* contract is consequently only a lease, but a perpetual lease as long as the conditions of payment are observed exactly, and a lease for a term when the conditions of payment cease to be observed exactly'. The notarised acts we have consulted from the Vernon region all contain a clause on maintaining the enfeoffed property in good condition.

In his studies of buildings in the city of Rouen, Jean-Pierre Bardet also leans to rental as he distinguishes 'three types of rental contract [...]: perpetual *fieffe*, long term *fieffe*, short term rental' (Bardet, 1971 & 1983: 178 ss). He adds: 'the expression *fieffe* is Norman; it should be translated as emphyteusis' (Bardet, 1971: 363). The *fieffe* is thus not a transfer of ownership but a transaction with the same effect as a long-term lease; that is to say, the lessee is responsible for all the repairs and improvements necessary to maintaining the revenue from the property.

However, a whole range of evidence seems to contradict this definition of the *fieffe* and assimilate this type of contract to a sale. We should first note that *fieffes* were registered by the administration of the *Centième denier*[4], which was responsible for collecting the duties on all acts transferring ownership, whether sales, cessions, collateral successions[5] or *fieffes*. Thus the *fieffe*, from the point of view of the royal administration, was considered as a real transfer of ownership since it had to be registered and taxed, while leases were exempt[6]. In the same way, in this region, the *vingtième* rolls[7] imposed the tax on the *fieffataire* and not on the *fieffant*, as if the lessee were really the owner. Further, notarial acts in Vernon in the second half of the eighteenth century contain only perpetual *fieffes*. The term of these rentes was never limited, except when they were referred to as redeemable (*racquitables*) and where this possibility was really used. In that case, the *fieffe* was transformed into a sale to the *fieffataire*, who paid a sum equal to the value of the property, which was estimated about twenty times the value of its annual payment.

3 For a more detailed account of Houard's legal arguments on the *fieffe*, Boudjaaba (2007: 757-775).

4 For a very complete history of the *Centième denier* and its archives, Vilar-Berrogain (1958).

5 Direct successions did not have to be declared.

6 Article 507 of the Coutume de Normandie states that; 'rentes in money, although they may be redeemable, are immovables'. In the case of the *fieffe*, it was certainly a *rente* and not a *fermage*.

7 A.D. de l'Eure, C 90 and C 91.

Long-term *fieffes* such as Bardet described in Rouen, did not exist in Vernon[8]. Their absence no doubt contributed to make the *fieffe* closer to a sale than to a rent in our region. Finally, the *fieffataire* could exercise a certain number of rights that he shared with the owner. The notarial acts, as they are formulated, suggest that it was closer to a sale than a lease, even a long-term one. Trichard, a notary at Vernon, generally used the following formula: the *fieffataire* has 'ownership, possession and use' of the property.

These different ways of interpreting the status of the *fieffe* are somewhat disconcerting. Houard saw that; the Rouen archives and those of Vernon present two divergent realities. Gérard Béaur, in his work on the Norman *bocage*, and more specifically on the Domfront region, saw the *fieffes* as contracts that 'are part of [...] the rental system' (Béaur, 1992: 77-87). These *fieffes*, 'a kind of emphyteutic lease or *bail à rente*, provided for a definitive cession of ownership in return for the payment of a perpetual rent termed *rente foncière*'. The author here does not make a clear choice between the two options; he prefers to classify this type of contract under the heading 'hybrid mutations'.

The *fieffe* is thus a complex formula which depended both on the rental market and the property market; however we need to pay attention to the environment in which this type of contract is used. In Rouen, the *fieffe* took on the aspect of a rental contract. This was a very specific market as the *fieffes* almost all concerned buildings, and very rarely land, in an urban property market. At Vernon, on the other hand, they were mostly agricultural lands. In these conditions the *fieffe* was a very flexible formula which allowed for adaptation to the nature of the property and activity in question. In an urban context, the *fieffe* functioned as a perpetual or long-term rental and the 'cession' of the property did not have the definitive nature that it had in the countryside, whether at Vernon or in the Domfront region. An urban building and a piece of agricultural land were turned to account in different ways. From one point of view, when an urban building was used to house the *fieffataire* it did not bring anything in and represented a loss for him; he had to maintain the building in the state he received it. The charges that normally fell on the owner – for example replacing the roof – fell on him. However, it was always possible to get rid of this burden. On the other hand, working land held as a *fieffe* was most often a source of revenue for the *fieffataire*. In these conditions he wanted secure, lasting and indeed perpetual possession of the property on the profits of which he lived. It was in his interest to improve it to the extent that he was able to transmit it to his heirs, conditional on making the regular payments.

The *fieffe* thus had different interpretations according to whether it was in an urban or rural context and this seems to be explained mainly by the purpose given to the property held in *fieffe*. This is why a strictly juridical

8 This observation is based on both the analysis of *fieffes* contracted before Trichard, notary at Vernon, and on the *fieffes* registered in the *Centième denier* between 1760 and 1789.

approach to this kind of emphyteusis is not adequate to explain why an individual preferred a *fieffe* to a sale or rental or why a local market tended to favour one of these three types of transaction. This is why it is necessary to look at what happened in practice.

II. The *fieffe* in the countryside: a contract concerning all kinds of property

The *fieffe* appears to be a common type of property transaction in the Norman Vexin and the Seine valley[9]. There seem to have been a significant number since, in the periods 1761-1780 and 1786-1789, where all the *Centième denier* registers have been analysed, there were 1,291 *fieffes* for 3,599 sales, one *fieffe* for 2.8 sales[10]. *Fieffes* thus made up more than 17 per cent of all types of property transfer. These figures are close to those obtained by Béaur for the region of Domfront between 1771 and 1790 (Béaur, 1992: 85). In that part of the *bocage*, the *fieffe* made up 15 per cent of transactions. On the other hand, Béaur found only one *fieffe* to 4.4 sales. This practice was thus relatively more widespread around Vernon than in the *bocage* where the simple sale had a much bigger share in transactions overall. These differences, though not always easy to interpret, show that the land market in Normandy was not homogenous and that, according to the region, one or other type of transaction was more or less preferred. The *fieffe* had the advantage of creating credit, where there was a lack of abundant cash. The *fieffataire* partly financed his acquisition by way of the perpetual rent. It is hard to know whether money and credit were more lacking in the Vexin than in the *bocage*. However, several features in the environment of the two markets provide useful clues. Different agrarian structures implied different modes of settlement. The Domfront region was a 'zone of high demographic pressure... with a density close to 100 inhabitants to the km^2, in an almost exclusively rural setting' (Béaur, 1992: 78). In the region of Vernon[11], the density was noticeably less, about 60 inhabitants to the km^2 (80 if the town of Vernon is included). In such an environment, the pressure on the buyer was no doubt less. It was easy to negotiate a *fieffe*, while for a sale one had to have on hand the total sum necessary for the purchase. In the Domfront region the difficulty was not necessarily the lack of money to make an acquisition but more the lack of property to buy, in a context made more competitive by demographic pressure.

---

9 An overall view of structures of ownership in the villages of the Seine valley, characterised by microcultivation and the presence of vines, can be found Boudjaaba (2009: 371-390).

10 The *Centième denier* office covered the town of Vernon and about forty villages, a little more than 20,000 hectares.

11 Within the boundaries of the canton.

This procedure for acquiring a property continued to be used in Vernon all through the second half of the eighteenth century. Between 1765 and 1788 the annual volume of sales doubled, from just under a hundred to more than two hundred a year, while at the same time the *fieffes* went from about forty to more than seventy. Of course the number of *fieffes* grew less rapidly than that of sales but their increase kept pace with the general rate of growth in the property market during the last two decades of the Old Regime (Boudjaaba, 2007). The evolution of this practice seems to be specific to the region of Vernon. In the Domfront region, according to Béaur, it appears to have been regressing and the same was true of Beaumesnil according to Bernard Garnier[12].

In the end, it was not until the Revolution that the place of the *fieffe* in the land market was transformed. Then the new formulation of property law made unnecessary a transaction halfway between rental and sale. The notion of full and complete ownership and the abolition of feudalism made it impossible to maintain a perpetual rent on landed property; that would have been to maintain the disassociation of dominium utile and dominium directum. However, many people continued to be attached to this type of property transfer; thus, in the canton of Vernon, the administration registered *fieffes* drawn up before notaries as late as 1815.

Was emphyteusis used for all types of property or was the *fieffe* preferred for certain types only? In order to answer this question we have compared the range of property transfers under a contract of *fieffe* with the range of property transfers by sale or rental on the land and rental markets (Table 6.1). The first thing we learn is that emphyteusis was not a contract for only one kind of property. The category 'others', which Table 6.1 does not list in detail, includes just as wide a band of transactions for *fieffes* as it does for sales or for short or medium-term rentals. The comparison of one term with another is not always easy, particularly with leases. The source of information for leases is different from that used for both sales and *fieffes*. For leases, we have only the very concise tables of lessors and lessees. For this reason we do not know the type of properties leased in a large number of cases. *Fieffes* and outright sales, on the other hand, were registered in the *Centième denier*, which rarely failed to give at least a rough indication of the type of property sold or enfeoffed. Nevertheless, it seems clear that emphyteusis was preferred for houses and buildings in general (houses, parts of houses but also 'buildings', the latter often for agricultural purposes). More than 40 per cent of *fieffes* were for houses against less than a quarter of sales. For leases, we should not take too much notice of the percentages because of the large number of unknowns and the under-registration of certain leases (mostly for parcels of land that were often made orally), but there was also a tendency to use emphyteusis for buildings. The reasons for this preference may be found not in the immediate

12 See Garnier, 1986: 121-140. The author notes that the proportion of *fieffes* in the estates of landowners in Beaumesnil diminished between 1754 and 1780.

needs of the participants, such as the lessors' urgent desire for large sums of cash, or the lessees' need of credit for purchase, but in the specific and inherent burden posed for the lessors by buildings. By leasing property as a *fieffe* rather than as a simple lease, the owner-lessor (*fieffant*) avoided the often heavy maintenance costs lessors incurred under normal leases, mainly the cost of heavy reconstruction needed to maintain the property.

Table 6.1 Distribution of type of property for each type of contract 1750-1800

	fieffe	sale	leases 1755-1789
Farm	0.0	0.1	4.59
House or part of house	39.0	24.3	30.39
Land	16.1	27.0	10.60
Heritable property	18.4	17.4	14.13
Vineyard	6.1	10.8	4.59
Other parcels	18.8	18.4	10.25
Nature unknown	1.6	2.0	25.44
Number of cases	510	1533	283

We have been looking at the role of emphyteusis in the overall operation of the land market and its interactions with the economic situation. From this point of view emphyteusis seemed to meet two requirements. It compensated for the absence of institutionalized credit by permitting the lessee (*fieffataire*) to acquire property without having on hand the amount equivalent to the full value of the property. On the other hand, it allowed the *fieffant* to lease his property without bearing the full burden that rested on the owner in the normal type of lease, and this explains the attraction of this type of divided ownership in the case of buildings.

However, many owners who did not want to make a definitive sale preferred a simple lease to emphyteusis, even for houses and buildings. Many of those in search of property turned to other modes of acquisition, either full and complete ownership, or short-term rental. In this sense the overall characteristics of the Old Regime market, the absence of credit institutions and the relative shortage of cash, are not sufficient to explain all of these choices. That is why it seems necessary to shift our focus to the individuals who chose this type of contract. The purpose was to find out how emphyteusis corresponded to a certain number of social and demographic attributes characteristic of the parties to the contract. By going beyond the legal and global approach to the study of the *fieffe*, analysis at the individual level gives a better grasp of the motivations and stages of the life cycle that explain why they preferred this formula to outright sale.

III. *Fieffe*, sale, lease and life-cycle

The analysis of the individual parties to these contracts was made possible because there is a demographic database of the population of Vernon and surrounding villages between 1690 and 1836[13]. We started by identifying anyone in the database who participated in a *fieffe* contract between 1760 and 1800, whether as a *fieffant* or a *fieffataire*; obviously the two parties had very different motives and behaviour. We have done the same for sellers and buyers of property and also for lessors and lessees under short and medium-term leases.

The average age of lessors was noticeably different from that of lessees: 48.3 years for the former, 40.7 for the latter. This difference was not unexpected but it is quite pronounced. The *fieffants* wanted to enhance, or at least preserve, the value of their property estate through the revenue from the rent; this means that they could not, or did not wish to, improve their property themselves. Advancing age and increasing difficulty in carrying out field work may explain these choices. The *fieffe* assured them of an income for their old age. The formula may be considered more advantageous than a regular sale as it provided an income for life rather than a capital sum, which might prove inadequate for the remaining years of life. At the same time it avoided reducing the inheritance; the children or other heirs of the *fieffant* would receive the income in their turn. The *fieffataires* on the other hand were on average younger as they had the burden of working the property. They were also younger because the *fieffe*, unlike the act of sale, did not require savings or an inheritance to acquire it.

An analysis of the median age has similar results: 50 years for the *fieffants* and only 40 for the *fieffataires*. This is a significant difference and clearly shows the advantages of the *fieffe*: income for the old, access to property for the young. In a traditional rural economy the *fieffe* partially made up for the absence of a pension system as well as for problems of access to credit. It was a better solution to an individual's life cycle than a simple sale.

However, the average age of participants in the market does not take account of all aspects of the life cycle. The distribution by age of the contracting parties, as shown in Table 6.2, takes us farther towards understanding the relation between this particular type of ownership and the demands of the life cycle.

Of the *fieffataires*, more than 60 per cent were between 30 and 50 years of age. It was in this period of 'full activity ' that individuals most often took a *fieffe* of landed property. Ageing, and the difficulties that could accompany it, no doubt explain why fewer and fewer individuals over 50 acquired a *fieffe*. After 60, it was very rare to become a lessee (*fieffataire*).On the one hand, it was less and less suited to the physical capacities of the individuals and on the other, the *fieffants* were probably not inclined to entrust their property to

13 This is a database of 210,000 individuals at the Centre Roland Mousnier under the supervision of Jean-Pierre Bardet and Jacques Renard. There is a general review of the methods and objectives of the enquiry (Renard, 1998: 239-246).

Table 6.2 Distribution by age of those contracting a *fieffe* between 1750 and 1800 in the Vernon region

Ages	*Fieffants*	*fieffataires*
Under 30	15.1	16.7
30-39	15.8	29.7
40-49	17.8	31.7
50-59	24.3	16.6
60-69	16.4	4.8
70+	10.5	0.5
Number of cases	152	186

someone already old. This would imply putting the property at great risk of a rapid turnover of *fieffataires* since property held in *fieffe* was transmitted in the same way as any other piece of landed property. In this case the property would pass to one or more heirs, with little chance of as good a guarantee of their managing the property well. There was a great risk that the enfeoffed property might, albeit temporarily, fall into joint ownership by the lessees, or that difficulties would arise when the inheritance was divided up. To make a *fieffe* over to a sixty-year-old was to run the risk of seeing the conditions of the contract modified in the near future while what the *fieffant* wanted from the contract was a 'perpetual' income, paid regularly.

The age distribution of the *fieffants* covered a much greater span. More than 40 per cent of them were over the age of 50. The age group of people in their prime, [between the ages of 30 and 49], on the other hand, made up less than 34 percent. The institution of the *fieffe* thus made it possible to adapt estates to the life cycle. Ageing transformed a productive capital, land, into a rente. Unlike the act of sale, this process avoided the need to sacrifice capital to income, since, if the clauses of the contract were not respected, the property returned to the *fieffant*.

It is more surprising to see the high proportion of young people among the *fieffants*. People under 30 made up more than 15 per cent of these 'sellers' and, surprisingly, there was almost the same proportion of *fieffants* as *fieffataires* (16 per cent). Why were so many young people attracted by a fixed income? Certainly a rent had many intrinsic attractions. The profession and place of residence may explain this choice: occupation and distance prevented many of them from cultivating their property themselves. However, the rent for a *fieffe* was a fixed amount. The younger the *fieffant*, the greater was the risk of a sharp decline in revenue if prices rose. The rent was perpetual and therefore not renegotiable. In these conditions, if one was not able to manage the property oneself, it probably seemed prudent to use a formula that was not perpetually binding. The ordinary lease, normally for a period of nine years, would seem to have been a much more advantageous formula since the rent was renegotiated with each new lease. If the charges on the lessor still seemed too heavy these young people could still sell rather than continuing to draw a fixed income from the *fieffe*, which might not amount to much by the end of their life.

But if we look more closely at these individuals we can understand why this formula was popular with the young as well as the old. There are 23 *fieffants* under the age of 30 in our sample or, more precisely, 19 individuals under 30, who were parties to 23 *fieffes*. Four of them were town-dwellers looking for a safe income from the *fieffe* of their property without all the normal charges incumbent on the owner of a tenant farm. There were a tailor, a wigmaker and two inhabitants of Vernon, one of whom was referred to as a *bourgeois*. The choice of putting their property out as a *fieffe* is explained by their occupation or social position. There were also two women among the 19 *fieffants*, both unmarried, who no doubt were unable to earn money directly from property themselves, and preferred to have a safe income without the responsibilities of a normal lease. Finally, among these 19 lessors under the age of 30, five held their land in joint ownership. Laurent Lavenant, *ayde de pont* (a kind of bargee) was twenty in 1783 and, with his mother Jeanne Cartier, put 60 perches of vines (around 1.900 m^2) at Giverny into *fieffe*. In another instance, four minors made an act of *fieffe* together with one or more older brothers. When there was co-ownership the *fieffe* provided a simple way to manage landed property and preserve capital. The co-ownership was continued as long as any of the brothers were minors. In these circumstances it was difficult to manage a property; a sale was not a solution because in that case the older brother would hold the capital in cash and the younger brothers had no assurance that he would use it for their benefit. The *fieffe* made it possible to tie up the capital in order to protect the interests of the minors, without depriving the co-owners of the revenue.

As we can see, the strong presence of people under thirty years of age among the *fieffants* is explained by a series of circumstances that can only be discovered by looking at the individual cases. Out of the 19 cases, four can be explained because the formula was best suited to their geographic and occupational situation. For seven others, it was suited to their age or matrimonial situation: five minors and two unmarried women. The *fieffe* certainly fits a general situation, characteristic of traditional rural societies, in which older persons, if they had means, tended to seek an income (Moriceau, 1985: 127-144) while the young were inclined to acquire a property they could work. But beyond this general schema the *fieffe* was also a way of coping with certain difficulties of the life cycle. From the broader perspective, these 'fragile' situations merit detailed examination, as they demonstrate how useful hybrid types of ownership could be in a rural society where land remained the principal basis of patrimony and income.

Does a comparison of these emphyteutic contracts with those for sales and short and medium-term leases confirm these conclusions?

Table 6.3 Average and median ages of parties to contracts by type of transaction

	Fieffe		Vente		Baux	
	Fieffataire	Fieffant	Buyers	Sellers	Lessees	Lessors
Average age	40.7	48.3	41.4	45.3	41.9	49.6
Median age	40	50	41	45	39	49

If we compare the average and median ages of people who signed the three types of contract (Table 6.3) it is clear that those who concluded *fieffe* and ordinary lease agreements did not come from precisely the same group of individuals as those involved in simple sales. Though lessees, *fieffataires* and buyers were around forty years old on average, it was not the same for lessors, *fieffants* and sellers. Sellers were on average five years younger than lessors and *fieffants*, the former were around forty-five and the latter nearer to fifty.

The age distribution of individuals according to the type of act and role in the contract opens the way for a more precise analysis (Figures 6.1 and 6.2). It is clear that, in comparison with the sellers, *fieffants* and lessors were over-represented among those over 50 and especially among those over 60 years of age. On the other hand, an emphyteutic type of sale was much less frequent among those who were between 30 and 49 years old. From this point of view, it is clear that the *fieffe* was a legal tool more favoured by older people, as was renting. It was a simple way to secure an income. But for the intermediary ages (30 to 49) the ordinary lease and emphyteusis seemed to follow a different logic. Lessors were proportionately more frequent in this age group than *fieffants*, which can be interpreted to mean that social groups were not equally involved in the *fieffe* and the lease. While the *fieffe* and the lease could seem to be solutions well adapted to the needs and weakness of old age, as they provided an income that it was becoming difficult to supply with labour, putting property out to rent at a younger age was likely to be the result of a more advantageous economic situation on the part the lessor. In short, the group of lessors probably contained more rentiers, living off income from the land, than those letting out land as a *fieffe*. The latter was more a solution for people made more vulnerable by their advancing years, who sought a convenient way to secure an income, without incurring the burdens of ownership, even if this meant obtaining relatively less revenue. This interpretation is supported by the age distribution of the sellers compared to that the *fieffants*. There were proportionately far more sellers in the 30 to 49 age group than those among their 50s and even more so those in their 60s, the converse of the *fieffants*. This result may seem surprising, since according to the life-cycle hypothesis, one would expect to see a significant part of sales being made by the oldest group. But this distribution reminds us that the simple sale was also a product of dynamic activity by the 30 to 49 year-olds in the market; they sold, to be sure, but often in order to buy again, rather

Figure 6.1. Age distribution of those ceding property, by type of transaction

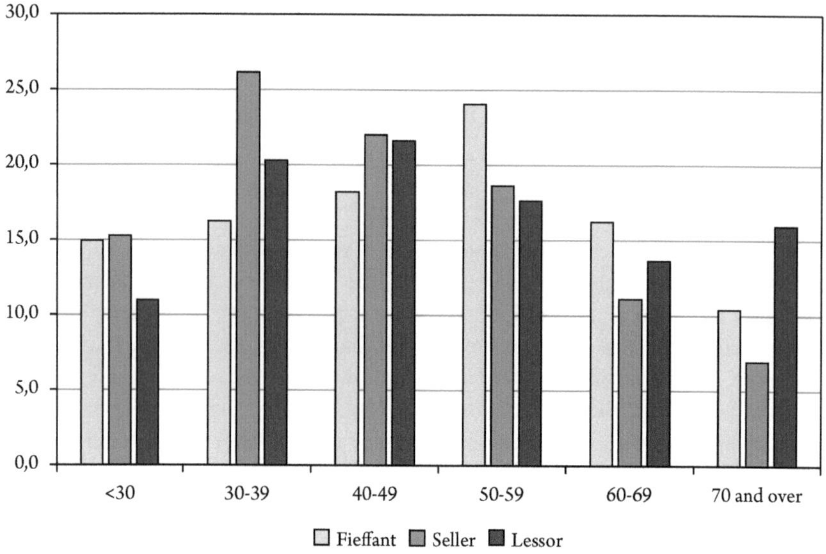

than to obtain liquidity, as the *fieffants* were doing[14]. In short, when the sellers parted with a property it was often the result of an 'offensive' attitude, a desire to reconstruct the patrimony, while the *fieffe* was more often used by *fieffants* in a 'defensive' position, looking for a safe income at a more advanced age, rather than hoping to improve their productive patrimony.

When we examine the age distribution of individuals according to whether they took on a lease or a *fieffe* or bought a property (Figure 6.2), the age variable seems less evident in the choice of emphyteusis as opposed to another type of tenure. The average and median age of buyers, *fieffataires* and lessees (Table 6.3) shows the similarities between the three groups, all three having an average and median age situated around 40 years, with no discernable difference between them. However, it seems that emphyteusis was chosen relatively more frequently than simple sale by the 30 to 49 year-old group, as was renting by the under 40s[15]. From this point of view, both renting and emphyteusis seem to have provided possible ways for the youngest to have

14 In fact, buying a property in the year *n* has a positive effect on the fact of selling in the same year.Selling in the year *n* on the other hand, has a negative effect on buying in the same year. This result is only apparently contradictory, as there were necessarily more individuals in economic difficulty among the sellers, while among the buyers the sale was often part of a process of reorganisation of their estate (Boudjaaba, 2008: 164-167).

15 The situation of the under 30s is always difficult to interpret because it includes minors, where the choice of action is often made by other individuals, older brothers or relations, in the context of joint ownership. See above.

Figure 6.2. Age distribution of those taking on a property by type of transaction

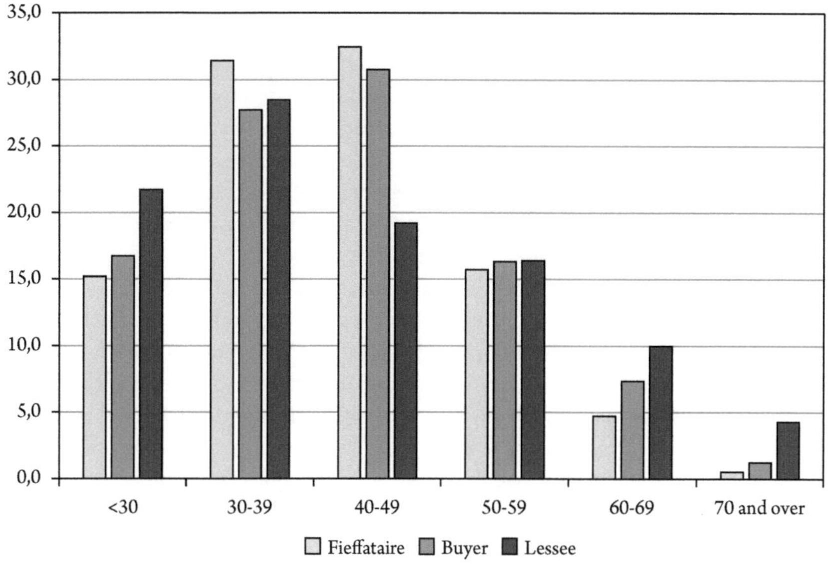

access to land. If they did not have sufficient savings to buy land or a house outright, emphyteusis was a convenient way of financing an acquisition, given the difficulties of obtaining credit.

In general, resorting to emphyteusis was not a neutral choice and the different age groups did not turn to it equally or for the same reasons. However, the specifics of the choice of emphyteusis can be seen most clearly in those ceding the property.

IV. Emphyteusis, a tool at the service of the widow and the orphan

When we look at the individual situations of those ceding their property by emphyteusis, it becomes easier to understand these estate management choices, as a qualitative approach to the signatories casts light on the effects of the life cycle revealed by the quantitative analysis.

Among the 470 *fieffants* in our sample there are 65 women, nearly 14 percent of the total. Widows make up more than two-thirds of this group (46). On the other hand, among the *fieffataires* there are only 19 women, 13 of them widows, or 5 per cent. This disparity is not surprising, but needs to be compared with that found among the simple sales. In the latter case, women made up 5 per cent of buyers and 10 per cent of sellers, that is, twice as many. This should be compared to the women among the *fieffants,* who were three times more numerous as women *fieffataires*[16]. It seems that women saw the *fieffe* as a procedure, distinct from the sale in the strict sense, for coping with difficult economic situations; the women who appear in these sources were unmarried and, mainly, widows. Emphyteusis provided a formula where the type of payment and the needs of a woman in one of these two situations coincided. Women who placed a property in *fieffe* obtained from it a regular income rather a capital sum, which they might not have known where to invest, since the possibilities for investment other than land were very limited in a society of small peasants. But mainly, thanks to the *fieffe*, they were sheltered from the burdens incumbent on a lessor who rented out land on a short or medium-term lease[17].

We should also notice how participants in emphyteutic contracts were often co-owners. This reflected another type of vulnerability among *fieffants*: the difficulty of day-to-day running of property by several people when it had to be managed for the collective good and the profits had to be divided among several individuals. Cases of joint ownership are unequally divided between *fieffants* and *fieffataires*: there are 39 cases, out of the 445 in our sample, where there are several *fieffants* on the same contract while only 21 *fieffes* had several *fieffataires*. Logically this suggests that joint ownership was a burden to be borne rather than a choice to be made.

Studying cases of joint ownership helps understand why the *fieffe* appealed to *fieffants* in that situation. The most usual type occurred when there were several siblings. Out of the 39 *fieffes*, 17 concerned brothers or brothers and sisters. Though this figure is weighted upwards by the case of two widowed sisters who put properties in *fieffe* eight times, it is also an underestimate, because of insufficient information in the registers of the Enregistrement[18]. In 13 other cases, joint ownership concerned people with the same surnames not identified in the demographic database, at least some of whom were likely to be brothers. However, these sibling groups did not have exactly the same profile as that of the *fieffataires*. Out of nine groups of brothers and sisters, where the ages at the time of the contract are known, seven included one or more minors. This particular family situation – quite common – in which children inherited from their parents before they had reached the age of majority, posed problems for managing the patrimony. Some of the owners

16 Data for the years 1761-1789.

17 The same was true for the towns; Bardet demonstrated this using the example of the Hôpital Général. The institution 'is incapable of managing its property estate because it lacks sufficient financial reserves'; it used the *fieffe* systematically because this formula provided access to new money while avoiding the expense of major repairs that were incumbent on the owner of the building. The reasoning was probably similar for women in the countryside around Vernon. If their property included buildings and they chose to lease, rather than put it in *fieffe*, the cost of repairs could be unbearable; in the vineyards in the Seine valley there was no lack of wine cellars …

18 It was common for the name of the second *fieffant* in the notarial act to be omitted in the *Centiéme denier* and the Enregistrement.

were too young to take part in the daily management of the property. At the same time, all decisions about the property had to be put off because of the minority of the youngest. It was difficult to divide the inheritance until all the heirs could take over control of their shares. In these conditions the *fieffe* was an intermediate type of ownership, well adapted to the circumstances.

One *fieffe* contract signed 16 May 1773 before Trichard, a Vernon notary[19], is particularly interesting in this context. Jean Nicolas Gambard and Nicolas Bernard ceded land at Giverny in *fieffe* to Pascal Saintard for an annual rent of nine livres. The notarized act tells us that Jean Nicolas Gambard shared his half of the property with his brother Louis and gives details of his reasons for the contract.

> The inherited property belongs half to the said Bernard and the second half to the said Jean Nicolas Gambard and the said Louis Gambard, minor, his brother. They gave their two sisters their legitimate share [*leurs légitimes*]; what is left in common to them is in total ruin and decadence. As the joint ownership is an obstacle to the said proprietors making the necessary repairs, they have chosen to give it in *fieffe* so as not to let it fall into decay and lose all its value, these being the compelling reasons thus to give it in *fieffe*. And it is agreed that if the minor Gambard wishes to take possession of his quarter, the said *fieffataire* [Pascal Saintard] will satisfy him either by way of *licitation* [sale of jointly owned property by auction] by law or otherwise, but always in such manner that the said Saintard his [Louis'] guardian may not be disturbed or contested because should there be a claim on behalf of the said minor, the said Saintard as *fieffataire* will take reimbursement from him [Louis] for what he paid for the upkeep.

Here joint ownership appears to be an obstacle to managing the property because it made it necessary to share the decisions and obligations. The *fieffe* made it possible to draw an income from the property without having to undertake expensive renovations. By this procedure the older brother made it possible for him and his brother to have a permanent income. The minor was protected because the capital was in a way immobilised by the creation of a rent. If a sale had taken place there would be a risk of the older brother's depleting the capital. For the guardian, the *fieffe* was a way of preserving the minor's property without having to manage it.

In general, the fact that women frequently used this hybrid form of ownership and that brothers in co-ownership resorted to this judicial procedure clearly demonstrates the advantages of the *fieffe* over renting or simple sale at certain stages of life or in certain complex family situations[20].

---

19 A.D. de l'Eure, cote 4 E 27-115.

20 This was also true for the *fieffataires*. Some properties were taken as a *fieffe* jointly by relatives who would not have been able to provide the guarantee (a mortgageable property) necessary to aspire to buy a *fieffe*. See Boudjaaba, 'La fieffe ...'.

V. Conclusions: Was emphyteusis an intermediate solution between lease and sale? It was that, but also more

Was Norman emphyteusis just an intermediary, divided form of ownership, of the sort so common in customary law, midway between a simple sale and a normal short or medium-term lease? The *fieffe* certainly had a number of characteristics that made it an intermediate legal instrument; its length, from very long to perpetual, the possibility for both the *fieffant* and the *fieffataire* to transmit it, its entry in the official register in the same way as a sale: these all brought it closer to a sale and to simple appropriation; however, the annual payment made it closer to a lease. On the other hand, the almost complete absence of burdens on the *fieffant* and freedom of usage for the *fieffataire*, are closer to a sale. It was an intermediary procedure then, but one which, particularly at Vernon, because the *fieffe* was *irraquitable* (unredeemable), makes us much more inclined to consider it a sale rather than a rental.

But beyond the hybrid character of emphyteusis, the *fieffe*, with its variants, mainly corresponded to a type of economic environment and to an organisation of the productive system particular to traditional rural areas. It should be emphasised firstly that the *fieffe* was not used in the same way in all parts of Normandy. In the towns, it broadly resembled a very long-term emphyteutic lease. In the countryside it was really an eventual transfer of ownership; the limited-term *fieffe* was almost unknown. These two conceptions of the *fieffe* are largely explained by the nature of properties on the market. In the towns, the market was almost entirely made up of buildings; from a certain point of view this was unproductive capital that the *fieffataire* could more easily part with in hard times; hence this type of contract had some similarity to rental leases. In the countryside on the other hand, the *fieffataire* took possession of assets, usually land, from which he would obtain an income, and wanted to have the ownership 'in perpetuity'. However, it is difficult to see the *fieffe*, at least in the second half of the eighteenth century, as a response to a specific environment, in the physical sense. Unlike like other regions where emphteusis was widespread, the Vernon region, and Normandy in general, were not considered difficult areas; they did not need repopulating or bringing under cultivation. On the contrary, population density was relatively high and the general quality of the land was such that owners did not have to offer particularly advantageous conditions to find farmers. Anyway, the *fieffe* contracts did not contain an improvements clause.

On the other hand, this hybrid property right offered a solution to the state of the credit market and the level of money circulation in Old Regime France. Of course a real credit market did exist in late eighteenth-century France (Postel-Vinay, 1998) but, in the context of the small peasant holdings in the Vernon area, the *fieffe* was no doubt a more effective way of financing a property acquisition. Payment in the form of an annual ground rent (*rente foncière*), had the double advantage of making it possible to buy a property without previous savings and avoid the difficulty of accumulating cash. In an economy where a large part of the production of small peasant owners was not commercialised, but consumed by themselves, it could be difficult to accumulate the amount necessary to pay outright for a piece of land. This hybrid property right thus helped to make the property market more fluid. However, this formula only helped to round out one's holdings, and not to make the first step to ownership. Every *fieffataire* in effect brought his property holding as a mortgage guarantee for regular payment of the rent.

Lastly, emphyteusis offered a solution appropriate to certain difficult moments in the life cycle. In particular, the *fieffe* provided recourse for those individuals in awkward situations in a productive system where land was the principal resource and where ground rent was the main guarantee against the difficulties of life. Without examining the social and demographic situations of individuals, we cannot understand why a *fieffant* would chose to exchange property in return for a fixed income. There were no charges on the *fieffant* as long as he retained direct ownership. This was a considerable advantage for those in vulnerable situations – old people, widows and minors – since it enabled them to keep both an income and the capital it produced. It was a very useful formula for transmitting heritages. The rent could be transmitted like any other landed property. The *fieffant* was assured of an income for his old age and kept the property to be handed on, whereas if he sold the property and lived a long time afterwards he might have nothing left to leave to his heirs. Certainly, the long-term rise in prices might reduce the real value of the fixed rent but in the medium term the *fieffe* was a useful compromise between the demands of the individual life cycle – an income in old age when there was no pension system – and those of the family life cycle – transmitting a patrimony to the children.

The disappearance of emphyteusis as a common method of property transfer occurred in a few years as the Revolution, confirmed on this point by the Code Civil, preferred simple, undivided ownership. Apart from a few acts of *fieffe* contracted between 1800 and 1810 it seems that this disappearance was carried out without much difficulty. This may seem surprising since in the 1780s it was still one of the most common methods of transaction, responding to both the relative weakness of the credit market and shortage of cash on the one hand and to a certain number of difficult family situations, which did not disappear like magic with the Revolution, on the other. There is no explanation to cover all aspects of this problem. However, we can point out that, even before the Revolution, individuals were already tending to prefer simple ownership; the development of the property market from the 1770s on occurred because of the increasing value of simple sales while the number of *fieffes* increased less in terms of absolute value[21]. Inflation during the Revolution no doubt reinforced this tendency to prefer cash in hand or a lease that was renegotiated at term rather than a perpetual rent that could potentially shrink to almost nothing with devaluation.

Bibliography

BARDET, Jean-Pierre (1971), 'La maison rouennaise aux XVIIe et XVIIIe siècles. Économie et comportements', in Jean-Pierre Bardet, Pierre Chaunu, Gabriel Désert, Pierre Gouhier and Hugues Neveux, *Le bâtiment, enquête d'histoire économique, XIVe-XIXe siècles*, Paris-The Hague, Mouton, 1971.

BARDET, Jean-Pierre (1983), *Rouen aux XVIIe et XVIIIe siècles: les mutations d'un espace social*, Paris, SEDES, 2 vols.

BÉAUR, Gérard (1992), 'Le fonctionnment du "marché-père": la circulation des propriétés dans le bocage normand au XVIIIe siècle', in Rolande BONNAIN, Gérard BOUCHARD & Joseph GOY (eds), *Transmettre, hériter, succéder. La reproduction familiale en milieu rurale. France-Québec XVIIIe-XXe siècles*, EHESS – Presses Universitaires de Lyon, 1992, p. 77-87.

BOUDJAABA, Fabrice (2007), 'La fieffe, les usages familiaux d'une spécificité normande du droit de propriété', in Jean-Pierre POUSSOU & Isabelle ROBIN-ROMERO (eds), *Histoire des familles, de la démographie et des comportements. Mélanges offerts à Jean-Pierre Bardet*, Presses de l'Université de Paris-Sorbonne, p. 757-775.

BOUDJAABA, Fabrice (2008), *Des paysans attachés à la terre? Familles, marchés et patrimoines dans la région de Vernon (1750-1830)*, Paris, Presses de l'Université de Paris-Sorbonne, p. 164-167.

BOUDJAABA, Fabrice (2009), 'La distribuzione delle fortune fondiarie in Francia alla fine dell'Ancien Régime: un approccio dimamico a partire dall'esempio della Normandia', in Guido ALFANI & Michela BARBOT, *Ricchezza, valore, proprietà in Età preindustriale. 1400-1850*, Venezia, Marsilio, p. 371-390.

GARNIER, Bernard (1986), 'Problèmes de reproduction économique et sociale dans le bocage normand au XVIIIe siècle', in Joseph GOY & Jean-Pierre WALLOT (eds), *Evolution et éclatement du monde rural, France-Québec, XVIIe-XVIIIe siècles*, Paris-Montréal, EHESS-PULyon, p. 121-140.

HOUARD, David (1780-1782), *Dictionnaire analytique, historique, étymologique, critique, interprétatif de la coutume de Normandie*, Rouen, 4 vols Article 'fieffe', p. 319-344.

21 There was also no change in the market of ordinary leases (in general 9 years) where the number stagnated until at least the 1820s, according to the Registers. It therefore seems as if simple sale was more and more preferred to emphyteusis during this period, but the same is not true of the simple lease (Boudjaaba, *Des paysans*, 2008, p. 428-429).

Ikni, Guy-Robert (1980), 'Recherches sur la propriété foncière: problèmes théoriques et de méthode (fin XVIIIe – début XIXe siècles)', *AHRF*, 52, 3, n. 241, juill-sept, p. 390-424.

Moriceau, Jean-Marc 'Un système de protection sociale efficace: exemple des vieux fermiers de l'Ile-de-France (XVIIe-début XIXe siècle)', *Annales de Démographie Historique*, 1985, p. 127-144.

Postel-Vinay, Gilles (1998), *La terre et l'argent. L'agriculture et le crédit en France du 18e au début du 20e siécle*, Paris, Albin Michel.

Renard, Jacques (1998), 'Les enquêtes de démographie historique du Centre Roland Mousnier', *Annales de Démographie Historique*, 1998, p. 239-246.

Vilar-Berrogain, Gabrielle (1958), *Guide des recherches dans les fonds de l'enregistrement sous l'Ancien Régime*, Paris, Imprimerie nationale.

ROSA CONGOST, PERE GIFRE,
ENRIC SAGUER

7. More than just Access to Land

*Emphyteusis and the Redefinition of Property Rights in North-East Catalonia (Eighteenth and Nineteenth Centuries)**

I. Introduction

Emphyteutic contracts, which survive from the Middle Ages onwards, played a key role in the agrarian transformation of Catalonia during the eighteenth and nineteenth centuries (Vilar, 1966; Ferrer, 1987; Congost, 1990a; Vicedo, 1991; Tello, 1997; Fabregat, 2008). Research has emphasised not only the importance of this contract but also the diversity of forms it acquired during this period. At either end of the spectrum are two clearly differentiated types of emphyteusis: first, those contracts that dominated in the interior of Catalonia around Lleida, where the *senyors directes* or holders of dominium directum led the colonisation of the soil through the grants (*establiments*) of large estates, and second, the emphyteutic practices of north-east Catalonia, where throughout the eighteenth and nineteenth centuries the *senyors útils*, that is, those who held the dominium utile of *masos*[1], took the lead in ceding small plots of land via emphyteutic grants (*subestabliments*)[2]. A different situation prevailed in the central and coastal districts where the most common

* This paper is part of the research project HAR2014-54891-P, financed by the Spanish Ministry of Science and Innovation.

1 A *mas* was a kind of catalan farm, with a farmhouse, which guaranteed the subsistence of the family who lived on. See Congost (2015).

2 The division of rights over land generated by emphyteusis led to a variety of terms and concepts that appear in the sources. the *senyor directe* held the dominium directum, whereas the holder of the dominium utile was known as the *senyor útil* or *senyor útil i propietari*. The dominium utile was acquired via an emphyteutic grant (*establiment*), whereby the *senyor directe* granted these rights in exchange for an entry payment, which could be a symbolic payment, and an annual rent, usually a fixed quantity in either cash or kind. The *senyor útil* held the land in perpetuity, without any obligation save that of recognising the *senyor directe* in declarations of title (*capbrevació*) and payment of a fine, the *lluïsme*, every time the use-rights changed hands. This fine could be up to a third of the price in cases of sales of land. As will be discussed in the text, if the *senyor útil* transferred the land to someone else, this should properly be termed a *subestabliment*, since the land had been granted once already.

Agrarian Change and Imperfect Property, ed. by Rosa Congost and Pablo F. Luna, Rural History in Europe, 15 (Turnhout, 2018), 133-154
 DOI 10.1484/M.RURHE-EB.5.116122

contract was the *rabassa morta*[3], which can be seen as a variant of emphyteutic contract, but one specifically associated with vines[4].

Which factors were responsible for the different forms that emphyteusis took in different areas and from when? In the Girona region, which constitutes our case study, neither the transfer of land by *senyors directes*, nor *rabassa morta* contracts were unknown. Indeed, both types were not only to be found in the area, but were, as we shall see, the dominant forms of contract during the first half of the eighteenth century. Both, however, gradually declined in importance as the century wore on, while emphyteutic *establiments* (probably fraudulently[5]) or *subestabliments* realised by the owners of dominium utile came to dominate. This substantial change coincided with an overall expansion in the number of emphyteutic contracts.

Emphyteusis in the eighteenth and nineteenth centuries, in contrast to the medieval period, did not involve the creation of new *masos*, despite their significance in this region, but rather its fragmentation into small parcels which even today have still left their imprint on the landscape[6]. Why did the transfer of small parcels come to be the norm in the Girona region?

It is very important to note that, despite the historiographical common view, the liberal revolution did not cause any significant break in emphyteutic practices, even within the new legal framework for regulating property rights. Given that the changes described cannot be ascribed to legal reforms, our main hypothesis is that the gradual dominance of emphyteutic *subestabliments* in the final stages of the Ancien Régime reflects important changes in the appropriation of resources. From this perspective, the decided preference for the *subestabliment*, whether explicit or hidden, of small parcels, should not be explained in terms of legal tradition, nor in terms of a strategy by some landowners to maintain themselves mid-way between renting and selling, but as the reflection of a dynamic process whereby property rights over land were created and recreated. In this process of creation and redefinition, the hunger for land of the poorest sort was as important as the initiatives of the more powerful.

---

3 For more on the *rabassa morta*, see the section below: 'From the *rabassa morta* contract to emphyteusis in perpetuity' and also the chapter by Ferrer & Moreno in this volume. See also Giralt (1965); Colomé (1990); Valls (2007a and 2007b); Moreno (1995 and 1997); and Ferrer (1987).

4 These were the three most common forms of emphyteusis in rural Catalonia, but not the only ones. In Barcelona and its hinterland, sub-emphyteusis led to the emergence of middlemen landowners (*senyors mitjans*), between the owners of *dominium directum* and the holders of dominium utile, with the right to claim part of the fines paid for the sale or transfer of land. Lawyer Jaime Tos, in his treatise *Tratado de la Cabrevación*, written in 1784, refers mostly to this form of emphyteusis (Tos, 2008).

5 Fraud was practised in notarial documentation with regard to the recognition of the rights of holders of *dominium directum*. See Congost (2007: 159-190).

6 72% of the land transfers between 1768 and 1862 were less than one hectare and less than 2% were more than 5 hectares.

Figure 7.1. The case study region

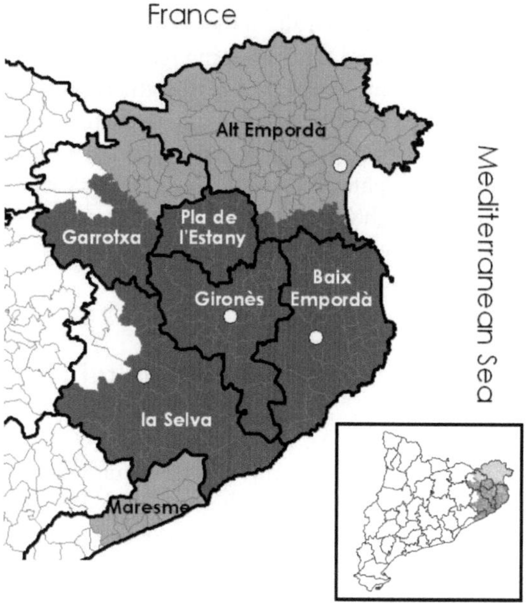

Sources: The darker zone corresponds to the area for which we have a complete series from the *Registro de Hipotecas*, while the two grey zones are those for which there are gaps in the series (see note 10). The white dots indicate the four notaries used in the sample created in order to extend the study beyond the period for which the *Contaduría de Hipotecas* (1768-1862) existed. For a better understanding of the map, see the section on methodology.

Emphyteutic *subestabliments* were particularly important in two aspects of this process: a) the gradual disappearance of so-called common rights, associated with an important change in the notion of property rights, which justified the privatisation of lands that had previously been considered as not subject to privatisation by individuals, b) the loss of power by some *senyors directes* in the face of the growing strength of some *senyors útils*, that is, those who felt themselves to be sufficiently strong and powerful to stand up to the *senyors directes* and to suggest new rules of the game.

Both aspects anticipate the modern notion of property enshrined in liberal law: private, individual property rights divested of feudal dues. Insofar as 'emphyteutic' has often been taken as synonymous with 'feudal', the role played by emphyteusis in the consolidation of this new property rights might appear paradoxical. We should not be deceived, however. That the victors in this process should have called, *a posteriori*, and successfully, upon the principle of absolute property rights in order to justify and ensure their own property rights tells us absolutely nothing about how such rights were created.

By contrast, an interesting finding that emerges from the analysis of historical case studies is that the ability to adapt emphyteutic practices to different historical contexts depended above all on the ability to relativize and thus redefine property rights to land. For this same reason, the need to keep an open mind when examining property rights in the context of emphyteusis makes the study of emphyteutic practices an excellent way in to understanding the processes of social appropriation which are hidden behind the redefinition of property rights[7]. Put another way, the success of different practices of emphyteusis in eighteenth-century Catalonia provide us with important information on the conflict and bargaining between different and emerging social groups.

II. Reconstructing a chronology: methodological issues

This study proposes, first of all, to establish the chronology of emphyteutic contracts throughout the eighteenth and nineteenth centuries within the Girona region. Our aim is not to establish a complete chronology, for which we would have to go back to the medieval sources, but to date the changes in the format of these contracts during a period in which their use extended enormously. Throughout the eighteenth and nineteenth centuries, more than 28,000 hectares of land, or 7.2% of the area under consideration, were transferred by emphyteutic grant, not including the hectares covered by many contracts which did not specify the extension of the holdings in question. We should not forget, however, that the major part of the transferred lands were located inside *masos* that had been subject to the emphyteusis regime since the Middle Ages (Congost, 2015).

The results presented here correspond to several stages which need to be explained in detail. The reconstruction is based on two different sources, each of which has been sampled in a different manner. The starting-point has been a source which corresponds to the central decades of the period studied, namely, the volumes of the *Registro de Hipotecas* for Girona and Figueres, a source which centralised the notarial contracts of all the districts between 1768 and 1862[8]. These offices registered all notarial acts relating to property

---

7 See, for example, the role played by emphyteusis in the consolidation of *latifundia* in southern Portugal (Santos & Serrao, 2013).

8 On the historical origins of the *Registro de Hipotecas*, see: Peset, 1978, Serna, 1996 and, specifically on Catalonia, López & Tatjer (1984). The implications of this institution for the functioning of the land market are discussed in Congost (2007) and Villalón (2008). For a detailed discussion of the *Registro de Hipotecas* as a source, see López (1974) and Congost (1990).

subject to some kind of a charge or mortgage[9]. The surviving volumes provide information on 30,620 emphyteutic grants. If we add an estimate for the contracts that would have been drawn up by the Figueres office between 1774 and 1805, the approximate total would be 34,000. This figure is high given that the population of the region in 1787 was around 133,000 and in 1860 around 270,000. These registers have been exhaustively transcribed and analysed (Congost, 1990a & 1990b).

To extend the time series and to see the importance of emphyteutic contracts before 1768 and after 1862, that is, before and after the *Registro de Hipotecas*, we have taken samples from the notarial records of four localities from the Girona region (Girona-IV, La Bisbal d'Empordà, Castelló d'Empúries and Santa Coloma de Farners). The sample consisted of taking all notarial deeds recorded in years ending in 0 and in 5 for the periods 1700-1765 and 1865-1910[10]. In total, for the period before 1768, we have obtained 261 emphyteutical grants (with an average of 15 contracts per year), while for the period after 1862 the sample size is 312 (approximately 35 per year). The sample has its limitations; one limitation, among others, is that at a local level the number of contracts could vary greatly from year to year. Nonetheless, the results allow for a first estimate of the total number of transfers for the period 1700-1900, as shown in Figure 7.2.

In order to integrate the series for the *Registro de Hipotecas* into the notarial sample, we have estimated the number of contracts for all the notaries of the region based on the weight of the sample within the entire set of contracts registered in the *Registro* in selected years. For the period before 1768, we have estimated that the contracts signed before the notaries in our sample represent 30% of the total; this figure is the average of the weight of the four notaries within the total number of contracts registered in the *Contaduría de Hipotecas* between 1768 and 1771. For the second period, we have estimated a slightly lower percentage (25%), based on the contracts signed in 1841.

Figure 7.2a shows that the rise of emphyteusis in the Girona region coincided with the creation of the *Registro de Hipotecas*. A valid question is therefore whether the use of two different sources and two different

---

9 For Girona, a complete set of registers survives. The records for the district of Figueras are incorporated into the Girona registers for the first six years (1768-1773), along with the records of some municipalities of the Maresme district. Registers for both these districts disappeared after this date due to a reorganisation of the district boundaries for these offices. For the district of Figueras, apart from the six years already mentioned, we thus only have the registers for the years 1806-1862. In order to homogenise the area under study, the records for the Maresme district have been omitted and estimates interpolated into the series for Figueras in order to cover to a certain extent the gap for 1774-1805.

10 The series ends in 1910 because Spanish law restricts access to notarial records until at least 100 years after the date the record was created. For the later period, from 1907, we only have figures published in the annual reports *Anuario de la Dirección General de los Registros Civil y de la Propiedad y del Notariado* which are aggregated at the provincial level and thus give only a very summary account of the creation and removal of emphyteutic rents.

Figure 7.2. Chronology of emphyteutic grants

a. Whole time period

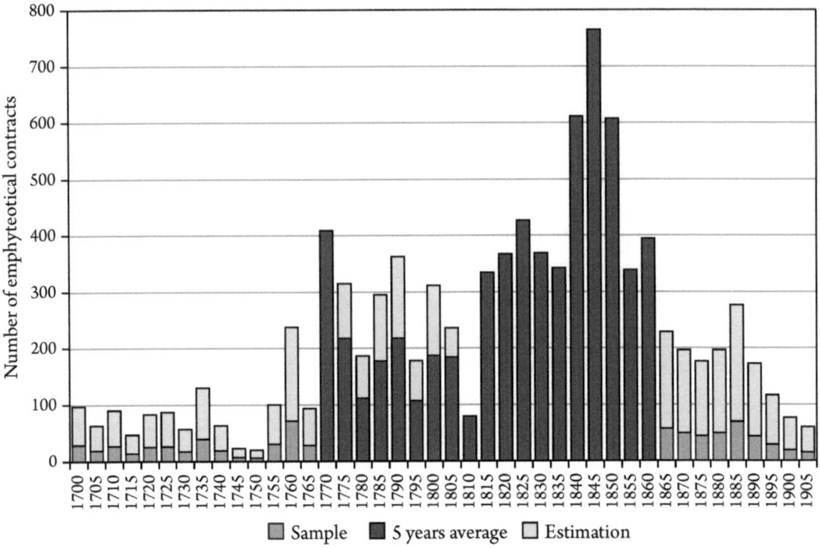

b. Detail for the period of overlap of the sources (1755-1780)

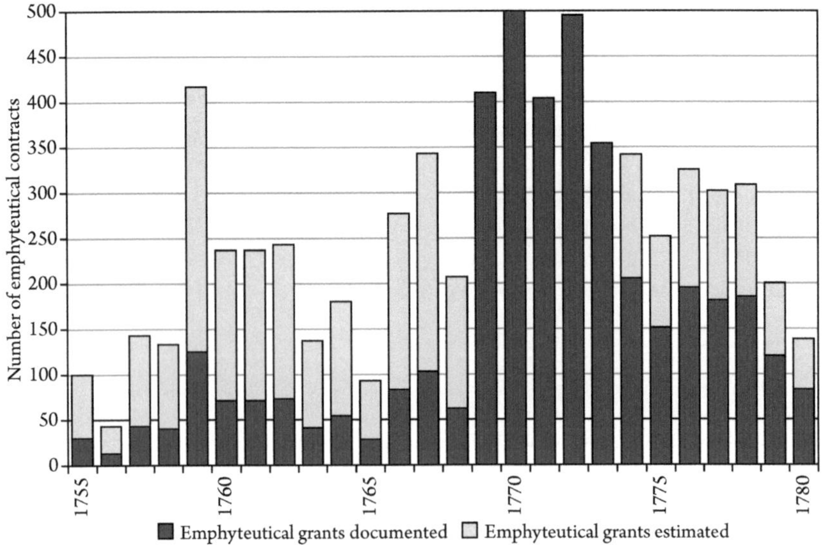

Sources: Arxiu Històric de Girona, Notarial, Girona-IV, la Bisbal d'Empordà, Castelló d'Empúries and Santa Coloma de Farners; Arxiu Històric de Girona, Comptadoria d'Hipoteques, Girona and Figueres

methods may distort our results. In order to discount the possibility that the chronology shown here can be explained simply by the change in source and methodology rather than reflecting a real change, we have undertaken a more detailed study of the transitional phase of the first period. Figure 7.2b shows this detail alongside Figure 7.2a, and confirms that the years in which the *Registro de Hipotecas* were created did indeed coincide with the beginning of a boom in emphyteutic contracts.

The series we have reconstructed shows that there was a particularly intense period between 1768 and 1772. This level of activity was not reached again until the years immediately following the Napoleonic Wars (1815-1830), reaching a peak in the 1840s. The golden age of the emphyteutic contract was thus the second half of the eighteenth century and the first sixty years of the nineteenth century, that is, the period of operation of the *Registro de Hipotecas*. During the second half of the nineteenth century, the number of contracts fell gradually. By the beginning of the twentieth century, the number of contracts registered in the province of Girona was only a quarter of what had been recorded by the *Registro de Hipotecas* of Girona and Figueras (covering a smaller geographical area) in the last five years of their existence, and this number continued to decline throughout the first third of the twentieth century. Although the notarial records cannot be consulted after 1910, the summary statistics published by the *Registro del Notariado* from 1907 supports this image of decline. Even though the legal concept of the emphyteutic rent survives today, and was actually ratified by the Catalan Parlament in a law of 28th February 1990, since the Civil War (1936-1939) its use as an instrument for the transfer of ownership has been minimal and residual[11].

The presentation of the time series represents the first step, to be followed by a closer examination of important qualitative changes in the forms of emphyteusis that the series alone cannot reveal. The majority of the emphyteutic land grants of the first half of the eighteenth century were instigated by *senyors directes* and many of them were associated with viticulture through the medium of the *rabassa morta* contract. The majority of emphyteutic land grants during the period from1768 to1862, by contrast, were *subestabliments* and, although many were also associated with viticulture, they mostly took the form of emphyteusis in perpetuity. The following sections will discuss these qualitative changes.

III. Who owned the uncultivated land? Emphyteusis as a means of appropriating resources

Is it possible to establish a relationship between the expansion of emphyteutic practices and the decline of common rights, or, to put it another way, the rise

11 On the end of such charges, see Congost (2007: 191-216).

Figure 7.3. Emphyteutic contracts concerning uncultivated land (as a %)

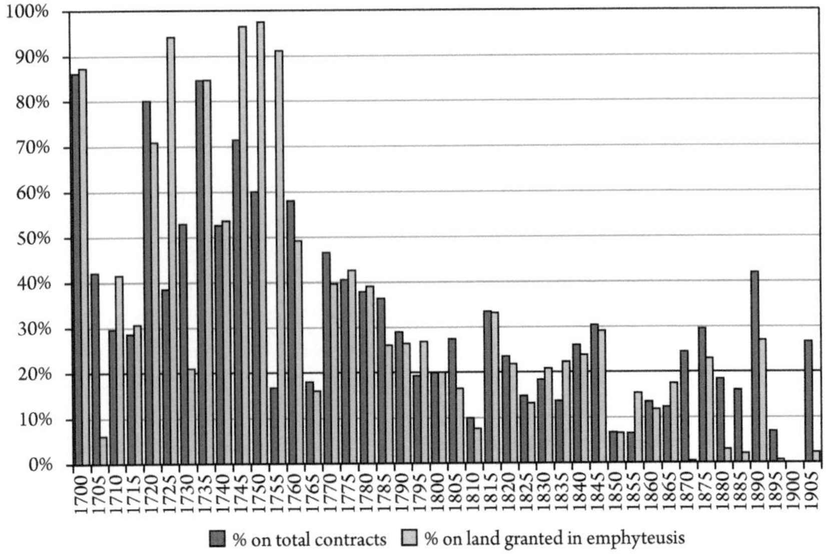

Sources: See Figure 7. 2.

of agrarian individualism? Yes, provided that we bear in mind that emphyteusis was the main method used to break up and bring under cultivation fallow and wooded land. The grant under emphyteusis of these lands also satisfied one of the conditions that in theory defined an emphyteutic transfer, namely, the obligation to improve the land. Leaving aside emphyteutic grants of arable land, common in the middle decades of the nineteenth century, where the contract became much closer to tenancy pure and simple, and those transfers of land rights, particularly at the end of the nineteenth and beginning of the twentieth centuries, where land was granted for building purposes (again, the aim of converting old plots of land into urban real estate counted as substantial improvement), we will focus our analysis on the transfer of fallow and wooded lands, the main use of emphyteutic contracts during the whole of the eighteenth century.

The low percentage of uncultivated land in 1735 is explained by the fact that the village council of Garriguella recognised in that year, via written contracts, the grant of an important number of plots of land that had already been occupied, broken up and, in some cases, planted with vines by local inhabitants. The contracts described the land in terms of the crops being grown, but did make clear in some cases that it had previously been uncultivated.

Many of these contracts, and not just those that were *rabassa morta*, include the obligation to plant vines or olives; in some the cultivator was obliged to plant fruit, almond or chestnut trees. In other cases, the parcelling-out of uncultivated land meant the expansion of arable land or the spread of market gardening; in others the occupation of river banks or the draining of lakes.

From the end of the seventeenth century onwards, some nobles, some ecclesiastical institutions and some village councils[12] granted via emphyteusis a large number of small plots of uncultivated or wooded land in the Girona region. To what extent was this process a novelty? We can only answer this question by first reflecting on the ownership of – and, by extension, the market for – such uncultivated or wooded land. The *Usatge Stratae* recognised that barren and uncultivated land belonging to the lords, not for their own benefit, but so that local residents coud enjoy their use[13]. Many historians have seen in this *Usatge*, which survived until the liberal revolution, a recognition of common property and common rights. The process of large-scale transfer of uncultivated land, insofar as this signified the appropriation of land that was formerly held collectively, could be seen as an attack on common rights. Equally, however, insofar as it guaranteed the occupation of small plots by a multitude of individuals, most of whom were of humble origins, it could also be considered as a process of land redistribution among local inhabitants.

Both perspectives are necessary for understanding all the processes of land transfer organised *by senyors directes*. For example, the 172 land grants carried out by the Count of Peralada between 1683 and 1693 in Cabanes were very unequal, though contracts associated with small plots dominated. There were 80 individual beneficiaries, 79 of whom were local inhabitants, who thus increased the amount of land they held. Soon afterwards, the village council of Cabanes initiated a suit questioning the grants, which ended, as was ofen the case in these situations, with the signing of an agreement among all parties. In this agreement, signed in 1700, the parties were three council representatives, 78 inhabitants and the Count. The Count, although he renounced most of the grants he had made between 1671 and 1700, was authorised to repeat the process. The village council, for its part, received the explicit setting aside of common pasture lands and a guarantee of market garden plots of .1 hectares. Among the documentation generated by this suit we find the testimony of one inhabitant denouncing the Count's attempts to manipulate the process by offering emphyteutic grants of land to certain inhabitants in exchange for votes in his favour. This testimony is interesting in that it reveals a perverse

12 Village council here translates the Catalan term *Universitat* (literally: 'university') which is a term of medieval origin used in Catalonia for town and especially village councils or assemblies during the Ancien Régime.

13 The *Usatges* are a compendium of laws published for the first time in the twelfth century which were officially recognised by the *Corts* (Estates) of Barcelona in 1251. The *Usatge* or *Strate* law laid down the following: 'The public highways, running water and fountains, meadows, pastures, woods, forests and oak trees, and the rocks of this country belong to the lords, but are not of their domain, so that they can be at all times enjoyed by all people without obstacle or opposition and without being subject to any service' (Vives, 1864: I, 259).

use of emphyteusis in order to divide opinion among the inhabitants of a community (Bosch, Congost & Gifre, 1996: 130-138; Gifre, 2009: 386-390 and 661).

Another interesting legal suit is that that took place between the *senyors directes* and the village council of Cervià de Ter, some 3.5 hours distance from the city of Girona. In this instance, the conflict had begun with the occupation by the local inhabitants, during the 1640s, of the lands near to the river Ter, lands known as *Comuns* (Commons). The two *senyors directes* of this village, a noble and a prior, protested to the courts. Finally, after many struggles, an agreement was reached whereby the lords signed contracts transferring small plots for a modest rent, to all the inhabitants of the village. What is interesting to note, however, is that the inhabitants of Cervià de Ter, throughout the occupation of land denounced by the lords, also fought to prevent the owners of *masos*, that is, the rich peasants of the village, from taking these lands (Congost, 2000).

The two examples we have just described show emphyteutic grants as a practice that weakened common rights while at the same time satisfying the demand for land of labourers and smallholders, some of whom were carrying out the occupation of land. In these cases, to which we could add many more examples, the private nature of emphyteutic land grants had much in common with the redistribution of land by local inhabitants that was taking place in some neighbouring villages[14].

Over the course of the eighteenth century, however, village councils and *senyors directes* increasingly lost ground to the *senyors útils* of *masos*, that is, the traditional holders of land via emphyteusis, when it came to the granting

14 During the eighteenth and nineteenth centuries, village councils used both the mechanism of egalitarian and free redistribution of land and that of emphyteutic grants of small plots of land to allow inhabitants access to land. In 1740, for example, the council of Bordils, very near to Cervià de Ter, decided to share out common land among all inhabitants for the same reasons given by the inhabitants of Cervià de Ter: they wanted to ensure that not only the rich could benefit from them. In this case, we stress, the land grant was not subject to any charge. On other occasions, however, the village councils were motivated by high levels of debt. We have detailed knowledge of the case of Torroella de Montgrí: in 1718, the council shared out in a 'fair distribution' small plots of land near the river among 187 individuals. A similar process was carried out in 1725, this time among 336 people. In both cases the aim was to plant trees and prevent the harm that flooding of the banks could do to common land. At the same time, however, in order to address its debts, the council made several grants (in 1729, 1735 and 1736) of small plots of land situated in the commons that resulted in a marked increase in viticulture in the village. A later (1855-1859) and much more complicated case was the redistribution by the council of 90 hectares of the lagoon at Ullastret. The council alleged that it lacked the means to carry out a drainage project that had been authorised since 1818 and thus distributed the land in exchange for a entry payment and annual rent, but in the form of shares in a society known as 'La Laguna', formed by those taxpayers in the village who wished to be part of the enterprise. The high costs of the latter meant that, although initially portrayed as an egalitarian redistribution of land, within a short while the land in question was concentrated in the hands of ten large landowners (Saguer, 2007).

of land. The emphyteutic contract can thus be interpreted not just as a way of being a property owner, but also as a means of becoming one, that is, as a mechanism for the appropriation of uncultivated lands. It was not the only mechanism available. The *senyors útils* from the mid eighteenth century onwards sought and obtained from the Real Audiencia, the supreme court of justice in Catalonia, many edicts (*bans*) that prohibited entry to the uncultivated lands of a village for the inhabitants. These edicts thus automatically became outright titles to property (Bosch, Congost & Gifre, 1997; Pellicer, 2007; Congost, 2007: 219-252). Emphyteutic contracts became one of the standard means by which such property rights were exercised. In the same way that the Count of Peralada had tried to buy votes from some inhabitants through the offer of land, so many owners of *masos* also offered plots of land to inhabitants and outsiders eager for land, and in so doing consolidated the final division of many communities.

IV. From *establiments* to *subestabliments* and vice versa: the strategies of the *domini utilis* and of the *domini directi*

The notarial sample analysed for the period before 1768 allows us to see an important change in the central decades of the eighteenth century, that is, a reversal of the roles played among those ceding land, whether through *establiments* (initial transfers of *dominium utile*) or through subsequent *subestabliments*. As the figures show, ecclesiastical institutions, the nobility and the village councils were no longer in the majority in this regard from the last quarter of the eighteenth century. Instead, they gave way to 'plebeian' groups, among them the *hisendats* and *propietaris*. These two labels appear late on in the sources and are applied basically to individuals who would previously have been described simply as farmers (*pagesos*), that is, those who owned the dominium utile of *masos*. From the second half of the eighteenth century the predominance of this group in emphyteutic transfers is unquestionable.

From a legal point of view, we need to distinguish between *establiments* and *subestabliments*. With *establiments*, the holders of the dominium directum had the right to claim the *lluïsme*, a fee payable each time the land changed hands. With *subestabliments*, whoever ceded the land only had the right to claim the annual rent. What differentiated one type of contract from another was thus the inclusion of clauses containing reference to the dominium directum. In Figure 7.5, we quantify as establiment contracts all those in which the individual or institution ceding the land claimed to be the holder of the dominium directum or reserved those rights to himself, while those cases in which the individual or institution transferring the land either referred to a third person or institution as the holder of the dominium directum, claimed not to know who held dominium directum or used the formula 'reserving the rights of dominium directum for whoever shall prove it with his title' are *subestabliments*.

Figure 7.4a. Those transferring land (*estabilients*): church, village councils and nobility

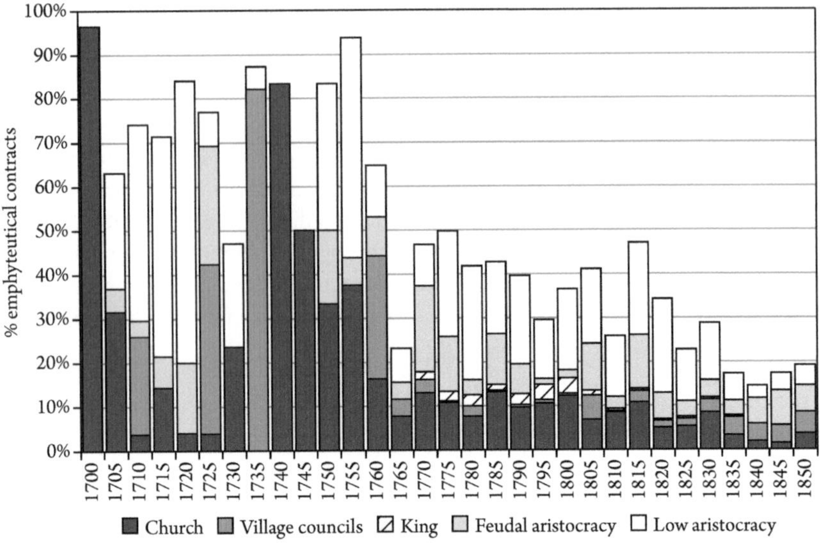

Figure 7.4b. Those transferring land (*estabilients*): individuals without a noble title

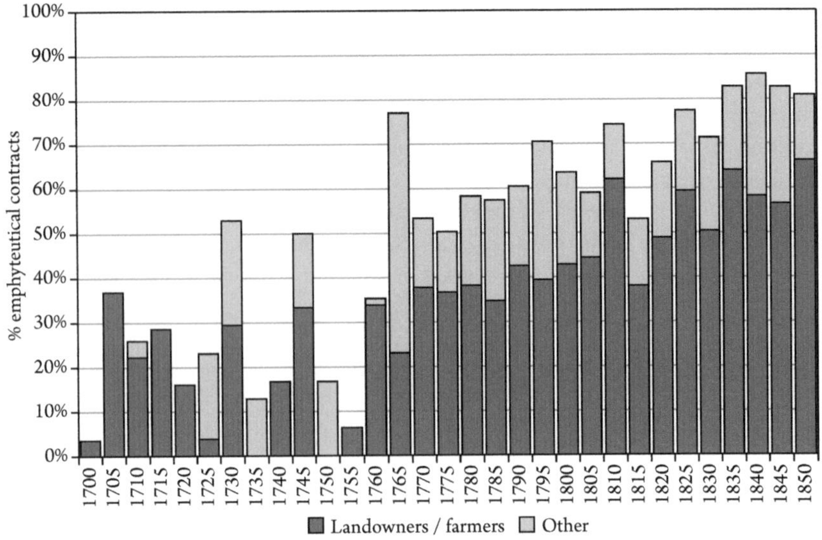

Sources: See Figure 7.2

Figure 7.5. Recognition of dominium directum

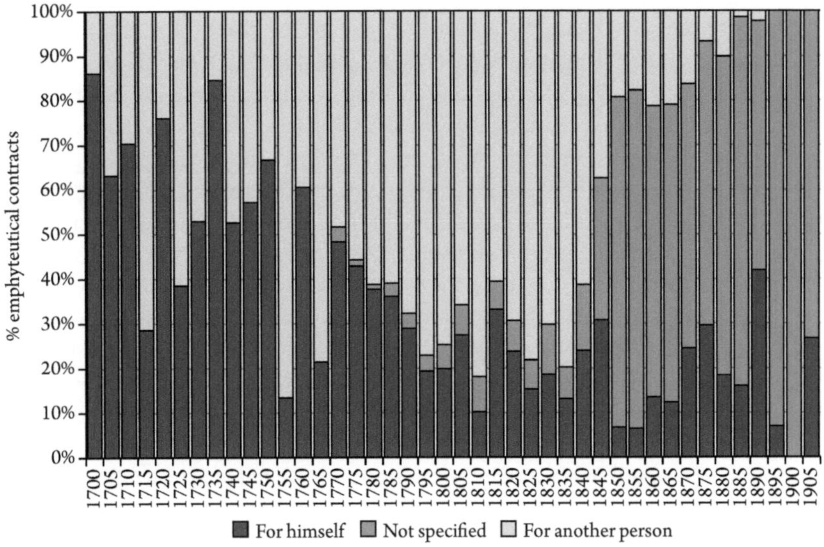

Sources: See Figure 7.2.

The U-shape of the figure at first sight suggests a rise and decline in the practice of *subestabliments*. In fact, it is a mirage which hides a much more complex reality. This reality can be seen more clearly when we analyse those contracts in which the person granting the land claimed the dominium directum for himself, that is, those contracts which, on paper, were undeniably emphyteutic *establiments*. During the first half of the nineteenth century the number of holders of dominium utile of plebeian origins who, at the moment of granting land, claimed either to hold the land freely or the dominium directum, or simply made no mention of dominium at all in the contract, multiplied. It is this tendency that explains the apparent rise of *establiments* at the expense of *subestabliments* after the middle of the nineteenth century.

The heyday of *subestabliments* that were declared to be such was thus limited to the final quarter of the eighteenth century and the first four decades of the nineteenth century. At this time the massive appropriation of dominium directum by the owners of dominium utile had barely started, though it rapidly intensified from the mid-ninteenth century onwards. Prior to this, however, the claims associated with dominium directum had begun to be questioned and, indeed, usurped, a process that is undeniably more important and interesting. Those who held only the dominium utile were nevertheless the driving force behind the colonisation of uncultivated land. The key question is therefore when and how did the *domini directi* allow the owners of dominium utile, who, after all, held these rights from them in the first place, to take control? If the chronology of these changes shows that this trend clearly predated the liberal revolution, a close examination of particular cases reveals that the trend was by no means unidirectional.

On the one hand, there is clear evidence that, from the mid-nineteenth century onwards, many holders of dominium utile felt strong enough to cede land to others, either recognising that the dominium directum belonged to a third person, or claiming that the land was freehold, or that they did not know who held dominium directum. In doing so, they began a clear process whereby the rights associated with dominium directum could be challenged and, in some cases, usurped. How did the holders of dominium directum react in the face of such behaviour? To demonstrate dominium directum over land was not always easy. Moreover, the two legal mechanisms whereby the *senyors directes* could claim a stake in the sale of land, namely, the claim to a percentage of the sale price (*lluïsmes*) and exercising the right to take back the land (*dret de fadiga*) were of little use where the land was not sold, but ceded by *establiment*. Even if payment of the *lluïsme* was agreed in the contract, it often only applied to the entry fee paid by the cultivator, which was often merely symbolic[15]. As for the *dret de fadiga*, it was not a viable option with *subestabliments*, as can be illustrated by a specific example. On 8th April 1780, the widow of a *Ciutadà Honrat de Barcelona* (a minor noble), ceded to a smallholder from Cervià de Ter 0.44 hectares of land, reserving the dominium directum for 'whoever should prove his title or, if no one should come forward, for herself'. On the 23rd of April of the same year, the Marquis de la Torre tried to exercise the *dret de fadiga* over this plot of land. The result was humiliation for the nobleman, who had to accept the status of taking on a 'new' *subestabliment* as the cultivator, with the same conditions as had been imposed in the first *establiment*, conditions that were fairly onerous. In the same contract in which the smallholder renounced all claims to the *subestabliment*, the Marquis took it on, promising to pay an entry payment of 75 *lliures* and an annual rent of two *quartans* of grain. In 1796, a rich peasant from Cervià de Ter, who in the *capbreu*[16] of a few years before had recognised the Marquis as *senyor directe*, carried out eight *subestabliments*, using the same formula as the widow had done: the dominium directum for whoever could prove his title or for himself. This time, the Marquis did not react (Congost, 2000: 77).

The silence of the *senyors directes*, however, could also reflect a change in strategy in the face of the evidence that in many cases in which they also received the tithe, *subestabliments* could result, without any administrative costs, in a considerable increase in annual income. As well as the tithe, the

---

15 A payment of 2 *sous* and 6 *diners* for every *lliure* paid as entry payment was agreed in the settlement signed in 1750 between the Marquis of Aitona and the town councillors of Llagostera, Caldes de Malavella and Santa Seclina. In the preceding law suit, the Marquis had demanded 6 *sous* and 8 *diners*.

16 A *capbreu* (*cabrevación* in Spanish) was a declaration before a notary whereby the holder of dominium utile recognised the rights of *dominium directum* that belonged to the lord and the rents or services that derived from these. For a more detailed account, see Tos, 1786.

holders of the dominium directum for whoever could prove his title or for himself could also claim *lluïsme* on all future transfers of land, and even, in some cases, on the entry payments of *establiments*.

Indeed, we know that some *senyors directes* actually encouraged the attempts at *subestabliments* on the part of the owners of dominium utile to their properties, through a reduction in the amounts that could be claimed as the *tasca*. According to legal texts, in the diocese of Girona, the *tasca* was an eighth of the harvest, once the land had been cultivated, and the tithe paid (Tos, 1786; Gifre, 2011). During the eighteenth century, the *tasca* was often reduced to a fixed payment in cash or kind. In some cases, this reduction can be correlated with the practice of *subestabliments*. One example is the agreement between the Duke of Hijar and Don Francisco March y de Jalpí, which specified a reduction in the *tasca* for the land attached to the Mas Agut, in the village of Grions, to a fixed annual payment of half a *quartera* (36.16 litres) of grain. The reduction was conditional upon the transferral of land via *subestabliments* within a short period of time[17]. We know this case was not unique, since in the mid-eighteenth century, the village councillors of Llagostera, Caldes de Malavella and Santa Seclina complained to the Duke of Medinaceli, their lord, because he refused to reduce the *tasca* as, they claimed, other lords were doing, which they alleged to be the reason why much of the land in these villages remained uncultivated[18].

V. From *rabassa morta* contracts to emphyteusis in perpetuity: the importance of negotiation from below

The *rabassa morta* was a contract involving the transfer of land in order to plant it with vines. Unlike other emphyteutic transfers, it was explicitly tied to the cultivation and life of the vines. This form of contract was key to the expansion of viticulture in Catalonia over the eighteenth and nineteenth centuries. In the Girona region, in contrast to other areas, the *rabassa morta*

---

17 Arxiu Històric de Girona, Comptadoria d'Hipoteques, Girona, book 3, f. 578. In the contract signed on 6th March 1770, the duke reduced the *tasca* for uncultivated lands belonging to the Mas Agut of Griona to the benefit of Don Francisco March y de Jalpi. In the contract, it was recognised that seven years previously Francisco March's father had negotiated this reduction in return for the obligation to cede the lands to cultivators. He had died without payment and the duke in 1770 conceded a space of one year in which to carry out the *subestabliments*.

18 Arxiu Municipal de Llagostera, *Llibre de Resolucions del Ajuntament de Llagostera, començant lo any 1813*. A document dated 8th August 1824 contains the following: 'On this matter of payment of the *tasca* it is accepted that this charge has greatly increased and is a burden for those who hold land subject to it and that it may be the reason why so many fields remain uncultivated, unless Your Excellency should be pleased to reduce or at least lower slightly the charge, as other landlords have done.'

contract seemed to have been less used. This study shows that while the *rabassa morta* contract was not only known in the region, but even enjoyed a notable presence there during the first half of the eighteenth century, it was in clear decline by the second half of and especially by the start of the nineteenth century, giving way to another contractual form: the *establiment or subestaliment* in perpetuity. Why?

Before continuing, some words are needed on the emphyteutic nature of this contract. The notarial documentation leaves this in no doubt: all *rabassa morta* contracts are *establiments* or *subestabliments*, with the same kind of conditions concerning the rent and the entry payment, except for the specific rule that the death of the vines signals the end of the contract and the recovery of the land by the person who had ceded it. From this perspective, a clause which tied the end of the contract to the death of the plant (either all the vines or two-thirds) could be interpreted more as a warning than as a fixed time limit. With this clause, the previous owner warned the *rabassaire* of the need to keep the vines alive. It was surely this clause that underlined the emphyteutic nature of the contract for the *rabassaire*. In the lawsuits before the Reial Audiència of Catalonia between *rabassaires* and landowners from 1765 onwards, the former always fought for the contract as being in perpetuity. They did not win in the Catalan courts, which in 1778 fixed the length of the contract at 50 years with the land returning to the previous owner at the end. The conflict continued, since the *rabassaires* appealed to the Council of Castile, but in many districts of Catalonia the *rabassa morta* contract began to be of fixed term (Giralt, 1965).

With this in mind, the decline in the proportion of *rabassa morta* contracts among emphyteutic contracts in the Girona district takes on a particular meaning, suggesting a certain degree of bargaining ability among those taking on land in this area, who were mostly agricultural labourers and smallholders[19]. We have indeed found several cases in which a *rabassa morta* contract was transformed, by agreement between the two parties and usually with a small sum paid in compensation, to an *establiment* in perpetuity. Here we describe two examples that involved various landowners.

In 1771, the nobleman Francisco de Jalpí authorized the conversion of 57 *rabassa morta* contracts in Peralada to perpetual contracts. The former *rabassaires* agreed to pay a tithe on all crops and a perpetual rent of 1 *sou* and 6 *diners* per *vessana* (0.34 *lliures* per hectare), plus 6 *lliures* entry payment[20]. Two years later, in exchange for recognizing the baron's direct dominion over their land, the residents of the village of Capmany won important concessions, including permission to rid themselves of the obligation to grow vines and convert the vineyards into croplands. This transformation entailed the de facto annulment of the time clause in the *rabassa morta* contracts. At the

19 See Congost & Saguer, 2015.

20 Arxiu Històric de Girona, Comptadoria d'Hipoteques, Girona, 1771, Book 6, f. 877r.

Figure 7.6. Proportion of contracts that were *rabassa morta*

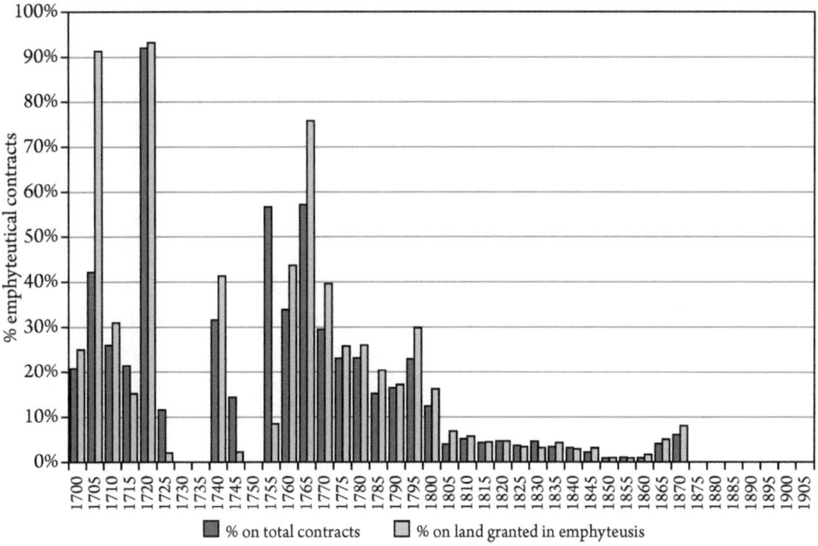

Sources: See Figure 7. 2.

same time, those residents who had old vineyards under the *rabassa morta* agreement were also allowed to replant them within a period of five years under the same conditions that had been paid until that date.

These examples reveal several interesting points. First, the conversion of *rabassa morta* contracts in perpetuity permitted the cultivators to escape enforced viticulture, which may have allowed them greater freedom in those years in which the conditions for viticulture were particularly difficult. Second, it is likely that this flexibility may in the long run have encouraged landowners to extend emphyteusis to areas where this would never have been an option had emphyteusis been restricted to the planting of vines. The process of *establiments* had resulted, by the middle of the nineteenth century, in the parcelling-out of the arable land of many *masos*, without this implying a change in crops grown. Whatever the implications, we would stress that the very fact of contracts in perpetuity supports the idea of a marked bargaining capacity among the cultivators.

VI. The revaluation of uncultivated land

The perpetual nature of emphyteutic contracts, by establishing yearly rents over the long term, make it impossible to interpret any increase or decrease in the amounts required as an increase or decrease in rent. For instance, the cultivator who had agreed to pay an annual rent of 2 *sous* continued to pay this years later, even if his neighbour were paying 20 *sous* for a similar holding. Moreover, any meaningful comparison would need to include the value of the entry payment.

Nevertheless, the same characteristics that make emphyteutic contracts unsuitable as a means of studying trends in rent provide useful information on important changes in property rights. This can be demonstrated via two simple exercises, based on the analysis of contracts for wooded and uncultivated land which have been the main focus so far.

The results of the first exercise are shown in Figure 7.7, and are based on only those contracts, whether for *establiments* or *subestabliments*, of uncultivated land for which the size of the holding is given and both the rent and the entry payment are in cash. The value of land has been calculated adding the value of the entry payment to the rent capitalized at a rate of 3%. The graph shows very low values for those contracts before the beginning of the *Registro de Hipotecas*, contrasted by a sustained increase in the amount payable afterwards. The low value is consistent with what we know about the Catalan economy at that time from Pierre Vilar's work, and with the fact that in some districts there was a seizure of uncultivated land, considered to be common land (Vilar, 1966, III: 569-570; Fabregat, 2008). What stands out the most and certainly requires explanation is the abrupt leap in price as we switch from one source to another. Does this mean we should view the change in source as the only reason for such a pattern? As discussed above, the notaries sampled for the earlier period were chosen because in 1768 and 1771, the years for which we are able to assess their importance of the different notaries within the whole range of emphyteutic contracts signed, these particular ones covered 30% of the emphyteutic contracts subsequently recorded in the *Registro de Hipotecas*. The graph thus indicates a real rise in the value of uncultivated and wooded land which coincided with the appearance of the *Registro*.

This thesis can be supported by the detailed analysis for the years prior to the *Registro* of those contracts for uncultivated land in which the owners required a share of the harvest, a frequent condition in *rabassa morta* contracts. In all the contracts available between 1700 and 1755, whether *establiments* or *subestabliments*, the share requested was one twelfth of the grapes. All the entry payments consisted of a pair of chickens, a pair of *capons* or a sum of money that was basically symbolic. After 1760, things begin to change; in 15 *rabassa morta* transfers carried out in that year by a rich peasant the rent was a tenth of the grapes and a third of the olives. An apothecary also demanded a tenth of the grapes. In 1765 we find, alongside rents still of a twelfth, the decision by a notary of Castelló d'Empúries to charge rents of an eighth share and to demand, for the first time, a fairly substantial sum of money by way of entry payment. This same notary carried out land transfers on a similar basis until 1770. He was not unique among landowners in imposing harsher contracts in the years immediately prior to the *Registro de Hipotecas*: in 1766, we find demands for a quarter of the grapes, a seventh of the grapes and a third of the olives and two-ninths of fruit as well as two-fifths of the grapes.

Figure 7.7. Evolution of the 'value' of *establiments* and *subestabliments* of uncultivated land

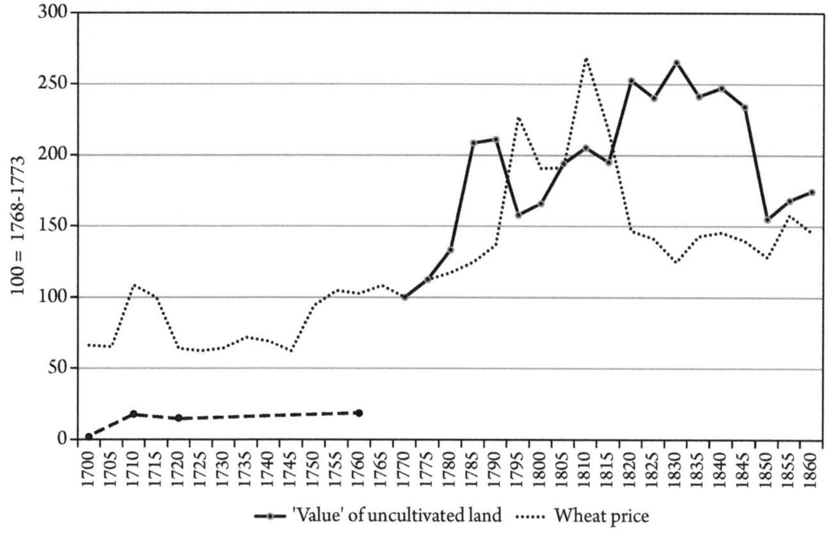

Sources: See Figure 7.2.

Both exercises suggest we are witnessing an important change in property rights. The sharp increase in the rents demanded, whether in cash or in crop shares, reflects a revaluing of uncultivated or wooded land or, what amounts to the same thing, the incorporation of such land into the land market[21]. The increase in rents was driven by the holders of dominium utile, who did not hesitate to demand much higher rents than those demanded in the first half of the eighteenth century by the *senyors directes* or the village councils. In taking on land from the owners of dominium utile, cultivators were often faced not only with rent, but also with the tithe that could be demanded by the *senyor directe*. In all probability, the similar increase in entry payments, which provoked complaints from the Reial Audiència on the grounds that it was a distortion of emphyteusis, was another aspect of the same process of revaluation (Vilar, 1966: III, 569).

VII. Final thoughts

Throughout the eighteenth century, many uncultivated lands in the Girona region were brought under cultivation, in small plots, via emphyteutic contracts. From the middle of the century onwards, however, not only did the number

21 On the need to analyse emphyteutic transfers alongside land sales, see CONGOST (2013).

of these transfers increase significantly, but important changes have also been demonstrated in terms of the parties to the contracts and the terms agreed. During the first half of the eighteenth century it was mainly the nobility, the Church and the town and village councils that granted emphyteutic *establiments* to labourers and smallholders in exchange for payments that were very small, both in terms of the rent and the entry payment. Gradually, the holders of dominium utile began to take over the process of land transfers, bringing about an important shift in that these transfers could no longer, in the eyes of contemporaries, be assimilated with the redistribution of land among residents. The rents demanded for the occupation of uncultivated land rose sharply and the new cultivators found themselves also obliged to pay higher entry payments. None of this means, however, that the cultivators did not have a role to play. They were undoubtedly responsible, throughout the period, for maintaining the transfer of small-scale plots, and the ones who forced the substitution of contracts in perpetuity across the region for *rabassa morta* contracts. In the long run, this type of emphyteusis allowed for the emergence and consolidation of a class of smallholders, even in grain-growing districts, who would be particularly active in a land market transformed by the introduction of uncultivated land.

Emphyteusis, therefore, was far from being an archaic form of property. Analysis of the practice has allowed us to see in the mid-eighteenth century, long before the institutional changes of the liberal revolution, the appearance of successful new ways of appropriating resources, that is, the appearance of new property rights. Above all, it allows us to place a process of bargaining and tension between different social groups at the very heart of these changes (Congost & Santos, 2010).

Bibliography

BOSCH, Mònica, CONGOST, Rosa & GIFRE, Pere (1997), 'Los *bandos*. La lucha por el individualismo agrario en Cataluña', *Noticiario de Historia Agraria*, 13, p. 65-88.

COLOME, Josep (1990), 'Les formes d'accés a la terra a la comarca de l'Alt Penedès durant el segle XIX: el contracte de rabassa morta i l'expansió vitivinícola', *Estudis d'Història Agrària*, 8, p. 123-143.

CONGOST, Rosa (1990a), *Els propietaris i els altres. La regió de Girona*, 1768-1862, Vic, Eumo.

CONGOST, Rosa (1990b), 'Una font poc utilitzada: el registre d'hipoteques', *Estudis d'història agrària*, 8, p. 201-234.

CONGOST, Rosa (2000), *Els darrers senyors de Cervià de Ter. Investigacions sobre el caràcter mutant de la propietat (segles XVII-XX)*, Girona, Documenta Universitaria.

CONGOST, Rosa (2007), *Tierras, leyes, historia. Estudios sobre 'la gran obra de la propiedad'*, Barcelona, Crítica.

CONGOST, Rosa (2013), 'The social dynamics of agricultural growth. The exemple of Catalan emphyteusis, eighteenth century', in Gérard BÉAUR, Phillipp R. SCHOFIELD, Jean-Michel CHEVET & María Teresa PÉREZ-PICAZO (eds), *Property Rights, Land Markets and Economic Growth in the European Countryside (13th-20th Centuries)*, Turnhout, Brepols, Rural History in Europe 1, p. 439-454.

CONGOST, Rosa (ed) (2015), *The Catalan Mas. Origins, transformations and the end of an agrarian system*, Girona, Documenta Universitaria.

CONGOST, Rosa & SANTOS, Rui (2010), 'From formal institutions to the social contexts of property', in Rosa CONGOST & Rui SANTOS (eds), *Contexts of Property in Europe: The Social Embeddedness of Property Rights in Land in Historical Perspective*, Turnhout, Brepols, p. 13-36.

CONGOST, Rosa & SAGUER, Enric (2015), 'De contractes de rabassa morta a emfiteusis perpètues: una negociació des de baix? La regió de Girona, 1700-1900', in Josep COLOMÉ, Jordi PLANAS & Francesc VALLS-JUNYENT (eds), *De la vinya a la fassina. Vinyes, vins i cooperativisme vitivinícola a Catalunya*, Barcelona, Publicacions de l'Abadia de Montserrat, p. 178-208.

FABREGAT, Emeteri (2008), 'Concessions, aprisions i emfiteusis: La formació de la propietat territorial al delta de L'Ebre (segles XII-XX)', *Estudis d'historia agraria*, 21, p. 49-78.

FERRER ALOS, Llorenç (1987), *Pagesos, rabassaires i industrials a la Catalunya Central (segles XVIII-XIX)*, Barcelona, Publicacions de l'Abadia de Montserrat.

GIFRE, Pere (2009), *En la prehistòria dels hisendats. De senyors útils a propietaris (Vegueria de Girona, 1486-1730)*, Girona, Universitat de Girona, PhD thesis.

GIFRE, Pere (2011), *Delmes, censos i lluïsmes. El feudalisme tardà a la CatalunyaVella (Vegueria de Girona, s. XVI-XVII)*, Girona, Documenta Universitaria.

GIRALT, Emili (1965), 'El conflicto rabassaire y la cuestión agraria hasta 1936', *Revista de Trabajo*, 7, p. 3-24 (also in E. GIRALT (2002), *Empresaris, nobles i vinyaters, 50 anys de recerca histórica*, València, Universitat de València, p. 114-139).

LÓPEZ, Marina & TÀTJER, Mercè (1984), 'Observaciones sobre la historia de los Oficios de Hipotecas en Cataluña (1768-1861)', *Revista Crítica de Derecho Inmobiliario*, 560, p. 131-150.

LÓPEZ, Marina (1974), 'Una nueva fuente para la Historia de Barcelona: el Registro de Hipotecas', *Estudios históricos y documentos de los Archivos de Protocolos*, IV, p. 345-363.

MORENO, Belén (1995), *La contractació agrària a l'Alt Penedès durant el segle XVIII. El contracte de rabassa morta i l'expansió de la vinya*, Barcelona, Fundació Noguera.

MORENO, Belén (1997), 'Del cereal a la vinya. El contracte de rabassa morta a l'Alt Penedès del segle XVIII', *Estudis d'Història Agrària*, 11, p. 37-56.

PELLICER, M. (2007), 'Los cercamientos de tierras en Cataluña. Fuentes para el estudio de una *revolución silenciosa*', in R. CONGOST & J. M. LANA (ed.), *Campos cerrados, debates abiertos. Análisis histórico y propiedad de la tierra en Europa (siglos XVI-XIX)*, Pamplona, Universidad Pública de Navarra, p. 249-292.

PESET, Mariano (1978), 'Los orígenes del Registro de la Propiedad en España', *Revista Crítica de Derecho Inmobiliario*, 54, p. 695-716.

SAGUER, Enric (2007), 'Dinàmica social i canvi ambiental: el dessecament de l'estany d'Ullastret durant la segona meitat del segle XIX', *El paisatge, element vertebrador de la identitat empordanesa*, Figueres, Institut d'Estudis Empordanesos, vol. II, p. 397-412.

SANTOS, Rui. & SERRÂO, José V. (2013), 'Property rights, social appropriations and economic outcomes: Agrarian contracts in southern Portugal in the late 18th century', in Gérard BÉAUR, Phillipp R. SCHOFIELD, Jean-Michel CHEVET & María Teresa PÉREZ-PICAZO (eds), *Property Rights, Land Markets and Economic Growth in the European Countryside (13th-20th Centuries)*, Turnhout, Brepols, Rural History in Europe 1, p. 475-494.

SERNA, Margarita (1996), *La publicidad immobiliaria en el derecho hipotecario español*, Madrid, Centro de Estudios Registrales.

TELLO, Enric (1997), 'Los usos de la enfiteusis en la Cataluña "Nueva" y la Cataluña "Vieja" (siglos XVIII-XIX)', in Eugenia TORIJANO, Luís Enrique ESPINOZA, Javier INFANTE, Amparo BEJARANO & Ricardo ROBLEDO (eds), *VIII congreso de historia agraria: preactas*, Salamanca, 28-30th May 1997, p. 525-538.

TOS, Jaime (1786), *Tratado de la cabrevación, Edició i estudi introductori a càrrec de Rosa Congost*, Girona, Documenta Universitaria, 2007.

VALLS, Francesc (1997a), 'Contractació a rabassa morta i conjuntura vitícola a Catalunya, 1720-1850', *Estudis Històrics: Documents de l'Arxiu de Protocols*, 15, p. 299-334.

VALLS, Francesc (1997b), 'La rabassa morta a la comarca d'Igualada en la transició de les velles a les noves formes de propietat. 1750-1850', *Estudis d'Història Agrària*, 11, p. 89-107.

VICEDO, Enric (1991), *Les terres de Lleida i el desenvolupament català del set-cents*, Barcelona, Crítica.

VILAR, Pierre (1962), *La Catalogne dans l'Espagne moderne.* Recherches *sur les fondements économiques des structures nationales*, Paris, S.E.V.P.E.N.

VILLALÓN, Sebastià (2008), 'Els problemes de la informació en una societat d'antic règim. Els notaris catalans davant la creació del Registre d'Hipoteques', in Rosa CONGOST (ed.), *Dels capbreus al registre de la propietat : drets, títols i usos socials de la informació a Catalunya (segles XIV-XX)*, Girona, Documenta Universitaria, p. 241-274.

VIVES, Pedro Nolasco (1864), *Los Usages y demás derechos de Cataluña, que no están derogados ó no son totalmente inútiles*, Barcelona, Librería de Emilio Font.

LLORENÇ FERRER-ALÒS,
BELÉN MORENO CLAVERÍAS

8. The Origins and Evolution of the *rabassa morta* Contract in Catalonia

Was It an Emphyteusis?[1]

What is the purpose of a chapter about the *rabassa morta* contract (literally, 'dead grapevine' contract) in a monograph on emphyteusis? This particular kind of lease transferred the *dominium utile* (beneficial dominion or ownership) of a parcel of land so that it was used for growing grapevines. Originally, from a legal standpoint, it was similar to an emphyteusis, although with certain peculiarities. The *rabassa morta* contract shared several elements with a traditional emphyteusis: a shared dominion over the land, the possibility of alienating beneficial ownership, an entrance fee, the right to charge for any improvements, etc. However, they differed in terms of their duration. Unlike in the case of the Catalan classical emphyteusis, whose terms were in perpetuity, the *rabassa morta* contract was a long-term contract with an undefined duration. For example, it could be valid until the first grapevines planted by the *rabasser* – the lessee – died (hence the name 'dead grapevine'), that is, for approximately fifty years. Some techniques – such as the use of *colgats i capficats*, which will be explained below – allowed the life of the vines to be extended indefinitely, thus *rabassa morta* contracts were passed on from father to son, generation after generation.

Which advantages did this contract offer to landowners? Once the demand for wine and distilled spirits increased, and with it the price of wine products, many landowners decided to cultivate unused lands in order to benefit from the economic growth. The problem lay in the time lag between cultivation and any economic returns, which involved a significant investment of both time and labour. Therefore, landowners – many of whom did not outright own the land but held themselves an emphyteutic lease on it – found in the *rabassa morta* contract the ideal legal instrument to sublease out the cultivation of the land without making a costly investment. Landowners could not use other methods such as the regular land lease (*arrendament*) and the sharecropping (*parceria*) because these were short-term contracts. No *rabasser* would be willing to invest years of work on uncultivated land to then immediately lose their right of use. The *rabassers*'s work would only be rewarded if they were

1 This paper is part of the research project HAR2014-54891-P, financed by the Spanish Ministry of Science and Innovation.

Agrarian Change and Imperfect Property, ed. by Rosa CONGOST and Pablo F. LUNA, Rural History in Europe, 15 (Turnhout, 2018), 155-181

DOI 10.1484/M.RURHE-EB.5.116123

able to hold beneficial ownership for at least half a century. In exchange for this, the lessor would receive a share of the annual production, as well as other payments and rights that will be discussed below.

This chapter will address the emphyteusis, the different kinds of legal formulas for the planting of vineyards, and the earliest identified *rabassa morta* contracts. Additionally, it will analyse the importance of the *rabassa morta* contract in different areas of Catalonia, the evolution of its conditions and clauses, and how *rabassa morta* contracts changed once landowners started to model them after other exploitation systems, such as the *parceria* or the *arrendament*. Finally, it will examine – albeit briefly, due to space constraints – the social conflicts generated by these changes.

I. Some ideas about the emphyteusis, the subemphyteutic contract, and the contracts for the cultivation of grapevines

The history of both rural and urban Catalonia cannot be understood without the emphyteusis. In this region, property rights were divided between the landowner, who ceded the land but retained its dominium directum, and the person who farmed it, who held the dominium utile. The landowner received a rent, whether monetary or in kind, and could also exercise the right of *fadiga* (the right to recover the dominium utile if the land was sold to a third party, and to do so for the same price) and receive the *laudemium* (a percentage of the purchase price every time the beneficial ownership changed hands). The holders of the beneficial ownership had leave to farm the land in exchange for a payment, as well as to bequeath the property to their descendants or even sell the exploitation rights as if they belonged to them[2].

Any contract regulates a relationship between unequal parties, and that also applied to the emphyteusis. There were differences between the medieval emphyteusis (in which the payment included a fraction of the crop, and whose duration was longer, although it was limited to one or two generations) and the emphyteusis that emerged in Catalonia after the War of the *Remences* in the mid-fifteenth century and the *Sentència Arbitral de Guadalupe* in 1486 (Serra, 1980; Gifre y Lluch, 2001; Montagut, May 1986). The new regulations reflected the change in the relationship between landowners and those who held the beneficial ownership, and the balance of power shifted to favour the latter. Tenants paid a fixed *cens* (rent), which devaluated over time, and had leave to hand beneficial ownership to their descendants, generation after generation. Therefore, in practice, they became quasi-owners of the land and true protagonists of the agrarian transformation. The medieval *mas*

---

2 See also the chapter on emphyteusis and land transfers in Catalonia by CONGOST, GIFRE, and SAGUER in this book.

(plural *masos*) was an agricultural holding that consisted of a house where the farmer's family and the labourers lived, some other buildings, arable lands, and uncultivated and forested lands. In the Early Modern period, the accumulation of abandoned lands turned the *mas* into a property of around 80-100 hectares. *Mas* farmers (*pagesos*, sing. *pagès*) held an emphyteutic lease and with it the beneficial ownership of the land, which ensured they were in charge of its exploitation. On many occasions they accumulated a significant amount of properties, usually geographically dispersed, and therefore they needed to use different kinds of contracts in order to secure their cultivation[3].

Since the rights over the land were already divided into dominium directum and dominium utile, an additional long-term lease entailed a legal problem that was solved by creating a second-order dominium utile. This is known as *subestabliment* or *nua percepció* emphyteutic contract. The new sublessee paid a fixed rent in kind, or a share of the yield plus an entrance fee. Also, he could bequeath the land to his descendants or sell his right (Broca, 1987: 278-279). This new division of property rights led to a period of economic stability for peasants, which now had legal access to land. This volume also includes a study concerning the growth in Girona of these contracts – indefinite contracts with a fixed *cens* (rent) to be paid in money or in kind – which provided thousands of peasants with access to the land (Congost, 1998). In the areas where wine became a commercial commodity, the *rabassa morta* contract was the most favoured agreement.

The *rabassa morta* contract was a contract that required the lessee to pay a rent – a share of the harvest – and a variable entrance fee. They also had to settle the payment of the *laudemium* with the landowner at the beginning of the contract. In exchange, they could transfer the dominium utile as long as they respected the landowner's right of *fadiga*, and the sublease lasted as long as the grapevines were alive, that is why it is called *rabassa morta* (dead grapevine) contract. This type of lease was key to the expansion of viniculture throughout large areas of Catalonia between the eighteenth and twentieth centuries, despite the problems regarding its legality.

The central role played by *rabassa morta* contracts raises many questions, particularly, why did the vast majority of farmers who held the beneficial ownership of a property decide to use legal agreements such as the emphyteutic sublease and the *rabassa morta* contract itself, which meant ceding their propriety rights, instead of using other methods such as sharecropping?

Growing grapes is very different from growing cereals. Cereals have an annual cycle: they are sown, harvested, and then the plant dies thus restarting

3 The farmers of these landholdings used the *masoveria* contract when they were not able to farm the *mas* by themselves (Congost, Gifre et al., 1999). However, when they wanted to exploit new lands, which required intense deforestation, they used other agreements such as the *boïga*, the emphyteutic sublease or the *rabassa morta* contract. This chapter will focus on the latter.

the process again. The capital is the land itself. Planting grapevines, however, requires hard work, especially if it is done in a forested or uncultivated land. It is necessary to chop the trees down, uproot the stumps, weed, remove the stones and, once the land is ready, dig a hole two-to-three handspans wide and deep to plant the vines. Additionally, it takes four years for the grapevine to be fully productive. All this hard work does not result in a short-term harvest in the first year, as is the case of wheat, but in a crop that could last up to eighty or ninety years. Once planted, the grapevines became part of the land's value as much as the land itself. Due to the enormous cost of planting vineyards, and the need to wait a few years until they started to yield fruit and reach full production, the contract provided a long time frame and the ability to transfer the exploitation rights as a means of compensation[4]. In Catalonia, vineyards expanded over uncultivated and mountainous lands in the eighteenth and nineteenth centuries, during which time, there was a clear predominance of long-term agreements. One of them was the *rabassa morta* contract[5].

II. The Earliest *rabassa morta* Contracts: from the Medieval *complantatio* to the establishment of the *ad plantandum*

One of the most characteristic contracts for planting grapevines during the Middle Ages was the *complantatio*, also known as *ad medietatem plantationes* or *ad medium plantum*, which can be translated as a planting contract between two parties. The landowner leased a piece of land to a peasant who was obliged to plant grapevines within the first five, six, or seven years. Later, the vineyard was divided into two equal parts, one for the landowner and the other for the peasant. Therefore peasants were given half of the land as remuneration

4 This was a recurring problem when planting grapevines. The need to reward the farmer's work and the fact that it resulted in increasing the immovable capital – the vines – led to the creation of long-term contracts. For instance, in France the most common agreement was the *bail à complant*, which was probably very similar to the *rabassa morta* contract. It started as a *complantatio* (the peasant was given ownership rights over a parcel of land as remuneration) and evolved into a land transfer in perpetuity in exchange for a portion of the vintage. The *bail à complant* disappeared as vineyards spread, but it was still in use in the region of Nantes at the beginning of the twentieth century (Grand, 1917). In order to encourage the expansion of vineyards, other agreements were created, such as the 'perpetual tenancy' (*locatairie perpetuelle*) in Montpellier (Grand, 1917: 100). The *complantatio*, or similar contracts, created to promote growth in viniculture were also used in Spain until the nineteenth century (Piqueras Haba, 2007). On these contracts, see Costa, 1981.

5 A variant contract was used in the regions of Sitges and Garraf (Moreno Claverías, 1995) and the area of Tarragona (Andreu, 1994): the 'ploughing contract.' The holder of the beneficial ownership subleased a piece of land to a peasant who would plant grapevines there. In exchange, the peasant held the land for ten to fifteen years and kept the harvest. After the established period passed, the vineyard would return in full to the landowner. This contract was not emphyteutic in nature.

for their work. This was traditionally considered a medieval contract, but it is now known that it was still in use up to the nineteenth century (Piqueras Haba, 2007). In other words, the *complantatio* was not a relic of the past but a type of agreement that continued to be used at either party's discretion[6].

In the Old Catalonia (roughly the area north of the Llobregat river) the *complantatio* contract was widespread in the tenth century (Aventín and Salrach, 2000: 459). The sources for the period indicate that the land was actually divided between both parties. In his work on the New Catalonia, J. M. Salrach (Salrach, 2001) found *complantatio* contracts from the twelfth century that also stipulated the real division of the land.

The *complantatio* contract was problematic for landowners: by reducing the size of their landholdings, they limited the number of times they could engage in this kind of arrangement. That is why the right of *fadiga* was introduced[7]. In some instances, a clause was added that prevented the peasant from selling his part of the land to noblemen and clerics (Salrach, 2001: 235). However, this situation also begs the question: was the cost of planting grapevines worth ceding the ownership rights over half the property? It could be argued that peasants solely profited solely from what the grapevines produced, which could allow for the vineyard to be divided between the two parties as long as the plants were alive. Once the grapevines were dead, the land should return to the landowner. In this context, during the twelfth and thirteenth centuries, several clauses began to appear which sought to ensure that the property returned to the landowner. Although the vineyard was actually divided in two, in 1168, for instance, the monastery of Poblet determined that the property held by the peasant could be bequeathed to his progeny, but only until their deaths, when the vineyard would return to the monastery[8]. If the vintage was considered remuneration for the peasants' work, then, once the plants were dead, those peasants no longer deserved to be compensated and everything went back to the starting point. This example could be the origin of the *rabassa morta* contract: the property was actually divided but the peasant had to return his half once the plants were dead.

In the context of *complantatios*, there were some institutions that had no interest in directly exploiting the vineyards, so they started to implement other

6 In France this contract was known as *complant*, *meplant* or *mi-plant* and was used mostly during the medieval period. For instance, in Poitou, it was commonplace to divide the land in half but in the eleventh century the usual was the division of the harvest. In Provence the division lasted for the tenant's lifetime, however they also adopted a system of paying with a portion of the harvest (Piqueras Haba, 2007: 8).

7 In 1072, the right of *fadiga* was institutionalized to around thirty days. Before this date it was only exercised when considered convenient. Pere Benito affirms that it was this agreement that allowed the landowner to recover his property (Benito, 2003).

8 In 1021, the vineyard was shared in exchange for an annual rent during the farmer's lifetime. Once the farmer died, the property would return to the landowner (Aventín & Salrach, 2000).

forms of agreements. Sometimes the land was transferred for cultivation, but once peasants planted the grapevines the property was no longer divided between both parties. Peasants accepted to farm the whole vineyard in exchange for three quarters of the produce. Actually, it was a fair exchange. If the peasant had the right to half the land and harvest when the property was divided, with this contract he obtained his full share plus half of the landowner's (who benefitted from not having to work on the land). The landowner, in return, was entitled to a quarter of the land's production and a cultivated vineyard, which would return to him once the grapevines were dead.

These conditions indicate that the *rabassa morta* system evolved from the medieval *complantatio*, which was problematic and contradictory, and resulted in solutions that were similar to the eighteenth-century *rabassa morta* contract.

III. Farming Contracts and the Expansion of Vineyards in Central Catalonia during the Seventeenth Century

During the seventeenth century there was an increase in the demand for wine, which led to the uneven expansion of viticulture in Catalonia (Valls Junyent, 2004). Farmers who held beneficial ownership, or owned allodial lands, were interested in increasing the amount of land that could be cultivated; in other cases, they wanted to benefit from the higher demand for vintage by receiving a share of the production. This impulse drove farmers to look for contracts to expand vineyards over uncultivated and forested lands, which resulted in different legal solutions. The *rabassa morta* contract was one of these solutions, albeit not the only one. Nevertheless, it became the most prevalent contract almost everywhere in the eighteenth century.

The planting contract between two parties: One of the methods landowners used to expand their cultivated lands was employing the updated version of the medieval *complantatio*. The land was still divided, however the peasants only enjoyed their property as long as the grapevines survived or for a predetermined period of time. The labour force at this time was scarce in Catalonia due to low population, and the peasants' interest in having their own vineyard favoured this type of contract.

Complantatio has been frequently overlooked – mostly because it was considered an exclusively medieval practice – but it is constantly mentioned in studies analysing the spread of viniculture. In 1601 in Mataró, Bartomeu Marc ceded two forested areas for the purpose of planting grapevines. The grapevines had to be cultivated over a twelve-year period, and once they were planted, the property would be divided in half: one for the landowner and the other for the farmer. The agreement clearly stated that the landowner did not have money to plant the grapevines, which is why he would compensate the peasant for his work by transferring half of the property. There was also an additional stipulation, which was frequently present: the *rabassa morta* clause, that is, once the grapevines died, the peasant's half would return to the landowner (Giménez Blasco, 1998: 219)[9].

Are these isolated examples? Nowadays it is impossible to tell because this issue has not been researched exhaustively, but we believe that a significant part of the expansion of viniculture was carried out through this legal formula. The data from the region of Bages, in Central Catalonia, seems to confirm it.

From the planting contract between two parties to planting for a share: We have analysed the *capbreus* (inventories of the lords' patrimony and the peasants' obligations) of several villages in the area around Bages so we could determine the evolution of farming contracts in this region. The Navarcles *capbreu* of 1635 mentions planting contracts between two parties for thirteen landholdings in Navarcles, Valldelshorts, and Olzinelles[10]. In all these cases, the contract specified that once the grapevines were planted, the property would be divided in half, but on condition that once the grapevines were dead (*soca perduda* or *rabassa morta*) the land would return to the landowner.

Over the years, a new legal formula emerged, which was known as the 'right to plant for a share' (*concessió a plantar a certes parts*). It seems likely that at first *mas* farmers were interested in having their own vineyard, and planting contracts between two parties facilitated this. However, as time went by, *masos* already had the vineyards they needed, and there was an increase in both the available workforce and the pressure of peasants who wanted access to the land to plant grapevines. All these elements brought about a change in the terms of the contracts. Vineyards were no longer divided up; now peasants farmed the entire property surrendering a quarter of the vintage and the land only returned to the landowner once the grapevines died (*a soca morta*). This type of agreement is the one which most closely resembles the *rabassa morta* contract, although it still lacked the emphyteutic terminology[11].

Although this legal formula was commonplace, there were issues concerning the legality of some of its aspects. Could peasants sell their part of the land to someone else? Did they have to inform the landowner of the decision even though they considered the land as theirs? The right of *fadiga* could have remedied these problems, but the contracts of the period do not mention it. Did these new landholdings, developed within an emphyteutic context, have to pay the *lluïsme*? Did they have to pay a part of the rent owed by the *mas*

---

9 Other examples can be found in Argentona (Badosa Coll, 1979) in 1666 and in the Alt Penedès in 1626 (Parés, 1944).

10 We have used the Navarcles *capbreus* of 1635 and 1687 (Archive of the Monastery of San Benet de Bages, and Archive of the Monastery of Montserrat), the Artés *capbreu* of 1697 (Cathedral Archive of Vic) and the *capbreus* of Sant Iscle de Bages (which were kindly provided by Marc Torra).

11 The Artés *capbreu* of 1691 (Arxiu Capitular de Vic) contains thirteen examples of this type of contracts. These include mentions of 'planting between two parties' from 1663, 1675, 1675, 1676, 1678, 1682, 1693, and of 'planting for a share' in 1669, 1681, 1687, 1687, and 1693. The second formula was commonly used in the later years.

farmer who held the emphyteutic lease? It is easy to imagine how emphyteusis solved these situations. Besides, the transition from the 'planting for a share' system to the emphyteutic sublease was relatively easy.

Agrarian contracts in this period increasingly used this formula. In 1674, in the parish of Viladecavalls, there was an example of a sublease contract with a *rabassa* clause. Jaume Tapias, a farmer, heir to *mas* Tapias, in Viladecavalls, transferred (*establia*) an uncultivated land of the size of one *quartera* (0.294 ha.) to Valentí Oliveres, a farmer from Navarcles, with the stipulation that Oliveres had to grow grapevines there for eight years. The latter had to pay a fifth of the production, ferment the grapes in Tapias's vats, accept a weight control during the wine harvest, and pay eighteen *diners* to help Tapias defray the rent he owed[12]. This contract had the same nature as the 'planting for a share' agreement but it already introduced the verb *establir* (literally, 'establish', a usual term in emphyteutic leases) and stipulated that the peasant who received the land had to help the sublessor pay their own rent.

In order to find the ideal formula to channel the expansion of viniculture in the seventeenth century, the 'planting contract between two parties' was replaced by the 'planting for a share', which later evolved into the *rabassa morta* sublease. By the end of the seventeenth century, the new contracts already used the term emphyteusis, they lasted as long as the grapevines were alive (*a rabassa morta*), and the peasant had to pay a share of the grape harvest and an entrance fee to the sublessor[13]. However, we are not sure whether this formula was used in other regions[14].

---

12 The peasant had to help the beneficial owner to pay the direct lord, because the peasant cultivated part of the *mas*. Notarial books of Viladecavalls, 11 March 1674, Parish Archive of Calders.

13 In other areas such as Anoia and Penedès the peasants were obligated to plant a certain number of grapevines every year in order to increase the vineyard's size (JORBA SERRA, 2011: 222-259). This was a mechanism used to expand the vineyards, and it also stipulated who was responsible for planting.

14 Historians have found very few examples of *rabassa morta* contracts in the sixteenth century. For example, in Argentona, a *capbreu* from the second half of the sixteenth century mentioned a land transfer that included clauses for planting grapevines: paying a quarter of the production and returning the property once the plants were dead (*cuiusdam pecie terre quam dictus quondam vir meus vendidit durantibus vitis sive rabases in eadem plantatis*) (AVENTÍN and SALRACH, 2000: 496-497). Eva Serra's works confirm the use of *rabassa morta* contracts in Sentmenat (SERRA, 1988: 351-352). An example from 1661 stipulates: ... *Stabilio et emphiteosim do et concedo... usque ad primas rabatias tantum instrumentum ut dicitur a rabassa mort et non amplius...* The text clearly indicates that there was a land transfer (*establiment*) and a *rabassa morta* clause. This assertiveness cannot be found in any other document. In the Penedès region the first contract of this kind dates to 1623 (PARES, 1944) and the same formula was used in another contract from 1670 (MORENO CLAVERÍAS, 1995).

IV. The *rabassa morta* contract

The evolution of the emphyteutic formula was a logical step in light of past experiences and the philosophies regarding the compensation of peasants for planting grapevines. Although these contracts included the *rabassa morta* clause, they also allowed the aforementioned technique of '*colgats i capficats*' to keep the grapevines alive and producing fruit[15]. There was a long tradition of dividing property rights into different dominions. Therefore, in the eighteenth century, it made no sense to question whether the *rabassa morta* contract was an emphyteusis or not. Beneficial owners felt adequately remunerated by a system that allowed them to obtain a share of the production with minimal oversight and expense.

- In the eighteenth century the *rabassa morta* contract was very similar to the emphyteutic lease from a legal point of view (Giralt, 1965: 6). There is significant overlap between these two kinds of agreements, as the analysis of hundreds of surviving contracts from the eighteenth century shows:
- The most common expression used by notaries when writing a contract had a strong emphyteutic component: 'establishes and is granted in emphyteusis *ad primas vittes*, commonly *rabassa morta*'
- It involved the transfer of the dominium utile to the *rabasser*, a basic and definitive characteristic of any emphyteutic contract. For example, in the postmortem inventories of *rabassers* the grapevines were included as immovable goods, while for their sublessors they were listed as a right, similar to the right of subemphyteutas[16].
- The *rabasser* paid an entrance fee (a few chickens, a certain amount of money, etc.) that symbolized the alienation of the beneficial ownership of the property. Later, this entrance fee changed and became dependent on the prevailing economic situation (the higher the price of the wine, the higher the entrance fee).
- As with the emphyteutic lease, there was a fixed fee, in addition to a fraction of the production, which consisted of a few chickens, a set amount of grain or money.
- Like in the emphyteutic lease, the *rabasser* was obliged to make improvements to the land he received. He had to follow the 'uses and customs of the good farmer' (*a ús costum de bon pages*). This meant the *rabasser* should practice the technique of the *colgats i capficats*, which could extend the lifespan of the grapevines indefinitely (Giralt, 1965: 3-24).

---

15 The '*colgats i capficats*' was a technique which consisted of replacing a dead grapevine with the vine shoot of a living one. That way, it was understood that the vineyard was continuously reproducing so the contract became indefinite.

16 During the second half of the eighteenth century, more than 70% of the landless peasants are described as *rabassers* in the inventories from Penedès. However, it must be noted that only an approximate 15% of the people in the region had inventories written after their death (Moreno Claverías, 2004).

During this period of expansion and dominance of the *rabassa morta* contract, notaries had no doubts about its emphyteutic nature. For instance, in 1784, Jaume Tos i Urgellès insisted that this type of contract, which was terminated after the death of the first grapevines planted, was emphyteutic. Tos stated that the emphyteutic contract could be either in perpetuity or temporary, and that it could include additional agreements or conditions. It also required the payment of an entrance fee and a rent, which could be paid either in money or in kind (Tos, 1786: 101; Moreno Claverías, 1995).

However, some jurists, many of whom also owned great vineyards and were sublessors themselves, assimilated this contract to a regular land lease or a sharecropping agreement, an interpretation accepted by some historians. For instance, Juan Carmona and James Simpson argue that the *rabassa morta* contract is not emphyteutic. They believe that the *rabassa morta* system, similar to French and Italian sharecropping contracts (Carmona and Simpson, 2003: 147-176)[17]. only gave the peasants rights over the grapevines, not the land, and only for a limited period of time – until the death of the plant. This is the same argument that some sublessors used in order to recover their lands once the price of wine became very tempting, but not before. Nevertheless, if this were so evident, landowners would not have had so many problems incorporating the *rabassa morta* contract into other legal formulas, such as the land lease or the sharecropping agreement, which became more desirable after the boom in the wine industry.

Moreover, if the *rabassers* were unsure about their ownership rights over the land – not just the grapevines – they would not have had enough incentive to maximize the output of the land. Dominium utile could be sold, used to guarantee a loan and, more importantly, bequeathed to their descendants. This issue was clearly discussed in a report on 'the means to maximize the use of the land', written in 1796. The text stated that a father believed he had left his son a good inheritance when he bequeathed the exploitation rights to him. Also it said that many young labourers did not wait for anything else in order to get married; and that single women thought they have reached the height of their happiness when they married a man who held a *rabassa morta* contract over a vineyard[18]. Although this contract was not a cure-all (the landholdings were small required a significant amount of work, and the payments and fees were expensive[19]), it is evident that it provided landless

17 The legal formula that presents more similarities with the rabassa morta contract is the *bail a complant* and its analysis shows the difficulties to differentiate between the rights of the landowner and those of the peasant (Grand, 1917).

18 Dn. Maximiliano Oliveras de Plana (1796): 'Memoria sobre los medios de sacar la mejor utilidad de la tierra o sobre los diferentes medios de cultivarla'. Arxiu de la Reial Acadèmia de Ciències i Arts de Barcelona, Libro de Actas, 1764-1815, 3rd volume, box 1.

19 During the second half of the eighteenth century in the region of Penedès, the average size of a smallholding transferred through a *rabassa morta* contract was approximately one hectare. Although some peasants held exploitation rights over several holdings, land concentration

peasants with the economic stability that a traditional sharecropping contract could not.

In the second half of the nineteenth century, most jurists were absolutely clear about the fact that the *rabassa morta* contract was neither a regular land lease nor a sharecropping agreement. For instance, Félix María Falguera, the author of *Formulari de Notaria* (1862), stated that in Catalonia *rabassa morta* contracts had never been regular land leases. He also added that all notaries labelled the *rabassa morta* contract in their registers as a temporary emphyteusis. They used the term *establiment*, which is the informal Catalan term for the emphyteutic contract. The reason behind this decision was that all these contracts entailed the payment of a fee but also recognised the *rabasser*'s dominium utile over the land[20].

V. Expansion and Chronology of *rabassa morta* Contracts

It is not easy to define the chronological and geographical spread of the *rabassa morta* contract. As previously discussed, by the end of the seventeenth century it was clearly defined in the region of Bages, in central Catalonia. There are also some examples, however scarce, in Sentmenat, the Western Vallès, Maresme, and the Upper Penedès (Serra, 1988; Roca Fabregat et al., 2001). The *rabassa morta* formula was central to the spread of vineyards in the regions of Bages, the Western and Eastern Vallès, Maresme, Garraf, Anoia, and the Alt and Baix Penedès. Its presence was not as strong in the areas of the Lower Llobregat and the Alt and Baix Camp, which were dominated by short-term sharecropping contracts.

One way of simultaneously analysing the chronological expansion of vineyards and *rabassa morta* contracts is to count the number of contracts registered by different notaries each year. This method can be problematic because there were several oral contracts that were only legalized a few years later, and some other contracts actually covered the replanting of a landholding. Several historians have used this methodology, although with different criteria; here we provide our own estimation.

---

was very exceptional. Nevertheless, a *rabasser*, unlike an emphyteutic lessee, could not exploit a substantial amount of land under this legal formula, see Moreno Claverías (2004: 620).

20 Cited by B. Jané i Jané (Jané i Jané, 1934). Other authors from the nineteenth and the beginning of the twentieth centuries also saw the *rabassa morta* contract as a temporary emphyteusis. Cardellach, Comes, Brocà, Duran i Bas, Benach i Sonet, Maspons i Anglasell, and Parès i Borrell defend the right of the emphyteutic lessee over the land. This legal tradition affected Supreme Court resolutions, which follow this interpretation. By including a chapter about emphyteutic contracts (*De los foros y otros contratos análogos al de enfiteusis*), the Civil Code from 1889 confirmed that these contracts implied the existence of two separate dominions (Article 2, Title 7, Book IV).

Figure 8.1. *Rabassa morta* contracts in Catalonia in the nineteenth century

The spread of viniculture throughout Catalonia (see Table 8.1) began at different times in different regions. In Bages, the *rabassa morta* contract appeared at the end of the seventeenth century, while in the Alt and Baix Penedès, Anoia, and the Baix Camp these contracts only emerged in significant numbers in the mid-eighteenth century. However, this gap in the regional development of viniculture did not prevent the Upper Penedès from becoming the area with the highest number of registered contracts. In fact, the amount of contracts signed in that region was greater than the contracts signed in the rest of the areas combined (1040 *rabassa morta* contracts between 1790 and 1800, or 95 per year on average). Does this hint at a process of contract specialization? Everything points in that direction, although there were also some oral contracts (years or decades old) that were now being registered by the notaries. Viniculture expanded during the last third of the eighteenth century and the first half of the nineteenth century.

Table 8.1. *Rabassa morta* contracts signed in different regions of Catalonia (18th-19th centuries)

	Bages	Index	Piera (Anoia)	Index	Valls	Index	Baix Penedes	Index	Sentmenat Palau Solita (E Vallès)	Index	Alt Penedes	Index
	n	1790-1799 = 100	n	1790-1799 = 100	n	1790-1799 = 100	n	1790-1799 = 100	N	1790-1799 = 100	N	1790-1799 = 100
1700-1709	10	4.5		0.0							5	0.48
1710-1719	175	78.8	1	0.5							0	0.00
1720-1729	244	109.9	3	1.6							45	4.33
1730-1739	82	36.9	16	8.8			4	1.8			10	0.96
1740-1749	262	118.0	57	31.3	3	1.4	23	10.5			290	27.88
1750-1759	301	135.6	79	43.4	28	10.6	58	26.4			340	32.69
1760-1769	148	66.7	139	76.4	100	34.1	189	85.9			490	47.12
1770-1779	316	142.3	290	159.3	238	144.7	275	125.0	78	40.6	520	50.00
1780-1789	176	79.3	87	47.8	87	51.6	133	60.5	27	14.1	360	34.62
1790-1799	222	100.0	182	100.0	164	100.0	220	100.0	192	100.0	1040	100.00
1800-1809	112	50.5	33	18.1					83	43.2	267	25.67

	Bages	Index	Piera (Anoia)	Index	Valls	Index	Baix Penedes	Index	Sentmenat Palau Solita (E Vallès)	Index	Alt Penedes	Index
	n	1790-1799 = 100	n	1790-1799 = 100	n	1790-1799 = 100	n	1790-1799 = 100	N	1790-1799 = 100	N	1790-1799 = 100
1810-1819	412	185.6	57	31.3					62	32.3	751	72.21
1820-1829	277	124.8	188	103.3					98	51.0	966	92.88
1830-1839	137	61.7	175	96.2					1	0.5	761	73.17
1840-1849	58	26.1	415	228.0							1131	108.75
	2932		1722		620		901		541		6926	

Source: Plans Maestra (2010); Valls Junyent (1996); Andreu (1994); Querol (2001); Garrabou & Tello, (2004); Moreno Claverías (1995); Colome Ferrer (1990)[21].

21 These estimates present some problems. For instance, in the region of the Alt Penedès there is only extant information for the contracts signed in the years that end in 5 and 0. In order to homogenize this with the other data sets, we have multiplied the number of documents by 5, except between 1790-1800 when the real data have survived. Therefore, these numbers are just an estimate. In the case of Bages we are not sure if our calculations include all surviving notarial registers. In Sentmenat there are only extant contracts from 1770 onwards, but we do not know whether there were earlier contracts. Moreover, we cannot determine how many oral contracts were made or how many of the surviving contracts were written by the notary years after the original agreement took place. Nevertheless, we believe that this trend and chronological evolution has been shown clearly.

Table 8.2. Landholdings subleased under the terms of *rabassa morta* contracts in some villages according to the *amillaraments* (1860-1872)

	Rabassers	% of the town's land cultivated under *rabassa morta* contracts	% of vineyards planted under *rabassa morta* contracts
BAGES			
Artés	295	40,6	60,1
Calders	461	27,2	67,5
Castelladral	264	8,2	74,7
Rajadell	266	14,3	79,7
Rocafort	184	32	80,7
Santpedor	454	32,6	55,9
Sallent	1261	22,25	68,1
Sant Fruitós de Bages	604	30,07	36,05
ANOIA			
Piera	618	32,1	41,5
Pierola	607	59,1	84,1
Masquefa	388	63,8	75,5
PENEDÈS			
Santa Margarida i els Monjos		52,7	75,-
Gelida		37,05	72,8

Source: (Ferrer Alòs, 1987; Colome Ferrer, 1996; Valls Junyent, 1996; Carmona and Simpson, 1999). We gathered the data for Sant Fruitós de Bages, Santpedor, and Sallent ourselves.

How much land was cultivated under the *rabassa morta* contract? The *amillaraments* – taxation reports drafted between 1853 and 1872 that recorded ownership rights over the land – highlight the importance of this type of agreement. Some of these documents also mention the *rabassers*, which makes it possible to calculate the amount of land subleased in certain villages (Table 8.2).

In the villages with extant data, the amount of landholdings subleased under a *rabassa morta* contract represents a variable percentage of the total area of the town. The town's forested lands and the active vineyards influence this ratio. Therefore, it is more relevant to analyse the percentage of vineyards that were cultivated under the terms of such agreements, which, in most towns, oscillates between the 60% and 70%, although this number could be lower in some areas where small landholders opted to exploit their own lands.

Table 8.3. Land exploited under *rabassa morta* contracts in Piera, Pierol, and Masquefa (Anoia) in 1860

	Landowners	Land size (ha.)	Land directly exploited (ha.)	% land directly exploited	Number of *rabassers*	Size of land exploited with a *rabassa morta* contract (ha)	% of land exploited with a *rabassa morta* contract	% vineyards of land exploited with a *rabassa morta* contract
0.1-5 ha.	252	406.10	382.83	94.27	21	25.5	6.3	8.1
5-10 ha.	45	321.13	206.43	64.28	74	114.7	35.7	46.1
10-20 ha.	30	416.11	338.73	81.40	43	77.4	18.6	21.9
20-40 ha.	22	590.37	328.74	55.68	138	261.6	44.3	63.3
40-80 ha.	30	1729.79	1097.32	63.44	269	632.5	36.6	53.5
80-160 ha.	19	2074.066	883.56888	42.60	511.00	1190.5	57.4	78.5
More than 160 ha.	10	2491.707	1125.79848	45.18	557.00	1365.9	54.8	67.3
	408	8029.26	4363.41	54.34	1613	3668.1	45.7	60.6

Table 8.4. Land exploited under rabassa morta contracts in Sant Fruitós de Bages, Sallent, and Artés (Bages) in 1872

	Landowners	Land size (ha)	Land directly exploited (ha.)	% land directly exploited	Number of *rabassers*	Size of land exploited with a *rabassa morta* contract (ha)	% of land exploited with a *rabassa morta* contract	% vineyards of land exploited with a *rabassa morta* contract
0.1-5 ha.	512	816.5	795.3	97.4	20	21.1	2.6	2.9
5-10 ha.	51	344.6	313.6	91.0	27	28.1	8.2	8.7
10-20 ha.	15	217.2	124.7	57.4	62	89.3	41.1	49.4
20-40 ha.	21	609.3	365.7	60.0	195	238.5	39.1	58.0
40-80 ha.	28	1564.3	1016.3	65.0	386	546.7	34.9	64.5
80-160 ha.	27	3010.7	1749.1	58.1	836	1261.6	41.9	72.5
More than 160	13	2835.5	1605.5	56.6	754	1229.9	43.4	85.8
	667	9398.0	5970.2	63.5	2280	3415.2	36.3	59.6

Source: *Amillaraments* of the aforementioned towns, ACA; the data from Anoia was provided by Francesc Valls[22].

22 We used the *amillaraments*, a source which registers the landholdings owned by landwoners and, in certain cases, whether they were cultivated under the terms of *rabassa morta* contracts. The main methodological problem comes from the fact that some large landowners also possessed lands in other towns, so the difference between a small and a large landholder becomes a bit blurred. This could distort the data presented in this table.

Table 8.3 shows the properties' size, and the percentage of vineyards operating under *rabassa morta* contracts in relation to the size of the landholding in three towns in Bages (Sallent, Sant Fruitós, and Artés), and three in Anoia (Masquefa, Piera, and Pierola)[23]. Small landowners cultivated the land themselves (94% and 97% respectively), but as the size of the landholding increased, the percentage of land subleased under *rabassa morta* contracts is between 40% and 55% of the properties. These percentages are very significant, especially considering that these landholdings usually included forested and uncultivated lands kept in reserve so that they could be exploited in the future. Therefore, the most relevant percentage is that of the vineyards cultivated under the terms of *rabassa morta* contracts. In this case, it can be seen that the increase in the percentage of *rabassa morta* contracts was directly linked to the size of the landholding, so much so, that 80% (or more) of the largest properties used this legal formula. To say it in other words: large landowners only cultivated a small portion of their properties subleasing the remaining land to a second party. This table shows how large landowners match the *masos* in the area, which were the ones behind this strategy for growing vineyards.

VI. The Corruption of *rabassa morta* Contracts

From the mid-eighteenth century onwards, the foreign demand for wine and distilled spirits and the rising price of wine made vineyards a very profitable business[24]. As the number of *rabassa morta* contracts multiplied, they became the most commonly used formula; however, wine's increasing profitability affected the *rabasser*'s conditions, especially the fraction of the production they had to pay and the entrance fee. *Domini utilis* started to introduce changes to these contracts. If the demand for wine was high, it was logical to demand a higher percentage of the production or a higher entrance fee. This focus on economic factors explains the regional and chronological differences. Additionally, there was a growing interest in ensuring the land's optimal cultivation (even introducing eviction clauses) and in guaranteeing the quality of the final product (setting the day of the wine harvest, the kind of grapevines to be planted, etc.)

During this period, the increase in the benefits yielded by vineyards and demographic growth (which resulted in an increase in the demand for land) led to stricter clauses in *rabassa morta* contracts, especially in relation to their duration and emphyteutic nature. P. Vilar clearly stated

---

23 We want to thank Francesc Valls who provided us with the data for these villages.

24 On the importance of foreign demand for Catalan wines and distilled spirits see Giralt Raventos (1952); Vilar (1962); Torras Elias (1997); Torras Elias (1976); Valls Junyent (2004).

that the transfer of *rabassa morta* exploitation rights from father to son was convenient for both parties only in times of limited population growth, a surplus of empty lands, mediocre benefits, and when vineyards were just for seasonal cultivation. Once the growing population made the land scarcer and more expensive, the relationship between landowners and peasants deteriorated and these contracts became sources of conflict (Vilar, 1962: 571).

In the region of Penedès the formal analysis of the contracts and their clauses during the eighteenth century shows the deterioration of the economic and legal position of the *rabassers*. Some examples of this deterioration were:

1. As the eighteenth century progressed, the legal formula was modified, separating this type of agreement from the emphyteusis and moving it closer to a sharecropping contract. Early examples stated that the transfer was emphyteutic in nature and would last 'for the lifespan of the first grapevines, that is, what was commonly known as *a rabassa morta*'. In mid-eighteenth century it was established that the land was transferred *a rabassa morta*, and finally, in the last decade of the century contracts only stipulated that the land was granted 'for a share' as long as the grapevines lived. Half of the contracts signed between 1790 and 1800 used this formula (Moreno Claverías, 1995: 67-70). Moreover, the first *rabassa morta* contracts with a fixed duration of forty or fifty years started to appear in the Alt Penedès in the 1770s, according to the rulings of the *Reial Audiència* (the Royal Appellate Court). However, in other areas of Catalonia they did not appear until later[25].
2. Over time, *rabassers* had to pay the landowner increasingly larger portions of their harvest. In the Alt Penedès, it was common in the 1750s for rent payments to be between a sixth and a seventh of the production, although this rate tended to disappear when more contracts demanded a third of the production (50% of the contracts in 1780 and 60% in 1795). Valls shows how in Piera – in the region of Anoia – the percentage of the grapes paid by the peasant to the landowner increased from 17% in 1750 to 27% in 1759 (Valls Junyent, 1995: 104). In the contracts signed by the family Pedró, from Igualada, the landowner's share of the production increased from 20% to 28.7% after 1778 (Torras Ribe, 1976: 671). Querol detects a similar trend in the *rabassa morta* contracts from the Baix Penedès during the second half of the eighteenth century (Querol, 2001)[26].

---

25 In Bages, for example, they did not appear until the second half of the nineteenth century (Ferrer Alòs, 1987: 459-462).

26 When studying the percentage of production demanded by landowners in the nineteenth century, it should be noted that tithes had been abolished. A change from a quarter to a third of the harvest can be interpreted as hardening conditions, but it could mean the assimilation of the old tithe. Paying a third of the production was the same as paying a quarter plus the tithe (Colomé, 1995: 62).

3. The entrance fee, which symbolized the payment to the landowner for the alienation of the landholding's *dominium utile* as seen in the traditional emphyteutic contracts, decreased throughout the century (it was required in 70% of the contracts in 1745 and in only 40% in 1795). This was another way of separating the *rabassa morta* contract from the traditional emphyteusis. Nevertheless, in those cases where the entrance fee survived, the traditional two chickens were substituted for an increasingly larger amount of money in order to compensate for the price increases of both land and wine. It could be said that the entrance fee acted as a means of regulating the wine economy.
4. The obligations of *rabassers* multiplied over time. These included: trimming the vine shoots of the sublessor's vineyard and transporting them to his house at their own expense; transporting the share of the wine harvest they had to surrender; paying for the right to use the sublessor's wine cellar and vats; repairing the roads, making terraces and *formiguers* (sing. *formiguer*, a pile of dry wood covered with dirt, which is burned and spread as fertilizer); allowing the sublessor's cattle to graze on their lands; working on the landowner's property if he needed help; paying an additional amount of money to hire one or two labourers so they could make sure the produce was evenly distributed, etc.
5. Concurrently, sublessors actively intervened in the exploitation of the vineyard. While the early contracts only specified that the *rabasser* had to cultivate the land following 'the good uses and customs of a good farmer', these contracts increasingly stipulated which specific tasks had to be done and which did not. For instance, they insisted upon a specific method of planting the grapevines – normally *a rasa oberta* (open ditch) – and they determined the distance between grapevines and between each row of plants, as the following example shows: 'he has to grow ten thousand grapevines with five handspans between each of them and ten between rows'. They forced the *rabasser* to notify the landowners of their activities at certain times (always during the planting season and during the grape harvest) and they threatened them with eviction if they did not fulfill certain tasks: 'if the *rabasser* spends more than a year without trimming the grapevines or three years without digging them, the sublease will end' (Moreno Claverías, 1995: 92-97).

In conclusion, landowners wanted to ensure their control over the lands leased out by highlighting the temporary nature of the agreement. Meanwhile *rabassers* suffered the increase of the payments and obligations over the land that they considered theirs until the grapevines died; which, thanks to the technique of the *colgats i capficats*, never actually happened. The conflict between landowners and *rabassers* was ready to ignite.

VII. The '*rabassers* Conflict'

In 1765 some landowners started to interpret the contract differently. As previously discussed, they were interested in toughening the conditions of the contract and obtaining a higher percentage of the production or a larger entrance fee. They also tried to improve their benefits by recovering the land and exploiting it under other legal formulas. Their desire to obtain more favourable terms and conditions explains their willingness to do away with the *colgats i capficats* technique, which effectively made the *rabassa morta* contract an indefinite one. In 1765 a group of landowners presented and won a lawsuit before the *Reial Audiència* demanding the prohibition of this technique.

These first rulings were completely ignored because they did not benefit anyone. Waiting for the grapevines to die meant that grapevines would steadily produce less fruit during their last fifteen to twenty years, which meant that both landowners and tenants would reap fewer profits. The solution was to challenge the contract's duration: in 1778, a ruling from the *Reial Audiència* authorized the use of *colgats i capficats* but limited the duration of the contracts to fifty years[27]. However, this time limitation did not appear in the notarial registers for many years. In the Alt Penedès, for example, the *rabassa morta* contracts with the fifty-year duration clause were not predominant until 1860-1870. In the region of Bages the contracts maintained their traditional conditions during most of the nineteenth century: they only ended with the grapevines' death and they allowed the use of *colgats i capficats* technique.

Neverthelees, *rabassers* defended the emphyteutic character of their agreement since the beginning of the conflict. In 1793 they wrote the first *rabasser* report (*memorial*) to the king (Carlos IV) in order to complain about the rulings pronounced by the *Reial Audiència* regarding the duration of *rabassa morta* contracts. They defended the use of the *colgats i capficats* technique and the fact that the contract was in perpetuity: 'To Your Majesty they humbly beg... that you order and arrange that the emphyteutic contracts... should remain in force as long as, with the work and industry of their owners and the help of the new shoots, the vines remain fruitful and able to support the expenses of their cultivation and the rents or the part of the harvest that were imposed at the time of its granting'[28].

In 1805, Martorell, El Papiol, and other villages wrote to the King making explicit reference to the landowners' opportunism and stressed the emphyteutic character of the contract: 'But it is in this flourishing state [of the exploitation] when to the true or apparent lord of the land, ignoring or not taking care of what there was before and of the sweat and blood that has

27 For an excellent and rigorous summary of the *rabasser* conflict see Giralt (1965).

28 The plea was made by representatives from Caldes and other towns (Arxiu de la Corona d'Aragó, Audiència, *Acordadas*, 1014, ff. 568-574).

made it beautiful to look at, this canon, that in another time was so lavish to his ancestors, seems short'[29].

In the nineteenth century there was another debate concerning property rights that also affected *rabassa morta* contracts. The liberal revolution tried to simplify the rights over the land in order to progress towards full property rights, but the emphyteusis presented a real problem. The rights over the landholdings were divided between the person who owned the property (dominium directum), the holder of the first beneficial ownership, and a third party who held a second-order dominium utile (the *rabasser*). Who should become the full owner of a landholding according to the parameters of the liberal revolution? Could the *rabasser* become the owner? (Ferrer Alòs, 2001: 78). Each group used the arguments that benefitted them the most: landowners started to introduce a fixed duration into the contracts, changed the name of the agreement, eliminated any emphyteutic reference, and denied its emphyteutic nature, etc. *Rabassers* joined egalitarian movements such as federal republicanism, and continued to defend the contract as emphyteutic, as it had always been.

During the nineteenth and the beginning of the twentieth centuries, the reports (*memorials*) in defence of the rights of the *rabassers* grew, showing an increasingly stronger class conscience. In 1861, for example, the *Ressenya en defensa de las vinyas a rabassa morta y modo pràctich de amillarar-las* (Review in Defence of *rabassa morta* Vineyards and a Practical Way of Improving Them) clearly shows the two sides of the debate surrounding the contracts' duration. The document shows how landowners wanted the emphyteutic *rabassa morta* contract to last only sixty years. However, the *rabassers* or *emfiteutes* considered that this clause did not affect them or their contracts. They considered that the limitation on the duration of the contract conditioned those agreements in which the landowner only leased the right to use the land, which was not their case 'since they had also been transferred property or dominium utile over land'. Therefore, *rabassers* believed that a law imposing short-term contracts 'only affected regular land leases, which lasted as long as the first grapevines were alive but not their own *rabassa morta* contracts, which they considered emphyteutic' (D.D.A.A., 1861: 5-28). For instance, the *rabassers* from Rubí reached an agreement to defend the indefinite duration of *rabassa morta* contracts on the basis of the *colgats i capficats* technique. They also considered that such duration provided the legal grounds for the payment of rents (*cens*) and the 'redemption' (*redempció*) (Jané i Jané, 1934: 255-271).

The conflict revolving around property rights was partly settled after the arrival of the phylloxera plague in Catalonia in 1879. This pest had a significant impact on the struggle over land rights. If the grapevines died, the *rabassa morta*

---

29 The plea was made by representatives from Martorell and other towns (Arxiu de la Corona d'Aragó, Audiència, Acordadas, 1023, ff. 52-76. 1805).

contract ended, so the holders of the first dominium utile recovered the land[30]. Arguing that the grapevines were dead, they benefitted from the situation because it allowed them to get back the dominium utile they had subleased. Later, they transferred the land again in order to replant the grapevines but under different formulas which did not involve the legal complications of the *rabassa morta* contract, such as regular land leases or long-term sharecropping agreements (*parceria*). Therefore, the phylloxera plague signalled the end of the traditional *rabassa morta* contract and its emphyteutic nature (Giralt, 1965: 126).

VIII. Conclusions

The emphyteutic contract provided access to land in Catalonia since the Middle Ages. However, from the sixteenth century onwards, dominium utile evolved becoming hereditary, demanding smaller rents, turning farmers into quasi-owners of the land, and giving them the initiative to work the property as they saw fit.

The expansion of vineyards in the seventeenth century emerged despite the lack of capital needed to invest in big plantations and the need to look for alternative solutions. Vineyards required a substantial amount of work and money and they did not yield any fruits for the first four years. It became necessary to reward this investment. There were several legal formulas that facilitated the expansion of vineyards: farmers having to plant a certain number of grapevines each year; the 'ploughing contract' (*contracte de rompuda*), which set aside some land for cultivation; profitting from the vintage for a period of time before returning it to the lessor; and the *complantatio*, which implied planting the grapevines and dividing the property in half between the lessor and the farmer.

The formula of the *complantatio* was always limited by the idea that the farmer could only benefit from his share of the land as long as the grapevines were alive. Once the vines died, the land would return to the landowner. In some areas, the fact that *masos* could not further expand their vineyards, joined with the population growth, and the increase in demand for wine led to the evolution of the *complantatio* into the 'planting for a share' contract (*plantació a certes parts*). The farmer now planted and worked the entire vineyard in exchange for a fraction of the harvest (usually a quarter). The idea of returning the land to the landowner, the one who held the first dominium utile, once the plants were dead (*rabassa morta*) was still present. By the end of the seventeenth century, these practices contributed to the terms and conditions of the *rabassa morta* contract that the landowners used to plant grapevines. It had a clear emphyteutic nature so the peasant obtained a second-order dominium utile.

30 For the eviction process following the arrival of the phylloxera plague see (Ferrer Alòs, Álvarez Arroniz et al., 1992) (Planas Maresma and Valls Junyent, 2011).

During the eighteenth century a series of problems and debates arouse. The rise in the price of wine led to a clash between both parties regarding the rent and the increase in the percentage of the harvest paid to landowners. Eventually, this spurred a conflict over the duration of the contract. The terms *rabassa morta* were very ambiguous, especially because the farmer could replant the grapevines so that they technically never died. Once the liberal revolution began, and the socialists and anarchists emerged with ideas that challenged current property rights, those who held rights over the land tried to extend their control over the entire property. Any method was valid: challenging the emphyteutic character of the contract, changing the contract's clauses to limit its duration, and altering emphyteutic formulas. The clash between those who leased the lands (who wanted to be sure that they would be able to recover them in the future) and the *rabassers* (who did not want to lose the land) led to a very long conflict in rural Catalonia.

The *rabassa morta* contract was a 'subemphyteusis', that is, an agrarian contract in line with the legal traditions of Catalonia. The changes experienced since the end of the eighteenth century put this formula into question; however, it was the phylloxera plague – that killed the grapevines and subsequently terminated most of the contracts – which finally ended the emphyteutic debate. Nevertheless, landowners used again long-term leases with similar clauses to those of the *rabassa morta* contract, but without using emphyteutic terminology. They wanted to benefit from the advantages offered by the traditional *rabassa morta* system, while simultaneously eliminating its inconveniences. Thus, the *rabassa morta* contract evolved into a long-term sharecropping agreement.

Bibliography

Andreu, Jordi (1994), *El Camp de Tarragona i el Priorat durant els segles XVIII i XIX*. Barcelona, Univeritat Autònoma de Barcelona.

Aventin, Mercè & Salrach, Josep Maria (2000), 'La explotación de la viña y el mercado de la tierra vitícola en la Catalunya medieval', en M. D. Passano, *La vite e il vino. Storia e diritto (secoli XI-XIX)*, Roma, I, p. 453-500.

Badosa Coll, Elisa (1979), *Actituds i comportaments econòmics d'un sector del clergat barceloní (1670-1835)*, Universitat de Barcelona.

Benito, Pere (2003), *Senyoria de la terra i tinença pagesa al comtat de Barcelona (segles XI-XIII)*, Barcelona, CSIC. Institució Milà i Fontanals.

Brocà, Guillem Maria (1987), *Historia del derecho de Cataluña especialemnte del civil y exposición de las instituciones del derecho civil del mismo territorio en relación con el código civil de España y la jurisprudencia*, Barcelona, Generalitat de Catalunya.

Carmona, Juan & Simpson, James (1999), 'A l'entorn de la qüestió agrària catalana: el contracte de rabassa morta i els canvis en la viticultura (1890-1929)', *Recerques*, 38, p. 105-124.

CARMONA, Juan & SIMPSON, James (2003), *El laberinto de la agricultura española. Instituciones, contratos y organización entre 1850 y 1936*, Zaragoza, Prensas Universitarias de Zaragoza.

COLOMÉ FERRER, Josep (1990), 'Les formes d'accés a la terra a la comarca de l'Alt Penedès durant el segle XIX: el contracte de rabassa morta i l'expansió vitivinícola', *Estudis d'Història Agrària*, 8, p. 123-144.

COLOMÉ FERRER, Josep (1995), 'La viticultura catalana durant la primera meitat del segle XIX. Notes per a un reflexió', *Recerques*, 30, p. 47-68.

COLOMÉ FERRER, Josep (1996), *L'especialització vitícola a la Catalunya del segle XIX. La comarca del Penedès*. Barcelona, Universitat de Barcelona.

CONGOST, Rosa & al. (1999), 'L'evolució del contracte de masoveria (Girona, s. XV-XVIII)', en Rosa Congost & Lluís To, *Homes, masos, història. La Catalunya del Nord-est (segles XI-XX)*, Barcelona, Publicacions de l'Abadia de Montserrat, p. 269-298.

CONGOST, Rosa (1988), *Els propietaris i els altres. Anàlisi d'unes relacions d'explotació. La Regió de Girona (1768-1862)*, Universitat Autònoma de Barcelona.

COSTA, Joaquín (1981), *Derecho consuetudinario y economía popular de España*, Zaragoza, Guara Editorial.

D.D.A.A. (1861), *Ressenya en defensa de las vinyas a rabassa morta y modo pràctich de amillarar-las*, Barcelona, Impremta de Joaquin Bosch, Barcelona, 1861.

FALGUERA, Félix María (1862), *Formulario completo de Notaría*, Barcelona, Impr. y Libr. Politécnica de Tomás Gorchs

FERRER ALÒS, Llorenç (1987), *Pagesos, rabassaires i industrials a la Catalunya Central (s. XVIII-XIX)*, Barcelona, Publicacions de l'Abadia de Montserrat.

FERRER ALÒS, Llorenç (2001), 'Viticultores no comerciantes. Notas sobre la evolución de la viticultura en la Catalunya Central', en Juan CARMONA, Josep COLOME, Juan PAN MONTOJO, & SIMPSON, James, *Viñas, bodegas y mercados. El cambio técnico en la vitivinicultura española (1850-1936)*, Zaragoza, Prensas Universitarias de Zaragoza, p. 69-88.

FERRER ALÒS, Llorenç, C. ALVAREZ ARRONIZ, et al. (1992), *Vinya, fil.loxera, propietat i demografia a la Catalunya Central*, Manresa, Centre d'Estudis del Bages.

GARRABOU, Ramon & TELLO, Enric (2004), 'Constructors de paisatges. Amos de masies, masovers i rabassaires al territori del Vallès (1716-1860)', en D.D.A.A., *Josep Fontana. Història i projecte social. Reconeixement a una trajectòria*, Barcelona, Crítica, p. 83-104.

GIFRE, Pere & LLUCH, Rosa (2001), 'Continuïtats del mas català abans i després de la Sentència Arbitral de Guadalupe (segles XV-XVI)', en Maria Teresa FERRER MALLOL, Josefina MUTGE VIVES & Manuel RIU RIU, *El mas català durant l'edat mitjan i la moderna (segles IX-XVIII): aspectes arqueològics, històrics, geogràfics, arquitectònics i antropològics*, Barcelona, CSIC, p. 593-610.

GIMÉNEZ BLASCO, Joan (1998), *Continuitat i canvi a les estructures econòmiques de la Catalunya del segle XVII. Mataró (1580-1710)*, Barcelona, Departament d'Història Moderna de la Universitat de Barcelona.

GIRALT RAVENTOS, Emili (1965), 'El conflicto rabassaire y la cuestión agraria en Cataluña hasta 1936', *Revista del Trabajo*, 7, p. 51-72.

Giralt Raventos, Emili (1952), 'La viticultura y el comercio catalán del siglo XVIII', *Estudios de Historia Moderna*, II, p. 159-176.

Grand, Roger (1917), *Le contrat de complant depuis les origines à nos jours*, Paris, Librairie de Recueil Sirey.

Jané i Jané, Benjamí (1934), 'Conferències sobre varietats comarcals del dret civil català', Barcelona, Acadèmia de Jurisprudència i Legislació de Catalunya p. 255-271.

Jorba Serra, Xavier (2011), *Odena. Segles XVI i XVII*, Barcelona, Parnass Edicions.

Montagut, Tomàs de (maig 1986), 'La Sentència arbitral de Guadalupe de 1486', *L'Avenç*, 93, p. 54-60.

Moreno Claverías, Belén (1995), *La contractació agrària a l'Alt Penedès Durant el segle XVIII. El contracte de rabassa morta i l'expansió de la vinya*, Barcelona, Fundació Noguera.

Parés, Sebastián (1944), 'Contratación notarial agraria en el Alto Penedés durante el siglo XIX', *La Notaria*, p. 366-387.

Piqueras Haba, Juan (2007), 'La plantación de viña a medias en España', *Eria*, 72, p. 5-22.

Planas Maresma, Jordi & Valls Junyent, Francesc (2011), *Cacics i rabassaires. Dinàmica associativa i conflictivitat social. Els Hostalets de Pierola (1890-1939)*, Vic, Eumo Editorial.

Plans Maestra, Jaume (2010), 'Els establiments a rabassa morta probable causa de la construcció de tines al Bages al segle XVIII i XIX', *Coordinadora Entitats de Pedra Seca. Butlletí Digital*, 3, p. 15-19.

Querol, Joan (2001), 'La vinya al Baix Penedès a partir dels contractes de rabassa morta (1750-1800)', en Ramon Arnabat Mata, *Els moviments socials al Penedès. Actes del II Seminari d'Història del Penedès*, Vilafranca del Penedès, Institut d'EStudis Penedesencs, p. 151-174.

Roca Fabregat, Pere, Sallas Puigdellivol, Carles, Joan et al. (2001), *Can Deu. De mas a parc*, Sabadell, Fundació Caixa de Sabadell.

Salrach, Josep Maria (2001), 'La viticultura de la Catalunya Nova després de la conquesta: societat i mercat en el segle XII', *Acta Historica et Archaelogica Mediaevalia*, 22, p. 229-256.

Serra, Eva (1980), 'El règim feudal català abans i després de la Sentència Arbitral de Guadalupe', *Recerques*, 10, p. 17-32.

Serra, Eva (1988), *Pagesos i senyors a la Catalunya del segle XVII. Baronia de Sentmenat 1590-1729*, Barcelona, Crítica.

Torras Elias, Jaume (1976), 'Aguardiente y crisis rural. Sobre la coyuntura vitícola (1793-1832)', *Investigaciones económicas*, 1, p. 45-67.

Torras Elias, Jaume (1997), 'Productes vitícoles i integració mercantil a Europa. Ss. XVI-XVIII. Una panoràmica', *Estudis d'Història Econòmica*, 14, p. 23-33.

Torras Ribé, Josep Maria (1976), 'Evolución de las cláusulas de los contratos de rabassa morta en una propiedad de la comarca de Anoia', *Hispania*, 134, p. 663-690.

Tos, Jaime (1786), *Tratado de la cabrevación, Edició i estudi introductori a càrrec de Rosa Congost,* Girona, Documenta Universitaria, 2007.

Valls Junyent, Francesc (1995), 'La rabassa morta a la comarca d'Igualada en la transició de les velles a les noves formes de propietat (1750-1850)', *Estudis d'Història Agrària,* 11, p. 89-108.

Valls Junyent, Francesc (1996), *La dinàmica del canvi agrari a la Catalunya interior. L'Anoia 1720-1860,* Barcelona, Publicacions de l'Abadia de Montserrat.

Valls Junyent, Francesc (2004), *La Catalunya atlàntica. Aiguardent i teixits a l'arrencada industrial catalana,* Vic, Eumo.

Vilar, Pierre (1962), *La Catalogne dans l'Espagne moderne.* Recherches *sur les fondements économiques des structures nationales,* Paris, S.E.V.P.E.N.

ANTÒNIA MOREY TOUS,
GABRIEL JOVER AVELLÀ

9. From 'Feudal' to 'Common' Emphyteusis in Rural Mallorca, Eighteenth to Twentieth Centuries*

I. Introduction

Numerous studies, both legal and historical, have emphasised the wide-ranging effects in the Balearic Islands of the legal concept of emphyteusis (Masot, 1979, 1985). Emphyteusis was a feudal institution in origin, derived from Roman law, and introduced to Majorca after the Catalan conquest of 1229 (Portella, 1998). In the twelfth and thirteenth centuries, Catalan jurists used the concept of emphyteusis to normalise and legitimise the rights over land and over surplus peasant produce that lords and barons had appropriated during the centuries of the formation of feudalism (Pons i Guri, 1989 and Freedman, 1988). The aim of the jurists was to impose a hierarchical structure on the web of relationships between lords (king, barons and knights)[1] and peasants (free and unfree)[2], as well as to normalise 'rights' over the appropriation of surplus product (rent) and over land. This process of normalisation was not free of social and legal conflict, as recent studies have shown (Wickham, 2000; Arnoux, 2012). Emphyteusis defined a set of land rights that were shared, yet strictly hierarchical, in which the direct lord claimed a rent (known as *censo* or *tasca*) in return for ceding the land he held. He also had the right of reversion (*fadiga*) and claimed an entry fine (*laudemium*) every time the land was sold or transmitted via inheritance. In some cases, as in Majorca, the same lords also held other rights over the lands in their domain, such as tithe and monopolies, and in other cases had also succeeded in restricting the personal freedoms of the families in their demesnes through different forms

* This paper is part of the research project HAR2014-54891-P, financed by the Spanish Ministry of Science and Innovation.

1 The ideological justification of this hierarchy was manifested in the three orders of feudal society (Duby, 1992). Even this hierarchy, however, acknowledged the role of the peasantry (Arnoux, 2012).

2 Feudal normalisation had to reconcile custom with Roman law, since the former recognised a wide gradation of servitude, whereas Roman law basically distinguished simply between free men and slaves (Freedman, 1988: 156).

Agrarian Change and Imperfect Property, ed. by Rosa Congost and Pablo F. Luna, Rural History in Europe, 15 (Turnhout, 2018), 183-206
© BREPOLS PUBLISHERS DOI 10.1484/M.RURHE-EB.5.116124

of serfdom[3]. Nonetheless, emphyteusis allowed these peasant families to sell or sub-let their land, wholly or partially, in return for rent, subject to the lord's permission. Subletting created another, distinct level of emphyteusis, in which the peasant had a right to claim rent, but could not intervene in the management of the land to the same extent as the direct lord. From the thirteenth century, this sub-emphyteusis became increasingly important in the division of landholdings and creation of new structures of property rights and exploitation of land[4]. For others, acquiring direct or full rights over land also became, in later periods, a means of consolidating property rights over land held by themselves or by others where existing property rights were divided, such as common lands (Congost, 2007).

The distinction between the two levels of emphyteusis is fundamental to understand the property rights evolution in the island. The feudal colonisation of Majorca was carried out using all the judicial means characteristic of Catalan feudalism (Romero, 1983; Montaner, 1986; Montaner, 1989; Soto, 1991 and Portella, 1998). However, emphyteusis did not imply *a priori* any particular class structure (structure of property rights and land exploitation) in the countryside. Indeed, the same legal construct that permitted the establishment of the *mas* (family farm) in Catalonia[5], also facilitated the consolidation of great estates and large farms (*possessions*) in Mallorca (Suau, 1988; Suau, 1991: 159). These same differences in landholdings in fact required legal institutions imported from Catalonia to be adapted to new social conditions. In particular, the protection of great estates was enforced by the creation of a form of tie to land, strict settlement (*fideicomiso*). The insular *fideicomiso* system does not require feudal rights over land. Unlike Castilian *Mayorazgo* (another form of *fideicomiso*), in Majorca the *fideicomiso* sistem did not require feudal property rights over land. Therefore, since the fifteenth century most of the new *fideicomiso* agreements were stablised over only the dominium utile of lands[6]. The old 'feudal' institution of emphyteusis was reshaped during the

3 On the origins of serfdom in Catalonia, see Freedman (1993) and To (1997). For later periods, see Lluch (2005).

4 For Catalonia, see Benito (2003), and for Majorca: Soto (1999); Portella (1994); Romero (1983, 1989); Suau, (1988: 152-153).

5 These different outcomes put paid to traditional (*pairalista*) claims that credit emphyteusis with the rise of a substantial peasant class (Congost, 1990: 267-293, 2009).

6 *Fideicomiso* is a type of entail of land ownership specific to the Crown of Aragon, in which heirs are named in succession, all of whom inherit just the usufruct of the land and are expressively forbidden to alienate this property without the express and special permission of the Crown (via the Council of Aragon). In practice, although *fideicomiso* differed from other land bonds, as *mayorazgo*, it had the same objective: to prevent the break-up of property (Zaforteza, 1992; Morey, 1999, 2007). In Majorca its widespread use by landowners is key to understanding the survival of large estates. It shielded large-scale property and reinforced the economic strategy of the nobility, which prioritised increasing income over production, see Morey (1999).

liberal revolution to become the key means of access to land for the peasantry (Bisson, 1977; Cela Conde, 1979 and Rosselló Verger, 1981).

Thus in Majorca we can distinguish between two historical processes of emphyteusis. The first occurred in the period following the conquest, and played a key role in the formation of a feudal hierarchy and the first colonisation of the land. A second phase occurred in the fifteenth and sixteenth centuries when a new aristocracy consolidated extensive landholdings, some of which they held as dominium directum but most of which were held under emphyteutic and sub-emphyteutic tenure. In the following centuries, conflicts over land and over *fideicomiso* were bound up with feudal emphyteusis, used to parcel out land by aristocracy and peasantry alike. Until the liberal revolution, 'feudal emphyteusis' (whether in the first wave of land cessions or in later subtenancies) and closely tied to the rights of dominium directum, dominated access to land. The second process of emphyteusis, termed 'modern' or 'common' by legal theorists, became divested of feudal rights and became the most common form of access to land in the second half of the nineteenth century and until well into the twentieth. Nonetheless, the failure to abolish dominium directum as a form of property rights would force feudal emphyteusis to reassert itself in later years, and it even continues to prove a source of conflict today.

This article will analyse the role that emphyteusis played during the period of liberal reform and the process of large-scale fragmentation of estates (from the end of the nineteenth to the first third of the twentieth century). The first section will briefly describe the development of feudal emphyteusis, and the next will address the debates generated by emphyteusis and *fideicomiso* during the period of enlightened reform and liberal revolution. The third section will analyse the impact of the break-up of large estates through the medium of 'common emphyteusis' and the conflicts that resulted from the insistence of landowners in claiming their feudal rights. In the fourth section we will focus on the survival of certain emphyteutic rights until very recently and, at the end, by way of summing-up, we will emphasise the continuing debate surrounding the still incomplete abolition of feudal emphyteusis.

I. Feudal emphyteusis: agrarian colonisation and formation of large estates

On the island, emphyteusis – according to 'the custom of Barcelona', the phrase used by manorial surveys and feudal treatises – was initially used to distribute land, rents and jurisdiction among the king and the four great feudal Catalan lords (the bishop of Barcelona, the count of Roussillon, the count of Empúries and Gaston de Montcada). This first distribution divided the land into five large baronnies, to each of which was assigned supreme jurisdiction and dominium directum over the land and its inhabitants. Later, within each area came a second wave of land divisions involving three different forms of transfer of rights:

- The king and his barons created manors or lordships, known in Majorca as *caballerías,* to the members of the petty nobility who made up their retinue. With these processes of feudalisation they created over a hundred small manors endowed with local jurisdiction, dominium directum and, later, partial tithe rights over the inhabitants and land (Montaner, 1986: 42-64; Portella, 1994 and Jover & Soto, 1998: 217-275).
- An important part of royal lands and those belonging to the barons were ceded *alou franc* or in dominium directum to members of the rural elites that fell under the jurisdiction of the magnates[7].
- The third means of transferring property rights over land was the use of the emphyteutic transfer: in exchange for the payment of rent and other dues to the lords of the manor, the tenant had the dominium utile over the land, including the right to sell, sub-let and bequeath it (Jover & Soto, 1998).

Over time, most of the land held by the barons, a large part of the small manors (*caballerías*) and allodial lands were ceded via emphyteusis to the settlers who accompanied the lords during the conquest or joined the first waves of migration to the island. In general, land was ceded in large units, which may have corresponded to the original Andalusí structure of landholding before the conquest. Later, the beneficiaries of these large farms, which adopted the existing Arabic names of *alquería* and *rahal,* ceded parts of their lands to other settlers, many of whom, in their turn, sub-let parts of their holdings to other peasants. This process resulted, overall, in a structure of landholding dominated by medium and large farms which became fixed between the boundaries of villages and hamlets, with small peasant holdings tending to crystallise around these settlements[8].

It was on these medium and larger peasant holdings that the crisis of the fifteenth century and the accumulation of land by the aristocracy erupted. According to the *catastro* surveys of 1576 and 1581, a new landed aristocracy took over nearly half the land, either the use-rights to it, or full title (Moll & Suau, 1979; Montaner & Le Senne, 1980 and Jover & Morey, 2003). The aristocratic great estates embedded lands either in *dominium utile* or full property. This aristocracy organised its estates into large farms (called in Majorca *possessions*) which were either administered directly or rented on short-term contracts to a stratum of peasants. These large farms employed a great number of waged

7 This *dominium directum* included rights to rent and entry fines, as stipulated in the manorial survey of Terrassa in 1750 (S45, f. 19v-20). However, these rights could be commuted to fixed rents.

8 The extent to which the *alquerías* became fragmented was very uneven. In western Majorca (Raiguer and the valleys of the Sierra de Tramontana), the *alquerías* were rapidly broken up into relatively small holdings, whereas in the centre and east of the island, large estates remained intact until the fifteenth century. In some cases, the process was reversed in that instead of breaking up, holdings became concentrated into larger units. See Soto (1990, 1991), Portella (1985: 331-343) and Rodríguez (1985: 371-387; 1994: 367-403).

labourers (permanent and temporary) hired from among the small peasants whose holdings were insufficient to guarantee subsistence, or from among the landless[9]. From fifteenth to eighteenth centuries emphyteusis became the means by which these great estates alloted land plots to the peasants. This was the way, along with purchase and inheritance, by which peasant families had access to land. The large farms or the common lands of the villages were allotted when they were indebted or suffered financial troubles. These allotments of lands continued throughout the seventeenth and eighteenth centuries, albeit in neither a continuous nor cumulative fashion. Rather, it occurred in various waves that alternatively broke down and built up landholding, without ever being sufficient to undermine the basic characteristics of Majorcan agrarian society: the hegemony of the nobility as landowners and the polarisation of the structure of property rights.

II. Defending emphyteusis in the context of enlightened and liberal reforms

At the end of the eighteenth century, despite a growing hostility towards feudal property rights in general and *fideicomisos* in particular, seen by some in society as an obstacle to economic growth, the structure of landholding remained sharply polarised. Cadastral sources demonstrate that in the final phase of the Ancien Régime, the nobility controlled more than a third of landed wealth, which implied holding in practice more than 40% of the surface area of Majorca. The *possessions* continued to dominate agrarian society, bordered by smallholdings, the owners of which (small peasants) had little option to meet their subsistence needs but to take up seasonal labour on the large farms. The majority of these small peasants were, moreover, only the holders of use rights to the lands they cultivated[10], land which, in general, they held through emphyteutic tenancies inherited from previous generations.

For these reasons, by the end of the Ancien Régime, inalienable rights and particularly entail, were presented by enlightened authors as a barrier to agricultural and economic progress: they prevented the cultivation of extensive areas while at the same time ensuring that a growing proportion of the rural population did not possess sufficient land on which to fully employ their labour. In the late eighteenth and early nineteenth centuries, therefore, when agrarian growth was beginning to show signs of exhaustion, the authors

9 Numerous studies have emphasised this feature. There is not space here for an exhaustive list, but pioneering studies that are particularly worthy of mention are those of Moll & Suau (1979) and Suau (1991).

10 This is a characteristic that has persisted almost to the present day. However great the effort from the second third of the nineteenth century to break up the large noble estates, the erosion of large-scale property was slow, lasting almost a century, and took the form, as we shall see, of transferring small plots by perpetual rent.

of many treatises presented inalienable property rights as one of the main explanations for why the cultivated surface area had diminished, and proposed by way of solution the breaking-up of large estates via emphyteutic transfers that would still enable the landowners to maintain dominium directum over the divided holdings and to receive an annual income. In Majorca, a pioneering work in this vein was that published in 1788 by Antonio Juan Caimari, *síndico personero* of the town council of Palma[11]. He argued that inalienable property rights created numerous ill-effects: abandonment of large farms, low investment in improvements, an abundance of lawsuits and conflicts, little land in circulation and so on. He proposed that the Council of Castile[12] should permit the owners of entailed land to cede them via emphyteusis without needing to acquire permission first, as had hitherto been the case. His proposals, however, met with firm resistance from the island's institutions and the landed nobility[13]. In general, both this and other similar treatises for other regions received little attention until the early years of the nineteenth century. In this case, not until the 29th of October 1800, when Bartolomé Muñoz, in name of the Council of Castile sent the Audiencia of Majorca[14] a copy of the treatise by Francisco Hurtado, member of the Sociedad Vascongada de Amigos del País[15], on the benefits of permitting the exchange and transfer of lands entailed via emphyteusis or fixed-term lease without the need to obtain prior approval. Both the judge and the heads of the Audiencia of Majorca approved the proposal. At that time, the head of the Despacho de Hacienda[16] was a Majorcan, Miguel Cayetano Soler, who ordered an inquiry into the state of the Spanish economy and the obstacles to its growth. His aim was to undertake a thorough fiscal reform (Morey, 2002). Against this background, the issue of entail and of the benefits of promoting agrarian wealth through land transfers was thus brought to the fore again by figures of authority within certain Majorcan institutions. Particularly vocal in this regard were the mayors of those towns and villages where large land holdings predominated. They proposed, as a means of increasing wealth and

11 The *síndico personero* was the member of the town or village council who represented guilds and similar bodies.

12 The Consejo de Castilla (Council of Castile), despite the name, was the supreme body of government for the whole of the Spanish kingdom.

13 Juan Caimari defined this type of transfer as 'a type of empyteusis in which fixed propoerty is transferred in exchange for a small cash payment, and the creation of a fixed rent to be paid to the 'seller' and his heirs… it is very common in Majorca, and a means whereby in the future great gains may be had from entailed property' (Zaforteza, 1992a: 40; Morey, 1999: 81).

14 The Audiencia of Majorca was the regional government and law court for the island.

15 The Sociedades de Amigos del País (literally: Societies of Friends of the Country) were enlightened societies set up to promote various kinds of debate and proposals for reform, usually at a regional or provincial level (in this instance, the Basque Country).

16 The Ministry of the Treasury.

population, to split up and transfer via emphyteusis the uncultivated areas of the large estates[17].

Nonetheless, circumstances favouring the erosion of large-scale holdings did not emerge until after 1815, when various factors (war, the collapse in prices and land rents, noble indebtedness, the blocking of old forms of credit, the failure of fiscal reform and political conflict) created the context for more far-reaching reforms: liberal revolution and agrarian reform. Even so, as is well known, the process of reform was drawn out and marked by numerous episodes of conflict[18]. Among all the liberal reforms relating to landed property produced by the liberal revolution (disentailment, abolition of feudal rights, abolition of tithe, suppression of settlements, etc.) the reform that was most important in Majorca was that relating to the limitation of entails and settlements (1836/1841). This law was the starting-point for breaking up of landholdings on a massive scale and, although the intensity of this varied dependening on the needs of particular landowners and to the changing economic climate, what emerged from a previous study of transfers of noble property recorded in the land registers (1768-1862), is that the land market did not become active in any meaningful sense until after the definitive publicaton of the 1841 law.

The analysis of this source, the land registers, has revealed that Majorcan landowners made use of emphyteusis, both in the strict sense and that of sub-emphyteusis, and regardless of whether it constituted a permanent transfer or not. The following table shows clearly that such transfers were far more important than sales of land. In this regard, it should be remembered that a sale differed from an emphyteutic transfer in that the former implied the exchange of both types of rights, dominium utile and dominium directum, whereas emphyteusis only meant the transfer of dominium utile. In the latter case, the lord received payment of an entry fee and the remainder was paid at intervals, subject to a fixed rate of interest, usually 3%. The clauses of these contracts stipulated the following: the entry fee, which could be paid as a lump sum or in instalments, but if the latter subject to an interest rate of 6%; the mortgage attached to the land; the rent to be paid to the former owner; the conditions surrounding payment of rent, with interest usually fixed at 5%; the rules and customs to which the land might be subject, such as boundaries, rights of way etc., and finally the new cultivator took on the costs of drawing up the deeds of transfer, registering them, payment of taxes and entry fines[19].

---

17 Some of the mayors' replies have been transcribed in MOREY (1999: 92).

18 By liberal revolution, we mean the complex of transformations that brought about the collapse of feudal structures and changed the rules of the game in a way favourable to the development of capitalist relations of production. See GARCÍA SANZ (1985: 7-99). On the political and social situation on the island during this period: DE LOS SANTOS OLIVER (1982), ROMERO (1983, 1989) and ROURA (1985).

19 On the types of transfer during the nineteenth century, see ROSSELLÓ VERGER (1981, 2012). From the middle of the century, when the process of alienation of large estates became more intense, contracts were drawn up by notaries, using a printed template. On this template

Table 9.1. Types of land transfer carried out by the landed nobility (1768-1862)

Type of Contracts	Number	%
Emphyteusis	3,371	72.38%
Sales	1,286	27.62%
Total	4,657	100.00

Source: Morey (1999: 248)

The predominance of emphyteutic transfers also confirms that the issue of divided property rights remained even after the liberal agrarian reforms. Despite emphyteutic rents supposedly being, like other dues, an obstacle to the transfer of property according to liberal thinking, we can confirm that not even after the revolution did sales outnumber emphyteutic transfers. Moreover, this pattern remained despite the publication of the 1805 law (a law which suffered from the ebb and flow of property reform, and was to be amplified by the laws of 1811, 1823 and 1837), proposing the abolition of all rents derived from 'old' (usually feudal in origin) and 'new' emphyteutic transfers. In practice, the process of abolition appears to have been slow, since the interest payments on most fixed rents had not risen and thus it was cheaper to pay the rent than to gather the funds needed to buy out the owners of dominium directum (Peset, 1982: 100). This hypothesis, however, remains to be confirmed for Majorca, though the land registers also record the liquidation of mortgages. What the evidence gathered so far does suggest, however, is that entry fines were not always low (Habsburg-Lorena, 1982-1993; 5: 34-35). To a certain degree, many of the transfers carried out in those years by Majorcan landowners approximated more to sales[20]. Many landowners demanded high entry fines and annual payments that were low and even symbolic; fundamentally because they were driven to the land market by a lack of ready capital, seeking the largest sum possible in cash. It is because of these characteristics that such transfers are commonly described in contemporary sources as 'modern' or as 'common emphyteusis', in order to

would be noted, by hand, the name of the individual receiving the land, the extension of the holding, its number on any maps, the boundaries, the amount payable as entry fine and as annual rent. These contracts are abundant among the papers of many notaries of the period, such as Miguel Ignacio Font, as even a superficial glance through the catalogue of the notarial papers held by the Archivo del Reino de Mallorca will confirm. It is also common to find such contracts in the private archives of noble families, especially among those who, for want of ready cash (following the abolition of *fideicomisos* in 1836-1841) with which to pay debts or inheritance taxes, were forced to sell off part of their estates (Morey, 2007). A particularly rich example of this is that of the marqués de Ariany in the Archivo Municipal de Palma, and particularly the deeds relating to the alienation of his Son Vaquer estate (register 372).

20 This is in contrast to the situation described for Girona by Congost (1990: 128-129), where those ceding land tended to demand more in entry fees that in land rents.

distinguish them from 'old emphyteusis' or, as we have referred to it, 'feudal emphyteusis' (Morey, 2007: 136-140).

Table 9.2 shows that 93% of plots of land transferred between 1768 and 1862 were 5 hectares or less, and the majority were smaller than a *quarterada* (0.71 hectares)[21]. It is hard to assess whether these smallholdings were sufficient for the reproduction of the peasant family, since this depended not just on the surface area, but also on the quality of the land, the intensity with which it was cultivated and the trends in relative prices of different agricultural products. Moreover, that these smallholders were listed in the 1860 census as labourers suggests that many continued to work for wages as well. Emphyteutic transfers and sales thus may have created independent forms of peasant tenure, but equally they may have facilitated the continuity of large farms managed by wage labour[22].

Table 9.2. Size of land plots transferred between 1768 and 1862

interval in hectares	**- 5**	**0-0,5**	**0,5-1**	**1-2**	**2-3**	**3-4**	**4-5**	**% Total**
nº of land plots	4,182	903	1,573	1.046	433	105	122	93.30%
interval in hectares	**5-15**	**5-6**	**6-7**	**7-8**	**8-9**	**9-10**	**10-15**	
nº of land plots	182	47	25	31	16	21	42	4.10%
interval in hectares	**15-45**	**15-20**	**20-25**	**25-30**	**30-35**	**35-40**	**40-45**	
nº of land plots	78	31	14	13	6	12	2	1,80%
interval in hectares	45-50	**45-50**	**50-100**	**100-200**	**200-300**	**300-400**	**400-500**	
nº of land plots	37	5	13	10	7	1	1	0.83%
nº of land plots	4,479							100.0%
More than 500 ha: 5 *possessions (great farms)* transferred without any division of holdings.								

Source: Morey (1999: 244)

21 Not all contracts that were registered specified the dimensions of the plots in question. Sometimes the land was a plot for building houses, in which case dimensions were often not recorded. In other cases, the contract noted that that dimensions could not be calculated because the plot was an irregular shape. When large estates were transferred, often without subdivision, some landowners claimed not to know the dimensions. Nonetheless, this table is based on a representative sample of 4,484 contracts (just over 96% of the total).

22 For the debate on this issue, see Tello (1983), Romero (1989), Suau (1991: 230-284), Manera (1990, 2001) and Jover & Morey (2003).

The land registers do not record consistently the quality of the land. We only know this in 2,224 records, approximately 47% of the total. This reduced sample is overwhelmingly concentrated in the period after 1845 and does not show any definite trend over time. What is apparent, however, is that the land transferred by emphyteusis was usually poor, essentially unirrigated and without trees.

Table 9.3. Type of land transferred (1768-1862)

Type	Number of Cases	Percentage
Uncultivated, wooded or shrubs	495	22.3
Non-irrigated without trees	1,466	65.8
Vines, olives and other trees	186	8.4
Irrigated land	77	3.5
Total	2,224	100.0

Source: Morey (1999: 246)

In reality, the smallholders who took on this poor land had no option other than to cultivate it intensively. This intense farming, according to some contemporaries, increased production, initially of wheat and other cereal crops and then of fruit and olive trees. One illustration of this is an account published by the Diputación Provincial de Baleares[23] in 1839 which argued that the grain and vegetable harvest had been greatly increased by the parcelling-out of land via emphyteutic contracts, to the extent that the island was now self-sufficient in grain (Morey, 1999: 117-118). Over time, the new pattern of landholding also led to an increase in planting of trees and some authors, among them B. Canut (1865) and F. Satorras (1878) did not hesitate to attribute the expansion of almond, fig, and carob trees to the success of large farms. Subsequent studies have also shown a clear increase in cereal, vegetable, fig, carob bean, and almond crops between 1835 and 1860. At the same time, a close relationship is evident between these increases in production and the process of division and subletting of large farms (Bisson, 1977: 220-223; Cela Conde, 1979: 55-62; Suau, 1991; Manera, 2001: 82, 2001; Jover & Manera, 2009).

From the landlord's point of view, it is worth bearing in mind that the decision to transfer all or part of an estate did not, in principle, require any substantial change in its management. The majority of these estates continued to be managed via rent contracts, often without even a change in stewardship. In general, all that happened was a renegotiation of the rent that the steward would be required to pay for the reduced holding and a series of clauses in the contract stipulating the further obligations of both parties should further reductions take place. These clauses begin to appear in some contracts during

23 The Diputación Provincial was the regional government that replaced the Audiencia and other governing bodies of the Ancien Régime during the early years of the nineteenth century.

the Trienio Liberal[24] and reappear with increasing frequency from 1836-1841. Amongst other points, they refer to the possibility that both the landlord and the steward may appoint trusted agents to assess the value of the land and the new obligations to which stewards would be subject following any subdivision[25]. The most frequent of these would be the obligation to collect on behalf of the landlord the rents and other dues that the new cultivators of the land would be required to pay each year[26].

III. Law suits concerning and 'renegotiation' of rents and other feudal dues associated with emphyteusis

The way in which large estates were gradually eroded via emphyteutic transfers that involved the payment of entry fines, an annual rent and often other feudal dues such as entry fees or right of reversion made rent collection complicated for previous landowners[27]. In part, this was because over time many of these rights were contested, and lawsuits over whether they were 'old' or 'new' rights began to multiply. At the same time, the new landholders often tried to evade payment of rents and other charges. Numerous sources testify to these proceedings, but here we cite as a typical example, the clause concerning alodial property[28] included in the 1893 will of the fifth *marqués* de la Romana. His father, Pedro Caro y Salas, had been one of the island's biggest landowners but around 1858 had had to move to Madrid because of his Carlist activities. For this reason, he had alienated most of his property and, unlike most of the Majorcan nobility, had done so by selling most of it, only using emphyteusis in very specific cases. In all likelihood, he foresaw

---

24 The three-year period of constitutional government from 1820 to 1823.

25 A good example is the contract for the Rafalet *possessió* signed in 1826 with the notary J. Oliver (Archivo Villalonga-Escalada, lease folder).

26 This fact confirms for Majorca, as for elsewhere in Spain, that the division between dominium directum and dominium utile remained the unfinished business of the liberal revolution in the countryside (García Sanz, 1985). Even after the definitive establishment of the liberal state, the percentages of sales remained below that of emphyteutic transfers and some of the obligations associated with the latter, such as *laudemio* or *retracto*) remain active today.

27 As emphasised by Moll & Suau (1986: 83).

28 From a legal standpoint, the term *alodio* (in Catalan, *alou*) should only be used to refer to property that was free from feudal obligations, that is, where the owners held both dominium directum and dominium utile. In practice, however, it came to be used and still is today, to refer to the bundle of obigations (rent payments in cash or kind, right of reversion, entry fees and so on) derived from the transfer of use rights via emphyteutic contracts. For a discussion of terminology, see Mas and Planas de Oleza (1990), and to understand how the owners of alodial land (initially both those who owned dominium utile and those who owned dominium directum) transferred their land, see in particular the introductory and final sections of this paper.

that claiming rents and dues would be much more difficult from outside Majorca, as indeed proved to be the case for his eldest son, Pedro Caro y Maza de Lizana for those rents he did inherit[29].

It is clear that many landowners responded to dilatory and non-payment of rents and other dues by appointing trusted individuals to act on their behalf as rent collectors, normally in return for a proportion of the sum they managed to collect. The latter were usually endowed with 'special powers' to travel to the villages where the landholders lived and pursue those who failed to pay with threats of seizing the land they had worked so hard to acquire and cultivate. There are numerous examples of this (Morey, 2007: 135-143). Particularly striking is the progressive importance, as land transfers became common, attached to rent collectors (*perceptores de censos*). These individuals are easily identifiable in tax records from the time. For example, the registers of the *Contribución industrial y de comercio de Palma*[30] from 1852 onwards, show that from the mid-nineteenth century, when land division became more important, to the 1920s when land transfers peaked in intensity, the number of professional rent collectors rose steadily. Nominal linkage of these registers with other sources shows that the majority had legal training as notaries or lawyers, further proof of the fear of large estate owners that liberal reforms might threaten their rights and thus, in the short-term, their sources of income. It was precisely to prevent such an eventuality that they hired the services of these professional rent collectors who, as well as monitoring the payment of their rents and other dues, also advised them on legal matters and defended them should conflicts with their tenants reach court.

The increase in emphyteutic transfers also obliged landowners to keep their documentation up-to-date. In order to claim the various rents and dues which might be owed on the lands they had been dividing up and transferring, they had to put their archives in order. They frequently had new *capbrevaciones* or registers of emphyteutic tenants and mortgagees compiled, keeping these up to date in order to monitor the precise moment when such debts would expire. These records were grouped in sheaves of paper or loose folios, headed with the name of the farm on which the plots of land in question were located, the names of the rent payers and the payments they were required to make[31]. Sometimes the records also included a copy of the original deed of transfer[32].

The reorganisation of archives and the appearance of new series of documents coincide with another feature of great significance, which we

---

29 *Testamentaría por el fallecimiento de D. Pedro Caro … Hijuela de Álvaro Caro Szechenyi … por Bernardo Pascual Ruilópez a 25 de mayo de 1893*. (Private archive, unregistered document).

30 These were lists of industrial and commercial taxpayers.

31 As one example of the many available, see the different records in the Archivo Municipal de Palma (Fondo Cotoner, registros: 665, 673, 884).

32 For a good example, see the annotations to the index of land transfers at Son Simonet for the last quarter of the nineteenth century (Private archive of J. Villalonga, unregistered document).

have discussed in previous research (Morey, 2007, 2013). This feature is the process whereby the new professional administrators, salaried or paid a percentage of what they were able to collect (Morey, 1999; López & Robledo, 2004), gradually crowded out the old administrators who had usually been part of the landowners' families or households. From the mid-nineteenth century the new administrators increasingly replaced kin, usually priests, who had traditionally kept accounts without, in most cases, having either legal or accountancy training. By contrast, the new administrators usually had sufficient knowledge of accounting to follow the practices recommended by contemporary experts. In addition, they were often established lawyers or notaries with sufficient reputation to gain the confidence of the landowners for whom they worked[33].

IV. Large-scale division of big estates and the survival of alodios

It has been calculated that in the last quarter of the nineteenth century there were around a thousand *possessions* in the Majorcan countryside (around 400 of which were more than 100 hectares in size) that were broken up, initially very slowly but very rapidly from the 1930s on. The following table shows for different administrative districts and the island as a whole the chronology of this fragmentation and, at the same time, highlights that this increased over time. It began in the 1890s, almost certainly as a result of the late nineteenth-century agrarian crisis and intensified from the early decades of the twentieth century.

Table 9.4. Trends in the fragmentation of large estates from the final decades of the nineteenth century (index numbers)

Periods	Mallorca	Palma	Inca	Manacor
1865-1890	23.65	2.65	40.4	24.93
1891-1910	104.77	83.73	77.08	158.01
1911-1930	150.53	139.16	228.76	123.78
1931-1950	186.61	226.51	127.76	151.7
1951-1970	34.48	47.71	25.98	41.98

Source: The index numbers have been calculated on the basis of average of the data of each serie as is explained in Jover and Morey (2003: 229-230, note 17). The division into sub-periods is conditioned by the data provided by Cela Conde (1979) and Florit Alomar (1983).

33 Intervention in the sales of estates by administrators was fairly common after the liberal revolution. The image presented of these administrators in popular Majorcan fiction is not exactly favourable (Peñarrubia, 2001: 199).

As is clear from the table, there were significant variations in the pace of land transfers across administrative districts. These differences can be explained by the desire of Majorcan landowners first to break up the estates furthest from Palma (the Manacor district), land which prior to subdivision was usually bare of trees and planted only with cereal crops. A combination of different factors explains why particular large farms were subdivided first: relative demand for land in different districts, population pressure, relative possibilities of the land for subdivision into smaller units, and so on.

As far as the type and size of the parcels transferred are concerned, in this period there are no significant differences from what was described above for earlier periods. Indeed, these aspects are the subject of now classic studies, such as those of Jean Bisson (1977) and Camilo J. Cela Conde (1979). However, it is worth noting here the widespread introduction of new crops from the 1920s onwards: carob beans, almond and figs trees, leguminous plants, vines, citrus fruits, vegetables and also the introduction of pig farming. These new products came mainly from small and medium holdings and their spread testified to the efforts of cultivators to participate in market networks and escape the control of the big landowners and their stewards. Nonetheless, not all products expanded at the same rate, since the very fact of their being commercial crops meant expansion could only be a function of international demand, a demand that was sometimes fleeting. Such was the case with viticulture in certain places on the island[34].

If any crop could be said to be directly tied to emphyteutic transfers, it was the almond. During the second half of the nineteenth century this crop spread to almost all land holdings that were suited to its cultivation. Between the end of the nineteenth century and 1920 the total surface area devoted to almond trees rose spectacularly from 5,134 hectares to 26,750 hectares, and in the space of a few years, almonds headed the list of exports from Majorca, in this case destined primarily for markets in France, Germany and England[35]. Other products, meanwhile, were also gaining importance in other locations, depending on their particular characteristics: citrus fruits in the Sóller valley, exported mainly to southern French ports, and the increase in irrigated crops in the districts of Palma, Muro, Sa Pobla and Campos (Manera, 2001: 199-204). The introduction of new crops on smallholdings was almost certainly not limited to these examples, since it is easy to understand that cultivators who had struggled to obtain small parcels of land would not stint on efforts (particularly labour) to ensure their survival and that of their families by adopting numerous and varied strategies. These ranged from diversifying

---

34 From the mid-nineteenth century, Majorcan wines gained in importance in French markets to the extent that France became the main destination for sales. However, the golden age of the wine business was short-lived, and exports fell from 1891 on once France began to recover from phylloxera (Morey, 2004: 143-144).

35 On almond cultivation, the classic work by Barceló (1964: 23) is still important, though mention should also be made of research in progress by Fornés (2013).

crops, and adapting quickly to changes in market demand, to changing occupations or residence when bad harvests or other misfortunes left them with no other option. What is clear is that from the 1860s onwards, agrarian society in Majorca was extremely dynamic. The liberal property reforms that emerged from the liberal revolution and particularly the system of plots land in perpetual rent adopted throughout the island from the mid-nineteenth century on encouraged the emergence of a new agrarian model characterised by small-scale holdings, market orientation and a great capacity to respond to changes in international demand. This dynamism of small-scale property was noted by contemporaries, especially in the reports of agricultural publications[36]. Also notable is the increasing importance of orchards, which in turn explains the appearance of clauses referring to trees in contracts relating to transfers and division of landholdings. The contracts drawn up in the first years of the liberal reforms did not include such contracts because, unlike the situation after 1910, the plots of land in question had no trees. These trees were mostly planted by the new tenants or cultivators[37].

Rather than focusing on new crops and new opportunities for commerce fostered directly or indirectly by land division, what stands out most, though, is that at the turn of the century emphyteutic transfers whereby the owner retained dominium directum and other rights gave way to outright purchases[38]. This shift does not imply, however, that *alous* disappeared. Although the liberal reforms (and earlier, if we recall the decree of 7th January 1805 cited above) granted the possibility that the holders of dominium utile could redeem the dominium directum, it is clear that in practice, most did not. That they did not explains why, despite the decline of emphyteutic transfers in the twentieth century, much land was still subject to dues of various kinds[39]. This is evident in the notarial deeds relating to sales, which always specify the dues to which

36 Particularly striking is the comment in the Boletín de la Cámara Agrícola Balear in 1911: 'without the division into small plots, it is doubtful that almond trees would have been planted and cultivated in Majorca, yet the almond crop is worth more than 15 million pesetas a year' (Creus, 1911: 213). See Morey (2007: 155).

37 Their descendents had to follow a new tactic when transferring this land, as can be seen from a clause in a sale contract from 1942: 'The fruit trees growing in these plots that may be less than the legally stipulated distance from the neighbouring plots must be respected by the purchasers of these same plots for as long as their roots or any grafting from these are still alive. The fruit from these trees belongs entirely to the owner of the plot in which the tree has its roots. With trees grown for wood, however, legal distances are to be maintained irrespective of when the tree was planted, and thus the owner cannot claim any right to keep the tree in situ.' (Archivo Tous Andreu, documento sin registrar).

38 From the beginning of the twentieth century, clauses stipulating some kind of rent, ubiquitous in the previous century, begin to disappear, to be replaced by clauses along the following lines: 'the sale of the plot in question is wholly free from all obligations, without exception, according to the provisions of Article 1,471 of the Civil Code.

39 Over time, it is likely that many holders of dominium directum stopped claiming these dues, particularly when these were largely symbolic (for example, half or quarter of a hen, a pound or a few shillings). Nonetheless, as late as 1950 many still had representatives in those areas

the land was subject, even when it was no longer clear who had the right to claim these[40]. This caution makes sense when we remember, as was noted early on by the land-registry authorities who were charged with the task of compiling the dossier that would be used to draw up the Spanish Civil Code of 1888-1889, that between 70 and 80% of property was subject to these dues. The authorities believed that all lands were still under some kind of feudal obligation, since they assumed that 'all were held in *alodio* by someone'. However, as we have seen, this was not the case. The overlaps of rights could occur not just because of questions concerning lordship, but also because land had been transferred according to the rules of common emphyteusis, regardless of whether those transferring the land were ecclesiastical or civic institutions, descendents of the old feudal nobility, landowners of noble origin whose ancestors had acquired use rights to large estates (*possessions*) in the fifteenth and sixteenth centuries, peasants or urban property owners who over time acquired the use rights to small plots of land with the intention of improving and cultivating them, or simply a small plot on which to build a house or have a vegetable garden or keep poultry. All these different situations were equally possible thanks to emphyteusis and, in practice, shared the obligation to pay dues of different kinds, commonly known on the island under the umbrella term of *alous*[41].

V. Final observations

This study has shown that, from the last stage of the Ancien Régime to the final triumph of the liberal agrarian reforms (1836), emphyteutic contracts, despite their feudal origins and despite the division of property rights they implied, were defended by both enlightened and liberal thinkers as a means of promoting agrarian growth and limiting the extent of large property. After the consolidation of the liberal state, emphyteusis was at the root of division of large estates and farms and the rise of a new class of small farmers who led a thorough reform of crop patterns. Our review emphasises that until the

---

where they owned such rights. These representatives in turn made sure to advertise, either directly or via the equivalent of the town crier, the precise date and place where dues would be collected, and carried out collections of rents in cash and kind (including hens).

40 For example, the following clause is from a division of a property amongst different heirs in 1930: 'a plot of land measuring one *cuartón* subject to the obligation to pay 2 *pesetas* and 50 *céntimos*, but to whom, where and when unkown' (Archivo Tous Andreu, register number not available).

41 Essential reading on this subject is the work of Pascual González (1979) on Majorcan civil law, a work which also covers the compilation of the civil code of the Balearic Islands as approved by the Law of 19th April 1961 and has a chapter by the noted Majorcan legal scholar Masot, titled 'The Majorcan civil code since its compilation', which illustrates the extent to which the new code meant revisions to the jurisprudence that had hitherto been practised in regard to dues.

beginning of the twentieth century emphyteusis remained the legal device by which the economic and social relations surrounding the access to and tenure of use rights over land were regulated. With the turn of the century, emphyteutic transfers began to lose ground to outright sales of land, but nonetheless, as the previous section made clear, some of the rights derived from emphyteutic transfers have survived to the present day. Since the 1960s, the massive urbanisation of the island as a result of tourism has witnessed a growing interest in the maintenance of such rights and the economic benefits derived from these.

Alous have enjoyed a similar longevity, despite the liberal revolution, and indeed, were incorporated into both the Spanish Civil Code and the Balearic Law Code of 1961 (*Compilación del Derecho Foral Balear*). Their legal interpretation, however, has led to numerous suits between holders of dominium utile and holders of dominium directum, and disputes between legal scholars[42]. In essence, according to Majorcan lawyers, the term *alou* should be used only to refer to contracts where the owners of the land transferred held it free from dues and thus owned both dominium directum and dominium utile. Such property was known as alodial precisely because it was free from obligations of any kind, and originated, as we explained in the introduction, in the grants of land made by the monarch to his vassals. As we have seen, however, what generally happened afterwards was that these landholders or their successors began transferring use rights to other tenants, who, in turn, transferred these to others. This process began immediately following the Christian conquest of the island and continued, with greater or lesser intensity depending on economic and other factors, throughout the centuries. It affected almost all landed property and all the institutions and social groups on the island. The process also gave rise to a complicated web of rent extraction which, aside from its economic implications, also complicated understanding of the different dues and obligations that derived over time from the emphyteutic contract 'imported' from Catalonia. Often, those charged with deciding such questions lacked a sufficient understanding of Majorcan law and tended to assimilate alodial property in the strict sense with other types of landholding. Nonetheless, Majorcan juridical doctrine has tended to agree almost unanimously and since the publication of the Civil Code and even before, on the existence of different types of dues that were incorporated into the Balearic Law Code. In our view, it is important not to lose sight of this fact when trying to understand the variety of outcomes to

42 Where legal experts and historians of different periods have disagreed is over the correct interpretation of the many dues and rents to which most land on the island has been subject since the thirteenth century until today. This difficulty results from the different levels of tenure described above and the common practice of sub-emphyteusis almost from the conquest of 1229. For legal studies on this question, particularly with regard to alodial property, see Lalaguna (1968); Masot (1985); Singala (1921, 1923) and Vaquer (1959, 1973).

which the legal fiction of emphyteusis has led in the Majorcan case[43]. For our purposes, the main aspect to emphasise is the coexistence throughout a long period of history of these different types of landholding, albeit that one or another form may have predominated at different times depending on different circumstances, such as whether the original holder of the land did indeed hold both the dominium directum and the dominium utile, or whether the new holder was able to avoid paying dues to the original owner, particularly if he, as the result of living abroad or for other reasons, found it easier to charge an annual rent rather than pursue other obligations. Other factors that might affect the stituation would be differences in economic context and the particular economic situation of both landlord and tenant.

The survival of alodial property rights until the present, and their revival as a consequence of the tourist-based urbanisation of the 1960s, which affected some estates where the owners of the use-rights had not paid the compensation originally required to the owners of the dominium directum, led to a surge of interest among legal experts and many property owners. In part this was the result of the surge in value of much property, which led the descendents of some of the original owners of the dominium directum to claim *laudemium* (percentages of the sale price) accordingly. The nature of such claims saw the rise of a similar professional class to that described earlier for the mid-nineteenth century, many of whom have only recently retired, who have dedicated their time to searching through archives and land registers for the title deeds to property, in return for a commission. These individuals had to be alert to various issues. One of these was to ascertain the real value at which land was registered, since if its value were underestimated, both the owner and the individual himself would receive lower percentages[44]. They also had to be alert to possible transfers that the holders of dominium utile could have made, since if the latter did not inform the holder of the dominium

43 The Compilación del Derecho Foral Mallorquín (Majorcan Law Code) distinguishes between: 1) the *censo reservativo* (the owner of dominium directum transfers full ownership without reserving the right to claim an entry fee but in return for an annual rent); 2) the *censo alodial* (the owner of dominium directum transfers the dominium utile but reserves the right to an entry fee but without the obligation to pay an annual rent); 3) the *censo enfitéutico* or *censo reservativo de establecimiento* (the owner of the dominium directum transfers the dominium utile, with or without reserving the right to an entry fee, but with the obligation to pay annual rent). Historians who have emphasised these different types of obligation include Juan Vidal (1985-1987) and Rosselló Verger (1981, 2012). On the legal side, and particularly the review by these authors of the situation surrounding these rents of the eve of the 1990 reform, see Mas and Planas de Oleza (1990).

44 In theory, the owner of the dominium directum had the right to demand 2% of the value of the land, including any buildings constructed upon it. This last point gave rise to many disputes, especially once significant buildings had been erected, such as hotels. As far as we can tell by word of mouth from people closely connected with these disputes, before the changes to the law in the 1990s, many property owners were able to demand much higher percentages on the basis of the potential value to be derived from tourism, as high as 7% in some cases.

directum, he had the right to claim *fadiga* or *retracto*, that is, to take back the holding or plot transferred for the same price for which it had been sold or, at least, registered.

Finally, the survival of alodial property until the present day[45] makes it easier to understand why there should be such an enormous literature on the subject, and that as recently as the 1990s, the Balearic government should have debated and approved various changes to modify the old feudal rents and remove the right to first purchase (*retracto* or *fadiga*). These changes to the law were the logical result of the economic changes brought about in Majorca by mass tourism, particularly its effect on real estate. Above all, the impact was felt on properties closest to the coast, originally transferred at low cost or given as inheritance portions to younger sons or to unmarried daughters because they were least suited to growing crops. Indeed, the changing uses of land in Majorca is a topic that is worthy of study in its own right, but beyond the scope of this essay.

Bibliography

ARNOUX, Mathieu (2012), *Le temps des laboureurs. Travail, ordre social et croissance en Europe (XIe-XIVe siècle)*, Paris, Albin Michel.

BARCELÓ, Bartomeu (1964), *El segle XIX a Mallorca*, Palma, Obra Cultural Balear.

BARCELÓ, Miquel & TOUBERT, Pierre (eds) (1998), *L'Incastellamento: Actas de las Reuniones de Girona: (26-27 noviembre 1992) y de Roma: (5-7 Mayo 1994)*, Roma, Escuela Española de Historia y Arqueología en Roma.

BENITO MONCLÚS, Pere (2003), *Senyoria de la terra i tinença pagesa al comtat de Barcelona (segles XI-XIII)*, Cosell Superior d'Investigacions Científiques, Institució Milà i Fontanals, Barcelona.

BISSON, Jean (1977), *La terre et l'homme aux Iles Baléares*, Aix-en-Provence, Edisud.

45 An interesting example is the recent lawsuit filed by the heiress of the Marqués of Campo Franco (now the director of the firm Roten Padura, SL, which deals primarily in real estate) with regard to the transfer of a plot of land, part of the Son Sunyer estate, in accordance with the following clause in the land register: 'only the use rights to the land are sold here. The dominium directum is reserved for the Marqués de Campo Franco, *if he should prove to be the owner*, or otherwise to whoever the owner should be, with the right to claim *laudemium* at 2% and other associated rights in law'. At the time of the contract, the notary apparently advised his client about this clause, declaring that there was no need to take it too seriously as the heirs of the holders of dominium directum rarely claimed such rights, a declaration which suggests he was ill-informed as to the extent of the conflicts such rights could and already had generated. A few years later, the heiress claimed 1800 euros as *laudemium* from the owners of the use rights, who defended themselves against this claim with numerous documents and even a formal petition to the Balearic government with a number of signatures, requesting the abolition of alodial rights. Further proof, if any were still needed, of the repercussions that emphyteusis continues to have on the island. See *Diario de Mallorca*, 30 nov. 2013.

Canut, Basilio (1865), *Memoria sobre los medios de promover el incremento de la riqueza agrícola y pecuaria de Mallorca atendidos los recursos y las condiciones de su territorio*, Palma de Mallorca, Imprenta de Felipe Guasp.

Cateura, P. (1997), 'Las cuentas de la colonización feudal (Mallorca, 1231-1245)', *España medieval*, núm. 20, Madrid, p. 57-143.

Cela Conde, Camilo (1979), *Capitalismo y campesinado en la isla de Mallorca*, Madrid, Siglo XXI.

Clavero, Bartolomé (1974), *Mayorazgo: propiedad feudal en Castilla: 1369-1836*, Madrid, Siglo XXI.

Clavero, Bartolomé (1983), 'Revolució i dret de propietat: interferència de l'emfiteusi', *Estudis d'Història Agrària*, núm. 7, p. 9-23.

Congost, Rosa (1990), *Els propietaris i els altres. La regió de Girona: 1768-1862*. Barcelona: Eumo.

Congost, Rosa (1991), 'Enfiteusis y pequeña explotación campesina en Cataluña, siglos XVIII-XIX', en Pegerto Saavedra & Ramon Villares (eds), *Señores y campesinos en la Península Ibéria: Os señores da terra*, Barcelona: Crítica, vol. 2, p. 63-87.

Congost, Rosa (2007), *Tierras, leyes, historia. Estudios sobre 'la gran obra de la propiedad'*. Barcelona: crítica.

Creus, G. (1911), 'La propiedad rústica en Mallorca', *Boletín de la Cámara Agrícola Balear*, núm. 14, p. 210-213.

Duby, Georges (1992), *Los tres órdenes o lo imaginario del feudalismo*, Madrid, Taurus.

Fernández de Pinedo, Emilio (1983), 'Els contractes emfitèutics al País Valencià', *Estudis d'Història Agrària*, núm. 7, p. 27-40.

Florit Alomar, Francisca (1983), *Les transformacions del paisatge rural i de la propietat de la terra al Pla de Mallorca (s. XIX-XX)*, Tesi doctoral inédita, Universitat de Palma de Mallorca.

Forcadell Álvarez, Carlos (1983), 'La redempció de censos a Aragó: el cas del terme municipal de Zaragoza (1855-1856)', *Estudis d'Història Agrària*, núm. 7, p. 41-50.

Fornés, Jaume (2013), *El cultiu de l'ametller a Mallorca*, Memòria de investigación leída en la Universitat de les Illes Balears, Departament de Ciències de la Terra.

Freedman, Paul H. (1988), *Assaig d'història de la pagesia catalana (segles XI-XV)*, Barcelona, Edicions. 62.

Freedman, Paul H. (1993), *Els orígens de la servitud pagesa a la Catalunya medieval*. Lleida, Eumo.

García sanz, Ángel (1985), 'Crisis de la agricultura tradicional y revolución liberal', en *Historia agraria de la España contemporánea: cambio social y nuevas formas de propiedad*, Barcelona, Crítica, p. 7-99.

Garrabou, Ramon (1985), 'La crisis agraria española de finales del siglo XIX: una etapa del desarrollo del capitalismo', en *Historia agraria de la España contemporánea: expansión y crisis (1850-1900)*, Barcelona, Crítica, p. 477-542.

Garrabou, Ramon, Planas, Jordi & Saguer, Enric (2001), *Un capitalisme impossible? La gestió de la gran propietat agrària a la Catalunya contemporània*, Barcelona, Eumo.

GARRABOU, Ramon, PLANAS, Jordi & SAGUER, Enric (2002): 'Procuradores, administradores y apoderados: una aproximación a las formas de gestión de la gran propiedad agraria en la Cataluña contemporánea', en Hilario CASADO & Ricardo ROBLEDO (eds), *Fortuna y negocios: formación y gestión de los grandes patrimonios, siglos XV-XX*, Universidad de Valladolid, p. 301-322.

HABSBURG-LORENA, Luis Salvador (1982-1993), Las Baleares por la palabra y el grabado, Palma de Mallorca, Caja de Ahorros de Baleares 'Sa Nostra', 10v.

JOVER, Gabriel (1996), 'Endeutament, desigualtat econòmica i despossessió pagesa. El cas de la parròquia de Petra, 1443-1524 (Mallorca)', *Recerques*, 33, p. 9-32.

JOVER, Gabriel (1999), 'Crisi agrària i endeutament nobiliari. La casa Gual-Despuig, Mallorca 1650-1750', *Randa*, nº 42, p. 11-46.

JOVER, Gabriel & MANERA, Carles (2009): 'Producción y productividad agrícola en la isla de Mallorca, 1590-1860', *Revista de Historia Económica*, núm. 3, p. 463-498.

JOVER, Gabriel & MOREY, Antònia (2003), 'Les possessions mallorquines: una modalitat d'organització de l'espai agrari i l'explotació del treball', en Rosa CONGOST, Gabriel JOVER & Giuliana BIAGIOLI (eds), *L'organització de l'espai rural a l'Europa mediterrània: massos, possessions, poderi*, Girona, CCG, p. 127-238.

JOVER, Gabriel & SOTO, Ricard (1998), 'Els dominis feudals a la Mallorca baixmedieval (segles XIII-XVI)', *Revista d'historia medieval*, (8), 217-274.

JOVER, Gabriel & SOTO, Ricard (2002), 'Colonización feudal y organización del territorio, Mallorca, 1230-1350', *Revista de Historia Económica*, nº 3, 2002, p. 437-475.

JUAN VIDAL, Juan (1985-1987), 'Los censos en la Mallorca moderna: su tipología', *Mayurqa*, núm. 21, p. 197-215.

LALAGUNA PIÑEIRO, Eduardo (1968), *La enfiteusis en el derecho civil de las Baleares*, Pamplona, Universidad de Navarra.

LEMEUNIER, Guy & PÉREZ PICAZO, Maria Teresa (1983), 'Cens emfitèutic i colonització agrària a Múrcia (1450-1900)', *Estudis d'Història Agrària*, núm. 7, p. 51-97.

LLUCH, Rosa (2005), *Els remences: la senyoria de l'Alamoina de Girona als segles XIV i XV*, Girona, Documenta Universitaria-Biblioteca d'Història Rural.

LÓPEZ, Santiago & ROBLEDO, Ricardo (2004), 'El administrador de los antiguos patrimonios agrarios según la teoría de la agencia', *Información Comercial Española*, núm. 812, p. 105-124.

MANERA, Carles (1990), 'Resistir i créixer. Canvi econòmic i classes socials a la Mallorca del segle XVIII?', *Randa*, núm. 26, p. 7-83.

MANERA, Carles (2001), *Història del creixement econòmic a Mallorca (1700-2000)*, Palma, Lleonard Muntaner.

MANERA, Carles & MOREY, Antònia (2006), 'La empresa en Baleares: flexibilidad y capacidad de adaptación al cambio económico (1850-2000)', en José Luis GARCÍA RUIZ & Carles MANERA (Dirs.), *Historia empresarial de España. Un enfoque en profundidad*, Madrid, LID, p. 79-112.

MAS COLOM, M. A. & PLANAS DE OLEZA, A. (1990), *L'alou i la seva reforma*, Palma, Institut d'Estudis Baleàrics.

Mas Fornés, Antoni (2008), 'Endeutament pagès i alienació de la terra a Mallorca durant la segona meitat del segle XV. L'exemple del terme de Maria de la Salut', *Butlletí de la Societat Arqueològica Lul·liana*, núm. 64, p. 89-114.

Masot, Miguel (1979), *El derecho civil de Mallorca después de la compilación*, Palma, Ereso.

Masot, Miguel (1985), 'Els censos i els alous, la sala de mòmies del Dret Mallorquí?', *Palau Reial*, feb. 1985, p. 31-37.

Molina de Dios, Ramon (2003), *Treball intensiu, treballadors polivalents (Treball, salaris i cost de la vida, Mallorca 1860-1936)*, Palma, Govern de les Illes Balears.

Moll, Isabel (1990), 'Els circuits de la terra (Mallorca, 1768-1814)', *Randa*, 26, p. 133-152.

Moll, Isabel, Albertí, Antònia & Morey, Antònia (1993), 'Tierra de fideicomisos: las consecuencias de la ley de desvinculaciones en Mallorca (1768-1865)', *Áreas*, núm. 15, p. 13-31.

Moll, Isabel & Suau, Jaume (1979), 'Senyors i pagesos a Mallorca (1718-1860/70)', *Estudis d'Història Agrària*, núm. 2, p. 95-191.

Moll, Isabel & Suau, Jaume (1986), 'Canvis i permanència de les institucions senyorials mallorquines durant el segle XIX', en Ramon Garrabou (ed.), *Terra, treball i propietat: classes agràries i règim senyorial als Països Catalans*, Barcelona, Crítica, p. 66-106.

Montaner, Pedro de & Le-Senne, Aina (1980), 'Nobleza, comercio y corso en la Mallorca moderna: Los "negocis per mar" de los Sureda', Mayurqa: revista del Departament de Ciències Històriques i Teoria de les Arts, n. 19, p. 233-243

Montaner, Pedro de (1986), 'Les cavalleries mallorquines (segles XIII-XVIII)', en Ramon Garrabou (ed.), *Terra, treball i propietat: classes agràries i règim senyorial als Països Catalans*, Barcelona, Crítica, p. 42-65.

Montaner, Pedro de (1989), 'Las franquicias de una baronía mallorquina: Sant Martí d'Alanzell', *Bolletí de la Societat Arqueològica Lul·liana*, núm. 45, p. 299-315.

Morey, Antònia (1998), 'El mercat de la propietat nobiliària a Mallorca entre la crisi de l'antic règim i la consolidació de l'estat liberal', *Estudis d'Història Económica*, núm. 15, p. 93-114.

Morey, Antònia (1999), *Noblesa i desvinculació a Mallorca als segles XVIII i XIX: les repercussions de la legislació desvinculadora sobre els patrimonis nobiliaris*, Palma, Universitat de les Illes Balears, Abadia de Montserrat.

Morey, Antònia (2002), *Els interrogatoris del ministre Soler (1800-1802). L'economia mallorquina a la fi de l'Antic Règim. Mallorca*, Documenta Balear.

Morey, Antònia (2004), 'Les transformacions econòmiques al segle XIX', en Ernest Belenguer (Dir.), *Història de les Illes Balears*, Barcelona, Edicions 62, vol. 3, p. 139-160.

Morey, Antònia (2006): 'Continuïtat i canvis en les formes d'explotació i ús de la Gran Albufera de Mallorca (segles XVI-XX)', en Ramon Molina de Dios (ed.), *S'Albufera de Mallorca. Aspectes geogràfics, històrics i socioeconòmics*, Palma, Conselleria de Medi Ambient, Govern de les Illes Balears, p. 37-64.

Morey, Antònia (2007), 'La legislación desvinculadora: una oportunidad para racionalizar la gestión de los patrimonios nobiliarios mallorquines y retrasar su desmembración', en Ricardo ROBLEDO & Santiago LÓPEZ (eds), *¿Interés particular, bienestar público? Grandes patrimonios y reformas agrarias*, Prensas Universitarias de Zaragoza, p. 129-157.

MOREY, Antònia (2013), 'Les comptabilitats nobiliàries: el cas de la noblesa mallorquina als segles XVIII i XIX', en *Comptes de pagès, comptes de senyor*, Girona, Associació d'Història Rural de les Comarques Gironines, p. 171-194.

OLIVER, Miquel dels Sants (1982), *Mallorca durante la primera revolución (1808-1814)*, Palma, Luis Ripoll, 3v. Ed. fascímil de la edición de 1901.

PASCUAL GONZÁLEZ, Luis (1979), *Derecho civil de Mallorca. Herencias y otras especialidades forales*, Mallorca, Ereso.

PEÑARRUBIA, Isabel (2001), *L'origen de la Caixa de Balears. Els projectes d'una burgesia modernitzadora (1882)*, Palma, Documenta Balear.

PÉREZ PICAZO, María Teresa & PÉREZ DE PERCEVAL, Miguel Ángel (2004), 'El mercado de la tierra en Murcia, 1836-1862', *Historia Agraria*, núm. 32, p. 57-84.

PESET, Mariano (1982), *Dos ensayos sobre la historia de la propiedad de la tierra*, Madrid, Editoriales de Derecho Reunidas.

PESET, Mariano (1983), 'L'emfiteusi al Regne de València. Una anàlisi jurídica', *Estudis d'Història Agrària*, núm. 7, p. 99-126.

PESET, Mariano (1989), 'Censos y propiedad de la tierra: los orígenes de la propiedad burguesa', en *Estructuras agrarias y reformismo ilustrado en la España del siglo XVIII*, Madrid, Ministerio de Agricultura, Pesca y Alimentación, p. 293-329.

PONS I GURI, Josep Maria (1989), *Recull d'estudis d'història jurídica catalana*, Barcelona, Fundació Noguera.

PORTELLA, Jaume (1994), 'Les baronies i cavalleries de Mallorca deis segles XIII i XIV. In feudum ad consuetudinem Barchinone', Afers, n. 18, p. 427-441.

PORTELLA COMAS, Jaume (1998), 'Cómo se exporta el feudalismo: el caso de Mallorca', en Miquel BARCELÓ & Pierre TOUBERT (eds), *L'Incastellamento: Actas de las Reuniones de Girona: (26-27 noviembre 1992) y de Roma: (5-7 Mayo 1994)*, Roma, Escuela Española de Historia y Arqueología en Roma, p. 85-98.

ROMERO, Joan (1983), 'Notas comparativas entre el señorío valenciano y los territorios de la antigua Corona de Aragón. Dos elementos básicos: la ausencia de población morisca en Cataluña y las Islas y la peculiaridad del modelo insular', *Estudis*, núm. 10, p. 151-164.

ROMERO, Joan (1989), 'Señorio y propiedad en mallorca en el tránsito de los siglos XVIII al XIX', en DD. AA., *Estructuras agrarias y reformismo ilustrado en la España del siglo XVIII. Actas del seminario de Segovia sobre Agricultura e Ilustración en España (14, 15 y 16 de septiembre de 1988)*, Madrid, p. 349-365.

ROSSELLÓ VERGER, Vicenç Maria (1964), Mallorca el Sur y el Sureste (municipios de Llucmajor, Campos, Ses Salines, Felanitx y Manacor), Palma de Mallorca, Cámara Oficial de Comercio, Industria y Navegación.

ROSSELLÓ VERGER, Vicenç Maria (1981), 'Canvis de propietat i parcel·lacions al camp mallorquí entre els segles XIX i XX', *Randa*, nº 12, p. 19-60.

ROSSELLÓ VERGER, Vicenç Maria (2012), 'La possessió, articuladora de l'espai rural. Imatge i realitat d'un sistema d'explotació esvaït', en Antònia MOREY

& Gabriel Jover (eds), *Les possessions mallorquines: passat i present*, Edicions Documenta Balear, Palma de Mallorca, p. 19-46.

Roura, Lluís (1985), *L'Antic Règim a Mallorca: abast de la commoció dels anys 1808-1814*, Palma, Conselleria d'Educació i Cultura del Govern Balear.

Satorras, Francisco (1878), *Informe sobre el estado de la agricultura en la provincia de las Baleares*, Palma, Imprenta de Pedro José Gelabert.

Satorras, Francisco (1887), *Memoria sobre el estado de la agricultura en la provincia de Baleares*, Documento inédito sin foliación.

Serra, Eva (1983), 'Notes sobre els orígens de l'emfiteusi a Catalunya', *Estudis d'Història Agrària*, núm. 7, p. 127-138.

Singala Cerdà, Miguel (1921), *Imprescriptibilidad del capital de los censos y de sus últimas 29 pensiones*, Palma.

Singala Cerdà, Miguel (1923), Nuevos datos sobre la imprescriptibilidad del capital de los censos y de sus últimas 29 pensiones. Palma.

Soto, Ricard (1991) *L'ordenació de l'espai i les relacions socials a Mallorca en el segle XIII (1229-1301)*, PhD thesis, Universitat Autónoma de Barcelona.

Soto, Ricard (1996), 'Conquesta, repartiment i colonització de Mallorca durant el segle XIII. Un estat de la qüestió', *Anuario de Estudios Medievales*, nº 26, p. 605-646.

Soto, Ricard (1999), 'Colonització i diferenciació pagesa a la Mallorca del segle XIII', en Miguel Gutierrez (ed.), *Doctor Jordi Nadal. La industrialització i el desenvolupament econòmic d´Espanya. Barcelona*, Publicacions de la Universitat de Barcelona, p. 375-491.

Suau puig, Jaume (1988), 'Els patrimonis nobiliaris mallorquins al darrer quart del segle XVIII i primeres dècades del segle XIX', *Estudis d'Història Agrària*, núm. 7, p. 139-160.

Suau puig, Jaume (1991), *El món rural mallorquí*, Barcelona, Curial.

Tello, Enric (1983), 'La producció cerealícola a les petites explotacions pageses del Pla de Mallorca (1850-1851)', *Estudis d'Història Agrària*, núm. 4, p. 167-194.

To figueras, Lluís (1997), *Família i hereu a la Catalunya nord-oriental (segles X-XII)*, Barcelona, Abadia de Montserrat.

Vaquer salord, Miguel (1959), 'La imprescribdibilidad de los censos mallorquines', *Revista Crítica del Derecho Inmobiliario*, núm. 369, p. 89-93.

Vaquer salord, Miguel (1973), 'Los alodios y la imprescriptibilidad de los censos', *Jornadas de Derecho Foral Balear*, Palma, Colegio de Abogados.

Villares, Ramón (1983), 'Els foros de Galícia. Uns quants problemes i comparacions', *Estudis d'Història Agrària*, núm. 7, p. 161-185.

Wickham, Chris (2000), *Legge, Practiche e Conflitti: Tribunali e risoluzione delle disputen ella Toscana del XII secolo*, Rome, Viella libreria Editrice.

Zaforteza, Luz (1992a), *La compilación de 1961 a través de su proceso formativo: antecedentes, documentos y actas*, Palma, Universitat de les Illes Balears.

Zaforteza, Luz (1992b), *El fideicomiso en el derecho civil de Mallorca y Menorca*, Palma, Ajuntament.

Zaforteza, Luz, Mut, Antonio & Oliver, Manuel (1995), *Tratados de notaría en el Reino de Mallorca*, Guadalajara, Colegios Notariales de España.

PEGERTO SAAVEDRA

10. *Foros*

*Land Tenure as a Source of Income and Conflict in Early-Modern Galicia**

I. Basic characteristics of the *foro*

From the eleventh through the thirteenth centuries, institutions and social relationships were established or consolidated in Galicia that remained in force during the entire Ancien Régime. These underwent transformations of varying intensity and a few, such as the *foros* or land tenures, survived into the twentieth century with more than a residual presence. Demographic and agrarian growth and expansion brought with it the creation of many hamlets and the establishment of large estates granted to the nobility and the church, among them the Benedictine and Cistercian monasteries. The *foro* emerged as a widespread legal instrument by which lords could bring land under cultivation. Hamlets were formed by assigning small plots to peasants, with tenure assured for generations. All these developments in the heart of the Middle Ages gave birth to a society of peasants and lords destined to last for centuries[1].

Foros and seigniorial rights were modified between the sixteenth and eighteenth centuries, in tandem with other changes brought about by the assertion of royal power. Greater royal control over seigniorial rights increased the significance of law in social relationships. In the late Middle Ages, the *foro* was often emphyteutic: a perpetual tenure under which tenants paid a rent usually proportional to the harvest. They also contributed with other work and were beholden as 'servants and loyal vassals' of the institution or feudal family with dominium directum over the land; who exercised immediate and sometimes arbitrary power over rural communities[2].

* This research has been carried out within the framework of Research Project HAR-2014-52667-R, financed by the Spanish Ministerio de Economía y Competividad.

1 This is shown in Ermelindo Portela's book on Cistercian colonization. See Portela Silva (1981).

2 When the land *foros* were not perpetual in nature, they often lasted four or more generations. See Rodríguez Galdo (1976) and Portela Silva (1976). On the arbitrary nature of seigniorial powers and excesses of some aristocrats and prelates in the fourteenth and fifteenth centuries, see García Oro (1977).

Agrarian Change and Imperfect Property, ed. by Rosa Congost and Pablo F. Luna, Rural History in Europe, 15 (Turnhout, 2018), 207-235

DOI 10.1484/M.RURHE-EB.5.116125

In the new situation that emerged from 1480 to 1520, the monarchy put an end to the local freedoms of the lords. *Foros* remained the preferred method of tenure by which ecclesiastical institutions, the aristocracy, the landed gentry (or small nobility) gave peasants land to cultivate. Privileged estates were defined above all by their condition as collectors of agrarian rent, which some ecclesiastics saw as inevitable (Villares (1982a and b, and 1988). In the history of the powerful Cistercian monastery of Oseira, published in 1677, the author Fr. Tomás de Peralta feels compelled to explain that all the lands pertaining to the monastery were hired out to peasants, who paid rent in kind:

> There is nothing stable in this life; everything changes and is disrupted. Ownership should therefore go hand in hand with these alterations, and in accordance with the changing times. The monastery once had slaves, who worked the land with their families, and lay converts, distributed into *majorats* and farms where they were, who looked after them, and even the monks themselves, as we have seen, went to harvest the crops. None of this exists any more, and as all the monastery's possessions consist of land, it had to be given to someone to cultivate, and obtain some profit in return[3].

In any case, the sources we have for the late Ancien Régime show that peasants mainly paid taxes in the form of rent and tithes from the lands they cultivated. The Ensenada registry from the mid-eighteenth century assigned monetary value in *reales* to the 'agricultural surplus'. The figures, though approximate, leave no room for doubt:

Table 10.1. Appraisal value in *reales* of *foros*, tithes, the vow of St James, first fruits and landlord rights in 1752 (Ensenada)

Concept	*Reales*	%
Foros	12,096,226	47.1
Leasing	c. 3,000,000*	11.7*
Tithes	8,963,256	34.9
Vows and first fruits	1,242,46	4.8
Lordship rights	387,683	1.5
TOTAL	25,689,411	100.0

Source: National Archive of History of Madrid, Tax Authority, Registry of Ensenada, ledgers 7,440 and 7,441. * The figures are approximate because unlike the *foros*, the registry did not provide direct information

3 In Peralta, 1677: 229. In recent years historiography has questioned whether the Cistercians farmed their lands directly, or at least whether they actually did so with their own hands; cf. Alfonso Antón (1991).

The Ensenada registry does not reflect whether the land was owned by peasants, held under *foro* tenure or leased[4]. It does indicate, however, that roughly three-quarters of cultivated land was managed through *foros* owned by ecclesiastical institutions or noble families. The rest – especially in Cantabrian Galicia – was leased, privately owned or allodial. The pervasiveness of the *foro* system, and therefore of peasant rights as land users, is clearly evident in the fact that inventories and other records from the time did not value monastic and seigniorial land in terms of extension – which was often unknown – but rather in the annual rent collected. In the documentation of the time, the term *foro* referred to both the type of agrarian lease and the income it generated.

Like income from nine-year maximum leases, *foro* rents were fixed in kind. In the general summaries or registry 'maps' from Ensenada, income was appraised monetarily. The prices were probably estimated (low) by the residents themselves. If we use such values to convert the 25,689,411 *reales* into hectolitres of rye, we would obtain roughly 1,050,000 hl; indicating that each family would pay a total of about 3.61 hectolitres per year. These calculations point to the huge surplus generated by Galician smallholders: in the mid-eighteenth century, approximately 280,000 families supported an opulent secular and regular ecclesiastical class and nobility composed mainly of landed gentry with manor houses. The architectural heritage that remains today and was admired by certain eighteenth-century travellers bears witness to the wealth received through *foros* and tithes (Rey Castelao, 1985, 1993; Saavedra, 2003, 2007).

Alexander Jardine, an English Consul who came to Galicia in the second half of the eighteenth century, likened *foro* landholding to the English *copyholder* system. In the 1790s he observed:

> Unlike the rest of Spain, [*in Galicia*] the greater part of their farms and lands are too small, and the owners too poor to improve them; however, the way of landholding, the foros, is like our copyholders, and it is preferable, it would be much better for Spain if this were generally the case, especially if it could avoid the problems of subleasing, which are all too frequent here, as they are in Scotland and Ireland[5].

The English Consul had a point. Half-way through the nineteenth century, legal expert Basilio Besada gave a clear and simple definition of the *foros*, comparing them with leasing and emphyteusis:

> it is very easy to form an idea of the *foro* in Galicia. It is no more than a land owner transferring the use of his land to the colonist, thereby ensuring an

4 Concerning the problems arising from the land register, which are partly the result of different property rights being in force over the same plot of land, cf. Saavedra (2007).

5 In García Blanco-Cicerón (2006: 289). In general travellers described agrarian system in Galicia as preferable due to the stability that *foros* implied for crop growers.

> annual pension while the land is tended by the other; when this situation comes to an end, things go back to how they were before.

Besada underlines the differences between the *foro* and lease:

> Whoever holds land under a *foro* holds it in his own name; while land under lease is held on behalf of the owner; the former can transfer the land and its obligations to a third party, while the latter cannot; the former acquires ownership of use, while the latter acquires no ownership whatsoever.

Above all, he emphasises the difference between the *foro* and emphyteusis:

> The *foro* and emphyteusis are more similar [than the *foro* and the lease], and can easily be confused if not carefully defined. In both cases, the person ceding the land does so for a fee or yearly retribution, and the person receiving the land is obliged to pay this; in both cases *dominium directum* remains with the former while use is transferred to the latter; in both cases the recipient can transfer the use of the land with its obligations to a third party; thus, as in other circumstances, the effects of the two kinds of contract are confused.

However, the *foro* was temporary (as defined by the *Novísima Recopilación* in 1805, and the Parliamentary Law of 8 June 1813, when it is excluded from the redeemable perpetual census), and payment by seizure, the right of first refusal, or payment of *laudemium* (entry fines) could be applied[6].

Basilio Besada was right regarding the temporary nature of the *foro*, but erred in his affirmation that the direct owner could not demand the right of first refusal to recover an object being sold, or receive *laudemium* on objects sold (usually ten per cent of the selling price). We should not forget that Besada wrote in the mid-nineteenth century, after the abolition of feudal lordships. The *foro*, however, originated in the heart of the Middle Ages; the condition of the owners of these lands as *lords* was inextricable from the *foro*, especially with regard to the Benedictine and Cistercian monasteries. Galicia remained a 'feudal reserve' until 1811, with 90 per cent of the population living in territorial circumscriptions (jurisdictions) belonging to the nobility and ecclesiastical institutions[7]. Consequently, many who received rent from *foros*

---

6 In Artiaga & Baz Vicente (1997: 44-47). For comparisons with other agrarian censuses, cf. Villares (1988); Clavero (1980, 1986) and Congost (2007).

7 Legal expert Pla y Cancela wrote in *De los foros y contratos enfitéuticos*: 'The *foro* has always been a feudal institution, which consisted of granting inheritable land tenure to one or several vassals together, or an entire estate with all its land and water, *a montes e a fontes*, so that they may live thereon and cultivate it, making the usufruct their own and under the obligation to provide personal services, which constitute the essence of being a vassal, and pay a moderate canon to their overlords in recognition of their ownership. In old deeds we see that the words *loan* and *foro* are used indistinctly and that *tenant (forero)* meant the same as *vassal*'. In Artiaga & Baz Vicente (1997: 149), concerning the extension of the feudal lordship regime in the eighteenth century, cf. Eiras Roel (1989).

held jurisdiction over their tenants, who were also their vassals. However, most landowners were not *lords of vassals*; or if they were, obtained rent from other areas. But when it did occur, at least until the early seventeenth century, tenants were also 'servants and obedient subjects', obliged under the *foro* clauses to carry out the services demanded by their overlords, including hauling stones, wood and other materials.

The usefulness to landlords of demanding discretional or arbitrary service (until the Royal Tribunal limited them) was evaluated in the mid-1570s by a commissioner sent to Galicia by Philip II to divide and sell the jurisdictions of ecclesiastical institutions. He explained how the peasants in Galicia were poorer than those in Castile, but that did not mean that their lords obtained less benefit from them:

> these subjects on the whole are more useful to their lords than those in Castile, even though they are poorer, they are more useful, as they contribute to wealth with the regular and forced rights and services and the daily work they are accustomed to doing, whereas the vassals of Castile and other areas do not carry them out [sc. said services].

Around the same time, the Cistercian monks of Penamaior stated that their vassals under *foro* 'do what they are told in usefulness and benefit to the house' (Faya Díaz, 1999: 110; Saavedra, 2010a).

In the sixteenth through eighteenth centuries, the *foro* was characteristically a flexible agrarian tenure that served the interests of lords who operated huge tracts of land with virtually no investment; although it also fit with peasant strategy. On the one hand, the ecclesiastical institutions and the noble houses occasionally included fees in the *foro* deeds and land registries that tenant farmers had previously paid collectively as vassals. From the early sixteenth century, tenants often challenged these in the main royal tribunals, such as the *Audiencia de Galicia* and the *Chancillería de Valladolid*. The lords reacted by trying to incorporate the disputed services into *foro* deeds: including the payment of a death tax or the payment of the best cow upon the death of the head of the household, or other personal services. From that time on, such charges or duties were specified, agreed to and witnessed by a scribe, leaving tenants without recourse for refusing payment (Baz Vicente, 1996: 124-154; Saavedra, 2003: 95-97 and 103-104). On the other hand, peasants often ignored stipulations regarding the duration of the *foro* or others that forbid them to sell, exchange or divide the land among their heirs without permission from the direct owner. Furthermore, because of its duration and the rights granted to holders, the *foro* system favoured the creation of superimposed dominion by means of *sub-foros*. A person or family who received one or more plots of *foro* land could rent it to a third party at increased price. Thus a single plot of land could be subject to diverse rents owed to different people. The landed gentry or minor nobility obtained a greater or lesser part of their income from *sub-foros*, which is why they were sometimes called 'intermediate nobility' or 'middle lords', akin to the Irish *middlemen* (Villares, 1982b, 1999).

From the sixteenth century on, the medieval custom of fixing rent as a proportion of the harvest was only maintained in winegrowing regions and a few coastal locations. Monks debated endlessly over the advantages of fixed rent versus variable quotas based on production. In the early seventeenth century, a monk from Oia wrote that 'there are different opinions for everything in this world, and on this matter too'. He admitted that a fixed rent 'is charged with no work or unease, [sc. the tenants] bring it to the house at no expense'. Even so, in order to take advantage of agricultural expansion, he preferred 'portions' proportional to the harvest. In long-term tenures like the *foros*, this only happened when there was an organic link between rent and production[8].

However, proportional *foros* created problems for monastic communities. Peasants would conceal monastery ownership of land parcels and thereby evade the corresponding contribution of its produce. It is easily understood that collecting a fourth, a fifth or a sixth part of the harvest would require identification and inspection of the corresponding lands. In 1616, the San Clodio monk who was responsible for drawing up the monastery's cartulary bemoaned the often insurmountable difficulties he encountered in the different priories and farms due to confusion, deceit, vows, divisions and denials of ownership by tenants unconcerned with reprimands or excommunication:

> because if you grant a *foro* of four vineyards to someone today, tomorrow you will find it divided up, sold off and concealed. They do not wait for their children [or someone else] to deny it, but rather they themselves confess it [in] a registry and tomorrow sell it as their own tithes for God, and if a new registry is documented, they conceal and ignore it with the greatest ease.

A declaration by a witness was required for drawing up a registry document; and as with litigation, monasteries were hard pressed to find peasants who would bear witness in favour of the monks: 'I consider the [lands] of this house as lost', the monk concluded in dismay[9]. References to lost land and rights are constant in the cartularies and inventories of deeds preserved in archives. Even so, diverse priories of the San Clodio monastery, (along with those of Oseira, Sobrado and Monfero) maintained proportional *foros* in parts of their dominion. Their land was basically for winegrowing in the river valleys near the monastery. The monks preferred supervising plots of land and harvests, and avoiding delays by charging fifth and sixth parts at harvest time. Because the land was so subdivided and subleased, charging fixed amounts would involve collecting from multiple tenants in dispersed locations.

'Farming monks' and overseers of noble houses needed determination and patience to deal with peasant cunning and malice on a daily basis. With

---

8 National Archive of History, Madrid, Clergy, book 10,223 from Oia.

9 National Archive of History, Madrid, Clergy, Codex 224 from San Clodio, and Lucas Álvarez (1996).

scattered habitats and very small plots of land producing different crops, harvested at different times, came abundant opportunities for fraud; especially in paying proportional rent and tithes. If the landowners held jurisdiction over the tenants as vassals, diverse sources indicate that the capacity for control increased significantly. When Philip II had enquiries made concerning the vassals of ecclesiastical institutions, with a view to selling certain jurisdictions and properties, the monasteries did everything in their power to maintain the *status quo*, even if it meant paying large sums of money to the Royal Treasury. The monks of Sobrado, for example, claimed that the peasants were 'indomitable people – the only way you can collect rent from them is by throwing them into prison'. Those at Oia, who also had numerous proportional *foros*, complained that tenants 'run off with, deny payment, or keep their rents on a daily basis'. They warned that if the King's project to divide up and sell jurisdictions and reserves went forward, 'it is clear that monasteries will become depopulated, and they will not be able to survive, not even if compensated in other ways' (Faya Díaz, 1999).

In the second half of the sixteenth century and the first decade of the seventeenth, ecclesiastical institutions and noble houses drew up numerous land registry documents to supervise and defend their material and immaterial assets. Independent monasteries were incorporated into the Benedictine and Cistercian orders; and the monks in charge set compulsory rules for abbots, regarding the administration of properties, record keeping and the kind of books they were to draw up, namely cartularies and land registries. During the same period, absentee noble families bureaucratised the administration of their estates; assigning an *alcalde mayor*, or magistrate, to supervise the judges, scribes and administrators who enforced rents and feudal rights (Saavedra, 2003).

Drawing up a land registry was a complex and difficult task, especially if the people called to declare would not collaborate. With land subdivisions, exchanges, purchases and sales, changing crops and other incidents, many plots of land became unrecognisable within one or two generations; to the point that even owners and agents were incapable of identifying them. Peasant malice and changes in the agrarian landscape eventually rendered registry documents insufficient as 'proof of ownership' and few were drawn up after the mid-seventeenth century[10]. The 'essential' warning issued by a monk from Oia (*c.* 1700) concerning the tricks of tenants to obscure the monastery's dominium directum is illustrative:

> One of the main ruses is employed when the head of a household dies. Assets have to be reckoned, for example from the monastery chapter, from the church, from his own possessions, and from the monastery of Oya, to

10 Cf. Burgo López (1986); Baz Vicente (1996) for registry documents. In France *terriers* were still in use and in Catalonia Jaume Tos i Urgellès published a treatise on land parcel delimitation in 1784; which was re-published by Congost (2007).

> be precise. The heirs put them in common and divide them up amongst themselves. They do the same with pensions and rents, and whoever receives chapter property, for example, pays the monastery of Oya, and the one who inherits from Oya pays the church, and so on with the rest. They pay in this way for some years, unwillingly, and then they decide not to pay and the owner of the foro and the land makes recourse to the law or demands the land be given back to him. Then come their tricks: the landlord gets out his papers and documents, and it is recognised, for example, that the one who inherited from the chapter has not paid rent for many years, because another heir paid for him, late and unwillingly; and then the one who paid starts complaining that he has paid for so many years unfairly, without inheriting anything from the chapter (…). Their children then do the same, and then their grandchildren, on the death of each head of the household; and so over time everything gets confused and muddled with the land. This is what the labourers want, as turbulent waters make better fishing[11].

The landlords coped primarily by creating more detailed *foro* deeds, by controlling payment of rents in their annual register and voluminous accounting books and by appointing a *fiduciary*, a tenant responsible for collecting the *foro* rents from the other tenants and taking it to the landlord. Every now and then rents were prorated or redistributed among crop growers, and payments were adjusted according to changes in land possession from sales, exchanges and divisions. In the eighteenth century, compulsory proration was sometimes included in *foro* deeds, and often resisted by peasants[12].

II. Conflicts arising from the temporal nature of *foros*

The fundamentally temporary nature of *foros* differentiates them from emphyteusis under the monarchy of Aragon (Congost, 1990 and 2007), for example, and is at the root of the conflicts that arose between the direct owners of the land (dominium directum) and the owners of its dominium utile. A significant change took place in the seventeenth century that established the duration of *foros* by the lives of monarchs rather than by tenant lives or generations; which clearly favoured the landowners' capacity for control. Until then, in order to determine when a *foro* that had been granted for a certain number of lives – usually three – expired, the direct landowners had to actually know the history of the tenant families. Families often concealed the deaths of heads of household in order to prolong the duration of the *foro*

11 National Archive of History, Madrid, Codex 60.

12 We could give numerous examples for the monasteries in the province of Ourense, where sharing out inheritances led to extensive fragmentation of use and rent. On pro rata divisions in general, cf. Villares (1981a).

and avoid eviction or rent increases. Upon the death of a tenant, the heir was required to appear before the landlord in order to be recognised as the successor. This was very seldom respected; nor was the prohibition of selling rights of use or dividing up the *foro* among children without informing the landlord[13]. Various lawsuits for dispossession or eviction were presented by the monastery of Melón in 1749, arguing that the *foros* were 'vacant' or that the tenancy periods had expired. Some plots of *foro* land granted in 1570-1580 for three lives or generations had not been renewed for over 150 years. Given the life expectancy of the time, such lengthy extensions to the contracts could not be justified. By fixing the duration of the *foro* according the lives of kings – generally three – it was easy for holders of extensive lands, especially monasteries, to ascertain what land became available when a monarch died. For example, by simply opening the *foro* books upon the death of Charles II in 1700, they knew which *foros* had been granted during the life of his grandfather, Philip III (1598-1621). The land affected could be leased out or tenured again under *foro* to the previous tenants or to others.

Clarifying which *foros* were in force, however, did not prevent the rights of tenants from prevailing over those of the landlords. In the first half of the seventeenth century, the landed gentry presented a petition in the *Juntas del Reino*, the representative assembly of the Kingdom, asking the monarch for a law that would either make the *foros* perpetual or make compulsory their renovation in favour of the descendants of the first tenants. The nobles appointed to the 1626 and 1629 assemblies requested that:

> given that many estates in this Kingdom are ecclesiastical and secular *foros* by emphyteusis, and tenants improve the land they receive by *foro* (…), and once the lives come to an end the landlords take the land away from them and keep it for themselves, or give it to others (…), we beg Your Majesty to promulgate a general law, like the Law of Portugal (…), [so that] they may be renewed in all cases (…), for the great benefit of the people of this Kingdom.

In the 1630s, the official jurist Francisco de Salgado y Somoza supported the nobles' request, noting that among them 'there are few who do not have monastery *foros*'. Without a law making renovation compulsory, many noble houses would wane[14].

Debates about the renovation of *foros* became more intense after Charles II died in 1700 and until the death of Fernando VI in 1759. Printed sources indicate it to be a rather serious conflict that set the gentry and middle nobility against the Count of Altamira. The first two groups had inherited *foro* land from ecclesiastical institutions and the aristocracy, which they had in turn tenured

---

13 Similar situations are recorded in England, where peasants worked land under copyhold. Cf. Thompson (1995 [1991]: 184).

14 These and other texts can be found in Villares & Díaz-Castroverde (1997).

to peasants in *sub-foros*. They therefore defended the compulsory renewal of the *foros* in favour of the descendants of the original tenants through the institutions they controlled: the *Juntas del Reino* and the urban municipalities. The Count of Altamira wished to recover *foro* lands that had become vacant upon the deaths of monarchs in 1700, 1746 and 1759; in order to draw up new *foros* or lease the land. Peasants were also affected, and the monastic communities brought numerous petitions for dispossession and eviction against them in the Royal Tribunal, which dealt with lawsuits of this kind.

I consider peasant involvement decisive in a rigorous explanation of the intense *foro* conflict that occurred in the mid-eighteenth century, though historians disagree as to the causes. For some, the problems that arose in relation to the renovation of *foros* were no more than a confrontation between Benedictine or Cistercian monasteries and the landed gentry. The religious houses wished to recover and control their extensive, dispersed possessions; an enterprise the landed gentry opposed and hindered. The monks had a paternalistic relationship with the peasants, while the greedy nobles speculated with the land, charging very high rents to tenant working *sub-foro* lands[15]. For others, the conflict was more than a struggle between monasteries and landed gentry: the peasant communities were decisively involved, also using diverse strategies to resist monastic aims. The monasteries often sought to convert *foros* into leases, a development that significantly altered the traditional distribution of land rights. No doubt the monks did wish to recover and control their lands; and eliminating *foros* was in fact the best way to achieve this while also enabling tenants to subdivide, exchange, mortgage and sell those lands. Fr. Sarmiento said as much in a letter to Campomanes in February of 1767: monastery land could only be ceded to laypeople under 'pure leasing'. Otherwise it was like 'exposing ownership to a cesspool of never-ending lawsuits, which occurs with the absurdity of foros, something unheard of in Castile'[16]. In my opinion, this second hypothesis has more arguments in favour, and becomes more plausible upon closer consultation of legal documentation from the monastery archives or the Royal Tribunal (Villares, 1982a and b; 1989, 1997; Barreiro Fernández, 1985; Díaz-Castroverde, 1992; Villares & Díaz-Castroverde, 1997; Dopico, 1978; Saavedra, 2012).

During the first half of the eighteenth century, many monasteries and convents in western Asturias and Cantabrian Galicia converted *foros* into leases (Saavedra, 1985; Paz González, 1991)[17]. Mandates of visiting priests and other monastery texts from the 1740s allude to the advantages of leasing, or report how certain communities had transitioned from *foros* to short-term

---

15 Cf. esp. Eiras Roel (1972, 1981); Barreiro Mallón (1972, 1973); Pérez García (1979, 1995).

16 Copied from book 5,777 from the monastery of Vilanova de Lourenzá, clergy section at the National Archive of History, Madrid.

17 See also Luna in this book.

leases. Others (Melón, Oia, Sobrado) unsuccessfully called for the peasants threatened with dispossession to bid for lease of the land. It is also highly significant to note that the greatest number of lawsuits brought before the Royal Tribunal by monasteries did not correspond to the eighteenth century, but to the late sixteenth and early seventeenth centuries; when the various communities were mandated by their congregations to draw up land registries and cartularies and make recourse to the Tribunal in order to recover land or have possessions recognised as part of their domain. The number of demands brought before the court by eight Cistercian monasteries can be seen in the following table, and the trend is very clear:

Table 10.2. Total lawsuits brought before the Royal Tribunal by monasteries in Galicia and percentage of land claims among lawsuits presented by eight Cistercian communities

Years	Total Lawsuits by Monasteries	Annual Average	Total Lawsuits by Eight Cistercian Communities	Annual Average	Land Claims	Annual Average	% Land Claims
1560-1639	4,576	52.7	1,744	21.8	1,570	19.6	90
1640-1719	2,188	27.4	762	9.5	539	6.7	70.7
1720-1759	503	12.6	165	4.1	89	2.2	53.9
1760-1834	591	8.3	163	2.3	16	0.2	9.8
Total	7,858	29	2,834	10.5	2,214	8.2	78.1

Source: Catalogue of resident reports, Archive of the Kingdom of Galicia (A Coruña)

The figures show a clear and spectacular drop in the number of land claims after 1720; which leads us to ask why those relatively few demands in the mid-eighteenth century were so conflictive. I would suggest several reasons:

- a) Lawsuits from the sixteenth and seventeenth centuries sought tenant recognition of direct ownership in order to receive new *foros*, whereas in the eighteenth century there is a clear trend by the monasteries to transform *foros* into leases.
- b) Though lawsuits involving *foros* in the mid-eighteenth century were significantly fewer in number, just one of them affected hundreds of tenants; whereas previously each claim was made against a single family. Since by this time the duration of many *foros* was established by the lives of kings rather than tenant lives or generations, on the death of Philip V (1746) and Fernando VI (1759) hundreds of *foros* suddenly ended. Also,

due to the extensive subdivision of land through sale or partitioning among heirs, *foro* land that had originally been granted to a single family was being cultivated by dozens of people. In the most densely populated areas of Galicia, rent payment was so atomized that some monastery account books used the *conca* (approximately 1.33 litres) to measure grain rents[18].

– c) Tenants in the eighteenth century were much more belligerent in their disinclination to leave the land: because of the number of people involved in each lawsuit, because of their unwillingness to lease the land, and because they knew that the Court of Castile favoured agrarian stability and harboured little sympathy for the regular clergy. 'Monks have no homeland', wrote Grimaldi to Tanucci in August of 1764: 'from the moment they take their vows they should see themselves not only as foreigners but enemies of the State where they were born'[19].

These points are supported by diverse extracts from the more 'conflictive' lawsuits between monasteries and groups of tenant farmers. The latter adopted myriad resistance strategies now considered the typical 'weapons of the weak': refusal to collaborate, heads of household disappearing in order to avoid legal notifications, challenges to public officials and tax appraisers, disturbances, scandal intended to discredit the monasteries and their representatives, recourse to the king through reports or journeying to Court, etc.[20]. The writings of a monk from Oia who recorded the lawsuits between the monastery and its tenants/vassals in the first half of the eighteenth century reflect these strategies:

> To describe in detail the most important developments that took place over the twelve years [*c.* 1721-1733] that the main lawsuit lasted would fill this cartulary and only begin to describe the main points. The residents of these two parishes went four times to Madrid, into the presence of His Majesty; on the first occasion over ninty men and women went (…). The monastery was at the end of its means, as it could not collect any rents or even find anyone to sell eggs.

He goes on to explain that the monastery presented various lawsuits to collect its debts, rather than a global one: 'after consulting the best lawyers in Spain, who said it was not a good idea to say that the whole jurisdiction was in play,

18 The documentation from the monastery of Armenteira, in the Rías Baixas, provides numerous examples of claims involving many smallholding tenants and the extreme fragmentation of *foros* and rents. National Archive of History, Madrid, Clergy, book 9,928 (claims) and 9,975 (collection records).

19 In Barrio Gonzalo (1997: 78-79). For Secretary of State Grimaldi, the homeland of the regular clergy was Rome.

20 Concerning the 'weapons of the weak', cf. Scott (1985), and its application to rural Galicia, cf. Fernández González (1995); Díaz-Castroverde (1992) for the specific case of *foro* conflicts.

as this sounded very bad in all the courts'. In other words, peasant efforts at disturbances and scandals were effective and there was no end to the conflict. He writes that in 1751, when he wished to lease out land to residents of Loureza, who had farmed it previously under a *foro*, 'they all swore not to accept the lease and decided to go to Madrid with their wives and children to complain to the King'. In the end, 'to avoid further trouble' and put an end to the quarrel, the monastery 'granted the land under a *foro* again'[21].

In this kind of conflict, women played a fundamental role, which paradoxically derived from their condition of legal and political inferiority. Women were considered minors unless they were widows or self-employed spinsters; and married women required their husband's authorisation to sign a deed or take part in a trial, as is commonly known[22]. In civil lawsuits, this discrimination virtually granted them impunity. When local or legal authorities came to give notifications or enforce sentences, the bells tolled a warning and the male heads of household fled. Their wives either threw stones at the scribes and judges or simply claimed ignorance of their husbands' whereabouts day after day.

The Rubillón estate, a group of six villages in the north-west of the Ourense province, under the lordship and dominium directum of the monastery of Melón, serves as another example. In the 1740s, the monks drew up a registry document, which the residents managed to have annulled due to technicalities by the Council of Castile[23]. The monastic house then presented a claim at the Royal Tribunal, alleging that the *foros* had expired and that they were entitled to recover the land in order to lease it or grant new *foros*. The sentence was favourable to the monks and backed by two letters of execution from the Royal Tribunal in 1749 and 1753. In 1754 a scribe from the Royal Tribunal came to the village of Penedo to give the monastery possession of its land, and called on residents to declare which plots of land each of them farmed. When the first of them started describing which plots belonged to him, his wife came forward with various nieces, 'yelling and shouting, threatening him and telling him not to declare [the land], otherwise they would leave him'. The sensible man obeyed, 'and said that he would rather go to prison than declare the land'. The other residents followed his example, and the scribe realised that the men's refusal to declare 'depended on what their wives told them to do'. He then decided to move the legal audit to another village appointed by the monastery, to a room in the ordinary judge's house. In this isolated, enclosed place he intended to bring in the peasants one by one to declare a detailed inventory of their lands, under threat of imprisonment.

---

21 National Archive of History, Madrid, Clergy, codex 60 and book 10,223 from Oia.

22 Cf. the pertinent thoughts of Thompson (1995 [1991]: 345-379) on the prominent role of women in mutinies in eighteenth-century England.

23 The main incidences in Clergy book 8,661 from Melon at the National Archive of History, Madrid. Cf. also the Archive of the Kingdom of Galicia (A Coruña), Monasteries, mss. 88/15 and 81/45. Mention was made of this conflict by Villares (1989); Díaz-Castroverde (1992).

The scribe's strategy failed. On the many trips both he and the judge made to the village of Penedo, sometimes at dawn, they only ever found women and children: 'The men from Penedo all fled with their cattle, and it is clear that their actions are designed to make the effect of the royal letter of execution illusory and void'. The scribe had initially been commissioned for thirty days; which was extended by 150 days and then 300 more. In July of 1754, after accepting witnesses who were partial to the prior, the scribe gave the prior formal possession of the land, although effective possession would take much longer. The residents lodged complaints of abuse of power, arguing that they had been violently thrown out of their homes, 'driven to the hills in terror and under threat, left without food, [as] the scribe and his acolytes [were] creating disturbances with people whom he had rounded up and armed'. The tenants even made recourse to the King, who through the Council of Castile ordered the regent to investigate the complaints and bring the case before the plenary session.

In May of 1755, a year after the commissioned scribe had arrived, the prior still had not taken possession of the lands that had been granted in *foros* almost two centuries earlier:

> the [tenants] had no intention of obeying and Lameiro [the leader of a group] and his followers fled, leaving behind their wives and families with express instructions to 'sit tight' and keep on using the houses and land as if there had been no dispossession, and this is what they do. They do not wish to renew their rights, even though I hung notices on the door of the parish church inviting everyone who wished to lease or use the land under *foro* to come to me so that I could draw up their rights.

Some tenants accepted new contracts, provided they were *foros*, while others 'remained stubborn and kept away, with their wives and families in the village' and threatened those who were prepared to take their land: 'if they do so they will burn the land and destroy the crops they have sown, and fear of this brought the would-be tenants to a halt'[24].

Finally, on 1 June 1755, the scribe, accompanied by the prior, the ordinary judge and various hired men evicted a dozen women and children, who in the absence of their husbands and fathers, refused to leave the houses and lands they had been working. The women would not hand over the keys, and so the doors to the houses were nailed shut. Almost seven years had passed since the first notification of the sentence ordering dispossession, and eighteen months since the Tribunal had issued the second letter of execution[25].

---

24 National Archive of History, Madrid, Clergy, book 8,661 from Melon, devoted to this lawsuit. Cf. also the Archive of the Kingdom of Galicia (A Coruña), Monasteries, mss. 81/45 and 88/15.

25 The prior showed himself well-disposed towards those responsible for throwing the women and children out of their homes, as is explained in the monastery's lawsuit record book. From April of 1755 to April of 1756 3,462 *reales* were spent 'on the scribe, accompanying

The peasant families were now homeless, but all was not lost. They filed a poverty report before the Royal Tribunal, with witnesses who said they had seen them begging for alms at different houses. The Regent of the Tribunal urged the monks to renew the *foros*, which they did, making their decision out to be a work of charity: 'Legal formalities were undertaken by both sides, and meanwhile, the others [the dispossessed tenants] alleged the little justice they had received and agreed to ask for a resolution of the conflict, and the result was a letter from the Royal Delegate in La Coruña addressed to the abbot and the monks, requesting them to have pity on those poor people, to allow them back into their homes as would be just'[26].

The minor nobility, desiring to maintain the lands they had let out to peasants under *foro*, made the most of the conflicts between the monasteries and tenants. They had little difficulty convincing the Council of Castile – the highest royal court, which included Galician noble Pedro Martínez Feijoo – that monastic greed was leaving poor tenants homeless and bereft of the lands they and their ancestors had worked. It was outrageous that monks under vows of poverty and charity were living in opulence, without concern for the families who had been evicted from their homes and were wandering around the realm. The landed gentry insisted that the social order, and their essential place in it, would fall apart if their families were deprived of the *foros* they had held for generations. The great monasteries were so powerful, they argued, that ruin of the nobility would open the door to a kind of 'ecclesiastical monarchy' in Galicia. They alleged, truthfully, that the Archbishop of Santiago, Bartolomé de Rajoy Losada, was in favour of the renewal of the *foros* and supported the nobility; as had other clerics before him such as the Jesuit Juan Álvarez de Sotelo[27].

The nobles knew that *foros* were temporary tenures and that once the tenants or kings passed away, the land returned to its direct owners, and this was upheld by the jurisprudence of the Royal Tribunal. Their arguments for requesting perpetuation or compulsory renovation emphasized the injustice of dispossession, the conflicts it caused in the rural world, the outrage of monastic greed, and the difficulties involved in defining *foro* land that had been subdivided or sold over several generations. They asked the king to find

---

priest, scribe's servant, officers and other men who helped in the eviction of families in Penedo, on wine, beef, chocolate, bacon, fish, sardines, game, tobacco, etc.'. Locks and other material to close up the houses cost 127 *reales*. Provincial Historical Archive of Ourense, Clergy, book 400 from the monastery of Melón.

26 Provincial Historical Archive of Ourense, Clergy, book 400 from the monastery of Melón, accounts for lawsuit expenses from April 1756 to April 1757.

27 The Archbishop of Compostela's support for the landed gentry was highlighted by Barreiro Fernández (1985). The Archbishop belonged to a noble family from the area around the River Eume, and 75 per cent of his rents came from the *Voto de Santiago*. In the documentation from the monastery of Melón a great part of the clergy – parish priests and others – opposed the monastery in dispossession lawsuits (in Rubillón, Navío, etc.).

a remedy for these evils and prevent the monasteries from acquiring power that not even royalty could control. *La natural razón: por el Reino de Galicia contra los monasterios de la orden de San Benito y San Bernardo...* was written by the General Delegate of the Court, Antonio de Zúñiga y Losada, and the legal expert Antonio de Valladolid, and printed in 1767. It states that 'On seeing the opulence of the few (who profess poverty) who have become rich without scruple, and the nakedness of so many, one cannot help becoming inflamed with righteous anger (...). Let these poor people then have some breathing space, it is due to them that you are wealthy'. In *foros* still governed by tenant lives, the death of the head of household brought with it a death tax and eviction: 'when the tenants die, scarcely have they been mourned before the vassals are evicted and they lose their fertile and plentiful land'. The text, approved by the nobles, related how in the past conflict was rare between landlords and tenants, as all of them 'lived in the knowledge that the foro was perpetual, whether by law, equity or custom'. However, 'as time changes everything, there are new ideas and customs, more people, and simplicity has given way to luxury. In the end discipline has been relaxed, and to maintain the leisure and vain ostentation of many [clerics], their evil ways also increased'[28].

A significant portion of *foro* land, or the rent it produced, had been included in the property of overseers of noble houses; which was illegal, as *foros* were temporary and the majorat was not. Meanwhile, the peasants divided, exchanged and sold the land, which led to great confusion when it came to assigning rights over land that belonged to many people at the same time:

> Lawsuits are also highly complex, especially when related to old foros. Each foro holder has shared them out among his children, and then they are further subdivided when the children die. Many are linked to the family. Many established tutelage, memorials, chaplaincies (...). Others tax them [the *foros*] with census, pensions, and other encumbrances to obtain money. Others sell them, partially or wholly: out of need, convenience or caprice. Still others have confused them with their own inherited or titled land or land split off from adjacent uncultivated land (...). Two or three centuries later, where is this land, after so many changes and divisions? Recourse to documents is pointless. The poor, mostly rustic and unlearned, have only their own memory, common tradition and public use for monuments and archives. They believe they are safe with this: they hold the land in good faith, as their ancestors held it (Villares & Díaz-Castroverde, 1997: 249).

Documents from the above-mentioned monasteries indicate that nobles were not exaggerating on this point.

Monks after the mid-eighteenth century failed to understand why, when *foros* expired, they could not recover their land and draw up new *foros* or

28 This and other texts can be found in Villares & Díaz-Castroverde (1997).

leases as they had always done. Fr. Sarmiento, who started writing about this controversy in 1762, expressed it clearly:

> Look up any record from the Royal Tribunal of La Coruña, in which someone has been forced, whether he wishes or not, to renew an expired foro against his will (...); try to find in any *foro* a condition that expressly states to the satisfaction of both parties that once the *foro* expires, the land in question should not be handed over to the monastery (...). Finally, try to find in these records [of the nobility] a reason, even a suggestion, as to why people cannot do what they want with their own possessions.

The legal situation was clear for the monasteries and their lawyers, and their allegation was published as a *Legal Manifesto*; though diverse factors led the Council of Castile to intervene in order to put a check on monastic designs. Apart from certain specific dispositions issued in favour of groups of tenant farmers who were involved in complicated lawsuits, a decree dated 11 May 1763 forbid the processing of dispossession orders awaiting hearing at the Royal Tribunal. From April 1785 they were even denied hearing. For the Council measures – which were initially provisional – to make sense, it is important to note that dominium utile prevailed over dominium directum here and in other European countries where a kind of peasant ownership was consolidated, such as France. However, things were not as simple as Robert Brenner portrayed them: even in England the smallholding peasantry did not disappear before 1800. Yet large farms and peasant evictions were not unknown on the continent; nor did the prevailing emphyteusis preclude social polarisation and the use of shorter contracts that were more burdensome for the peasant[29].

The power of rights of use can be seen in the land registry of Ensenada (1749-1753); where the peasants rather than the landlords declare themselves the 'owners', unless they had leased the land or sub-contracted to sharecroppers. Significantly, in 1755, the residents of Portas, who were tenants of Sobrado, argued that the monastery could not change the rent it charged, as that would invalidate the operations in the accounts showing payments made up to that time. Furthermore, as Ángel García Sanz points out, the agrarian policy of the councillors of Charles III was oriented towards favouring peasant stability. Thus, the Council of Castile upheld the ban on dispossessions in the *Expediente General de Foros* (General Report on *Foros*) (García Sanz, 1996: 175-180). The members of the Council were not particularly sympathetic to the clergy, who were fractious and unsubmissive to royal control. Reformist political ministers were particularly bothered by the fact that monasteries and convents that held large tracts of land operated as 'farming agents', and in 1766 Campomanes mandated that certain priory monks temporarily return

29 Aston & Philin, eds (1988 [1985]). Concerning the survival of smallholding peasants in England, there are currently numerous studies: cf. Neeson (1993). For emphyteusis territories, cf. Congost (1990 & 2007), and for France Béaur (2000).

to living in their monasteries[30]. Ultimately, the landed gentry were firmly supported by the Council of Castile, which was composed of minor nobility, among whom was the Galician Pedro Martínez Feijoo, Count of Troncoso since 1762. All these factors lie behind the decree of 1763; and its significance in the evolution of agrarian relations was shrewdly noted by Ramón Otero Pedrayo. From that time on *foros* existed in a 'legal interim': though formally they were still temporary, tenants could not be dispossessed of their lands so long as they paid the rent. Though there were plans to remedy this provisional situation with legislative measures, it continued until 1926, when the *foro* redemption law became effective. The peasants' rights to ownership of use were thus consolidated, and the landed gentry could not abandon their status as landlords because they had impeded the direct owners from recovering the rights of use when the *foros* expired. The victories of the landed gentry from 1763-1785 subsequently limited them; they had to respect peasant rights, and the peasants ended up becoming full owners of the land in the first third of the twentieth century (Otero Pedrayo, 1958; Villares, 1982a and b, 1997).

III. *Foros*, crops and rents

Given that *foros* were long-term contracts, often in exchange for a fixed amount in kind, the rents they generated tended to remain stable. Landlords could not modify the rent in the short or medium term unless numerous *foros* expired at the same time. In the 1970s, when rural history entered a period of splendour, debate was quite heated regarding whether *foros* conditioned the crop system by requiring peasants to plant the grains named in longstanding rent stipulations: wheat, rye and millet[31].

Foro rents, whether proportional or for fixed amounts, do not appear to have decisively conditioned crop evolution. Crops seem to have varied more or less according to the climate and edaphological conditions, regardless of how the land was granted. In areas where corn was grown, fixed *foro* rents were not related to the composition of peasant harvests; though circumstances varied and some monasteries took advantage of contract renewals to update the grain rents. As the Early Modern Age advanced, peasants made increasing use of the legal possibility of paying cash for rents that were stipulated in kind, at prices determined by local justice authorities. They were also allowed to pay one kind of grain for another based on established equivalences, when

30 On 17 February 1767 Sarmiento sent the above-mentioned letter to Campomanes, asking him to take action to calm the 'new and unprecedented tempest' that had arisen against the longstanding Benedictine custom of administering 'the little land that lay people have left them'.

31 As examples of different positions, cf. García Lombardero (1973: 41 and 95). He sustains that *foro* rent stipulations determined the crops, while Pérez García (1979: 175-176) states that on the contrary, the agrarian system was transformed quite independently of *foro* rents.

certain crops were no longer planted. In 1828, just before disentailment was decreed for ecclesiastical lands, the monastery of Celanova started a new book for bread grains. The first few pages contain a series of warnings about how to collect rent; including two warnings regarding rye, which was becoming less frequent, and millet, which was no longer grown:

> Given that the rent for *foros* is generally paid in rye, and that as there is a scarcity of this crop, the tenants usually pay in corn instead of rye, and the measure *[of corn]* is greater than that of rye and should be filled to overflowing. Despite the fact that they do so freely and of their own free will, and for their own advantage, interest and use, they should be informed that they have no obligation but to pay their *foros* in kind or in rye, or the value thereof, according to the equivalences of the months of May and June. Likewise, the grain masters point out that when landlords receive corn for rye, even though the value of the former is greater, it places the monastery under the obligation of accepting it, even if rye is worth more in one year or for several years. This is only fair and just under a 'de facto' tacit agreement, based on the popular (but true) principle, *qui sentit commodum, debet sentire incommodum*. These warnings should always be taken into account…[32].

A solution also had to be found for rents stipulated in millet, when it was no longer grown in the area:

> Some *foros* and ecclesiastical patronages, apart from the rent in wheat, rye or barley, bring in *fanegas [a dry measure]* or *tegas [another variable measure]* of millet. When the *foros* were set up this grain was quite common, and was used as payment in kind for corn (or rye). This seed has not been planted for many years now (because of sparrows and other birds). And so payment has been changed accordingly…

According to Fr. Sarmiento, to avoid rent collectors taking advantage of its absence, peasants started growing millet again:

> All the old rent and grain in Galicia was measured in two-grain bread, which means 'half in rye' and 'half in millet'. But as little millet was sown, farmers paid millet in cash rather than in kind. Rent collectors therefore valued millet at higher prices each year, as not much was planted, and so extortion was rampant. The farmers realised what was happening and started planting millet again… (Sarmiento, 1762 ff.)

The presence of millet in the rent of some monasteries was still significant at the end of the eighteenth century. According to diverse sources, this crop was only residual or had disappeared from some areas by that time. No doubt the monks collected part of the *foro* rent in cash, at the prices fixed by the

32 Provincial Archive of History, Ourense, Clergy, book 234 from Celanova, see Introduction.

'evaluation committee', but not all of it. This can be seen in the real breakdown of costs in kind at various monasteries towards the end of the Ancien Régime:

Table 10.3. Income in grain at the monasteries of Poio, Tenorio and Lérez, and expenses from Poio, at the end of the *Ancien Regime*, with the average in hl/year

a) Income

Monastery	Years	Wheat	%	Rye	%	Millet	%	Corn	%	Total	%
Poio	1781-1784	158.5	8.5	717.3	38.5	548.6	29.4	440	23.6	1,864.4	100
Poio	1814-1824	253.1	13	774.2	39.9	606.1	31.2	309.3	15.9	1,942.7	100
Tenorio	1777-1784	8.9	1.4	118.2	18.6	104.5	16.4	404.9	63.6	636.5	100
Tenorio	1814-1818	9.9	1.6	124.9	20.4	98.5	16.1	378.7	61.9	612	100
Lérez	1814-1818	145.7	14.7	387.9	39.1	320	32.2	138.4	14	992	100

b) Outflow

Monastery	Years	Wheat	%	Rye	%	Millet	%	Corn	%	Total	%
Poio	1777-1784	244.1	(29.5)*	697.5	(59.2)*	539.1	(77.4)*	468.3	(57.6)*	1,949	(56.5)*
Poio	1814-1824	206.5	(2.4)*	634.9	(75.5)*	514.8	(92.7)*	280.3	(31.6)*	1,636.5	(69.2)*

* Sales as a percentage of total outflows. *Source*: Drawn up from digitalised document collections of the Benedictine Archive at Silos, incorporated by LÓPEZ VÁZQUEZ (2005).

At both Poio and Lérez, millet income accounted for almost a third of the total, and greatly exceeded corn income just prior to monastic disentailment. However, income at the small monastery of Tenorio, also located in the Rías Baixas area, was better adapted to the crops grown in south-western Galicia, possibly because it included a significant portion of tithes. If we compare percentages of sales to total outflow, we see that in Poio millet was the most commercialised grain: 77.4% from 1777-1784, and 92.7% just prior to disentailment was destined for the market. José Manuel Pérez García notes that in real terms, this meant that tenants paid their grain rents in cash; which the grain masters and overseers entered as sales, according to their accounting logic (Pérez García, 1979: 284-285). Millet was apparently sold more as it became scarce: indicating that peasants had started paying their rent 'at set values' or prices determined by local authorities. After many years of examining Cistercian accounting documentation, I have observed that overseers seldom differentiated between amounts actually sold and those collected in cash. For them it was irrelevant: the tenant farmer who paid in cash was in the end purchasing a portion of his own harvest[33].

The Cistercians at Armenteira were still fixing rents in rye and millet in *foros* drawn up in 1761. In this area of the Rías Baixas, the tithes collected by the monks in 1788 and 1789 consisted of 308.8 hl of corn, 41.6 hl of rye, 3.56 hl of wheat and 1.28 hl of millet. In other words, American grain accounted for 86.9% of total grain production[34]. The landlords – more specifically the monasteries – did what they could to adjust rent to changes in crops, so long as they incurred no losses. However, bearing in mind that the duration of *foros* had been 'perpetuated' since 1763 (and even a few years before, because of serious opposition to peasant evictions and dispossessions), the distance between rent and crops tended to increase in areas where agrarian change was greatest. Grain income at the monastery of Melón provides a good example of the sudden adaptation of *foro* rents to agrarian transformations, and rent stagnation is clearly evident:

Table 10.4. Annual average grain income (hl) at the Melón monastery

Years	Wheat	%	Rye	%	Millet	%	Corn	%	Total	**Index**
1677-1679	91.2	13.3	349.4	51	244.4	35.7	--	--	685	100
1680-1689	93.9	11.9	382.9	48.5	246.4	31.2	65.9	8.4	789.1	115
1690-1699	98.3	10.6	361.3	39	202.7	21.9	263.2	28.4	925.5	135
1700-1709	94.6	9.1	418.7	40.2	221.4	21.2	307	29.5	1,041.7	152
1710-1719	111.1	10.5	411.5	39	225.5	21.4	307.7	29.1	1,055.8	154
1720-1729	139.9	12.6	415.7	37.6	237.6	21.5	313.1	28.3	1,106.3	162
1730-1739	145.6	13.4	399.4	36.8	238.1	21.9	302.3	27.9	1,085.4	158
1740-1749	153.8	13.8	411.8	37	239.9	21.6	307.7	27.6	1,112.2	163
1800-1809	161.5	14.4	407.5	36.4	245.2	21.9	305.5	27.3	1,119.7	163
1823-1829	155.7	16.9	316.5	34.5	167.8	18.3	278.2	30.3	918.2	134
1830-1834	172.4	16.4	365.2	34.9	204.4	19.5	305.5	29.2	1,047.5	153

Source: Author's own from the Provincial Archive of History, Ourense, Clergy, book 387 from Melón.

Until 1687, income composition reflected the reality that rye and millet were grown more than any other grains: the former providing 177-182 and the latter

33 The recording of amounts actually sold and those collected in cash as the same item had other consequences, which affected, for instance, price homogeneity in account books. Items collected in cash were sometimes several years overdue, but were entered in the year they were collected, while the prices are those of the year in which the debt was generated. Hence the prices often lack homogeneity. This was addressed in Saavedra (2008b).

34 National Archive of History, Madrid, Clergy book 9,775 from Armenteira, showing the list of tithes; and book 9,959 listing *foro* conditions: including death tax, *laudemium*, rent transport, payment of rams and wax, and some stipulating rent in corn.

154-157 *fanegas* per year. In the accounts for April of 1688, the monk who oversaw grain warned that:

> the old agreements expired this year, and rent was collected in the fields according to the *foro* conditions (...), and it is important for the house to charge them at the same rate as this year (...), and more than what they paid in the year when we collected the least amount, adding corn, which they did not *[formerly]* pay at all.

In effect, the tithes and fifths for the 1687 harvest amounted to 191 measures of rye, 81 of millet and 154 of corn: a grain increase of 18% for the monastery compared to the previous five years. From 1688 to 1691, tithes from the parishes of Melón and Quines amounted to 124.25 measures of rye, 102.25 of millet and 200.1 of corn (almost 50% of production). The monks had begun to negotiate agreements with the tenants; and by 1698-1699 income was stabilised with only minor variations, as the tithes from leasing had been incorporated into the *foros*[35].

Monastery lands were dispersed and the breakdown of income could vary notably from one area to another. Houses with more land in the interior received more rent in rye, millet and corn from sheltered valleys, and in wine from priories close to the Sil and Miño rivers or their tributaries. The monastery of Oseira, for example, possessed 23 priories and farms; only one of which was on the coast, in Marín. The rest were located in the provinces of Ourense and Lugo, except for the abbey of Júnias de Pitões, in Tras-Os-Montes (Portugal). In the mid-eighteenth century, global income from these vast lands amounted to 6,725 hl of grain, and 2,500 hl of wine. Rye accounted for 89% or 94% of the total, wheat for 2-3% and millet and corn from 3-5.5%.

Rye income, 85% of which came from *foro* lands, varied little over the course of two centuries. Only in a few decades of the eighteenth century did it increase, by 22-24 per cent. It is significant that after three years of liberalism, the monastery collected its full rents just prior to the definitive monastic disentailment, indicating that social opposition was very limited compared to other parts of the Peninsula. However, millet and especially corn income rose considerably; corresponding mainly to winegrowing priories in the river valleys of the interior, where proportional rent prevailed. Corn was increasingly grown along the Miño, Sil, Arenteiro, Arnoia, Támega and Limia rivers from the 1680s until well into the eighteenth century, to the detriment

---

35 Provincial Archive of History, Ourense, Clergy, book 387 from Melón, accounts for April of 1687 and the following years. Fluctuations in rye and millet income derive from changes in first fruits, which were paid in these grains. The increase in wheat rent in the 1720s owes to the lease of a profitable water mill, which produced from 20 to 60 *fanegas* per year depending on the water level.

Table 10.5. Annual average composition and evolution of grain and wine income (hl) at Oseira

Years	Wheat	%	Rye	%	Millet and Corn	%	Total	Index	Wine	Index
1617-1619	109.6	2	5,055.9	93.4	248.9	4.6	5,414.4	100	1,561*	100
1650-1655	177.9	3	5,617.9	93.4	218.8	3.6	6,014.6	111	1,996	128
1672-1673	166.5	2.7	5,689.4	93.7	213.3	3.5	6,069.2	112	2,270	145
1738-1740	168.5	2.7	5,779.9	91.4	374.7	5.9	6,323.1	117	2,345	150
1791-1802	203.8	3	5,991.5	89.5	499.4	7.5	6,695	124	3,710	238
1828-1831	185.8	2.9	5,635.9	88.7	530.6	8.4	6,352.3	117	2,134	137

Source: Library of the monastery of Poio (Pontevedra), accounts book of the monastery of Oseira. *1617-1628.

Table 10.6. Evolution of annual average grain income (hl) at Sobrado and the coastal priories of Las Cascas and San Martiño do Porto

Years	Sobrado	Index	Las Cascas	Index	San Martiño do Porto	Index
1620-1649	2,334.6	100	269.5	100	81.3	100
1650-1699	2,337.9	100	341.1	127	114	140
1700-1749	2,346.9	101	411.9	153	155.4	191
1750-1799	2,291	98	444.5	165	236.8	291
1800-1834	2,251.6	96	440.7	164	234.5	288

Source: Archive of the Kingdom of Galicia (A Coruña), Monasteries, Books 19, 21, 237, 238, 123 and 132 from Sobrado.

Table 10.7. Composition of proportional rent at the priory of San Martiño de Porto

Years	Wheat	%	Rye	%	Millet	%	Corn	%	Total
1640-1649	20	24.6	39.7	48.8	7.7	9.5	13.9	17.1	81.3
1650-1659	18.2	23.5	36.8	47.5	11.9	15.4	10.5	13.6	77.4
1660-1669	18.2	15.9	36.8	32.2	6.9	6	52.4	45.8	114.3
1700-1709	6.9	5.8	36.3	30.3	8.1	6.8	68.4	57.1	119.7
1750-1759	6.4	3	21.1	10	0.8	0.4	182.9	86.6	211.2
1800-1809	13.4	6.1	13.2	6.1	--	--	191.9	87.8	218.5
1824-1834	12.7	5.2	4.4	1.8	--	--	226.7	93	243.8

Source: Archive of the Kingdom of Galicia, Monasteries, Books 123 and 132 from Sobrado.

of millet and winter grains. Wine rents were also largely proportional to the harvest and much more dynamic than those of rye[36].

In western Galicia, from the Betanzos coastland to the Miño valley, changes in the agrarian system and numerous *foros* proportional to the harvest had a very positive effect on monastery income, though there were clearly differences among majorats. This can be seen by comparing the powerful monastery of Sobrado with that of Oseira, the Cistercian house with the highest rents in Galicia. If we compare the evolution of income in the interior rye-producing areas with those of the coastlands, clear differences emerge:

The monastery maintained a stable grain income, virtually all of it rye, for over two centuries. This was attributable to fixed *foro* rents (accounting for 95% of total income) and lack of change in the agrarian system, which included no spring grains until the very end of the Ancien Régime. The coastal priories, on the other hand, with *foro* rents corresponding to one-quarter or one-fifth of the harvest and assorted tithes, forged an organic link between rent and production. It increased notably and especially after the expansion of corn, which in the long-term significantly transformed an agrarian system that had been dominated by wheat and rye. This is clearly evident in the breakdown by type of rent for the priory of San Martiño de Porto:

Corn accounted for 12-13% of priory rents in the mid-seventeenth century, but 93% just prior to monastic disamortization. By then, harvests were 16.25 times larger and monastic rents had trebled. This reflects the extensive, long-term transformation of the agrarian system, which led to profound changes in both the landscape and peasant nutrition[37].

IV. Conclusion

Diverse factors affected the composition and evolution of *foro* rents and proportional or fixed rents implied stronger or weaker organic links to production. These factors include whether the *foros* were renewed before widespread planting of corn, intense crop changes in coastal areas and river valleys versus scarce change in much of the interior until potatoes became widespread in the second half of the eighteenth century (potatoes were rarely included in *foro* rents), or other more specific and circumstantial conditions. In addition to the examples given we could mention the monasteries of Oia and A Franqueira. At Oia rent in millet disappeared half-way through the seventeenth century and was replaced by corn; while at A Franqueira the

---

36 Cf. Saavedra (2008b) for a detailed analysis of rent at Oseira, one of the most powerful Cistercian monasteries in the Iberian Peninsula.

37 Rent at Porto includes wine, but its production stagnated and lost importance in the agrarian system.

old spring grain, which accounted for two thirds of the harvest before 1640, held out much longer[38].

The *foro* is to all appearances an 'archaic' form of land tenure. Its lengthy duration and fixed rents prevented landlords benefitting from increased production and caused them great difficulties when it came to overseeing lands subjected to subdivision and other alterations. It also involved death taxes, *laudemia*, transport fees, payment in rams, capons, fattened pigs, etc. However, in an economic and social environment where smallholdings were universal and the urban world relatively unimportant, *foros* enabled the privileged classes to obtain benefit from the cultivation of their dispersed lands at almost no cost, and to include feudal taxes in deeds or assimilate them into the *foros*. Despite complaints about loss of land due to peasant malice, the account books show that monasteries were receiving virtually full rent at the time of disamortization[39]. The consolidation of tenant rights of use was, therefore, compatible with the strength of the landlords prior to the liberal revolution. This apparent paradox calls for detailed research into the social relations operating in rural Galicia, but lies outside the scope of this study.

Bibliography

ALFONSO ANTÓN, Isabel (1991), 'Cistercians and Feudalism', *Past and Present*, 133, p. 3-30.

ARTIAGA, Aurora & BAZ VICENTE, Maria Xesús (eds) (1997), *Propiedade da terra e reforma liberal*, Biblioteca de Clásicos Agrarios Galegos, vol. III, A Coruña, Xunta de Galicia/Caixa Ourense.

ASTON, Trevor H. & PHILPIN, Charles H. E.,., (eds) (1988 [1985]), *El Debate Brenner: estructura de clases agraria y desarrollo económico en la Europa preindustrial*, Barcelona, Crítica.

BARREIRO FERNÁNDEZ, Xosé Ramón (1985), 'A problemática foral no século XVIII. Unha nova interpretación', en Carlos BARROS (ed.), *Dende Galicia: Marx*, A Coruña-Sada, Edicións do Castro, p. 243-258.

BARREIRO MALLÓN, Baudilio (1972), 'La Pragmática de perpetuación de Foros. Intento de interpretación', *Compostellanum*, XVII.

BARREIRO MALLÓN, Baudilio (1973), *La jurisdicción de Xallas en el siglo XVIII: Población, sociedad y economía*, Universidade de Santiago de Compostela.

BARRIO, Maximiliano (1997), 'Madrid y Roma en la segunda mitad del siglo XVIII. La lucha contra las "usurpaciones" romanas', *Revista de Historia Moderna. Anales de la Universidad de Alicante*, 16, p. 69-82.

---

38 SAAVEDRA (2010b: 143-148). In the Lower Miño areas of both Galicia and Portugal, millet was the main crop until the introduction and spread of corn.

39 Numerous monasteries still collected all their rent after that three-year period. See SAAVEDRA (2007, 2010b).

Baz Vicente, María Xesús (1996), *Señorío y propiedad foral de la alta nobleza en Galicia (siglos XVI-XX): La Casa de Alba*, Madrid, Ministerio de Agricultura, Pesca y Alimentación.

Béaur, Gérard (2000), *Histoire agraire de la France au XVIII*[e] *siècle: inerties et changements dans les campagnes françaises entre 1715 et 1815*, Paris, SEDES.

Burgo López, Concepción (1985), *Un dominio monástico femenino en la Edad Moderna. El monasterio benedictino de San Payo de Antealtares*, Tesis Doctoral inédita, Universidade de Santiago de Compostela.

Clavero, Bartolomé (1980), 'Foros y rabassas. Los censos agrarios ante la revolución española. Primera parte', *Agricultura y sociedad*, 16, p. 27-69.

Clavero, Bartolomé (1986), 'Enfiteusis, ¿qué hay de un nombre?', *Anuario de Historia del Derecho Español*, LVI, p. 467-519.

Congost, Rosa (1990), *El propietaris i els altres: la regió de Girona, 1768-1862*, Vic, Eumo.

Congost, Rosa (2007), *Tierras, leyes, historia. Estudios sobre 'la gran obra de la propiedad'*, Barcelona, Crítica.

Díaz-Castroverde, Jose Luis (1992), *Conflictividad social y régimen de propiedad en Galicia: la cuestión de los despojos*, Tesis Doctoral inédita, Universidade de Santiago de Compostela.

Dopico, Fausto (1978), *A Ilustración e a sociedade galega. A visión dos economistas ilustrados*, Vigo, Galaxia.

Eiras Roel, Antonio (1972), 'El régimen subforal y la clase hidalga intermediaria (Prólogo)', en Maria del Carmen Quintáns, *El dominio de San Martín Pinario durante la desamortización*, Santiago, Universidade de Santiago de Compostela.

Eiras Roel, Antonio (1981), *La Historia Social de Galicia en sus fuentes y protocolos*, Santiago, Universidade de Santiago de Compostela.

Eiras Roel, Antonio (1989), 'El señorío gallego en cifras: nómina y ranking de los señores jurisdiccionales', *Cuadernos de Estudios Gallegos*, 103, p. 113-135.

Faya Díaz, María Ángeles (1999), 'Los señoríos eclesiásticos gallegos y la venta de jurisdicciones en tiempos de Felipe II', en José Luis Pereira Iglesias (coord.), *Felipe II y su tiempo*, Cádiz, Asociación Española de Historia Moderna, p. 101-115.

Fernández González, Ángel Ignacio (1995), *A fiscalidade eclesiástica en Galicia, 1750-1850*, Tesis Doctoral inédita, Universidade de Santiago de Compostela.

Finzi, Roberto (1998), *Civiltà mezzadrile: la piccola coltura in Emilia-Romagna*, Roma, Laterza.

García Blanco-Cicerón, Jacobo (2006), *Viajeros angloparlantes por la Galicia de la segunda mitad del siglo XVIII*, A Coruña, Fundación Pedro Barrié de la Maza.

García Lombardero, Jaime (1973), *La agricultura y el estancamiento económico de Galicia en la España del Antiguo Régimen*, Madrid, Siglo XXI.

García Lombardero, Jaime & Dopico, Fausto (1978), 'La renta de la tierra en Galicia y la polémica por la renovación de foros en los siglos XVII y XVIII', *Hacienda Pública Española*, 55, p. 193-199.

García Oro, José (1977), *Galicia en la Baja Edad Media: Iglesia, señorío y nobleza*, Santiago de Compostela, Bibliófilos Gallegos.

García Sanz, Ángel (1996), 'La reforma agraria de la Ilustración: proyectos y resultados. El precedente del arbitrismo agrarista castellano', en Ángel García Sanz & Jesús Sanz Fernández, *Reformas y políticas agrarias en la Historia de España*, Madrid, Ministerio de Agricultura, Pesca y Alimentación, p. 161-200.

López Vázquez, José Manuel (coord.) (2005), *Patrimonio, arte, historia y orden: Opus Monasticorum*, Santiago de Compostela, Xunta de Galicia.

Lucas Álvarez, Manuel (1996), 'Una aproximación a superficies y rentas en el patrimonio del Monasterio de San Clodio del Ribeiro de Avia (Ourense)', en *Humanitas: estudios en homenaxe ó Prof. Dr Carlos Alonso del Real*, Santiago de Compostela, Universidade, p. 463-474.

Neeson, J.M. (1993), *Commoners: Common Right, Enclosure and Social Change in England, 1700-1820*, Cambridge, University Press.

Otero Pedrayo, Ramón (1958), 'Evolución de la doctrina sobre el foro', *Cuadernos de Estudios Gallegos*, 13, p. 58-76.

Paz González, D. (1991), *El Monasterio de Santa María de Villanueva de Oscos: de la reforma a la exclaustración*, Oviedo, Universidad.

Peralta, Fray Tomás de (1677), *Fundación, antigüedad y progresos del Imperial Monasterio de Ossera, Orden del Císter*, Madrid, Melchor Álvarez.

Pérez García, José Manuel (1979), *Un modelo de sociedad rural de Antiguo Régimen en la Galicia costera*, Santiago, Universidade de Santiago de Compostela.

Pérez García, José Manuel (1995), 'El régimen subforal en la Galicia occidental entre 1740 y 1850. Muestreos comarcales', *Obradoiro de Historia Moderna*, 4, p. 71-93.

Portela Silva, Ermelindo (1976), *La región del obispado de Tuy en los siglos XII al XV: una sociedad en la expansión y en la crisis*, Santiago de Compostela, El Eco Franciscano.

Portela Silva, Ermelindo (1981), *La colonización cisterciense en Galicia (1142-1250)*, Santiago, Universidade de Santiago de Compostela.

Rey Castelao, Ofelia (1985), 'La renta del voto de Santiago y las instituciones jacobeas', *Compostellanum*, 30, p. 323-368.

Rey Castelao, Ofelia (1993), *El Voto de Santiago: claves de un conflicto*, Santiago, Universidade de Santiago de Compostela.

Rodríguez Galdo, María Xosé (1976), *Señores y campesinos en Galicia, siglos XIV-XVI*, Santiago de Compostela, Pico Sacro.

Saavedra, Pegerto (1985), *Economía, política y sociedad en Galicia: la Provincia de Mondoñedo, 1480-1830*, Madrid, Xunta de Galicia.

Saavedra, Pegerto (2003), *Señoríos y comunidades campesinas en la España del Antiguo Régimen*, A Coruña, Fundación Pedro Barrié de la Maza.

Saavedra, Pegerto (2007), 'Reforma fiscal y control del territorio: el Catastro de Ensenada – o la "confusión de Babel" – en Galicia', *Anuario de Historia del Derecho Español*, 77, p. 771-844.

Saavedra, Pegerto (2008a), 'Fiscalidad y agricultura en la España Moderna', en Rafael Vallejo Pousada (ed.), *Los tributos de la tierra. Fiscalidad y agricultura en España (siglos XII-XX)*, Valencia, Publicacions de la Universitat, p. 265-301.

Saavedra, Pegerto (2008b), 'Economías cistercienses del Antiguo Régimen: el Imperial Monasterio de Oseira', en Manuel Reyes García Hurtado (coord.), *Modernitas. Estudios en homenaje al profesor Baudilio Barreiro Mallón*, A Coruña, Universidade da Coruña, p. 161-190.

Saavedra, Pegerto (2010a), 'Les senyories monàstiques a la Galicia moderna', *Afers. Fulls de recerca i pensament*, 65, p. 113-141.

Saavedra, Pegerto (2010b), 'Trayectoria de las rentas monásticas y del sistema agrario de Galicia desde la segunda mitad del XVI a 1835', *Revista Portuguesa de Historia*, XLI, p. 105-156.

Saavedra, Pegerto (2012), 'As mulleres do couto de Rubillón fronte ó mosteiro de Melón a mediados do século XVIII', *Boletín Auriense*, XLI-XLII, p. 201-225.

Sarmiento, Fray Martín (1762 ss.), *Obra de 660 pliegos*, Transcripción del manuscrito realizada por el Consello da Cultura Galega, Santiago de Compostela.

Thompson, Eduard Palmer (1995 [1991]), *Costumbres en común*, Barcelona, Crítica.

Tos i Urgellés, Jaume (2007 [1784]), *Tratado de la cabrevación, Edició i estudi introductori a càrrec de Rosa Congost*, Girona, Documenta Universitaria - Associació d'Història Rural de les Comarques Gironines.

Villares, Ramon (1981a), 'Los prorrateos de tierras: su utilidad historiográfica', en EIRAS ROEL, A. *et alii*, *La Historia Social de Galicia en sus fuentes de protocolos*, Santiago de Compostela, Universidad, p. 387-406.

Villares, Ramon (1981b), 'La economía del clero regular gallego ante la desamortización', *Cuadernos de Estudios Gallegos*, 32, p. 81-139.

Villares, Ramon (1982a), *La propiedad de la tierra en Galicia*, Madrid, Siglo XXI.

Villares, Ramon (1982b), *Foros, frades e fidalgos*, Vigo, Xerais.

Villares, Ramon (1988), 'Los foros de Galicia: algunos problemas y comparaciones (Galicia, Portugal, Valencia)', *Ler Historia*, 12, p. 47-75.

Villares, Ramon (1989), 'Carlos III y la temporalidad del foro: los pleitos sobre despojos', en *Estructuras Agrarias y reformismo ilustrado*, Madrid, Ministerio de Agricultura, Pesca y Alimentación.

Villares, Ramon (1997), 'A provisión de 1763 revisitada', en *O padre Sarmiento e o seu tempo*, Santiago de Compostela, Consello da Cultura Galega-Universidade de Santiago de Compostela, t. 1, p. 209-224.

Villares, Ramon (1999), 'La nobleza gallega en los siglos XVI al XIX: la hegemonía de la hidalguía de pazo', en Maria del Carmen Iglesias (dir.), *Nobleza y sociedad, III. Las Noblezas españolas, reinos y señoríos en la España Moderna*, Oviedo, Nobel, 1999, p. 31-62.

Villares, Ramon & Díaz-Castroverde, Jose Luis (1997), *O conflicto foral nos séculos XVII e XVIII*, Ourense, Xunta de Galicia-Caixa Ourense.

PABLO F. LUNA

11. From *Foro* to Renting (and back?)

Emphyteutic Tenure at the Asturian Monastery of San Pelayo during the Old Regime

I. Introduction

The North and Northwest of Spain under the Old Regime, the area made up of the Principality of the Asturias and the Kingdom of Galicia, in all its local and regional diversity, is an excellent place to observe the defining crisis of ecclesiastical *dominium* that took place between the last third of the seventeenth century and the first decades of the nineteenth[1].

In relation to the overall situation of the Catholic Church in Spain, this was a medium-term crisis, with both internal and external origins, and it took place at varying rhythms, with periods of sharp confrontation followed by temporary lulls, according to the area, the institutions, and the social groups directly involved and under attack. However we can say that the crisis went on throughout this period, that it was probably not just a Spanish crisis and that different forms of the same process, can be detected and identified in other parts of Europe, and even elsewhere[2].

One way of looking at this crisis, though not the only one, is to recreate its phases and events from the point of view of the ecclesiastical bodies as they experienced it, taking care to place each of them in its own social, economic, local, regional and institutional framework, This should be done in individual monographs that are as complete as available documentation allows. The aim is to retrace the full individual development of these bodies before moving on to the stage of synthesis and interpretation.

1 This is generally termed a 'crisis of the regular clergy' but there was certainly also a medium-term crisis of the whole ecclesiastical order in Spain and Spanish America. There was still and ostentatious display of prosperity and a notorious increase in wealth in the short term. But it also seems that the tension between the social function and the societal role of the clergy, and the visibility of its temporal power increased significantly and became much sharper before the final crisis. See particularly Domínguez Ortiz (1973); Barrio Gozalo (1989, 2000); Rey Castelao (1991, 1993, 2007); Saavedra (2009). See also Bloch ([1939] 1989, [1931] 1999: Ch. 4).

2 For a comparison of Europe and America, see Landi (2004, 2005); see also Bodinier et al. (2009).

Agrarian Change and Imperfect Property, ed. by Rosa Congost and Pablo F. Luna, Rural History in Europe, 15 (Turnhout, 2018), 237-262

DOI 10.1484/M.RURHE-EB.5.116126

There is a flourishing literature in Spanish on this historical field and naturally the present study has been inspired by it[3]. For several years now we have tried to look at different ecclesiastical institutions in the Spanish Asturias involving regular as well as secular clergy during this period, and examining both their structure and their evolution. We have chosen to use two kinds of sources from the Archivo Histórico Nacional at Madrid: first, dossiers on conflicts over land holding between protagonists of different origins and secondly, notarial contracts for *foro* (see below) and leases, and their renewal by the religious institutions. An attempt has also been made to locate this review of the documentary evidence in the context of contemporary social and economic issues.

This paper presents the results of this reflection, this reconstruction and recasting of the investigative framework. It is bound to be partial and provisional. It shows how emphyteutic leases of land (*foro*) – typical of Galicia as well as the Asturias and even of some parts of the kingdom of Leon – erratically and gradually changed into renewable rentals for shorter terms. This evolution occurred through a process of adaptation, subject to temporary setbacks or reversals; and it was driven by Church institutions even though they were certainly not the only forces promoting it.

In order to present our results in a concrete form we have decided to concentrate on the Benedictine women's monastery of San Pelayo de Oviedo, one of the most important ecclesiastical institutions in the Asturias in the early modern period[4]. It was also one of the principal landowners during the period that interests us, and one of the main holders of ecclesiastical *dominium* in the Asturias. At the same time we will compare the evolution of San Pelayo with that of other ecclesiastical institutions in the Asturias, and also with some in Galicia, because there are important similarities and connections[5].

II. Ecclesiastical dominium

Before presenting and discussing the results for San Pelayo, we need to clarify some details and discuss our methodology in relation to the period studied and to the larger questions at issue.

---

3 In 2007, Ofelia Rey Castelao examined the achievements of this field of Spanish history over several decades, while emphasising the risks and limitations that such a success might incur. Rey Castelao (2007: 180-181).

4 On the history of the foundation and growth of the monastery of San Pelayo in the Spanish Asturias, see, among others, Sitges (1913); Alvarez Vazquez (1982); Fernández Conde (1978-1990, 1982); *Real Monasterio*, 1994; Faya Diaz (2007); Luna (2007).

5 On the development of Galician institutions of the regular clergy see, notably, Burgo López (1986, 1992, 1993); Martinez Ruiz & Suárez Grimón (1994); Rey Castelao (1991); Saavedra (2010).

The word dominium (*dominio* in Spanish) was clearly used by the social and institutional protagonists we studied as a fixed and polysemous term[6]. It refers to effective social control, to local power and to authority, exercised fully, in many ways, over land, people, animals, space, economic and social resources and activity. It evokes the reality of relations between the dominant and higher orders and those social groups and objects that were subordinate and dominated.

It was an authority, a power, a control, which was as much juridical as real, and took the form of possession and rights, in both the singular and the plural. These rights were exercised by material methods of coercion available as well as those to do with mentalities and beliefs; they were generally accepted by the different layers of society, by more or less tacit consent, within the somewhat precarious equilibrium of the Old Regime.

In the first place we have tried to define this notion and the changes it underwent by looking at how the term dominium was understood at that time in contemporary dictionaries of the Spanish language. It is obvious that there are inherent limits to this method since they clearly concentrate on the opinion of jurists and men of letters in the Spanish monarchy.

According to Covarrubias' dictionary of 1611[7], *dominio* or dominium is the right of the lord to have, possess, enjoy and dispose of something as he chooses, by ways defined by superior authority, in this case, the sovereign.

Thus dominium was a synonym of *imperium*, which was used to explain command and the fact of lordship over things, in the sense of a person exercising sovereignty and commanding.

In the same way, a century later in the *Diccionario de Autoridades* (1732), which we examined systematically (as well as in the editions of 1780, 1783 and 1791)[8] it seems that the term *domination* was the synonym of *imperio*, that it comes from the Latin *dominatio* and that it evokes lordship, or the *imperium*, exercised over a province or a kingdom[9]. But, after 1791 in the same source (and also the later editions of the *Diccionario*, 1803, 1817, 1822, 1832, 1837 and 1843) *dominium* is an attribute of the sovereign alone, that is, the King of Spain, and its applicability is more narrow than previously.

---

6 This question was raised in our first study of the monastery of San Pelayo, presented at the Actas del I Congreso de Estudios Asturianos (Luna, 2007). The term *dominium* was frequently used by contemporaries with the same meaning that it has here (see below). See, particularly, Bloch ([1931] 1999); Guerreau (2001).

7 The electronic edition of Covarrubias' *Diccionario*, has been used. It is widely available e.g. at: http://fondosdigitales.us.es/fondos/libros/765/1041/tesoro-de-la-lengua-castellana-o-espanola/.

8 The electronic edition has also been used. For all the editions of the *Diccionario de Autoridades*, see: htpp://buscon.rae.es/ntlle/SrvltGUILoginNtlle.

9 The noun *dominador*, dominator, therefore means the person who exercises domination, including that obtained by conquest or military victory. In the fifteenth century Antonio de Nebrija's definition evoked the control of the lord over his serfs, that is, an *amo de siervos*.

Between 1732 and 1791 the Castilian verb *dominar,* derived from the Latin *dominari,* also meant exercising command, *imperium* or seigneury, over goods (jewels, buildings, houses, land), over space, over provinces etc., over things of which one can freely dispose. But, from 1803 (and then later, in the 1817, 1822, 1832, 1837, and 1843 editions of the *Diccionario*) the definition changes, or rather, becomes more restricted and specific, with *dominio* seen as essentially the power of all persons to use and dispose freely of the goods that belonged to them. This was a significant change. It was as if the dominium was now the attribute of the sovereign alone (and no longer of others) and as if the *dominio* over things and objects was attributed to all who possessed them. Pursuing this line of inquiry, we see that between 1732 and 1783 it was explained that there were 'persons' who could be subject to dominium. Thus the children or wife were subject to the father of the family who exercised dominium over them. However these examples, though not the reference to personal subjection, disappeared in the 1791 version of the *Diccionario* and never reappeared in subsequent editions. Later, in the *Diccionario* of 1817 and after, the term *dominio* also included the land owned by the lord, or by the state under the majesty of a sovereign who disposed of the *domination* or the *res-publica,* the possession of the public thing. This tends to confirm the closer identification that took place over the first decades of the nineteenth century between *dominio* and possession or ownership, even personal, including that possession exercised by the sovereign.

The dictionaries suggested some other interesting distinctions. There is *dominio absoluto* when it is exercised completely and unaccountable to anyone. There is *dominio directo,* a derivation from the Latin dominium directum, to indicate the part of dominium retained by the person, individual or collective, who ceded a house or patrimony in emphyteusis or perpetual rent so that the house or patrimony could not be sold or given up without his consent[10]. In the 1732 edition it was even specified, while recalling the definitions of jurists from previous centuries, that dominium directum was indeed *propriedad.* However, all these indications, which were in the *Diccionario* throughout the eighteenth century, disappeared for good from the 1791 edition and later editions. From then on it was simply explained that dominium directum was what was retained by the person who ceded the dominium utile.

In the same way, dominium utile was that of the person who acquired a property, a house or land, by emphyteusis or by payment of a perpetual rent (*censo*), in order to enjoy its fruits, knowing that if he wished to sell it in his turn he would need to ask permission from the holder of the dominium directum. But, as in the previous case, this nuance disappeared from the 1791 and later editions of the *Diccionario.* It is as if the position of holders of dominium

10 Apart from other obligations favourable to the person who ceded the property and imposed on one who received the ceded property.

directum had weakened and the possession by holders of dominium utile had been correspondingly confirmed.

This, then, is what we learn from consulting contemporary dictionaries. They 'record' so to speak what was weakened and what was more precisely defined in the terms of possession and domain; and this is not without interest.

However, from documents of the period, which we have also worked on, it seems that *dominium* was simultaneously a power, an authority and a control that had progressively been challenged, both in its very foundations and in a practical, everyday way, by subordinate, subaltern and subject socio-economic sectors. This challenge did not come only from the traditional conflicts related to economic conditions, which were mostly isolated events; it was becoming more and more structural, even though there was no plan for a general transformation. Though the order expressed by the *dominium* appeared to be a 'stationary state', a peaceful and unchanging seigneurial world that was sometimes idealised[11], that order was breaking up and decomposing little by little under cumulated assaults from disparate groups and sectors of society who took the initiative in refusing to accept the existing state of affairs. These attacks came from the middle or minor nobility (*hidalguía*), from a certain type of nobility incrusted in local institutions (*nobleza concejil*[12]), and from sections of the bourgeoisie or proto-bourgeoisie who had recently acquired wealth and prosperity and sometimes sought 'progress' or justice. But it was also challenged by some of the peasant smallholders or those on uncertain tenancies, the rural poor and those who owned nothing and had to struggle to survive. This opposition force sometimes made noise but sometimes it remained unheard and unseen; however it makes its' presence felt in the archives we consulted. In order to understand these interventions and actions better we need to broaden the basis of our documentation.

Though it may seem strange, it was also true that the actual owners of dominium, those entitled to it and benefiting from it, could themselves take part in the erosion of their own power, the authority and control that they exercised over society. In fact, they were participating in changes to the existing order when they increased pressure on the land and on rents and thereby modified the prevailing balance of social forces. It is even possible that the projects for reforming the dominium, conceived and put into practice on their initiative, served to accelerate the decline, as we shall presently see.

Together with the dominium of the nobility, the dominium of the Church was one of the pillars of the existing order. Heir to a universal majesty dating from ancient and medieval times, endowed with great prestige, the ecclesiastical dominium, was a major element of the Spanish Old Regime,

---

11 It was also theorized and sometimes 'sacralised' by some of its defenders and even by reformers of the Old Regime.

12 The term is used in Paz González (1991: 74) to describe the specific circumstances of the Asturian *forera* nobility, since the late Middle Ages.

and one of the features that set it apart in Europe, although neither exclusive nor unique. The Church's presence in society was total and integral; it was different from that of the nobility. It was probably greater and more deeply rooted than the territorial presence of the Spanish state or the monarchy, in spite of the limited number of its personnel. Its institutional fibre and fabric penetrated the whole of society, with the structure of its corporations and their networks and with its two different bodies of clergy, plus the Holy Office. The ecclesiastical dominium was expected to last for ever (*para siempre jamás*); and it exercised its power, imposed its authority and maintained its social control in various ways. It possessed but also dispossessed, it acquired but it both ceded and conceded at the same time; it gave and it took away; it managed and it commanded; it judged and executed; it punished but equally it pardoned; it accorded asylum at the same time as it pursued and denounced crime and sin; it exonerated and compelled; it absolved and condemned; it paid but it collected; it bought and it sold; it was a creditor but also a debtor; it accumulated but equally redistributed; it sacralised but also excommunicated; it administered baptism at the entrance to life and later on it buried the dead; it recorded but it also concealed; it was feared but it brought consolation.

And yet this same ecclesiastical *dominium*, omnipresent and extremely powerful, was now systematically beginning to be singled out and questioned on many fronts and not just partially, as previously, or in certain specific situations. Of course this was not a complete, sudden or generalised dissatisfaction. Sometimes the challenge was to the judicial role of the Church, its jurisdictions and fiscal authority, or to its patronage, privileges and designation to benefices. Sometimes it was its accumulated patrimony or intervention in trade, financial or monetary activity which were targeted by those who contested it. Sometimes it was simply a matter of rejecting the presence in the active world of institutions that had been founded and had developed within the cloister, where they should have stayed or where they should return and remain.

It was also a cyclical questioning: some particularly difficult situations were followed by periods of relative calm, of muted protest, where the ecclesiastical dominium benefited from the resilience of society as a whole. It needs to be emphasized that it was its nature as a body exercising possession and temporal power, accumulating land, rents and wealth, which recurrently aroused thoroughgoing discontent and disapproval. And this was one of the visible characteristics of the Northern Spanish region we examined, the Asturian region.

III. The transition from *foro* to renting

The practice of ceding land by *foro*, in its different forms in Galicia, the Asturias and Leon, was clearly an emphyteutic practice, although it was also linked to local customary law and habits. The direct owner handed over the dominium utile, by a long-term cession; it had originally been perpetual and subsequently was based on 'lives' or 'voices' of the *foreros* who benefited from it, and later still on the 'lives' of the Spanish monarchs. The cession was carried out for various reasons and with various conditions, feudal and/or real, in space and time[13].

It was originally a medieval practice, even though it had lost its feudal features and characteristics over the years; it was related to, among other things, the need to repopulate and revive the areas conquered in the struggle against the Muslims. The *foro* practice continued naturally into the modern period, gradually losing its perpetual aspect and becoming a lease for a fixed term. It is fairly clear that in modern Spain the *foro* was capable of fitting, flexibly but permanently, into the demographic, social, and economic development characteristic of Northern and Western Spain. Of course, this does not mean that there were no periods of conflict.

According to the data and references that we are still gradually reconstructing, it seems that conflicts concerning ecclesiastical dominium clearly increased at the end of the seventeenth century and the beginning of the eighteenth. Two well-defined and opposite camps emerged, one defending and one against it. The possession and working of the land, as well as the appropriation of the rents it produced, were often at the centre of confrontation and opposition, but all aspects of the ecclesiastical dominium, were shaken by the conflict.

There are two telling signs of such a conflict. First, the profusion of collective or individual *paulinas*, edicts, ordinances, summons, under pain of excommunication, published by churches and parishes against villages or owners, families or individuals, who, in the view of the ecclesiastical institutions, were illegally and illegitimately occupying the clergy's land or space, or against 'sly' peasants who were supporting the usurpers of these properties[14].

But in the period under consideration, and even before, from the end of the sixteenth century on, there was also a renewal and updating of the *apeos generales*, the detailed inventories or surveys of clerical possessions. These were carried out on a very large scale, and tenants (*foreros* or tenants and *llevadores*, those in charge of the holding) themselves were forced to participate. This

---

13 On the *foro* see especially Jove y Bravo (1883); Villares (1982); García Fernández (1988); Gómez Alvarez (1993); Villares & Díaz-Castroverde (1997); Saavedra (1999). Improvement of the property, increase in number of trees, introduction of new crops, etc. were sometimes part of the conditions of cession.

14 Hiding, or pretending ignorance or inadequate knowledge, of titles and documents was not a new way for peasants to resist seigneurial claims. Bloch ([1931] 1999: 167) refers to peasants in the Auvergne who were accused of being *malin au dernier point*. In the Asturias in the early modern period, see notably Fernández Conde (1993: 190-191), on the 'tricks' of peasants in regard to the possessions of the Chapter of the Cathedral church of Oviedo. Another example is the refusal of the tenants of San Pelayo in the sixteenth century to pay rents and emphyteutic dues because 'there was no notarial act' to prove the cession, Alvarez Vazquez (1982: 477).

was done as an explicit reminder of who held the dominium directum of land and property and thereby to register clearly the rights of this dominium.

But, most importantly, this was also done in order to find real or presupposed proof of failed land management or simply of the expired concession periods, in order to declare many of the old concessions of *foros* to be *vacos* (or *bacos*) without title and attribution, or vacant. The purpose of this was not to reallocate them as *foro* on emphyteutic terms but to rent the land and property concerned on new and more advantageous conditions for the holder of the dominium directum. It is very likely that this was the response of the ecclesiastical dominium to what may be termed the movement towards the increased autonomy of dominium utile on lands ceded under *foro*. In other words, the holders of dominium utile believed that they had become completely direct owners (*dueños*). The *foro*, it should be recalled, was a long-term cession, renewable by tacit agreement in return for an annual and usually fixed payment by the holder of the dominium utile.

Over the course of centuries the *dominium utile* passed into the control of the *foreros* of the middle and upper nobility but also into that of the second order and the nobility of the *concejos*, nobility pertaining to an Old Regime administrative unit. Among these intermediary *foreros* there were also to be found members of the secular clergy, with family links to the nobility, who had gotten possession of the property of abbeys, convents and monasteries, which these institutions did not much like. There was thus a *de facto* concentration of ecclesiastical possessions and of their *utile dominium* in the hands of several types of nobility. However this process may also be regarded as a sign of a 'general contract' or tacit alliance between the ecclesiastical power and the nobility[15].

But it should also be pointed out that this movement towards an autonomous *dominium utile*, depending on the area and the particular circumstances of the ecclesiastical institutions, favoured a good number of small and medium peasants, running agricultural holdings on large or small estates, who behaved like smallholders and farmers, and wanted to maintain the stability and duration that *foro* contracts guaranteed.

All this created a mosaic of interests and a variegated social unit in which likely, though transitory, alliances could provoke opposition, resistance and even a challenge to ecclesiastical dominium. This was a challenge, in the first instance, to the soundness of the claim by the two types of clergy to be *domini directi* of the land, and then to the whole system of their privileges, attributions and position at the heart of society. Above all because in the Asturias, as in Galicia, though it seems to a lesser extent, there had also been a growing fragmentation of *foros* into sub-*foros* and other *acaseramientos* (family

---

15 A similar alliance can be seen in other parts of Galician and Asturian society. It is hard to believe that the Northern Spanish clergy had not noticed such a considerable medium-term transfer of patrimony.

establishments), a process which continued into the eighteenth century. This in practice led to a breakup of the patrimony, which made it difficult for the ecclesiastical institutions to exercise control as holders of dominium directum.

This also led to growing interest in land and a widening of the social fabric of the dominium utile, even though there was greater fragmentation of land, putting more pressure on the weakest and lowest links – a breakup of ownership and management resulting from the mechanisms of the *foro*. What this actually meant, from the point of view of the annual emphyteutic payment, was that where the divided domain was broken up, more rent had to be borne at its lower echelons, that is, by the lower levels of the peasantry[16].

Such subdivision of the *dominium utile* was strongly resisted by ecclesiastical institutions because for them it was a diversion, a 'leakage', of the rent which should naturally have come to the direct owners, i.e. themselves. But the main reason was that it 'obscured' their eminent possession; that is, it was an element in dissolving dominium directum, and a reason for expropriation in the medium term. Their institutional memory, stronger and clearer than that of individuals, could recall earlier times when their patrimony had been lost or stolen, particularly at the beginning of the early modern period.

For these two reasons, the *foro* contract, that particular Northern and Western Spanish form of emphyteusis, became the target of an offensive, or a reaction, from the ecclesiastical *dominium*, and from other quarters as well. The rental contract (*arrendamiento*, cession by rent), which was not based on divided ownership, which did not give up the dominium utile, and which reduced the period for renegotiating the contract conditions (rent, improvements, etc.) thus became the ideal substitute.

However it must be emphasised that the opposing sides to the conflict were not indissoluble blocs. In certain conditions, and in some parts of the Asturias, Church institutions managed to get support from 'poor peasants and tenants', as their own lawyer described them, against the 'rich and selfish *foreros*', proposing that tenants should negotiate directly for the concession of land and the rent payable without going through those who held the concessions. This short-circuited the social networks established by these *foreros*. What it meant was that the balance of power, which could be adjusted to the circumstances, could make it possible for negotiations that favoured certain groups among the peasants, tenants and farmers, or even among small and medium *foreros*. And this could be done not only by the clergy but also by the great landowning nobility, which behaved in much the same way[17].

16 See particularly Jove y Bravo (1883: 47-48). This evidence comes from the dossier (*expediente*) on the *foros* of the Real Audiencia of Oviedo.

17 It is therefore possible to say that the nobility reacted to the demands of tenants and those who owned the dominium utile. See Bloch ([1931] 1999), particularly the chapter on seigneurial reaction on large and small property: 162-180. The Asturian case is examined by Faya Díaz & Anes Fernández (2007: 190-200).

In the Asturias region the chronology of confrontation, the rhythm of protests and the responses of the *domini directi* have not yet been fully established. For certain ecclesiastical bodies the challenge to the *foro* came very early, as did the transition from *foro* to rent, from the last thirty years of the seventeenth century, or even before. For others the time of greatest conflict happened later. In some cases it was not until the last decades of the eighteenth or the first years of the nineteenth century that the same phenomenon occurred that had already been seen elsewhere.

We can say for now, however, that, in the Asturias as in Galicia, the middle years of the eighteenth century, between 1740 and 1770, witnessed a significant build-up of such conflicts and it is possible to speak of a real, medium-term, agrarian, rural crisis; this is true even though the conflicts in the Asturias, with a wide range of intensity, went on beyond the time limits indicated for Galicia.

The tenants responded vigorously to the legal challenges from the direct owners, particularly to the clergy, who hoped to dislodge or expel the holders of dominium utile (*foreros*) and oppposed renewing land concessions by *foro*. The direct owners were thereby openly attacking the *foro* contract itself. The holders of dominium utile defended their domain and the contract that favoured them and actively resisted the expulsions (*despogos y desalogos*) that were first decreed by the courts. The social block favouring the dominium utile came from a variable number of groups with interests in the land (both nobles and commoners). They came together or split up according to circumstances and carried out different forms of action, struggle and pressure.

The key years in the mid-eighteenth century were, beyond a doubt, doubly important for the challenge to ecclesiastical dominium. They began with the defence of dominium utile and the network of interests built around it, but then went beyond the mere issues of possession of land and distribution of land rent. It is not an exaggeration to say that the offensive attitude and conduct of those holding the dominium directum contributed largely, and paradoxically, to eroding the foundation of their own social hegemony.

We should also remember that it was just during this period of conflict that the Spanish monarchy's judicial authorities, doubtless fearing a widespread peasant reaction with far-ranging consequences, especially in the Kingdom of Galicia, promulgated a series of measures, notably a law on expulsions and on the *foro* as contract (Jove y Bravo, 1883: Chapters VIII, IX and X; Villares, 1982: 127-137; Villares and Díaz-Castroverde, 1997). This law was specially designed for Galicia and the Asturias and was adopted in stages, first in the one and then in the other. It particularly stipulated that all procedures for seizure and all expulsions by authority (*despogos*) should be suspended and ordered the restitution of their possessions to *foreros* who had already lost them.

In practice, the royal law (*Real Provisión*) of 11 May 1763[18] decreed, with regard to the possession and effective occupation of land, that there should be no changes

18 The text can be found in Jove y Bravo (1883: 325-327), among others.

(*no hacer novedad* in the terminology of the period) in the conditions of possession of the *foros*, that the existing system should be preserved and the *foreros*, tenants and those who worked the land should be kept in place by tacit renewal of the contracts, until royal authorities and the sovereign himself were able to take proper measures; measures and decisions which, of course, were never taken.

In this situation, the correlation between the balance of power and the approval for these measures and laws on land possession is quite clear. In the Asturias the Audience of Oviedo even took decisions and acted on the Galician model before the specific official provisions for the Asturias were in place. This obviously shows that practical measures imposed by the balance of power could be taken before the law was approved.

IV. The monastery of San Pelayo of Oviedo

This Benedictine monastery for women was one of the most important ecclesiastical institutions in the Asturias. It was founded in the tenth century and its urban and rural holdings had increased bit by bit since the Middle Ages in typical ways, by donations from families and from the faithful, by accumulating endowments and grants bestowed by benevolent monarchs, but also by buying property, in whole or in part, often after legal suits or by seizing the possessions of insolvent debtors.

Later San Pelayo also absorbed the goods, the rents and the members of other Asturian women's monasteries (Benedictines, Cistercians, and the like) when, in the context of the late fifteenth-century reform of the regular clergy, it became one of the centres designated by the Congregation of St Benedict of Valladolid to bring together Benedictine nuns, at the beginning of the sixteenth century[19].

With ups and downs, living through crises that usually were brief, and surmounting internal conflicts that reflected larger divisions within the families and clans of the Asturian nobility, the monastery increased and consolidated its holdings through the early modern period. This growth was focused in the territory at the centre of the Principality of the Asturias, around Oviedo, but it stretched beyond that, over a great number of *concejos* and parishes throughout the Asturias and into the kingdom of Leon.

The monastery's dominium was exercised fully and wholly[20]. It held title to jurisdictions in the areas ceded by the sovereign (*cotos*), in the parishes and churches, or as lord of vassals. It owned, directly and fully, lands bringing with them all possible varieties of dues. It collected and benefited from tithes, ecclesiastical benefices and other rents. It exercised rights of passage and customs. It owned houses, buildings, barns, woods and forests, rivers and

19 This reform affected almost all Benedictine institutions; see Egido (2007: 14). For its effects in the Asturias, see Martínez Vega (1994: 14-15; 307-310).

20 Luna (2007) examines a similar interweaving of powers, resources and rights, as does Alvarez Vázquez (1982).

the like; the capital it advanced made it a creditor, and it exercised rights over the mortgaged property. It held title to established rents (*censos*). It lay at the centre of a social network of power and influence. It functioned as the depository of justice and truth and much more.

The research on these collections of documents on the monastery, though still far from complete, has concentrated on conflicts over possession of land and payment of *rentes* and on rental and *foro* contracts, negotiated and renegotiated between the end of the seventeenth century and the beginning of the nineteenth. We have looked at dozens of dossiers on conflicts and more than 300 contracts of cession, but we are fully aware that a large part of the available documentation remains to be examined. These results are thus provisional and relatively limited.

In order to demonstrate the characteristics of this effective, though contested, ecclesiastical *dominium* in its worldly activities, we have grouped them under five headings: first, the increase in the landed property estate of the monastery during this period; secondly, the way the transition from *foro* to renting happened, without going into details of setbacks or reverses; third, the introduction into leases of precise details on the rented property; fourth, the steady increase in rent charged by the monastery of San Pelayo throughout the eighteenth century and beyond; and finally, the increasing indebtedness of the renters and tenants, and debtors, of the monastery that often built its prosperity on bankruptcies and property seizures.

IV.1. The increase in San Pelayo's landed property

Contrary to other great, and some small, ecclesiastical institutions in the Asturias, which, like the men's Benedictine monastery of SanVincente of Oviedo (Barreiro Mallón, 1982: 492, 498; Cuartas Rivero, 1983), had already established most of their property estate in the previous century. San Pelayo continued to build and extend its patrimony throughout the eighteenth century. This increase and consolidation of its landed property holdings, in the old and new Asturian *concejos* and parishes, seems to have been a deliberate choice, pursued consistently while taking advantage of opportunities afforded by changing circumstances.

There were four main ways used to carry out this qualitative and quantitative consolidation of property in the eighteenth century. The first was outright purchase, either with no divided domain, and/or eliminating the previous divisions[21]. The second was judicial purchase, after successful suits against

21 By way of comparison, in the Concejo de Nava alone: Archivo Histórico Nacional de Madrid, Clero Regular, Monasterio de San Pelayo [henceforth AHN. CR. MSP], Leg. 5065, Castañedo de la Cerra y Prado de la Riestra, Concejo de Nava, 09/09/1736; Casa de Curtia y Basoredo, Concejo de Nava, 23/03/1765; Prado de Pradellin, Concejo de Nava, 15/04/1790; Prado de la Bega, Piloñeta, Concejo de Nava, 29/01/1798.

debtors, whether or not they were former tenants of monastery possessions[22]. The third was the exchange of land on terms always advantageous to the monastery, so as to 'round out' certain properties, to gain entry into new *concejos* or parishes or to wipe out old debts[23]. The fourth was to take over improvements (*los perfectos*) that *foreros* or tenants carried out on their properties, without compensation[24].

The documents show that, for San Pelayo, there was no such thing as a small acquisition. Any property, any parcel, however small (any *quiñón* of land), however far away, even if it was surrounded by properties that did not belong to the monastery, was of interest to the Benedictine house. It did not worry about dispersion of property and did not try to concentrate its possessions on the map. Though there was always a rentier's logic in this practice, there may have been decisions that were motivated by other aims and objectives.

From this point of view, it is essential to look at the strategy of the monastery, and all the operations recorded in the available documentation, from three points of view[25]. First came the purpose of producing and accounting for rent (that is, economic and financial aims) though we know that San Pelayo did not suddenly discover the need to increase its property rents in the eighteenth century. But, secondly, we also have to take into account and understand that San Pelayo was an institution that sought to place itself at the centre of a totality of collective and individual social relations and links, in order to exercise its 'social function', its influence, its control and its power[26]. Thirdly, there was a last dimension, admittedly rather more insubstantial or vague, but which cannot be forgotten or neglected in examining any investment or property operation of the monastery: its nature as a religious house within the Catholic church, as part of an establishment, a social network but also as a institutional depository of the truth, of examples to be made, of beliefs to be upheld.

---

22 See particularly AHN, CR, MSP, Leg. 5064. Dossier Domingo González, Concejo Las Regueras, 1745-1801; Leg. 5046, Coto de San Bartholomé, Concejo de Nava, 1706-1785; the latter is a very full dossier with all the acquisitions made in the course of the eighteenth century.

23 e.g. AHN.CR. MSP, Leg. 5065, La heria de Lomedo, exchanged for la heria de la Espina, Concejos de Siero y Sarego, 1764-1777; La pradera de Sanrriella (La Rubiera y Riba), Concejo de Bimenes, 1765-1793. This last operation concerned an exchange in which the monastery cancelled and expunged outstanding debts in return for property.

24 Examples in AHN. CR. MSP, Leg. 5065, Prado de Silbota, Concejo de Llanera, 10/05/1749; Bienes de Cueto, Abadia de Zenezo, Concejo de Gijón, 01/08/1745.

25 A triple regard based on understanding the ecclesiastical *dominium*, explicitly criticised and condemned by the eighteenth-century enlightened authors, particularly, Rodríguez de Campomanes; see Luna (2005).

26 Some operations that may seem illogical or irrational from the point of view of the rent obtained, or its economic and financial consequences, may be explained by this. All this occurred over the long term, with the certainty of seeking and doing good, and of being in the right; see Luna (2007: 18-19).

IV.2. The transition from foro to renting

The documentation we have consulted on San Pelayo and the work we have done on other Asturian ecclesiastical institutions, make it possible to say with reasonable precision that there was a concerted attempt by the monastic authorities to replace the *foro* contract by a rental one. This process seems to start in the last third of the seventeenth century, as discussed above, but it appears to continue throughout the eighteenth century[27].

This was accompanied by another tendency that, as we have previously noted, consisted in declaring the *foro* vacant after three sovereigns' lives (at the death of Charles II or even after the death of Philip IV in 1665) or after the lives of three *foreros*, and then refusing to renew the *foro* in favour of the heirs of the last deceased beneficiary.

Sometimes a temporary manager of the *foro* was imposed, different from the *forero* in place, who had to be removed because he would not accept the transition, until they found a tenant who would take the property on a rental contract, with revised and renewable conditions, mostly concerning the rent[28]. But it is also interesting to note that there were other ecclesiastical institutions, such as the monastery of Santa Maria de la Vega in Oviedo, which had clearly started a similar process in the middle of the seventeenth century, or even before (Martínez Vega, 1994: 327-334)[29].

The transition from *foro* to rental was not undisputed. The monastery of San Pelayo had to deal with protests, as did other Asturian institutions. From this point of view it is interesting to note that the litigants, whether lay or ecclesiastical, who made claims against San Pelayo for the recognition of their *foros* and extension of their rights, had often profited from the prevalent terminological ambiguity, maintained by the monastery through the previous centuries, between *foro* and rentals. There is clearly confusion in the archival documentation, where we often find a bewildering mix of terms to describe the length of contracts and informal descriptions of certain cessions and transmissions of goods[30].

---

27 AHN. CR. MSP, Leg. 5046, Juguería de Ujo y Figaredo, Concejo de Lena, 1722-1803. The *foro* Emilia Rivera, at the origin of this property, and still in existence in the middle of the eighteenth century, was turned into a rental by judicial decision of 12/07/1767, and this had given rise to the claims of the presumed beneficiaries.

28 See especially AHN. CR. MSP, Leg. 5046, Arriendo de Villargusan, Concejo de Bavia, 1723; the property of the *foro* Juan Suárez de Arenas had been ceded to a temporary manager.

29 This among other practices aimed at reinforcing the *directum dominium*, at the expense of the existing social equilibrium.

30 There are some outstanding cases of this confusion, and of the judicial conflict it caused, sometimes favouring the monastery and sometimes working against it. See for example, AHN. CR. MSP, Leg. 5046, Foro Antonio de la Espiniela, Santa Cruz de Jove y Veriña, Concejo de Gijón 1718-1792. The monastery's lawyers did not hesitate to invent figures and formulas (annuity or rental *foros*, twenty-year *foros* and the like) designed to protect and safeguard the interests of San Pelayo, with generally favourable results.

The monastery of San Pelayo seems to have been successful in imposing rentals in place of *foros*, permanently and without exception. We have not yet found in the eighteenth century any cases where property was ceded in *foro*, and no *foros* were renewed. This was not the situation with some other Asturian ecclesiastical bodies, even at the beginning of the nineteenth century, as for example Santa Maria de Villanueva de Oscos, which had to re-establish *foro* contracts during a period marked by protest, intensive demands and litigation by peasants and other owners[31].

It seems that this characteristic, that is the return or not to forms of contract using the *foro*, may be one of the traits distinguishing Asturian ecclesiastical institutions from each other, according to their social influence, their ability to negotiate and their effective control over their patrimony. But this observation needs to be confirmed by much more extensive comparative studies.

At San Pelayo the very mention of the verb *aforar* disappeared from the attributes of the vicars administrating the estate and interests of the monastery[32]. This happened in the second or third decade of the eighteenth century, when, depending on the *concejo* or parish, this function disappeared for good from the notarial protocols setting out the functions of the vicars, who were usually Benedictine monks. But in general, the vicar's activities in all decisions concerning the possession of property were limited from then on to the collection and management of rents due.

The rental contracts at San Pelayo during the eighteenth century generally stipulated a term of nine, or, exceptionally, between four and eight years. These contracts possessed a certain formal uniformity, with the parties conferring mutual guarantees and the tenant foregoing his right to appeal to legislation; this has been termed the 'juridicial disarmament' of the tenant[33]. In the last third of the eighteenth century new conditions appeared in the contracts, which were no longer limited to the conditions under which the property was rented (see below).

During the last decades of the eighteenth century, there were also more contracts in which the monastery made collective agreements with a group of tenants, even though it recorded the share of the rent due from each of the

31 At Villaneuva de Oscos, there was a return to the *foro* from1797 (following the *Concordancia o Concierto de 1797*) with a decrease in the rent and the annual emphyteutic payments even in the medium term, after the peasants refused to take up the rental contracts that the monastery of Santa María de Villanueva de Oscos tried to impose. Paz González, 1991: 52, 60-61, 99 et seq. This was a temporary, though resounding, victory of *utile dominium* over *directum dominium*, and a general weakening of the ecclesiastical *dominium*.

32 e.g. the following dossiers, where this is particularly visible: AHN. CR. MSP, Leg. 5046, Renta y Arrendamiento de Enguil, Concejo de Gozón, 1722-1806; Juguería de Ujo y Figaredo, Concejo de Lena, 1722-1803 (in 1725 the verb *aforar* was replaced by *cuidar*, to take care of or oversee); Arriendo San Pedro de Beberino, Concejo de Gordón (León), 1720-1807; Juguería de Robledo, Concejo de Llanera, 1715-1806.

33 This formula is used by Paz González (1991: 45), among others. However this 'disarmament' never prevented conflicts or claims from the peasants and tenants.

individual signatories, including the name of the direct tenant At the same time it named a 'head' tenant (*cabezalero*) as collector and guarantor of the rent, a kind of lay sub-vicar of the monastery[34]. It even happened that some of the new tenants were made to dislodge and expel the old ones in order to take possession of the rented land.

IV.3. The detailed description of property

Another clear sign of San Pelayo's determination to reassert total possession over its rented property was greater precision in the description of rented land. This became very noticeable from the middle of the eighteenth century and characterized without exception all the rental contracts signed at the beginning of the nineteenth century[35]. This does not mean that no care had previously been taken to describe precisely the monastery's possessions, particularly in drawing up the *apeos generales,* that is, inventories or surveys of possessions, especially those done during the seventeenth century or even earlier[36]. The novelty was that such descriptions were now incorporated systematically in the rental contracts. From this point of view there was a clearly marked change between the first and second halves of the eighteenth century, as the 'descriptive itch' and the desire to measure the land rented out in a detailed way took hold.

From that time on rental contracts followed the model used earlier in the general surveys: after listing general characteristics of the rented land, its boundaries and limits were described in varying detail. Adjoining lands were specified along with the name of their owners (sometimes the monastery itself or the Benedictine order). The rented surface was also described, along with the ecological environment, the type of land, its present use, the type of produce harvested and so forth. For each part and parcel of land, some idea of its surface area was given, measured in days' labour of oxen (small or large), in wagons of grass, in *fanegas* of grain harvested, sometimes even in square measure (*varas cuadradas*) and so on.

Detailed descriptions were also given of land whose the ownership was 'obscure', no doubt with ulterior motives. This term meant that the lands owned,

---

34 It is useful to note that the *cabezalero,* who was generally from the lower or middle nobility was not a new figure in the eighteenth-century Asturian countryside, and may, as intermediary between the *directum dominium* and the work actually performed on the land, have been one of the agents by which some direct ecclesiastical owners had been dispossessed between the end of the Middle Ages and the Early Modern period.

35 This can clearly be seen in certain dossiers: AHN. CR. MSP, Leg. 5046, Renta y Arrendamiento de Enguil, Concejo de Gozón, 1722-1806 (for the desire to describe the smallest *quiñón* of land with precision); Arriendo de la Casería de Orizon y Oturu, Concejo de Nava, 1709-1815; Juguería de Carabiés en Lugo, Concejo de Llanera, 1719-1807.

36 AHN. CR. MSP, Leg. 5045, Dossier Apeos y Amojonamientos, 1488-1817; Leg. 5062, Dossier Renta Mayor de Noreña, Concejo de Siero, 1716-1824.

or supposedly owned, by the monastery at the time the rental contract was signed, were under the control of 'usurping' occupiers. The general surveys (*apeos*) of the seventeenth century were used as proof, particularly where these properties were described as owned by San Pelayo, and these were of course included with the mass of rented land.

In the last third of the eighteenth century, as we have already shown, rental contracts began explicitly to include a certain number of conditions previously unknown, or only mentioned in a general way. These new conditions formally prohibited the division, partition, separation or partial cession of the pieces making up the rented property, even to the close family of the beneficiaries, particularly to brothers. The contracts also prohibited mortgaging the land when the tenant needed a loan. And, in general, all actions of the tenants that could lead to 'obscuring' the title of the land were forbidden.

There were, on the other hand, conditions obliging the tenants and direct occupiers to make improvements and repairs, to construct new buildings, to enclose the limits, to restore the boundary markers, etc. These were known as 'improvements' (*perfectos*) of the holding; they were to be done without financial or other compensation to the beneficiaries by the monastery.

But sometimes the monastery obliged the tenants to retain or install principal tenants on certain pieces or parcels of the rented property, or force them to accept certain people to work the direct land *llevadores*) rather than others, or to increase the amount of land allocated to such and such a tenant[37]. With the exception of acts of Christian charity or special favour towards particular individuals, this no doubt meant that the monastic authorities were intervening directly in networks of local interests in order to defend their clientele or a local power group. And thereby fully exercising their ecclesiastical *dominium*, we may add.

IV.4. Rent Increases

The work done on the available sources seems to show that there was a noticeable increase in the rent received by the monastery during the eighteenth century, particularly in the middle of the century[38]. However we are not yet able to quantify by how much it increased and we have sources only for the proceeds from landed property rentals. The increase in rent seems to have

---

37 It is impossible to go into all of these in detail within the framework of a single article. Some cases can be found, especially at the end of the eighteenth and beginning of the nineteenth centuries, in the following dossiers: AHN. CR. MSP, Leg. 5046, Arriendo Santa Cruz de Jove y Beriña, Concejo de Gijón, 29/09/1803; Arriendo Santianes de Ceñero y Sandal, 1779-1807; Renta y Arrendamiento de Enguil, Concejo de Gozón, 1722-1806; Arriendo Olleros de Alva, Gordon (León), 1709-1804.

38 Including the monastery of San Pelayo's ventures into other parts of northern Spain, for example the Kingdom and Bishopric of Leon. See: AHN. CR. MSP, Leg.5045, Dossier de Renta de Alcabalas, Reino de León, 1730-1745.

been progressive and substantial, whether it was paid in money or kind[39]. This feature distinguishes San Pelayo from most but not all other Asturian ecclesiastical institutions.

This progressive increase in rent only seems to have slackened, and then very slightly, in the critical period at the end of the eighteenth and beginning of the nineteenth centuries and then resumed its upward course. The documentary evidence confirms that from then onwards the monastery preferred to take its rents in hard cash; there seems to have been a process of converting to money rents and refusing payment in paper currency[40].

As well as raising the rent in successive rental and renewal contracts, the monastic authorities also tended more and more to divide a piece of land into two or more physical parts, and rent it to two or more different tenants, thereby increasing the total rent received[41]. However, the documents we have reviewed do not provide details on the area of land divided up. Nor do they tell us about the reaction of these tenants, particularly those who had previously farmed all or part of the land, when they saw part of the holding go to others, apart from the fact that they signed and accepted the contract.

In addition to the raising the rent, as we have seen, the contract obliged the tenants to investigate, at their own expense, the parcels with 'obscure' title. Once the 'usurpers' or illegal possessors were identified the tenants had to initiate a lawsuit, also at their own expense, but in the monastery's name, and complete the process of expelling the intruders and recovering the land[42]. Though there are references to this all through the eighteenth century they are clearer and more urgent at the beginning of the nineteenth.

However, the documents also show that, when the judicial authorities ruled in favour of recovering the disputed land, and the pieces and parcels were reintegrated into the original property, the monastery retained the right to lease it to a different tenant or to increase the rent paid by the original

---

39 e.g. the following specific cases: AHN. CR. MSP, Leg. 5046, Arriendo san Martin de Podes, Concejo de Gijón, 1718-1802: the rent went up by 533% in less than a century, with a particularly steep rise between 1793 and 1802. AHN. CR. MSP, Leg. 5046, Arriendo Folenti y Valperi, Concejo de Gozón, 1722-1830 (incomplete dossier): the increase in rent between 1722 and 1782 was 290%, even though the property had been divided. The increase could also be expressed in quantities of cereals. AHN. CN. MSP, Leg. 8046, Arriendo de Perlavia, Concejo de Grado, 1715-1818; the rent went from 4 *fanegas* of cereal in 1715 to more than 66 in 1804.

40 e.g. the following different and individual instances of collection in AHN. CR. MSP, Leg. 5061, Dossier Iglesia de santa María de Tiñana e Iglesia santa María de Meres, Concejo de Siero, 1610-1831; Dossier Iglesia de santo Tomás de Feleches, Concejo de Siero, 1669-1827; Dossier Iglesia santa Eugenia de los Pandos, Concejo de Villaviciosa, 1670-1821.

41 e.g. AHN. CR. MSP, Leg. 5046, Arriendo de Mansos san Nicolás de Bañugues, Concejo de Gozón, 1772-1805: the division took place on 18/10/1772; Arriendo de los bienes del foro de Ballangas, Concejo de Nava, 1708-1787: division of property between 1786 and 1787.

42 It is impossible to list all these cases here, but see e.g.: AHN. CR. MSP, Leg. 5046. Arriendo de Bienes de Misiego, Concejo de Gozón, 1807; Arriendo san Martin de Pereda y Cañedo, Concejo de Grado, 1743-1830; Arriendo de Castiello en Lugo, Concejo de Llanera, 1732-1800.

tenant – even when the recovery had been carried out by the tenant, or thanks to him, and when these pieces had been part of the property originally rented by him under contract.

IV.5. Increase of tenant and renter indebtedness

The documents we have consulted also show that the monastery's tenants became perceptibly more indebted and that the conflicts linked to this financial situation became more acute. These conflicts took place when the tenants could no longer repay the principal of their debt and the interest on it, particularly in the last third of the eighteenth century. San Pelayo had long been accustomed to lending capital to its tenants when they were having difficulty in meeting their expenses, even rescheduling their debt payments. It is worth recalling that in the Asturias, many of the women's convents, more so than the men's[43], often devoted large sums of money to buying *censos* (interest-bearing perpetual securities or bonds) as well as making loans themselves. This is an aspect of the activities of religious bodies in the Asturias that needs to be systematically studied.

Even though we do not yet have a large body of evidence, there are indications in the documents that the tenants of San Pelayo faced considerable financial difficulties after the brutal upswing in rents imposed in the mid-eighteenth century contracts, although to complete the picture, we also have to take account of the actual agricultural conditions and price movements. Later on, but as early as the end of eighteenth century and during the first three decades of the nineteenth century, there was an increase in judicial proceedings[44] for bankruptcy, and seizure of goods and furniture (*ejecución judicial*) against the monastery's debtors[45]. This was not a new issue; the same things had occurred during the last decades of the seventeenth century and earlier, in the sixteenth century. But we can see in these procedures for debt and in the negotiations

43 There were even some Asturian men's monasteries that were net debtors rather than creditors, e.g. Santa María de Villanueva de Oscos, in the western Asturias, also a Benedictine foundation. Paz González (1991: 16-18).

44 The following is only one of such examples of a suit for bankruptcy and seizure of goods. AHN. CR. MSP, Leg. 5046, Arriendo de la Caseria del Sartero, Concejo de Langreo, 1787-1819: the *ejecución judicial* of the goods of Diego Hevia and his mother for unpaid debts.

45 It was also the case that after seigneurial jurisdiction was abolished by the liberals in Cadiz, between 1811 and 1813 and even later (after the return of Ferdinand VII), the San Pelayo monastery sought to re-establish the *finsos y mojones*, the boundary markers of its possessions, which had been overturned by the peasants and tenants physically to signal the end of ecclesiastical seigneury. AHN. CR. MSP, Leg. 5062, Dossier de supresión del Señorío Jurisdiccional, 1811-1815. See also AHN. CR. MSP, Leg. 5062, Dossier Reclamos, 1787-1816.

between the monastery and the debtors, that repayment schedules bound the debtors over a much longer period than did current rental contracts[46].

Presumably this means that the monastery authorities were taking account of the difficulties of the debtor tenant, even if they finally 'ejected' his goods and furniture later on. On the other hand, no doubt San Pelayo wanted to ensure that the rented land was worked productively and that it did not deteriorate from lack of activity. But it is also possible that the monastery doubted the capacity of its debtors to pay off all their obligations and that it sought payment of debt by seizing their goods, which were immediately useable or saleable.

V. Conclusion

At the end of this analysis we may conclude that the transition from *foro* to rental contract was one of the monastery's defence mechanisms in face of more and more open challenges to ecclesiastical dominium. In particular, it was a response to the increasing, and verifiable, autonomy of the *foro*'s emphyteutic dominium utile.

Behind the domimium utile, and in direct opposition to the transition imposed by San Pelayo, we have found a active social group, still in need of a more detailed description, that seems to bind together interests linked to the possession and working of the land.

It appears that the monastery had at least two basic aims:

- First, it wanted to reassert clear eminent possession of its property as direct and superior owner, showing its will to absorb the dominium utile, in order to prevent any new division of the dominium or dispossession, and the spread of social conflict inherent to it.
- Second, it tried to maintain a favourable balance of power, a socially dominant position which would allow it to exercise its authority, and social control and power, on a local and regional level, over and in other aspects of everyday life.

Although this clearly disturbed the balance of the *dominium,* the path they chose had the great advantage of increasing the institution's actual revenue by regularly renegotiating the annual rent from their developing landed estate, and

46 e.g. AHN. CR. MSP, Leg.5046, Arriendo San Bartholomé, Coto de Nava, Concejo de Nava, 06/05/1788: a debt repayment schedule of 18 years, in favour of María Pandiella, for a rental renewal contract of four years; for another example, see AHN. CR. MSP, Leg.5046, Arriendo Prado del Valle, Concejo de Nava, 1726-1814 containing a very large accumulated debt, an agreed debt repayment schedule stopped in 1791 and the seizure of the debtor's goods in 1810.

the conditions on which property was ceded[47]. This allowed them at the same time to face the erosion of their income by rising prices, and, more importantly, to counter the 'rent leakage' that came from the increased fragmentation of the dominium utile. This division of the dominium, an inevitable consequence of the *foro* system according to the monastery's lawyers, also led to the 'obscuring' of eminent possession dominium directum[48].

It should also be mentioned that the imposition of such a policy could not be expected to pass without reaction from the former *foreros* and new tenants. This fed structural challenges to the ecclesiastical dominium.

At the end of the Old Regime, retaining the *foro* in the North and West and, more generally, different forms of emphyteusis elsewhere on Spanish territory, as a way of holding and working the land, seems to have represented a kind of resistance or alternative, that was economic as well as patrimonial and social. The emphyteutic tenants and *foreros*, who had titles to different segments of dominium utile, appear to have chosen to struggle against the absorption of the dominium utile into dominium directum, not just by the Church but by all those who benefited and profited from the dominium in general. The contest over the perpetuation or the abolition of the *foro* crystallised the clash between the two social groups and called into question one of the pillars of ecclesiastical dominium.

In both cases however, that is, in the defense of each kind of domain, there seems to have been a gradual, sometimes tacit, sometimes even explicit, consecration of property rights and of property holders, traditional and potential, old and new, direct and indirect. This consecration clearly appeared in the assertion of absolute rights, brandished by both sides of the conflict. The French Revolution, a few years later, carried this process to its ultimate end by adding to the sacred character of these rights, the juridical force of nature and even natural law, plus the economic and civic necessity of introducing them[49].

It was as if the Revolution brought to completion a medium-term process which had been started some time before. The dominium – ecclesiastical, in this context – was to become, or become once more, absolute ownership, while at the same time losing its coherence and power in society. Thus began the final phase of its decline.

---

47 This also meant, as we have shown, that the monastery had the power to negotiate the incorporation of the *perfecto* (improvements made by the tenants), or to punish the tenants for running down the property, without going through the courts and without judicial costs. We should remember that this was in a period when rural conflicts and judicial processes were both rising steeply.

48 Furthermore, the Congregation of Saint Benedict in Valladolid advised resisting the division of *utile dominium*. See e.g. the interesting details in *Libro de anotaciones al govierno de hazienda del monasterio de la Vega*, in Martinez Vega, 1994, 322-334; this was a compilation of management advice directed at all Benedictine religious institutions.

49 This question is discussed in Béaur & Minard (1997: 9-12).

Archives

Archivo Histórico Nacional (AHN) de Madrid; Clero Regular (CR); Monasterio de San Pelayo (MSP)

- AHN, CR, MSP, Legajo nº 5045: *Contaduría Monástica*
- AHN, CR, MSP, Legajo nº 5046: *Arriendos*
- AHN, CR, MSP, Legajo nº 5061: *Patronato Eclesiástico 4*
- AHN, CR, MSP, Legajo nº 5062: *Diversos de Archivo*
- AHN, CR, MSP, Legajo nº 5063: *Jurisdicciones*
- AHN, CR, MSP, Legajo nº 5064: *Papeles Judiciales*
- AHN, CR, MSP, Legajo nº 5065: *Diversos de Archivo*

Bibliography

I Congreso Internacional del Monacato Femenino en España, Portugal y América, 1492-1992 (1993), León, Universidad de León, 2 vols

Real Monasterio de san Pelayo (1994), Oviedo, Real Monasterio de san Pelayo, 182 p.

Alvarez Vazquez, José Antonio (1982), 'La vida económica del Monasterio de san Pelayo en los siglos XVI y XVII', in *Semana de Historia del Monacato Cántabro-astur-leonés*, Oviedo, Monasterio de san Pelayo, p. 468-490.

Anes, Gonzalo (1988), *Economía y Sociedad en la Asturias del Antiguo Régimen*, Barcelona, Ariel.

Anes, Gonzalo (1989), *Los señoríos asturianos*, Gijón, Silverio Cañada editor..

Anes, Gonzalo (ed.) (1990), *Oviedo 1753; según las respuestas generales del Catastro de Ensenada*, Madrid, Centro de Gestión Catastral y Cooperación Tributaria.

Arango Fernandez, Jesús (2009), *Montes comunales en Asturias y otras cuestiones agrarias*, Oviedo, Ediciones KRK.

Barreiro Mallon, Baudilio (1982), 'El dominio de San Vicente en la Edad Moderna', in *Semana de Historia del Monacato Cántabro-astur-leonés*, Oviedo, Monasterio de san Pelayo, p. 491-529.

Barreiro Mallon, Baudilio (1990), 'Producto agrario y evolución de la población en Asturias, siglos XVI al XIX', *Bidea*, 133, p. 73-95.

Barreiro Mallon, Baudilio (1993), 'El monacato femenino en la Edad moderna: demografía y estructura social', in *I Congreso Internacional del Monacato Femenino en España, Portugal y América, 1492-1992*, León, Universidad de León, vol. 2, p. 57-74.

Barrio Gozalo, Maximiliano (1989), 'Sociedad, Iglesia y vida religiosa en la España del siglo XVIII', Anthologica Annua, 36, Roma, p. 273-310.

Barrio Gozalo, Maximiliano (2000), 'Reforma y supresión de los regulares en España al final del Antiguo Régimen (1759-1836)', *Investigaciones Históricas*, 20, Valladolid, p. 89-118.

Beaur, Gérard (2000), *Histoire agraire de la France au XVIIIe siècle: inerties et changements dans les campagnes françaises entre 1715 et 1815*, Paris, Sedes.

BEAUR, Gérard and Philippe MINARD (eds) (1997), *Atlas de la Révolution française*, Economie, Paris, EHESS.

BLOCH, Marc [1931] (1999), *Les caractères originaux de l'histoire rurale française*, Paris, Armand Colin.

BLOCH, Marc [1939] (1989), *La société féodale. La formation des liens de dépendance. Les classes et le gouvernement des hommes*, Paris, Albin Michel, XII.

BODINIER, Bernard & TEYSSIER, Eric (2000), *L'événement le plus important de la Révolution. La vente des biens nationaux*, Paris, Société des études robespierristes, Editions du CTHS.

BODINIER, Bernard, CONGOST, Rosa & LUNA, Pablo F. (eds) (2009), *De la Iglesia al Estado. Las desamortizaciones de bienes eclesiásticos en Francia, España y América Latina, Zaragoza*, Prensas Universitarias de Zaragoza.

BURGO LOPEZ, María Concepción (1986), *Un dominio monástico femenino en la Edad moderna: el Monasterio benedictino de san Payo de Antealtares*, Santiago de Compostela, Universidad de Santiago de Compostela.

BURGO LOPEZ, María Concepción (1992), 'El señorío monástico gallego en la Edad Moderna', *Obradoiro de Historia Moderna*, 1, p. 99-121.

BURGO LOPEZ, María Concepción (1993), 'Política económica y gestión administrativa de las entidades monásticas femeninas', in *I Congreso Internacional del Monacato Femenino en España, Portugal y América, 1492-1992*, León, Universidad de León, vol. II, p. 569-585.

CORTES PEÑA, Antonio & LOPEZ-GUADALUPE, Miguel (eds) (2007), *La Iglesia española en la Edad Moderna. Balance historiográfico y perspectivas*, Madrid, Abada Editores.

CUARTAS RIVERO, Margarita (1983), *Oviedo y el Principado de Asturias a fines de la Edad Media*, Oviedo, Instituto de Estudios Asturianos.

DOMINGUEZ ORTIZ, Antonio (1973), *Las clases privilegiadas en la España del Antiguo Régimen*, Madrid, Istmo.

Estructuras Agrarias y Reformismo Ilustrado en la España del Siglo XVIII (1989), Madrid, Ministerio de Agricultura.

EGIDO, Teófanes (2007), 'Historiografía del clero regular en la España moderna', in Antonio CORTES PEÑA & Miguel LOPEZ-GUADALUPE (eds), *La Iglesia española en la Edad Moderna. Balance historiográfico y perspectivas*, Madrid, Abada Editores, p. 9-37.

FAYA DIAZ, María Angeles (ed.) (2004a), *La nobleza en la Asturias del Antiguo Régimen*, Oviedo, Ediciones KRK.

FAYA DIAZ, María Angeles (2004b), 'El Occidente de Asturias a fines del Antiguo Régimen', in *Sulcum Sevit. Estudios en homenaje a Eloy Benito Ruano*, Oviedo, Universidad de Oviedo, p. 503-534.

FAYA DIAZ, María Angeles & ANES FERNANDEZ, Lidia (eds) (2007), *Nobleza y poder en la Asturias del Antiguo Régimen*, Oviedo, Ediciones KRK.

FAYA DIAZ, María Angeles (2007), 'La oposición al poder señorial del Monasterio de San Pelayo de Oviedo en el Coto de San Bartolomé de Nava', in *Actas del I Congreso de Estudios Asturianos*, Oviedo, Real Instituto de Estudios Asturianos, vol. III, p. 29-42.

Feo Parrondo, Francisco (1992), 'La economía del convento franciscano de Tineo (1758-1836)', *Bidea*, 139, p. 305-319.

Fernandez Conde, Francisco Javier, torrente, Isabel & de la noval, Guadalupe (1978-1990), *El Monasterio de san Pelayo de Oviedo*, Historia y Fuentes, Oviedo, Monasterio de san Pelayo, 4 vols

Fernandez Conde, Francisco Javier (1982), 'Orígenes del Monasterio de san Pelayo', in *Semana de Historia del Monacato Cántabro-astur-leonés*, Oviedo, Monasterio de san Pelayo, p. 99-121.

Fernandez Conde, Francisco Javier (1993), *El Señorío del Cabildo Ovetense: Estructuras Agrarias de Asturias en el Tardo Medioevo*, Oviedo, Universidad de Oviedo.

Garcia Fernandez, Jesús (1988), *Sociedad y organización tradicional del espacio en Asturias*, Gijón, Silverio Cañada editor.

Garcia Villoslada, Ricardo (ed.) (1979), *Historia de la Iglesia en España*, Madrid, Biblioteca de Autores Cristianos, 7 vols

Gomez alvarez, Ubaldo (1993), *La sociedad tradicional asturiana*, Oviedo, Universidad de Oviedo.

Guerreau, Alain (2001), *L'avenir d'un passé incertain. Quelle histoire du Moyen Âge au XXIe siècle ?*, Paris, Seuil.

Jove y Bravo, Rogelio (1883), *Los foros: Estudio histórico y doctrinal, bibliográfico y crítico de los foros, en Galicia y Asturias*, Madrid, Imprenta de la Revista de la Legislación.

Jovellanos de, Gaspar Melchor (1999), 'Descripción del Principado de Asturias', *Astura*, 8, p. 37-57.

Landi, Fiorenzo (2005), *Storia Economica del Clero in Europa, Secoli XV-XIX*, Roma, Carocci.

Landi, Fiorenzo (ed.) (2004), *Confische e Sviluppo Capitalistico. I grandi patrimoni del clero regolare in età moderna in Europa et nel Continente Americano*, Milano, Franco Angeli.

Lopez, Roberto J. (1985), *Oviedo: muerte y religiosidad en el siglo XVIII. Un estudio de mentalidades colectivas*, Oviedo, Servicio de Publicaciones del Principado de Asturias.

Lopez, Roberto J. (1989), *Comportamientos religiosos en Asturias durante el Antiguo Régimen*, Gijón, Silverio Cañada.

Lopez Iglesias, Florentino (1999), 'Vecinos, caseros, señores, amigos y parientes, en la Asturias del Antiguo Régimen', *Bidea*, 153, p. 109-157.

Luna, Pablo F. (2003a), 'Las reformas de la propiedad: los planteamientos del conde de Campomanes', in Dolores Mateos Dorado (ed.) (2003), *Campomanes, doscientos años después*, Oviedo, Instituto Feijóo de Estudios del Siglo XVIII-Universidad de Oviedo, p. 547-555.

Luna, Pablo F. (2003b), 'El régimen de propiedad en el pensamiento de Jovellanos', *Boletín Jovellanista*, IV, 4, p. 127-138.

Luna, Pablo F. (2005), 'El intocable dominio y las reformas de la posesión: los planteamientos de Campomanes', *Tiempos Modernos*, 12, 2, <http://www.tiemposmodernos.org/>.

LUNA, Pablo F. (2006), *La Reforma de la sociedad y la defensa de los derechos del propietario, según G.M. de Jovellanos, a finales del Antiguo Régimen*, Oviedo, Real Instituto de Estudios Asturianos.

LUNA, Pablo F. (2007), 'Prácticas y mecanismos del dominium y la posesión eclesiásticos. Asturias, segunda mitad del siglo XVIII. Monasterio de san Pelayo', in *Actas del I Congreso de Estudios Asturianos*, Oviedo, Real Instituto de Estudios Asturianos, vol. III, p. 13-28.

MARTINEZ, Elviro (1979), *Los documentos asturianos del Archivo Histórico Nacional*, Gijón, Colegio Inmaculada.

MARTINEZ RUIZ, Enrique (ed.) (2004), *El peso de la Iglesia. Cuatro siglos de Ordenes Religiosas en España*, Madrid, Actas Editorial.

MARTINEZ RUIZ, Enrique & SUAREZ GRIMON, Vicente (eds) (1994), *Iglesia y Sociedad en el Antiguo Régimen*, Las Palmas, Universidad de las Palmas de Gran Canaria, 2 vols

MARTINEZ VEGA, Andrés (1994), *El monasterio de santa María de la Vega. Historia (s. XII-XIX)*, Oviedo, Real Instituto de Estudios Asturianos.

MORO BARREÑADA, José María (1993), 'Propietarios y colonos en Asturias en el siglo XIX. Notas en torno a la propiedad y uso de la tierra', *Astura*, 1, p. 49-54.

MORO BARREÑADA, José María (1998), 'Análisis de una crisis agraria y sus consecuencias, Oviedo en 1803-1804', *Bidea*, 151, p. 113-141.

OCAMPO S-V, Joaquín (1990), *Campesinos y artesanos en la Asturias preindustrial (1750-1850)*, Gijón, Silverio Cañada.

PAZ GONZALEZ, Daniel (1991), *El Monasterio de santa María de Villanueva de Osco: De la reforma a la exclaustración*, Oviedo, Universidad de Oviedo.

QUIROS, Francisco (1978), *El crecimiento espacial de Oviedo*, Oviedo, Universidad de Oviedo.

REY CASTELAO, Ofelia (1991), 'La crisis de la economía de las instituciones eclesiásticas de Galicia', in *Simposio Internacional de Historia Rural de los siglos XVIII al XX*, Barcelona, Crítica, vol. 1: p. 261-303.

REY CASTELAO, Ofelia (1993), 'Las economías monásticas femeninas ante la crisis del Antiguo Régimen', in *I Congreso Internacional del Monacato Femenino en España, Portugal y América, 1492-1992*, León, Universidad de León, vol. 2: p. 105-129.

REY CASTELAO, Ofelia (2007), 'Las economías eclesiásticas en la Edad Moderna: Un estado de la cuestión de la historiografía reciente (1994-2006)', in Antonio CORTES PEÑA & Miguel LOPEZ-GUADALUPE (eds), *La Iglesia española en la Edad Moderna. Balance historiográfico y perspectivas*, Madrid, Abada Editores, p. 179-221.

SAAVEDRA, Pegerto (2009), 'El patrimonio y los ingresos de la Iglesia en la España de finales del Antiguo Régimen', in Bernard BODINIER, Rosa CONGOST & Pablo F. LUNA (eds), *De la Iglesia al Estado. Las desamortizaciones de bienes eclesiásticos en Francia, España y América Latina*, Zaragoza, Prensas Universitarias de Zaragoza, p. 45-76.

SAAVEDRA, Pegerto (2010), 'Les senyories monàstiques a la Galicia moderna', *Afers, fulls de recerca i pensament*, 65, Valencia, p. 113-141.

Saavedra, Pegerto (ed.) (1999), *Agricultura e Ilustración, Santiago de Compostela,* Xunta de Galicia.

Semana de Historia del Monacato Cántabro-astur-leonés (1982), Oviedo, Monasterio de san Pelayo.

Simposio Internacional de Historia Rural de los siglos XVIII al XX (1991), Barcelona, Crítica, 2 vols

Sitges, Juan B. (1913), *El Monasterio de Religiosas Benedictinas de san Pelayo el Real de Oviedo,* Madrid, Sucesores de Rivadeneyra.

Torrente Fernandez, Isabel (1982), *El dominio del monasterio de San Bartolomé de Naca (Siglos XIII-XVI),* Oviedo, Universidad de Oviedo.

Vilar, Pierre (1962), *La Catalogne dans l'Espagne moderne.* Recherches *sur les fondements économiques des structures nationales,* Paris, S.E.V.P.E.N.

Villares, Ramon (1982) La propiedad de la tierra en Galicia, 1500-1936, Madrid, Siglo XXI

Villares, Ramon & Díaz-Castroverde, José L. (1997) *O conflicto foral nos séculos XVII e XVIII, Santiago de Compostela,* Xunta de Galicia/Caixa Ourense

BENEDITA CAMARA

12. The *Colonia* Contract

Ambiguity between Sharecropping, Fixed Rent and Emphyteusis

Emphyteusis is a legal institution with historical character that has been registered in different types of circumstances. In the 1850s, Portuguese liberals sought to associate the Portuguese *colonia* contract from Madeira with emphyteusis. By the 1880s there was a shift in the focus but the valuation and property rights of the improvements of the *colono* remained the common element of political and legal debate. In line with recent studies which have suggested an agenda for researching the imperfect nature of land ownership, while pointing out that the historical changes that occurred in the property rights were not only the result of the changes introduced in the law (Congost, 2007), the thesis of this chapter is that those debates and attempts at reform were linked to the context of the time period between the 1850s and the 1880s, which was characterized by changes in relative prices that required adaptation to land use. This interfered with the incentives generated by the valuation of the improvements of the *colono* and the risks taken by the landowners in the *colonia* contract. There were similarities between a number of these issues and the ones being debated in England.

I. Introduction

In the present chapter we are concerned with the proposals about the classification of the ownership of the investments of the *colono* and the reform of the procedures to evaluate these investments. In our view, this cannot be dissociated from the historical context of the second half of the 19th century, which was characterized by agricultural difficulties. Among these difficulties we can highlight the loss of the importance of the external market for wine production, and the necessary adaptation of land use given the increase in the labour intensity of the product mix due to changes in relative prices.

Economists and historians have focused on explaining how the conventional property rights prevent transaction costs for landowners and they have ignored other property rights that existed within indirect forms of exploitation of land (Garrido, 2009: 462). The historiography inspired by neo-institutionalist theories has emphasized the connection between economic growth and the path toward full ownership (North, 1981: 5) and has not paid attention, for example, to problems concerning property of improvements – who owned

Agrarian Change and Imperfect Property, ed. by Rosa Congost and Pablo F. Luna, Rural History in Europe, 15 (Turnhout, 2018), 263-285

DOI 10.1484/M.RURHE-EB.5.116127

them and how they were evaluated. This view does not explain why a form of indirect exploitation of land, like *colonia*, was able to create conditions for investment in vines during the eighteenth century and early nineteenth century but lost this capacity between the 1850s and 1880s.

The case of the *colonia* contract in Madeira illustrates the difficulty faced by the liberal regime in addressing the issue of the classification of the property rights of the improvements of the *colono* and the procedures to evaluate them. It is also important because, in a sense, the property rights of the *colono* were recognized before the Civil Code (1867). We address how, during the second half of nineteenth century, the period between the 1850s and 1867, and from then until 1888, Portuguese liberals classified the property rights of the improvements of the *colono*. The ideological and political debate that occurred at national and at regional levels evolved until the Civil Code was drawn up (1867). An association between *colonia* and emphyteusis was successively produced and rejected. In 1888, the creation of a law to regulate the evaluation of the improvements of the *colono* was debated. Improvements were the central problem in both phases.

As sources we used draft laws, national parliamentary debates, decree-laws, pamphlets, newspapers, the minutes of the meetings of the local board of an administrative institution (Junta Geral), and an inquiry into the social and economic situation that occurred in 1888. In addition, we studied notary documents and private archives in order to substantiate the evolution recorded.

The *colonia* contract issue arose between the 1850s and the 1880s in local and national debates as a highly specific type of contract. This view was later transferred to historiography and to legal science. The defence of its specific nature increased around the time of the promulgation of the Civil Codes of 1867 and 1967 (which had different technical and political perspectives) when the issue was to find a solution for the conflict between the formal property right over the improvements and landlord's rights to the land.

Despite the specific nature of this contract, the issue of assessing the improvements was one similarity with the first known attempt at regulation in England, which occurred in 1875, via the law of tenants' right based on Lincolnshire custom. *Colonia* was a contract based on the share of the output, whereas in England fixed rent tenancy contracts prevailed. Notwithstanding several differences, until the end of the nineteenth century, some similarities can be seen in the problems and difficulties of assessing the compensation of the improvements.

In the second section, we characterize the conditions present in *colonia* contracts. We then compare the *colonia* contract with emphyteusis and with sharecropping, we show the changes introduced in the agriculture of Madeira between the 1850s and 1880s and we refer to the evolution of the incidence of *colonia* contracts. In the third section, we analyse the changes in the method of addressing the improvements in the *colonia* contract between 1854 and 1867 in the political debate at national and at regional levels. The suggested reform was to approximate *colonia* to emphyteusis, and we consider the interests of the landlords and the *colonos* in this solution. As *colonia* was not specifically regulated by the Civil Code (1867) and was framed for legal purposes under fixed rent and sharecropping contracts, in the fourth section we analyse the radicalism of the debate of the 1880s on the urgent need to write a law to regulate the valuation of the improvements of *colonos*. We present a number of issues debated in relation to the *colonia* contract and we refer the attempt made in England after 1875 (the Agricultural Holding Act: A.H.A.) to regulate by law the valuation of the improvements in order to compensate the tenant. We conclude that the agricultural changes that were required between the 1850s and the 1880s in order to adapt land use cannot be dissociated from the problems generated by the valuation of the improvements of the *colono*. The valuation of the improvements in Madeira had worked in the past as an incentive to the *colono*'s investment. In the context of the period between the 1850s and the 1880s, the conditions that allowed for a balance between the *colonos'* investments in fixed capital and the risks taken by landowners in permitting those investments on their lands underwent changes. The thesis is that the attempts to reform the valuation and the classification of the property rights of the *colono* cannot be dissociated from the agricultural problems of the time. The evolution of the regulation on evaluating improvements within the *colonia* contract was similar to the English case (tenancy rights) in that both were criticised by people at the time who thought that they were not protected by effective institutions.

II. Characterization of *colonia* contracts

II.1. Colonia contracts vs. emphyteusis and sharecropping

The *colonia* contract had no fixed term because *colonos* and landlords committed themselves and their heirs to complying with the conditions of the contract while it lasted. It was a long-term contract with no pre-established fixed term. A particular feature of the *colonia* contract was the fact that the *colono* took ownership of improvements – fixed assets other than land, such as buildings (supporting walls to build terraces, houses, barns and presses) or plants. In the *colonia* contract improvements were owned by the *colono* because they were a specific asset. The advantage of these being the property of the *colono* was related with their need to be continuously maintained. In the landscape of Madeira the supporting walls were vital to sustain the land of the terraces. In practical terms the *colono* could acquire ownership of improvements by reason of having made them. The *colono* could buy or sell the improvements to the landlord or to a third party. Improvements could be handed down by way of inheritance because the contract did not expire upon the death of the *colono* or of the landlord.

Valuation of the improvements of the outgoing *colono* was central to the *colonia* contract because it was an eviction contract. This was so because *colonos* were required to accept that the owner of the land had the right to terminate the contract at any time, provided that he paid compensation to the *colono* for his improvements (eviction). If there were crops still to be harvested this would be included in the valuation of the improvements to be paid for by the landlord prior to eviction. The reverting of the improvements to the landlord could be by mutual agreement (as is borne out by several notarial contracts) or through litigation (demonstrated by lawsuits).The landlord might take this step in order to punish the *colono* for his negligence or lack of success, but it might simply be the case that he wished to use the land for an alternative purpose[1]. In early *colonia* contracts the idea of useful investments was an important criterion for the landlords' commitment to indemnifying the *colono*[2].

Regarding emphyteusis we adopt the definition of a legal framework that established a relationship based on two levels of domain over a single piece of land – dominium directum and dominium utile. The right involves a relationship between the owner (the dominus emphyteuseos) and the lessee (the emphyteuta). The right consists of the legal power of the lessee to cultivate the land and to treat it as his own, on condition that he cultivate it properly and pay the owner (the dominus) a fixed sum (*canon, pension*, or *reditus*). This payment had a more or less symbolic character and was to be paid at fixed times.

According to the Old Portuguese law there were two types of contracts concerning the *dominium utile* which differed in terms of their duration in the hands of the holder of the *dominium utile. Dominium utile* could either be perpetual (*prazo fanteosins*), meaning remaining forever in the hands of the holder of the useful domain and his successors, or temporary (*prazo de vidas*) or for the duration of three lifetimes (Serrão, 2000: 429-438)[3]. The division between ownership of the land and ownership of the improvements was in a certain sense characteristic of the *colonia* – it could be associated with temporary emphyteusis – but in case of eviction the *colono* only had the right to the compensation for the investments after evaluation in a situation similar to the 'tenancy rights'[4] seen in England. In emphyteusis there was the division between dominium directum and dominium utile. Both contracts

1 This right of the landlord to have the *colono's* investments revert to him was a potestative right – a right of redemption – by means of which title to the soil and surface of the land was consolidated (Ascensão, 1971: 513).

2 In a *colonia* contract of 1756, landlords stipulated that the *colonos* 'should work very hard to produce lower-cost investments (buildings) which could be totally useful' (Sousa, 1994: 347).

3 Both types required that the holder of the dominium directum be paid an annual pension (forum).

4 According to Mcquiston, tenancy right concerns 'the claim of a farmer to compensation for any unexhausted improvement made by him and remaining on his holding at the end of his tenancy' (Mcquiston, 1973: 95). The expansion of Linconshire Custom throughout Britain was a difficult process. The Agricultural Holding Act of 1875 was – based on Lincolnshire – the first attempt to regulate tenant rights by law (Garrido, 2011: 73; Porter, 1986: 188-197; Perkins, 1975:1-22; Fisher, 1978: 15-25).

differed from the arrangements typical of the *censo* regime because in this case the landlord transferred the full domain to the tenant[5]. *Prazos de vidas* were unusual in Madeira, although perpetual emphyteusis was quite common (Azevedo e Silva, 1995: 196-198).

Moreover, *laudemium*, a proportion of the sale of any improvements, which was also a fine for alienation paid to the direct owner (*dominus*), was typical of emphyteusis but absent in the *colonia* contract. In terms of both perpetual and temporary duration, emphyteusis differed from *colonia*. In temporary emphyteusis, the end of the contract was stipulated as a number of lives of the tenant, but in the *colonia* contracts the use of the property was more flexible because it could revert to the landlord at any time provided the landlord indemnified the *colono*.

Sharecropping contracts and *colonia* contract had in common the characteristic of the share of the product between the *colono* and the landowner. However, when we compare sharecropping with *colonia*, we may note a difference insofar as in the former the duration was normally shorter and improvements usually belonged to the landlord and remained his property.

Improvements of the *colono* were subject to compensation by the landlord and could be traded. In 1776 a group of landowners that belonged to the nobility stated that owners allowed the *colono* to make the improvements considered necessary. Those improvements could be sold by the outgoing *colono* to an incoming *colono*. In the case of an eviction it was up to the landlord to indemnify the *colono* for the latter's improvements[6].

After 1776 there was an evolution in terms of a certain official recognition of the ownership of the improvements of the *colono* that we will refer to below. This is crucial for understanding the attempt to connect *colonia* with emphyteusis that occurred between the 1850s and the publication of the Civil Code (1867). The sharing of the product between the *colono* (tenant) and the landlord gave arguments to those who tried to identify *colonia* with sharecropping.

II. 2. Characterization of the agriculture of Madeira

The agricultural area of Madeira is limited to 31.3% of the total area (72,800 hectares). The degree of slope and configuration of terraces prevent alternatives to human labour. After a phase of expansion from the mid-seventeenth

---

5 *Censo* involved a total transfer of the domain providing the possibility for the *censuário* to sell the good or the land without giving any acknowledgment to the landlord, without the obligation to pay the *laudemium* (fine for alienation) and even against the landlords's will. Concerning the differences between the *censo* system and emphyteusis, Serrão (2000: 434-455, footnote 24).

6 Petition of the City Hall of Funchal (signed by nobles that were members) dated 25th May 1776 addressed to the king disagreeing with a previous petition written by *colonos* in 1773, Arquivo Histórico Ultramarino, Madeira, no. 449 in Sousa (1994: 364-365).

century until 1820, wine production decreased. Between the 1820s and the 1850s, the evolution in wine prices and in demand remained low, despite some fluctuations. As a result during the 1840s the economic agenda was focused on the need to reconvert crops. During the 1850s and 1860s, this situation was compounded as a result of the destruction of the vines by powdery mildew. The replantation of the vines was a slow process, due to the lack of trust given the market trends, the increasing cost of production, and also possibly to institutional aspects resulting from the failure to adapt the incentives provided to the *colono*. In this context, the cultivation of wheat and vines joined that of sugar cane in a limited area located in low-lying regions. Between the end of the 1870s and the beginning of 1880 vines and sugar cane were affected by diseases and pests (*phylloxera*). At the same time, besides the fall in the prices of wheat and wine, the increase in cultivation costs (due to the need for pesticides and fertilizers) led farmers to make adjustments. The agricultural area became more crowed, nodal crops tended to substitute the already scarce cereal crops, and the rearing of animals in stalls increased. This evolution was not synonymous with prosperity or dynamism for the external market. The requirement of more effort from the *colono* interfered with the working of the *colonia* contract.

The 1880s were a turning point in terms of the intensification of crops by area. Wheat production fell 64% from 1864, the quantity of potatoes produced tripled between 1853 and 1856 and between 1908 and 1913 and wine production more than tripled between 1868 and 1869 and between 1911 and 1914. Between 1855 and 1862-1863, the amount of sugar cane produced multiplied nine times and from then until 1910-1911 it increased again another four and a half times. Livestock rearing also grew, with meat production rising 30%. The labour element played a central role in this intensification process (Câmara, 2002: 148, 303-304, 148).

II. 3. Evolution of the incidence of colonia contract

In the past, access to land in Madeira was made possible by different means. *Colonia* began to spread from the mid-seventeenth century onwards. At that time, perpetual emphyteusis and a particular sharecropping contract (*contrato de meias*) which contained some elements of emphyteusis (*laudemium*, or fine for alienation) were common. Until the middle of the nineteenth century a significant proportion of land remained inalienable.

There is a lack of precise information regarding the incidence of *colonia* contracts over time. In Madeira, as was the case in many countries, most of the agricultural contracts were oral contracts. Some contracts were signed in the mid-eighteenth century and at the beginning of the nineteenth century. These are complemented by unofficial documents, such as lists of improvements used by the landowners until the 1860s as proof of ownership of the improvements or of their sale. The sale and mortgaging of improvements, specifically between *colonos*, had always gone on, often involving the use of a notary[7].

During the 1880s many purchases of improvements from *colonos* can be identified along with a considerable number of evictions. Specific references to the decline of the contract begin to appear beginning in 1916, it being noted that there were parishes without landlords because 'over time, the *colonos* had bought the lands where they owned improvements, (...) or [the land had] been purchased freely and without hindrance from the landlord' (*A Vida* ..., 1916: 20-21). In the early 1920s there are records of many sales of land to *colonos*. In 1929, we see another mention of the decline from the once almost universal *colonia* contract to a much reduced system (Pedro Pita: 13 and 70)[8]. Inflation during the war and a reduction in the protection given to sugar cane production (and to the export of sugar to the mainland) after 1918 helped to lower the incidence of the *colonia* contract. Institutional aspects resulting from the valuation of the *colono*'s improvements were not extraneous to the increase in the sales of land to *colonos*.

III. Colonia: debates from 1854-1867

III. 1. Historiographical/legal and political/ideological debates

Some analyses of the *colonia* contract have sought to draw a connection between this institution and other pre-existing ones on the mainland. José Manuel Azevedo e Silva (1995: 196-198) thought that the colonia evolved out of emphyteusis. He contested both its association with *morgadio*[9], and the idea of the *colonia* as an adulteration of the *sesmaria* contract, which was a mixture of sharecropping and emphyteusis, presented by Álvaro Rodrigues de Azevedo[10], a scholar who had an active voice in the political and ideological debate taking place in Madeira between the 1850s and 1880s.

7 Sousa (1994: 336-362); Arquivo Regional da Madeira (A.R.M.), Notaries and Family Archives (Ornellas e Vasconcelos; Torre Bela).

8 In 1965 an agricultural survey confirmed that the occurrence of the contract prevailed in the south of the island and in the central and eastern zones in the north and in the south. Fixed tenancy was residual and (very) small family farms prevailed. Within a total of 27,141 farms those classified as simple – with one single type of contract – made up 71.1% and the mixed ones totalled 28.9%. *Colonia* corresponded to 12.44% of the simple forms of exploration and 74.37% of the mixed forms. (Recenseamento ..., 1965, p. 3-5 and p. X).

9 Like Sousa (1994: 17-31). The author links the expansion of the vine with the *colonia* contract. For the connection between *colonia* and the entailment, see Freitas Branco (1987).

10 In 1873 Rodrigues de Azevedo (1825-1898) published a manuscript of the sixteenth century (Gaspar Frutuso: *As Saudades da Terra. História das Ilhas do Porto santo, Madeira, Desertas e Selvagens*). He was a bachelor in law that lived in Madeira and played a political

The specific nature of the *colonia* contract within the heart of the Portuguese legal system – due to the *colono*'s ownership of the improvements – was the subject of debate in the Portuguese Parliament in the 1850s[11] and was reaffirmed in 1888. The controversial issues linked to the evaluation of the *colono*'s improvements had a lot in common with the problems raised in England after 1875. In Madeira it was recognised by custom the right of the *colono* to be compensated but in England it wasn't. In England the process of guaranteeing the tenant's rights to be compensated for the improvements introduced took a long time.

In the sixteenth and seventeenth centuries, Portuguese legal doctrine tried to introduce a certain systematization in the legal framework relating to emphyteusis. This attempt continued between the late eighteenth century and 1867, when the Civil Code was passed by Parliament. In the debate that preceded the approval of the Code, Parliament considered what meaning ought to be given to the legal relationship that involved the transfer of the *dominium utile* of the emphyteusis on a temporary or on a perpetual basis. Regarding the matter of emphyteusis it is important to highlight the two opposing opinions of two import jurists. Basically, there were two different political ideas – enlightened despotism on the one hand and liberal ideas on the other. Pascoal de Mello Freire defined emphyteusis as a kind of property right at the end of the eighteenth century[12] and Carlos Alberto de Meneses defined emphyteusis as a contract in 1825[13].

---

role as a member of a political party (*partido popular*, situated on the right) in the riots that occurred in Madeira 1868 connected with the national political riot called *Janeirinha* (Silva e Meneses, 1878, vol. II: 384-385).

11 José Silvestre Ribeiro (footnote 16) defined the *colonia* contract as customary law and the Minister of the Kingdom (Fonseca Magalhães) agreed, referring to the special nature of the island customs, a 'sort of agrarian legislation' where 'ideas of land ownership, and property of the farmer, are uniquely understood' (*Diário da Câmara dos Senhores Deputados*, no 17, 25 February 1855). The particular character of *colonia* was expressed by António Correia Heredia a politician that belonged to party *progressista histórico* that was very active at local level in reforming the *colonia* contract (nt.19).He wrote about the astonishment of the historian Alexandre Herculano about the content of this institution (*A Discussão*, no.7, 22 March 1855). A legal trend stressed the view that the *colonia* was specific in nature. The historian Azevedo e Silva (1995: 196-198) reaffirmed this.

12 Pascoal de Mello Freire (1738-1798) was a teacher at the University of Coimbra and an important jurist that expressed political ideas of enlightened despotism. He was appointed to a commission to organize Portuguese legislation where he came into conflict with a colleague, António Ribeiro dos Santos, who had liberal ideas. He defined emphyteusis as a 'kind of proprerty right, in other words, the dominium utile that someone owns temporarily or permanently over someone else's landed property, paying, for that, a certain amount in order to recognise the dominium directum' (1965: 239). This author stated this thesis in 1789 in his work *Institutiones Juris Civilis Lusitani*, where emphyteusis rights are placed in part XI, published in Antologia (1965). On the debate of that time on this issue, see Serrão (1987, 2000: 430-431).

13 Alberto Carlos de Menezes, was a graduate in law who played a role in the government of the first liberal regime (1820-1823) considered politically radical and in the Parliament. He expressed this point of view about emphyteusis in his work *Plano da Reforma de Forais e*

Hespanha shows that the Civil Code of 1867, following some attempts adopted in the eighteenth century, took some steps towards instituting a 'general rule of the absolute nature of property.' The framework on which it was based prioritised the link between ownership and will. This excluded the possibility of limiting the rights of the owner with repercussions for several types of imperfect property rights on land. The Code expressly listed some of these forms and excluded certain figures of real rights, such as sub-emphyteusis (2004: 480). The act of making improvements on the land was a feature of emphyteusis that was silenced in the Civil Code of 1867 (Liz Teixeira, 1848: 85; Cordeiro, 2010: 110). Thereafter the classification of the improvements as a property right of the *colono* became more difficult.

III.2. Political and Ideological debates: association between the colonia contract and emphyteusis (1854-1867)

Until the Civil Code of 1867, there were two types of emphyteusis in Portugal, neither of which allowed improvements to be divided among heirs without the consent of the landlord. The Civil Code maintained the indivisibility of perpetual emphyteusis (Cordeiro, 2010: 108-110).

In 1854, José Silvestre Ribeiro[14], representing Madeira in the Parliament, presented a draft law proposing to extend the legislation which regulated succession in emphyteusis to the *colonia* contract (Ordenações, Book 4, title 96 § 23 and § 24). One of the main intended features of this law was the impossibility of dividing the *colonos'* improvements in succession transmissions in order to prevent the division of improvements between *colonos* (*Diário da Câmara dos Senhores Deputados*, session no. 15, 17 March 1854).

José Silvestre Ribeiro drew up a request to the Central Government, which he presented in Parliament, for an inquiry into the *colonia* contract. The argument most commonly repeated by the opponents of this inquiry was that the national legislation prior to the Civil Code already provided for the situations which would be addressed in the inquiry.. In other words, the *colonia* was not so specific and could be regulated by the national laws. In their view, the transfer of property rights from the landlord (the domain) to the tenant or to the sharecropper was addressed in the charter of 3 November 1757. It stipulated that in fixed rent tenancy contracts that lasted more than ten years, there could be no transfer because the origin of the contract was more important than its duration. The transfer of the contract to the heirs only

---

Direitos Banais, fundado em um novo Sistema enfitêutico nos Bens da Coroa, de Corporações e de outros senhorios singulares (Menezes, 1825).

14 José Silvestre Ribeiro was a politician that served the national political movement called *cabralismo*. He was governor of Funchal between 1846 and 1852. In 1847 he faced the riots that occured at national level during Maria da Fonte that had repercussions at local level, creating a regional alternative form of government – Junta Governativa da Madeira (Silva & Meneses, 1978, vol. II: 384, 194-195) in 1855.

happened with fixed rent tenancy contracts where the duration was stipulated in advance. All the other fixed rent tenancy contracts ceased when the tenant died. *Colonia,* as previously mentioned, had no fixed term.

This debate was important because it occurred at a time when the Civil Code was already being drawn up[15]. One member of Parliament, Moraes de Carvalho, linked the *colonia* contract with the sharecropping contract and another member, Mello Soares, confused the *colonia* contract with a tenancy type of contract. In so doing he equated the valuation of the improvements of the *colono* with the procedures used for fixed rent tenancy contracts, in which the improvements contributed to increasing the value of the land they had to be paid for by the landlord according to *Colecção de Legislação Portuguesa, Ordenações,* Book 4, title 45 (*Diário da Câmara dos Senhores Deputados,* no. 17, 25 February 1855)[16].

The local administrative authority that was consulted as part of the inquiry conducted by Silvestre Ribeiro was the *Junta Geral* of Funchal. One of the aspects presented in the inquiry was whether the manner in which the *colonia* contract was practiced at that time fully met the requirements of property rights and the interests of the landowner himself. This question returned a negative vote because the subdivision of the improvements of the *colono* to his 'heirs' was classified as an abuse that required repression (*ARM, Governo Civil, Actas da Junta Geral,* 6 July 1855, fl. 144-147v).

Concerning what basis ought to be adopted to ensure equal treatment for, and protection of, the rights and interests of both the landowner and the *colono,* the Board of the *Junta Geral* initially pleaded lack of time to discuss the issue, but afterwards its members voted by a majority to accept the draft decree of 14 March 1854, also written by the author of the inquiry, which equated the *colonia* contract with emphyteusis[17] (ARM, *Governo Civil, Actas da Junta Geral,* 6 July, 1855, fl. 144-147v).

The vote shows contention within the Board of the *Junta Geral.* In a declaration while voting against the Draft Law of 1854[18], the president of the *Junta Geral* stated that this solution would mean giving in to abuse in sharing the produce between *colonos* who had not paid for what they owned. In this sense, approving the Draft Law of 1854 would mean that the *Junta* recognized that the *colonia* contract was not a sharecropping contract. The vice president of the Board (José Vicente d'Antas) voted against adopting the

---

15 The issue of land ownership and property rights does not appear to have been discussed explicitly at the national Parliament during the debate about the Civil Code (Meneses Cordeiro, 1999: 66). For the difficulties that surrounded the revision and approval, see Cunha Gonçalves (1961, vol. I: 122-126) and Galvão Teles (1995: 143-145).

16 On the *Colónia* Right, see Helder Fonseca (1998: 391-392; 1992: 633-640).

17 *Relatório Apresentado à Junta Geral do Distrito do Funchal … (1864),* Lisbon, Imprensa Nacional, p. 43-45.

18 Gregório Medina was a prebendary of the Funchal cathedral. His annual rent was 600 réis and that of a large landowner was thirty times bigger.

Draft Law of 1854 because he considered that equating the *colonia* contract with emphyteusis would be impossible to enforce, given the ability that the *colonos* had demonstrated in dividing the improvements without the landlords being able to stop them (ARM, *Governo Civil, Actas da Junta Geral,* 11 July 1855, 149 v–150). This demonstrated that the *colonós* will was to divide the improvements. Emphyteusis would also mean that for the landowner it would be more difficult to evict *colonos*.

The debate regarding the basis of a future written law to reform the regime of the *colonia* contract was reopened in 1856 based on a proposal published in a local newspaper[19]. It reaffirmed the solution of equating *colonia* with emphyteusis already present in the Draft Law of 1854. The *Junta Geral* once again invoked lack of time and postponed preparation of the foundations of the draft law (ARM, *Governo Civil, Actas da Junta Geral,* 18 June 1856, fl. 170-174 and 21June 1856, 174v).

The amount of compensation that the landowner had to pay in order to evict a *colono* and the procedures required for valuing the *colono*'s improvements were recurring themes during the 1850s and 1860s (Contracto de Colonia [1855], p. 14; *Diario da Camara* ..., 17 March 1854; *Relatório Apresentado* ..., 1864, p. 43-44). In a sense this coincided with the defence of landowners´ interests.

In 1864, three years before the Civil Code was adopted, the *Junta Geral* proposed creating a commission to reform the *colonia* contract and as a result of this initiative, a draft law was written by two law graduates, one of whom had experience as a notary (J.A.Almada) and the other of whom was a conservative politician (Joaquim Ricardo Trindade de Vasconcelos)[20]. The *colonia* contract was defined as a sharecropping contract based on the Civil Code (Articles 1299 and 1301) and on the old Laws (Colecção de Legislação ..., Ordenações, Book 4 Title 45). The Civil Code omitted the *colonia* contract. In practice, the courts, in line with many aspects set out in this draft law, began to apply the rules of sharecropping and tenancy contracts to *colonia* contracts, in accordance with Article 1303, which set out the rights and obligations of the lessors and the tenants that applied to sharecroppers.

The draft paid significant attention to the valuation of improvements of the outgoing *colono*. Concerning the productive (agricultural) improvements the draft law created a limit. In addition it proposed that perennials such as vines should be valued in the traditional way (by classifying the various plants according to quality, age and agricultural condition). However, it introduced

---

19 The author of the draft – published in the local newspaper 'A Discussão' – was António Correia Heredia (footnote 14). His considerations about *colonia* evolved between 1848-1849 and 1888. In 1888 his main concern was the subdivision of the improvements. Thereafter the solution to create the perfect ownership was redemption of the *colonia* contract (of the land by the *colono* or of the improvements by the landlord).

20 Trindade de Vasconcelos was a member of the *histórico* party. *Relatório Apresentado à Junta Geral* ..., 1864, p. 45 and Silva & Meneses (1978, vol. III: 46-47). The *histórico* party (1852-1876) alternated power with the *progressista* party.

a new form of valuing sugar cane according to the costs of planting (Trindade e Vasconcelos & Almada, 1867: 32-37). This proposal differed from what was common practice as seen in probate inventories or mortgages, i.e. a valuation based on counting the number of plants and ratoons – in other words, usual practice was followed, adapting sugar cane to the process adopted for vines. Their argument emphasised that the costs of planting were more beneficial to the landlord´s interests. This was an old question in valuing agricultural improvements as a result of the change of crops. At the heart of the problem was how evalution worked as as an incentive to colono´s investments[21].

The draft law of 1867 classified the useful improvements (constructions like walls, houses, or barns) and confirmed the need for permission from the landlord for certain constructions. The usefulness of the improvements was a criterion which became increasingly necessary for landlords from the eighteenth century on in order to justify the compensation. The improvements were listed on rolls (a non-official document written by landlords) that existed in private archives until the 1860s, on official documents such as mortgages between *colonos* or on probate inventories. The Civil Code of 1867 (Articles 1614 and 1601) established the possibility for tenancy contracts with the tenant retaining the building until the compensation was paid. Article 1615 stated that in a tenancy contract the outgoing tenant had the right to receive compensation from the landowner for all useful improvements even if they were not authorised, except in the case of contracts disposed of in opposite direction. Concerning repairs to the land, Article 1611 provided that the tenant could require the landowner to make them, or could charge the landlord for them. It is possible that from then on it became more difficult to gain the landlord's written permission required for the construction, repair and enlargement of the houses, barns and warehouses. The written authorized permission to the *colono* became necessary for compensation in the case of eviction.

Classifying the *colono*'s improvements became a legal conundrum during and after the Civil Code. There is some evidence that a path towards some kind of official recognition of the ownership of the improvements of the *colono* occurred around 1822 when the Treasury recognized that the *colonos* were allowed to use their improvements as a guarantee to the state[22]. This

21 In 1822 the same issue had been discussed in petition and this was a demonstration of how the evaluation was an incentive to the investment of the *colono*. It was stated that in the evaluation of plants the cost of planting was not taken into account and if an income-based valuation method were adopted the *colonos* would stop planting vines (Arquivo Histórico Ultramarino, representations by Junta da Fazenda Nacional da Madeira to the Congress, 30th of May 1822, Box XIX, doc. 6476).

22 In 1822 in a document of the Financial Department of the central government it was stated that it was impossible to claim for certain payments since these had been secured by overvalued investments (A.H.U., Madeira Collection, Representation by the Junta da Fazenda Nacional da Madeira to the Congress, 30 May 1822, Box XIX, Ms. 6476).

recognition was reinforced in 1885 by two fiscal directives on the matrix tax (dated the 19th and 26th of January) that gave the property of the improvements owned by the *colono* legal existence that was autonomous from the land owned by the landlord[23].

Great changes occurred between 1854, when the *Junta Geral* agreed to apply the rules of hereditary transmission relating to emphyteusis to the *colonia* contract, and the passing of the Civil Code in 1867. As the latter classified emphyteusis as a contract, it meant that the possibility of defining the notion of ownership of the improvements as a right inferior to the right of ownership of the land was no longer plausible because the improvements of the *colono* under the *colonia* contract were not included in the list of imperfect forms of property listed.

Furthermore, this code limited emphyteusis to a single form, perpetual emphyteusis, thereby eliminating temporary emphyteusis. It also provided (in Article 1672) that the owner of the dominium directum could repossess the land in the event of the emphyteuta damaging it. This possibility was limited to cases where the value of the property fell to an amount lower than the annual fixed tenure plus one fifth (Cordeiro, 2010: 112). This form of assessment could not be applied to *colonia* contracts due to the absence of an annual fixed tenure. In this context, the draft law of Trindade de Vasconcelos and Almada (1867) affirmed the non-perpetuity of the *colonia* contract, but in reality it worked the opposite way. In fact, it was what some scholars classify as an eviction contract (Dutta, Ray & Sengupta, 1989; Bandiera, 2003)because there was no transfer of the dominium directum to the *colono* (as in the contract referred to above as *Censo*). This was a clear attempt to dissociate the *colonia* contract from emphyteusis because Article 1607 stated the conditions under which the lessor could evict a tenant before the end of the rent tenancy contract. This means that eviction was still allowed under the Civil Code since *colonia* contracts were regarded by the courts as equivalent to rent contracts.

Dias Ferreira, a commentator on the Civil Code, stated that the *colonos* were entitled to compensation for the improvements they owned in accordance with the law. This recognition – as *colonia* contracts and *colonos'* improvements were omitted from the Civil Code – was accompanied by the statement that the two property rights of the *colono* and the landowner could not be seen in equal terms. He added that the *colonos* could not acquire a share in the land that held their improvements on it because they did not own it (Ferreira 1894, vol. II, p. 516). At the heart of these comments was the conundrum concerning the classification of the property rights of the improvements[24].

---

23 See Decree 30-06-1870.

24 José Dias Ferreira defended the hierarchy between property rights – improvements and land – but Cunha Gonçalves (a professor of law of Coimbra University and Commentator of the Civil Code) opposed it. In his comments to the Civil Code published after 1929 he saw *colonia* as 'perpetual sharecropping', with local usage constituting tacit clauses in the contract regarding rustic improvements (plants) and urban improvements (buildings and supporting walls). From this legal perspective, the property rights of landowners and *colonos* had the

IV. Valuation of the improvement: debates in 1880s

IV.1. *An urgent need for a law*

In 1885, Augusto Fuschini, an advocate of socialist ideas, pointed out in Parliament that the *colonia* contract was one the most important problems that Madeira faced[25]. Two years later, the government appointed a committee of eleven members, some of whom were landowners, to conduct an inquiry to study the economic difficulties and propose some measures[26]. At the root of this initiative were a number of popular uprisings which had occurred in various parishes of the island during 1887 and 1888. The cause of the uprisings was administrative changes (the creation of Parish Juntas), but people also feared a tax increase (Silva & Meneses, 1978: 196-198). In Parliament, Fuschini emphasized the social conflicts that occurred in Madeira in 1887[27]. *Colonia* contracts took on a political dimension because they were classified as a cause of a kind of 'social war' between landlords and *colonos*. In the same vein, an opinion maker who had testified in the inquiry, considered the revolt of 1887 in Madeira as the harbinger of the approaching storm (Valle, 1888: 8-9).

As a result of the inquiry, various measures were taken[28], but those concerning *colonia* contracts were omitted (Valle, 1888: 4,23; *Inquérito* ...: 23). Despite this measure, the president of the committee decided that this part of the report,

---

same value (1933, vol. VII, P.370 and vol. IX, p. 55). Ascensão (1971) was closer to Dias Ferreira's point of view. Dias Ferreira had radical political ideas. He became the leader of a Party, o Constituinte. For its local members, see footnote 31. After 1865 he left the University of Coimbra and became a jurisconsult in Lisbon. He was a member of parliament in several legislatures and was Prime Minister from 1892 to 1893.

25 *Diário da Camara dos Senhores Deputados (1885)* 21 January, p. 203-204; 27 April, p. 1325; 1 May, p. 1374; 13 May, p. 1543.

26 The commission (appointed in December of 1887) was composed of nine members with different important functions in the local society. Two members were sent for three months from the mainland (the president Manuel Raymundo Valadas, a military man that was inspector of the Telegraph and the secretary, Gaspar Malheiro Pereia Peixoto, who was a bureaucrat in a district of the mainland (Viseu)). Another three civil servants were appointed: the director of the Finance Department; the Director of Public Works and the Agronomist. The President of the Board of the Junta Geral (Manuel José Vieira) and the President of the City Council of Funchal (Viscount of Ribeiro Real) were landowners, although they were not classified as such. The two names classified as landowners were Manuel Inízio da Costa Lyra and António Leite Monteiro, also Registrar of the Civil Register (*Inquérito* ..., p. 87). A member of Madeira Trade Association (Angelo Hermegildo dos Santos) and a businessman (Silvano de Freitas Branco) completed the list.

27 *Diário da Camara dos Senhores Deputados* (1888) 18 January, p. 171-172; 30 January, p. 263-264; 27 January, p. 250-202.

28 The document with the agenda of the future measures to solve the economic and social crisis of Madeira was signed by the Prime Minister and the Finance Minister and the important landowner Agostinho de Ornelas e Vasconcellos and the deputy Manuel José Vieira were with them (see note 28).

which had been signed only by him, should be brought to the attention of the government based on consultation with different bodies and local personalities.

Two opposite perspectives about the *colonia* contract can be detected in the report of the inquiry. In the first, the rules framed by the Civil Code of 1867 were considered adequate, based on sharecropping and rent contracts[29]. In the second, advocated by Fuschini and Valle, the sources of the social conflict were connected with the provisions of the Civil Code. Fuschini stated that the provisions of the Civil Code did not apply to *colonia* (it was only regulated by customary law).

The high value of the improvements in relation to the value of the land was somewhat contradictory for many – the low-lying areas had a better climate and the land required fewer improvements in the form of supporting walls, as outlined in the arguments used by the chairman of the commission in charge of the inquiry. Referring to the cases where the value of the improvements exceeded the value of the land he argued that the latter should revert to the *colonos*. The *colono* would compensate the landlord but if he did not have sufficient capital he should benefit from a capital allowance due to the extraordinary profits earned by the landlord for years. Secondly, if the *colono* depreciated the land under contract he should be excluded via a process that should be facilitated and, accordingly, the valuation of his improvements should be depreciated in proportion to what had happened to the land (*Inquérito ...*, 1888: 129-132). He advocated the prohibition of *colonia* contracts for the future.

In this same vein, a reformist of *colonia* contracts advocated expropriation in favour of the *colono* or in favour of the landlord, with the government providing money loans at a low rate of interest (Heredia, 1888, p. 3)[30]. A judge endorsed this solution but he removed the banks from the mix. The compensation payable to landlords would be paid annually in the form of an increase in property tax (Pinto de Andrade, *Inquérito ...*, 1888: 146-147). Valle suggested that after a valuation of the investments the *colono* would have to pay five per cent of the valuation on an annual basis. This would transform the *colonia* contract into a perpetual rent contract (Valle, 1888: 7). Fuschini also advocated an expropriation but, in practical terms, it was not clear whether the state would play a leading role or if he was mirroring Heredia's reform (Vieira, 1888: 19). In some of these proposals the state would play a role, namely by providing the financial means to allow the *colono* to buy the improvement[31].

---

29 A notary (José António de Almada), author of the draft of 1867, and the member of Parliament Manuel José Vieira (notes 28 and 29) agreed with the rules framed on the Civil Code. They both belonged to the party of José Dias Ferreira – the *Constituintes* that owned the local newpaper 'O Direito'. J.A. Almada became the local leader of another party (Progressistas) in 1885.

30 See footnotes 14 and 22.

31 At this stage the regulation of access to land on a private basis by the *colono* is less emphasized than the role played by the state. The right of first refusal in cases of the sale of the land by the landowner or of the investments by the *colono* was the focus in the 1910s and

Valle claimed that the difficulties that arose in valuing the improvements resulted from the fact that the Code of Civil Procedure of 1876 had not been applied in Madeira until that time, and he demonstrated that equating the *colonia* to the legal framework for fixed rent tenancy contracts was inadequate and that equating it to the framework for sharecropping contracts, namely Articles 1595 and 1596, could be considered illegal (Valle, 1888: 8-9). In short, according to these views the regulations were not binding. These factors prevented the law from ensuring that the valuation of the improvements was protected by rules set out in law (Garrido, 2011: 72)[32].

IV.2. Radicalism of the 1880s debate

In 1888, the debate was essentially ideological. Fuschini compared the social conflicts of Madeira to the ones in Ireland with the difference that the conqueror in the latter was replaced by the landlord in the former[33]. A member of Parliament from Madeira (Vieira) counter-argued with the differences that existed between Madeira and Irish landlords (Vieira, 1888: 3-4).

The reference to Ireland is evidence of the radical ideological burden introduced by Fuschini. Historiography has considered the land agitations which took place in Ireland, Scotland and Wales. Recent studies have stressed the great diferences between these processes, despite the fact that the land agitations may have originated from certain similar points of conflict. The English land question stands out since it was not associated with any mass movement. The agitations which took place in Madeira (although there have been few studies on them) appear to have a political and administrative root and are therefore different to the Irish case, which was marked by a high level of violence[34].

1920s (Ribeira Brava, articles 1 and 2 Diário da Câmara dos Deputados, 11-02-1916 and Pitta (1929: 17).

32 In the 1910s and 1920s the legal technicalities concerning court eviction proceedings were said to continue to be ambiguous (article 2 of the Draft Law, *Diário da Camara dos Deputados*, 1916, 11-02, p. 8 and Pitta (1929: 19-22).

33 He attributed it to the extreme concentration of land ownership which could be considered a mistake, see footenote 23 and Vieira (1888: 5, 19).

34 Concerning the differences of the land question and level of conflict between Ireland, Scotland, and Wales (Howell, 2013: 83-100). Collective conflicts connected with *colonia* are not studied in detail (for the petions see footnote 6). We have some evidence about difficulties of the landowner in terms monitoring the share of the output namely between the 1840s and 1850s. George Peacock (a professor of astronomy at the University of Cambridge that visited Madeira) stated that 'if a landlord resides upon his estate, and exercises too close an inspection of the productions of his tenants; he is subjected to annoyances and losses, which render his continuing among them uncomfortable (…) if not dangerous'. The 'practice of frauds (…) is equally difficult to prevent and detect' (Peacock, 1850: 277).

In England the common law prescribed for the improvements to revert to the landlord at the end of the fixed rent contracts. It differed from the norm in many places in Europe since everything that was placed on the land belonged to the tenant, especially trees and plants. The tenants' rights case (Lincolnshire custom) was special because after 1875-1883 an attempt was made to regulate the compensation for the tenant's improvements, as part of a long path towards making it compulsory. In Madeira, the compensation for the improvement (established by rules based on custom) was accepted by the landlord prior to the Civil Code. Thereafter, there was an attempt to regulate it by law. Before 1875, the fixed improvements (for instance, buildings or fences) of the English tenant contracts were supported by landlords (Garrido, 2011: 67, 70-71). This was an important difference when compared to the *colonia* contract.

In the nineteenth century there was a heated debate in England regarding how far local customs that guaranteed the tenant the right to compensation for the improvements ought to be regulated by law. This debate went through several stages, but the Agricultural Holding Act (A.H.A.) of 1875 meant that it was accepted that regulation was advisable, and many European countries eventually followed this route some decades later[35].

The A.H.A. of 1875 differentiated three types of improvements: permanent ones which required the landowner's permission for their construction, semi-permanent ones where there was an implicit understanding that the landowner would be informed so that he could monitor them, and those where there was no requirement of permission or to inform, for example the application of fertilizers. This logic can be found in the Civil Code of 1867 applied to fixed rent, and was applied to the *colonia* contract by analogy.

Somewhat before this time, in 1849, Silvestre Ribeiro pointed out the mountainous terrain of Madeira required heavy investments in fixed capital by the *colono*, which, in a context where wine prices were decreasing, benefited the landowner (Menezes, 1849: 70-72). This means that in relative terms the reproducible capital of the *colono* (vines that the *colono* was able to sell) was depreciating. It is clear through this statement that the subject of permanent improvements was brought to the fore in the debates.

The tight control of approvals by the landowner increased after the 1870s. It became common for the landlord's permission to be granted against the *colono*'s agreement to receive compensation at a previously agreed price. In the 1880s, the request to regulate the existing laws demonstrated that the landowners drew up agreements with their *colonos* in which they agreed to rules about compensation. For example, one stated that the authorization to

35 Prior to 1875, an important phase was linked to 'acts of husbandry' in compensation being replaced by 'unexhausted improvements'. For Valência custom see Garrido (2011: 72; Garrido & Catalayud, 2011). Lincolnshire custom was the basis for the tenancy right (see footnote 4).

build a house would be given against its price of evaluation remaining fixed in a future transaction.

The debate on the value of the improvements cannot be dissociated from the right of the *colono* to be compensated, nor can it detached from the fact that the property rights of the *colono* over the improvements had been recognized before the Civil Code of 1867 and even reaffirmed after that, as the registration of the improvements and the payment of taxes for cadastral purposes proves. In the 1880s, attention was focused on the courts' decisions regarding eviction. These tended to rule that the *colonos* could only be compensated for investments (buildings) if they had been authorized by the landlord in writing. In the case of permanent investments built prior to the Civil Code, payment was imposed unless there was a written document opposing the payment (Vieira, 1888: 14)[36].

The debate on unexhausted improvements did not receive the same level of attention as in England. Valle suggested extending Articles 1299 and 1303 of the Civil Code to regulate the landlord's participation in the input and the share earned (Valle, 1888: 6)[37]. Underlying this point of view were all the agricultural changes that occurred between the 1850s and the 1880s – the path towards intensification and dependency on irrigation in a context marked by the loss of the commercial dynamism – that increased the effort of the *colono*[38]. Landowners eventually entered into contracts with the *colonos* regarding their participation in the inputs of crops – the half of the expenses in irrigation water costs and fertilizers that landlords were supposed to pay – such as sugar cane, depending on the location and attractiveness of their land.

The A.H.A. of 1875, being based on the Lincolnshire custom, was associated with a difficulty in assessing the compensation; the basis of the calculation was not the result of the changes introduced on the farm but rather of the unexhausted improvements. The difficulties in implementing this calculation meant that from 1883 on it was accepted that various forms of calculation could exist in England (including local tradition) rather than 'one single rule sanctioned by law' (Garrido, 2011: 74).

36 A.R.M., caixa 13, doc 61, 12th of November 1900. For other conditions established between 1880 and 1900, see Caixa 13, documents 62-63; 45-47, 50; 52; 54; 57-59. The draft law of *colonia* presented by a republican, Visconde da Ribeira Brava, provided that such clauses in the contracts were invalid and forbade landlords from opposing the building of useful improvements by the *colonos* (Arts. 4 and 3 Diário da Camara dos Deputados, 11-02-1916, p. 8), a rule already established in the Civil Code of 1867 for rent tenancy contracts.

37 This situation was detected in some places but not in others (Funchal) in the family archive of the Ornellas e Vasconcellos. It seems that the investments of the landowner in inputs for certain crops were determined by the location of his lands. He did not invest where he thought it was worthless.

38 For the case of Valencia, Garrido & Calatayud (2011: 606) did not agree with Perkins about the long-term fixed tenancy contract being a predisposition of the tenant to make investments (Perkins, 1975: 4-6).

The regulations adopted in England for customary tenancy rights after 1875 and the regulations adopted for Madeira after 1867 were the subject of criticism at the end of the nineteenth century, namely because it was claimed that in both cases the evaluation of the property rights of the investments, ether by the English tenants or by the *colonos*, was based on institutions that did not operate effectively (Garrido, 2011: 80).

V. Conclusion

The decision not to apply the rules of the indivisibility of the emphyteusis in the case of transmission by inheritance to the colonia contract relates to the treatment given to emphyteusis in the Civil Code. This involved one formula that was reversible and another that was perpetual. The Civil Code simplified the emphyteusis, classifying the former as a rent contract and defining the latter as a perpetual contract. The refusal to equate the *colonia* contract with this resulted from the fact that it would neither be in the interest of the *colono* nor that of the landlord. Landlords wanted to keep the eviction as a way of having crops grown with greater monitoring of the sharing, and the colono wanted to have access to the property rights of the land.

In Madeira the custom of compensating the colono at the end of the contract was established before the Civil Code (1867). Recognition of the *colono*'s property rights was reaffirmed throughout the second half of the nineteenth century. In the English case it was only after 1875 that consideration was given to compensation in favour of the tenant at the end of the contract for the investments made. At the end of the nineteenth century, after regulation in both cases, there was criticism that the assessment of the investments was based on institutions that did not operate effectively.

In the case of Madeira, the system of incentives worked during the phase when wine prices and demand were high. The fact that the *colono* could sell the vines to another *colono* and that the system of evaluation was based on the number of plants (including their characteristics and state of development) was beneficial because it increased their commercial value. Between the 1850s and the 1880s, the difficulties in agriculture and the need to adapt to international prices led to changes in terms of intensification of labour. This additional effort that was a result of the intensification and maintenance of fertile land was not counted in the assessment.

The intensification of the crops, since it was associated with more constructions on the part of the *colono*, involved greater risks for the landlord in the case of eviction of the *colono*. On the other hand, as the *colono* supported the investments in constructions – unlike the situation in England before 1875 whereby, under tenancy rights, the landlord supported it – the high level of fixed capital owned by the *colono* benefited the landowner, as Sivestre Ribeiro stated in the 1840s. In addition, since the Civil Code brought *colonia* contracts closer to renting, it introduced some uncertainty as to how the courts would assess eviction cases and the valuation of improvements.

The *colono*'s improvements were at the centre of the debate during these four decades. The focus shifted from the division of the *colono*'s improvements in the case of transfer by inheritance to assessment, to achieve the perfect ownership of the land by the *colono* or by the landowner. This development of the *colonia* contract provides an example of the economic importance of the assessment of the investments in a long term and eviction contract – when the aim was to replace custom or frame it within a regulation of the Civil Code, even if by anaology – and how it goes beyond the legal formula for perfect property.

Sources and bibliography

A Vida Económica da Madeira. A Imprensa. Os Três Projectos, Funchal, 1916.

Actas Da Junta Geral, Arquivo Regional da Madeira (ARM), Governo Civil, Junta Geral do Funchal, 1854-1856, Livros 905-906.

Ascensão, José Oliveira (1971), *Direito Real*, Lisboa, Centro de Estudos de Direito Civil da Faculdade de Direito de Lisboa.

Azevedo e Silva, José Manuel (1995), *A Madeira e a construção do mundo atlântico (século XV-XVII)*, Funchal, Secretaria Regional do Turismo e Cultura, Centro de Estudos de História do Atlântico.

Bandiera, Oriana (2003), *Contract Duration and Investment Incentives: Evidence from Land Tenancy Agreements*, Department of Economics, London School of Economics Paper.

Brandão, Maria de Fátima (1994), *Terra, Herança e Família no noroeste de Portugal. O de Mosteiro no século XIX*, Porto, Edições Afrontamento.

Brandão, Maria de Fátima (1991), 'Propriété, loi et coutume : la diversité des campagnes portugaises', *Recherches en anthropologie au Portugal*, n. 3, 1991, p. 7-17.

Calatayud, Salvador, Millán, Jesús & Romeo, Maria Cruz (2006), 'Leaseholders in Capitalist Arcadia: Bourgeois Hegemony and Peasant Opportunities in the Valencian Countryside during the Nineteenth Century', *Rural History*, 17, p. 149-166.

Câmara, Benedita (2002), *A Economia da Madeira (1850-1914)*, Lisboa, Imprensa de Ciências Sociais.

Câmara, Benedita (2006), 'The Portuguese Civil Code and the colonia tenancy contract in Madeira (1867-1967)', *Continuity and Change*, 21, p. 213-233.

Congost, Rosa (2007) *Terras, Leyes, Historia. Estudios sobre 'la gran obra de la propiedad'*, Barcelona, Editorial Crítica.

Contrato de Colonia, [1855], Funchal, typographia nacional.

Cordeiro, António Menezes (2010), *Da Enfiteuse: Extinção e Sobrevivência, Estudos em Homenagem ao Prof. Doutor Martim de Albuquerque*, vol. I, Lisboa, Faculdade de Direito da Universidade de Lisboa, p. 101-129.

Cunha Gonçalves, Luiz da (1961) *Tratado de Direito Civil em comentário do Código Civil Português*, vol. I, Coimbra, Coimbra editora.

Cunha Gonçalves, Luís da (1993), *Tratado de Direito Civil*, Coimbra, Coimbra Editora, vol. VII, e vol. IX.

Diário da Câmara dos Deputados, (1916), Lisboa, Imprensa Nacional.

Diário da Câmara dos Senhores Deputados 1854-1855; 1885-1888 Lisboa, Imprensa Nacional.

Dutta, Bhaskar, Ray Debraj & Sengupta, Kunal (1989), *Contracts with Eviction Repeated Principal-Agent Relationships, apud Bardham*, P., The Economic Theory of Agrarian Institutions, Oxford, New York, Toronto and Melborne: Oxford University Press.

Feijó, Rui Graça, *Liberalismo e Transformação Social*, Lisboa, Editorial Fragmentos, p. 147-148 e p. 13.

Ferreira, José Dias (1894), *Código civil português anotado*, vol. II, Coimbra, Coimbra editora.

Fisher, J. R. The Farmers' Alliance: An Agricultural Protest Movement of the 1880's, *The Agricultural History Review*, vol. 26, no. 1 (1978), p. 15-25.

Fonseca, Helder (1998), Réflexions sur la communication de Margarida Durães, *Extrait des Mélanges de l'école française de Rome. Italie et Méditerranée*, MEFRIM – 110 (1), p. 389-393.

Fonseca, Helder (1992), *Economia e atitudes económicas no Alentejo Oitocentista*, Évora.

Freitas Branco, Jorge (1986), *Camponeses de Madeira. As bases materiais do quotidiano no Arquipélago (1750-1900)*, Lisboa, Dom Quixote.

Freire, Pascoal de Mello (1965), *Antologia de textos sobre a economia e as finanças*, Lisboa.

Garrido Herrero, Samuel (2009), 'Las imperfecciones de la propiedad perfecta, arrendamientos rústicos e indemnización por mejoras', Salustiano de Dios de Dios (coord.), Javier Infante Miguel-Motta, Ricardo Robledo Hernández, Eugenia Torijano Pérez (coords), *Historia de la propiedad: servidumbres y limitaciones de dominio: VI Encuentro Interdisciplinar: Salamanca, 17-19 de septiembre de 2008*, p. 433-469.

Garrido, Samuel & Calatayud, Salvador (2011), 'The price of improvements: agrarian contracts and agrarian development in nineteenth-century eastern Spain', *Economic History Review*, 64 (2), p. 598-620.

George Peacock, D.D., F.R.S., 'A Review of the State of Sgriculture and of the Tenure of Land', in James Sheridan Knowles (ed.) (1850) *A Treatise on the Climate and Meteorology of Madeira*, London: John Churchill and Liverpool: Deighton and Laughton, p. 277.

Heredia, A.C. (1850) *As contradições vinculadas pelo A. Das Breves reflexões sobre a abolição dos morgados na Madeira*, Funchal, Thypographia nacional, 1850.

Heredia, A.C. (1888) *Observações sobre a situação económica da Ilha da Madeira e sobre a reforma das alfândegas*, Lisboa, Typ Mattos Moreira, 1888.

Heredia, A.C., (1849) *Breves reflexões sobre a abolição dos morgados na Madeira. Oferecido à consideração da liga dos interesses materiais do paiz*, Lisboa, Typ da Revolução de Setembro.

Hespanha, António Manuel (2004), *Guiando a mão invisível. Direitos, Estado e Lei no Liberalismo Monárquico Português*, Coimbra, Almedina.

Howell, David W. (2013), 'The Land Question in nineteenth-century Wales, Ireland ans Scotland: a comparative study', *The Agricultural History Review*, (61) I, p. 83-110.

Inquérito Sobre a Situação Económica da Ilha da Madeira e Medidas Convenientes para a Melhorar ordenado por Decreto de 31 de Dezembro de 1887 (1888), Lisboa, Imprensa Nacional.

Menezes, Servulo Drummond de (compil), *Uma Época Administrativa da Madeira e Porto Santo, a contar do dia 7 de outubro de 1846*, 3 vols Funchal: Typ. Nacional, 1849-1852.

Modesto, José R. (2010), 'Costumbre y Coacción social. La formación del arrendamento rústico valenciano (1880-1940)', *Historia Agraria*, 51, p. 45-80.

Morais Carvalho, António de (1858), *Resposta á primeira apostilha do senhor António Luís Seabra*, Lisboa, Imprensa Nacional.

North, Douglass (1981), *Structure and Change in Economic History*, New York, Norton.

O'Brien, Patrick in Feijó, Rui Graça, *Liberalismo e Transformação Social*, Lisboa, Editorial Fragmentos, p. 10.

Perkins, J.A. (1975), 'Tenure, Tenant Right, and Agricultural Progess in Lindsey, 1780-1850', *The Agricultural History Review*, (23) I, 1975.

Pitta, Pedro (1929), *O contrato de 'Colonia' na Madeira*, Lisboa.

Porter, J.H. (1986), 'Tenant Right: Devonshire and the 1880 Ground Game Act', *The Agricultural History Review*, p. 188-197.

Rau, Virgínia e Macedo Jorge (1962), *O açúcar da Madeira nos fins do século XV. Problemas de Produção e Comércio*, Funchal, Junta geral do Distrito do Funchal.

Recenseamento das Explorações Agrícolas das Ilhas Adjacentes, Instituto Nacional de Estatística, Lisboa, 1965.

Rosenthal, Jean-Laurent (1992), *The Fruits of Revolution. Property Rights, Litigation, and French Agriculture, 1700-1860*, Cambridge University Press.

Serrão, José Vicente (1987), *Demografia e agricultura no Portugal do Século 18*, Lisboa.

Serrão, José Vicente (2000), *Os Campos da Cidade. Configuração das estruturas fundiárias da região de Lisboa nos finais do Antigo Regime*, Lisboa, ISCTE (mimeo) p. 478-480).

Silva, Fernado Augusto & Meneses, Carlos Azevedo, (1978), *Elucidário Madeirense*, vol. II e vol. III Funchal, Secretaria Regional da Educação e Cultura.

Solar, P. M. & Hens L. (2013), 'Land under pressure: The value of Irish land in a period of rapid population groth, 1730-1844', *The Agricultural History Review*, (61) I, p. 40-61.

SOUSA, João José Abreu de (1994) *História Rural da Madeira. A colonia.* Funchal, Direcção Regional dos Assuntos Culturais.

TEIXEIRA, António Ribeiro Liz (1848), *Curso de Direito Civil Portuguez*, 3 vols.

TELLES, Inocêncio Galvão (1995), *Introdução ao Estudo do Direito*, vol. I, Lisboa.

TRINDADE e VASCONCELLOS, J.R. & ALMADA, José António d' (1867), *Projecto de Lei Regulamentar do Contrato de colonia ou parceria agricola da Ilha da Madeira.* Funchal, Typographia da Gazeta da Madeira.

VALLE, Henrique F. F. (1888), *A Revolta da Madeira e A Comissão de Inquérito. Breves Considerações e Apontamentos*, Madeira.

VAN ZANDEN, J. L., (1991), 'The First Green Revolution: The Growth of Production and Productivity in European Agriculture, 1870-1914'. *Economic History Review* 45 (2), p. 215-239.

VIEIRA, Manuel José, *Discurso Pronunciado na Camara dos Senhores Deputados na Sessão de 7 de Julho de 1888*, Funchal, Typographia do 'Direito'.

VILLARES, Ramon (1988), 'Los foros de Galicia. Algunos problemas comparaciones (Galicia, Portugal y Valencia)', *Ler História* (12), p. 47-75.

VILLARES, Ramón (2009), 'A reforma agrária liberal em Espanha: algumas comparações com Portugal' in Miriam HALPERN PEREIRA, José VICENTE SERRÃO, Magda PINHEIRO, Maria DE FÁTIMA SÁ & Melo FERREIRA, *Desenvolvimento Económico e Mudança Social: Portugal nos últimos dois séculos: homenagem a Miriam Halpern Pereira*, Lisboa, ICS, p. 155-171.

ELEFTHERIA ZEI

13. *Emphyteotic* Practices and Relations of Power

An Approach of Social Conflicts in the Greek Archipelago, 17th-18th Centuries

The social transformations of the Greek peasantry under Latin and Ottoman rule has constituted quite a recent field of systematic research in Greek historiography, which has been long influenced by 19th century nationalistic trends that tended to regard modern social conflicts as early forms of 'national revolution'. The first contemporary studies concerning the subject appeared during the period of the 80s and 90s and focused on Venetian territories, the Ionian islands and the island of Crete in particular, which are much better documented in this direction, whereas the so-called modern 'peasant revolts' in the Greek Archipelago, particularly in the Cyclades, have barely been explored yet. On the other hand, contemporary historians have been quite preoccupied with peasant movements in late medieval and modern Europe. Discussions and debates have revealed a rich and diversified field of research concerning rural mentalities and cultures of violence, and models of resistance and discourse analysis, which also raise questions of social and political anthropology: the very term of 'revolt' has given much to consider[1].

In the above mentioned social revolts of the Greek Archipelago, the emphyteuticrights, emerging from a larger Mediterranean tradition of customary land relations based on 'the right to plant in the other's land'[2], appear to have

1 See a bibliographical selection (including a rich former and contemporary bibliography): Mollat & Wolff (1973); Fourquin (1978); Hilton (1988); Blickle (1993); Cohn (2004, 2006). See also larger approaches of social conflicts: Tilly (1996, 2004). And a recent problematic on violent cultures in modern Europe, where popular violence in rural Europe constitutes a special field of research: Carroll (2007); Avdela, D'Cruze & Rowbotham (2010).

2 The historical origins of emphyteusis in the Mediterranean have constituted the object of a historiographical discussion in Greek as well as in European historiography in general, included in the larger problematic concerning the interaction between the Roman law and seigniorial rights in late Middle Ages Europe. It seems that the term emphyteusis comprises different rights and practices dating since the Roman or Greek antiquity, having known several local variations both in Western and in Eastern Mediterranean, where they were generalized during the Byzantine period; on a social history of the emphyteutic relationships and practices in the Cyclades islands cf. Zei (2001: 228-300); cf. also the problematic on the*bail roman* [Roman lease]: Vallat (2003: 13-34). On a typology of emphyteutic relations in the Ionian islands which offers a very interesting field of comparisons cf. Argyrou (1995, 2003: 155-165).

Agrarian Change and Imperfect Property, ed. by Rosa Congost and Pablo F. Luna, Rural History in Europe, 15 (Turnhout, 2018), 287-296

DOI 10.1484/M.RURHE-EB.5.116128

served both as major instrument of power and as primary object of claim between conflicting social groups in the Cyclades during the seventeenth and eighteenth centuries: they offer, thus, an interesting case-study that could shed new light on social movements as well as on the formation of local elites in the complex and divided world of modern Eastern Mediterranean during a period of important transitions.

I. The historical context

Before approaching the above questions, we propose a quick review of the geographical and historical context. The Ottoman administration established in the Greek Archipelago in the beginning of the seventeenth century put an end to the long supremacy (since the thirteenth century) of the Duchy of Naxos, comprising the central-southern part of the Archipelago, that is the islands of Naxos, Paros, Andros, Syros, Milos and Santorini[3]. Submitted to the jurisdiction of Kapudhan-Pasha, the supreme maritime authority of the Ottoman Empire (Zachariadou, 2002), the above islands were since integrated in the Ottoman fiscal system, according to which their populations were generally obliged to deliver capitation, land tax and tithe on the production as a standard annuity (*maktu*), whereas they were granted the Ottoman right to individual property (*mülk*), regarding mainly vineyards and orchards. On the other hand, the Ottomans had largely maintained, at least until the first half of the 18th century, the status of seigniorial lands in the Cyclades (the status of *tópoi*, *afentótopoi*, *volés* or *feudal lands* according to the archives), which marked the long installation of the Latins and their descendants in the above islands. Thus, the agricultural populations of the islands were submitted to a system of multiple tax imposition, that of the Ottoman *maktu*, directly collected by Kapudhan Pasha or indirectly by Ottoman and later by Christian tax farmers (*voevods*), and that of the Latin landlords, including both monetary and natural values. On the other hand, at the end of the seventeenth century the Cyclades still remained under the economic control of the Venetian Republic, which, holding on to its most important, and henceforth unique, Eastern Mediterranean bastion, the island of Crete, added to the Archipelago's troubles with the levy of a special annual imposition, appearing in the documents as *caraggio*[4].

3 Regarding the passage from Latin to Ottoman installation: Slot (1991: 195-207); Lock (1995); Zachariadou (1992: 329-342).

4 Concerning transformations in the fiscal system of the Cyclades during the period of transition between Latins and Ottomans see: Slot (1982); Kolovos (2003: 317-321 and 2006: 34-85, in which the author contests several historiographical clichés about the Ottoman fiscal mechanisms and documents); Zachariadou (2004: 199-212).

We will focus on the most documented case of all, that of Naxos seventeenth- and eighteenth-century peasant movements[5], and we will try to show that the economic, social and political transformations indicated by different historical narratives portraying the principal actors of the above movements, could be largely illustrated or even explained by the evolution of emphyteutic relations, as reflected in emphyteutic contracts during the period in question.

II. Different historical narratives

An abundant contemporary literature concerning the above movements represent on the one hand the proliferate written reports of the local Councils ('Communities') of the island and their correspondence with the Ottoman administration, the Orthodox Patriarch and the Republic of Venice, all three called in as arbitraries, and on the other hand the Catholic sources, such as the Jesuit missionary reports[6], the archives of the Capuchin monastery, or the catholic archbishop's correspondence. The above sources generally make the distinction between the Community of the *Citadel* (Castro), the main fortified settlement of the island, inhabited by families of Latin origin and Catholic rite, particularly rich in land and agricultural revenues; the Community of the *Borgo* (Bourgo), which lay in the periphery of the Citadel and was inhabited by a native Orthodox population occupied in manufacture and commerce; and the agricultural Community representing 15 villages, the inhabitants of which worked the lands of the Citadel landlords. During the seventeenth century the Borgo Community seems to have provided the leaders of peasant movements, the most famous being Konstantinos Kokkos, a rich Borgo inhabitant, enjoying an alliance with the Catholic archbishop as well as the favors of Venice. During the eighteenth century new leaders seem to have emerged among the peasantry, members of local councils, small landowners experienced in the Ottoman courts of justice and enjoying very good relations with the Ottoman authorities (e.g. the well known Politis family), as shown in a rare document that particularly stresses the claim of emphyteutic rights by the peasants: in 1719 the Community of the villages presented 31 articles before the Council of the Citadel, by which they demanded not to be deprived of their 'ancient rights', to be liberated from certain particularly heavy taxes, and to be granted permission to 'plant

5 On social seventeenth- and eighteenth-century social conflicts in the island of Naxos: ZERLENTIS (1887: 408-427; 1925 (including published documents); TOURTOGLOU (1991-1993: 37-48, in which the author particularly stresses the fiscal aspect of the above confrontations). There are also two parallel approaches of Naxiot movements in KASDAGLI (1999: 185-194) and in ZEI (2001: 232-237). Cf. about similar conflicts in 18th century isl and of Kea: SLOT (1982: 267).

6 About the importance of missionaries' reports on the islands, see BORROMEO (2004: 123-144).

and enclose their vineyards and orchards, as well as to obtain property rights on the olive trees and branches which they have planted and grafted inside the seigniorial domains of the island[7].'

The seventeenth-century Catholic missionaries' reports enhance the doctrinal aspect of conflicts: *Greek* (meaning Orthodox) peasants, according to the Capuchins, *Roman* peasants according to the Jesuits, poor, abused and exasperated by the cruelty and injustice *of Latin* seigneurs, were led to slaughter like an innocent flock by their own leaders, who sought to prevail over the Latins and consequently were the only ones to blame for the riots. As the century drew to its end, the above leaders were said to have gained more and more power among the peasantry, to have become more and more reckless, eloquent and sly in their methods, as they spent most of their time in Ottoman courts and became familiar with their tricks[8].

The eighteenth-century Catholic discourse illustrates even further the social aspect of the above oppositions, which are described as conflicts of power between a dominating order, the 'notables and primates' of the Citadel, drawing legitimacy on the antiquity and perpetuity of land structures, and an agricultural milieu, considered clandestine because of their 'rebel' activities. In 1777, after a new peasant uprising in Naxos, Jovanni Battista Crispi, the archbishop of Paronaxia and the Aegean decrees measures against 'the barbaric and wicked *socmen*[9] of the villages', because they had the nerve to 'infringe on the ancient and customary obligations, which all *bondmen* and *socmen* ought to fulfill obediently'. According to the above decree, peasants were obliged to settle immediately all their debts and fulfill their fiscal obligations: 'in the future they would be refused every loan and would be excluded from every agricultural contract, if they did not accept to settle the ancient dues', whereas the leaders of this 'reckless revolt' faced the penalty of excommunication (Zerlentis, 1925: 93).

European travellers of the eighteenth and the beginning of nineteenth century (Tournefort (1717), Hope (1820), Blancard (1909), Yerasimos (1982), on the other hand, have particularly developed the innovating, revolutionary profile of the above leaders. They are described as a group of free, well-to-do owners of vineyards, orchards and pastures, with which they royally provided their daughters' dowries, moving constantly from their urban residence to the country to survey the harvest as well as the processing

---

7 The document is first published in Zerlentis (1925); Guinis (1966).

8 A first translation of the Jesuit Ign. Lichtle's report on Naxos in: Kremos (1891); see also Miller (1927-1928).

9 By *socmen* I translate the Greek term ζευγάδες [zevgàs/zevgàdes] in the document, which seems to bear similarities with the English medieval and early-modern category of rising free peasants working in seigniorial lands, opposed to that of *bondmen* [= bound to the lord of the land], as well as to the seventeenth-century free *laboureurs* of several French regions (Beauvaisis, Île-de-France etc.); relative to these comparative remarks see for example Bloch (1983: 227); Hilton (1988); Béaur (1998).

of the product, venturing new varieties and techniques of culture, and at the same time endeavoring to assimilate themselves to their land tenants in their everyday behavior and customs, to the point of sharing their meal on the field (a 'black, coarse barley bread'). A rising insular elite, those 'new rich' gradually prevailed over the Latin landlords, who are described as lords of ancient tradition, distant and intangible, isolated in the Citadel, considering themselves self-sufficient in their well-being, plunged in the traditional pleasures of their social order, such as hunting with falcons and offering grand dinners with rich dishes of pheasants to their guests, demanding that their duties, regardless their pains, regularly deposit the riches of their lands at their feet. Nevertheless, the above new elite does not seem to scorn the seigniorial cultural model: reproached as they were for their rough peasant origins, they answered with the construction of genealogical trees, the invention of coats of arms and titles of nobility, by wearing furs, laces and velvet clothes and hats, and showing themselves on every ceremonial occasional in the greatest possible luxury, often at the expense or despite their vulnerable revenues, exposed to the everyday risks of insular economy: the lack of cash, the heavy debts and taxes, the natural aridity of insular land, the frequent destructions of harvest by weather hazards, and the constant dangers at sea.

III. The evolution of emphyteutic relations

All the above documents seem to indicate the passage between two different and clearly distinguished insular societies: from a seigniorial society, based on the survival of long term land relations towards a society of petty free owners, who can obtain property rights on the land through their money and their labor, and who seem to develop a relation with the market through the realization of commercial cultures. Nevertheless, the picture drawn by the above narratives, although quite perceptive, bears strongly the mark of a long European debate on feudalism and individual property, generated by eighteenth-century economic and political theories. The study of the contracts and the contracting parties themselves in the notarial archives of the islands suggests that social mutations are not linear: a comparison, for instance, between the contracts of Naxos and those of Paros, would indicate that unlike Paros, eighteenth-century Naxos still clung onto seigniorial structures, a fact which partly explains constant claims upon ancient rights presented by the peasants, as well as the perseverance of social agitations during that century. We are thus led to discover that instead of bilateral oppositions between traditional opponents, such as Catholic-Orthodox, urban-rural population, landlord-tenant, we seem to deal with transformations of power relations inside the same composite and dynamic insular society.

The majority of seventeenth-century agricultural contracts in Cyclades[10] concern cases of land leasing based on mixed farming (cereals, vegetables, trees), concluded between *landlords* or *masters* (translations of the terms *àrchontes* or *aféntes*), of Latin origin or lineage, and their tenants. The principal object of contracts being vine plantation and viniculture, they also include arboricultures of other kind, among which a special place is occupied by citrus, fig and olive trees. Not demanding in natural humidity, the above cultures were particularly adapted to the dry climate and arid soil of the islands. Fig trees, olive trees and especially vines contributed to the natural drainage of the land, permitted an annual yield with a minimum of irrigation, a luxury in a world invaded by salt water. Furthermore, the above cultures mark the long history of insular agriculture with their slow rotation of fertility years (the olive tree) and the long continuity of traditional techniques such as grafting of the wild tree (olive) or pollination of the male tree (fig), by which they ensured the peasant's property rights to the tree or to the grafted branches.

The agricultural contracts of Naxos, as well as those of Mykonos (Petropoulos, 1960), insisted on the length of land leases: they generally ensured a short term lease of two to three years, which included vine plantation or growing, cultures of annual rotation (cereals, dry vegetables or green vegetables) fixed in time and space, reparation and construction of enclosures and wine presses that remained in the possession of the landlord. The same contract would also include permanent or long term leasing between tenants and landlords, generally extended over two generations. Finally they defined several obligations and duties towards the 'master' (transportation of the landlord on horseback to the field at the time of harvest, delivery of the first crop or fruits etc.), the regularity of which (annual, monthly, weekly) marked the insular calendar. The above contracts often anticipated the extraction of one half or two thirds of the production by the landlord.

On the other hand, the eighteenth century announces the distinction of two types of leasing. The emphyteutic contracts of Paros[11] seem to specialize all the more in wine vineculture, and to specify its practices, techniques and instruments, offering an extremely precious source of historical study on the 'rural civilization' of the islands, to apply a term introduced by Emmanuel Le Roy Ladurie (1973: 141-168). On the other hand, they announce a shorter lease of three to eight years, followed by the irregularity, even the abolition of former duties, whereas they tend to fix the land owner's participation in the expenses – the term 'landlord' is subsiding or is reserved for the more important landowners. Finally, at the expiration of the contract, not only the

---

10 Among the numerous corpuses and isolated notarial acts lying in the National Archives or scattered in various editions we note the more recent publication of a voluminous corpus of seventeenth-century acts of Naxos: Siphoniou-Karapas, Rodolakis & Artemiadis (1990).

11 NA doc. 212; for the analysis of the material, Zei (2001).

crop and the vintage, but also the field and the trees are generally divided in two parts, and so are the agricultural constructions, such as wine and olive presses, which were realized or repaired by the tenant.

But the most interesting transformation concerns the constitution of land rent: in seventeenth-century contracts, the tenant had to pay in advance an entry fine to the landlord (*embatiki*), which was supposed to correspond to the value of one quarter of the land in lease. The contracts being permanent or for two generations, the entry fine ensured a long term right of tenure, and a fixed land income to the landlord, independent of weather hazards and fluctuations of land prices on the market. In case the contract was prematurely dissolved, the entry fine ensured property rights on one quarter of the land to the tenant, provided that he fulfilled his obligations (planting, growing and constructing enclosures) according to the agreed terms.

The above entry rights, more virtual and symbolic in the seventeenth century, would become more real in the eighteenth century, as shown by the final division of the field after the expiration of the contract, offering the possibility of land investment outside the system of 'partible inheritance' and the land market, which moreover encouraged investment in commercial cultures, mainly in the vine. This appears more systematically in eighteenth century agricultural contracts: the emphyteutic lease tends to take the form of a fixed agreement between land owners. The entry fine, still appearing by the term *embatiki*, now defines an annual rent in the case of cereals, or an 'industrial capital' in the case of wine or tree growing which is generally to be paid off by the farmer after the expiration of the contract and the division of the field, but which can also be retained as 'gift orremunerationfor one's labors ' (Zei, 2008: 241-251). Nevertheless, one should not forget that land investment in the islands is closely connected with credit: the compared study of contracts and other notary acts show that throughout the seventeenth and eighteenth centuries emphyteutic contracts can very well conceal settlements of debt even between members of the same family.

Olive growing and oil production in the Archipelago, on the other hand, represent an entirely different story which will not occupy us at present: it is interesting to note, however, that while the petty production of the islands seems to be crushed under the protective measures of their authorities and the state farming of oil taxes in the eighteenth century Ottoman empire, only the islands which maintained seigniorial structures proved themselves capable of launching their production in the larger Mediterranean commerce: Syros, Andros, and of course Naxos.

IV. A new economic and political elite of the islands

In conclusion, the evolution of emphyteutic contracts in the seventeenth- and eighteenth-century Cyclades marks the slow and irregular generation of a new local elite whose income is largely based on viniculture and wine production.

According to their contractual activities, the eighteenth century heralds the strengthening of their economic position all over the Greek Archipelago: not only do they plant vines and buy real estate in all Aegean islands, but they also possess stores and deposits in insular ports, and sail among the islands with their own vessels, to try their fortune later, towards the middle of the century, in the larger Mediterranean and European commerce. They import new varieties of vine and develop new techniques for producing wine, which bring a creative and sensitive art of the land, described and commended by the abundant agronomic literature of this period[12], as well as a new period of fame for the Archipelago wines, such as the wines of Paros and Santorini, which according to European sources, dared even to compete with the legendary 'Venetian or Cretan wines'; they also import the new ideas and cultures of economic and political liberalism. On the other hand, since the first half of the century, the above elite enlarged their capacities as economic and administrative agents between different groups of power inside the Ottoman Empire: apart from their position as interpreters (*drogman*) to which they are constantly appointed, they become tax distributors, collectors and later tax farmers (Asdrachas, 1991: 245-264), estimators of land values, members of councils, agents of European commerce in the islands, important creditors who ensure the fiscal capacity of insular Communities and populations. By the second half of the eighteenth century, theyacquired a new responsibility, that of Community Commissioner and Port Commissioner [*Epitropos*], which permits them not only to negotiate and exercise their political influence on both insular and Ottoman authorities, but also to impose their proper economic policy in the Eastern Mediterranean by regulating the flow and prices of importations (mainly cereals and raw materials) in the Archipelago.

Bibliography

ARGYROU, Eustathia (1995), *Les baux ruraux dans l' île ionienne de Leucade au XVIIIe siècle*, 1-2, doctoral thesis, University of Paris I.

ARGYROU, Eustathia (2003), 'Les baux ruraux dans une île ionienne. L'exemple de Leucade au XVIIIe siècle', in Gerard BÉAUR, Mathieu ARNOUX & Anne VARET-VITU (eds), *Exploiter la terre. Les contrats agraires de l'Antiquité à nos jours, Rennes-Presses Universitaires de Rennes*, p. 155-165.

ASDRACHAS, Spyros I. (1991), 'Les communes dans les régions grecques de l' Empire Ottoman: fonctions fiscales et restrictives', *Byzantinische Forschungen* 16, p. 245-264.

AVDELA, E., D'CRUZE, Sh. & ROWBOTHAM, Judith (eds) (2010), *Problems of Crime and Violence in Europe, 1780-2000*, Lewiston/Queenstone/Lampeter-Edwin Mellen Press.

12 The most famous agronomic oeuvre being that of LANDOS, 1991 [1643].

BÉAUR, Gerard (ed.) (1998), *La terre et les hommes. France et Grande-Bretagne (XVIIe-XVIIIe siècle)*, Hachette Littératures.

BLANCARD, Thomas (1909), *Les Mavroyéni. Histoire d' Orient (de 1700 à nos jours)*, vol. 1, Paris.

BLICKLE, P. (1993), *Unruhen in der ständischen Gesellschaft 1300-1800*. Munich: Oldenbourg, 1988; W. Rösener, *Die Bauern in der Europäischen Geschichte*, Munich-C. H. Beck Verlag.

BLOCH, Marc (1983), 'The Rise of Dependent Cultivation and Seigniorial Institutions', in *Mélanges historiques*, vol. 1, Paris-Serge Fleury-Editions de l' EHESS.

BORROMEO, Elisabetta (2004), 'Les Cyclades à l' époque ottomane: L'insularité vue par les missionaires jésuites (1625-1644)', in Nicolas VATIN & Gilles VEINSTEIN (eds), *Insularités ottomanes*, Maisonneuve & Larose, Institut Français d' Etudes Anatoliennes, Paris 2004, p. 123-144.

CARROLL, St (ed.) (2007), *Cultures of Violence. Interpersonal Violence in Historical Perspective*, Chippenham and Eastbourne-Antony Rowe Ltd.

COHN, Samuel K. Jr. (ed.) (2004), *Popular Protest in Late Medieval Europe: Italy, France and Flanders, Selected Sources Translated and Annotated*, Manchester University Press.

COHN, Samuel K. Jr. (2006), *Lust for Liberty. The Politics of Social Revolt in Medieval Europe, 1200-1425*, Harvard University Press, Cambridge M.A and London.

FOURQUIN, Guy (1978), *The Anatomy of Popular Rebellion*, tr. A. Chesters, Elsevier Science Ltd.

GUINIS, D. (1966), *Περίγραμα Ιστορίας Μεταβυζαντινού Δικαίου*, Athens.

HILTON, Rodney (1988), *Bond Men Made Free: Medieval Peasant Movements and the English Peasant Rising of 1381*, London, Routledge.

HOPE, Thomas (1820), *Anastase ou Mémoires d'un Grec*, 1., Paris.

KASDAGLI, Aglaia E (1999), *Land and Marriage Settlements in the Aegean. A Case Study of Seventeenth-Century Naxos*, Venice, p. 185-194.

KOLOVOS, Elias (2003), 'Les documents ottomans de la Bibliothèque Kaïreios d'Andros (Grèce)', *Turcica* 35, p. 317-321.

KOLOVOS, Elias (2006), *Η νησιώτικη κοινωνία της Άνδρου στο οθωμανικό πλαίσιο*, Kaïreios Library-Andros, p. 34-85.

KREMOS, G (1891), 'Νάξος', *Απόλλων* 7.

LE ROY-LADURIE, Emmanuel (1973), 'Civilisation rurale', *Encyclopedia Universalis*, in *Le territoire de l'historien*, Editions Gallimard-Paris, p. 141-168.

LANDOS, Ag. (1991 [1643]), *Γεωπονικόν* [Geoponicon], Venice (and the edition by D. Kostoula, Volos.

LOCK, Peter (1995), *The Franks in the Aegean, 1204-1500*, London-Longman and New York.

MILLER, W. (1927-1928), 'Lichtle's Description of Naxos', *Byz.-Neugr. Jahr.*, 6.

MOLLAT, M & WOLFF, Ph. (1973), *The Popular Revolutions of the Late Middle Ages*, London-Allen & Unwin.

PETROPOULOS, G. (1960), *Νοταριακαί πράξεις Μυκόνου των ετών 1663-1779*, Athens-Monuments of Postbyzantine Law 3.

Siphoniou-Karapas, A., Rodolakis, G. & Artemiadis, D. (1990), *Ο κώδικας του νοταρίου της Νάξου Ιωάννου Μηνιάτη, 1680-1689 (National Archives, doc. 86)*, Athens-Academy of Athens.

Slot, B. J. (1991), 'The Frankish Archipelago', *Byzantinische Forschungen* 16, p. 195-207.

Slot, B. J. (1982), *Archipelago Turbatus. Les Cyclades entre colonization latine et occupation ottomane, c. 1500-1718*, 2 vols, Istanbul-Nederlands Historisch-Archaeologisch Instituut.

Tilly, Charles (1996), *European Revolutions, 1492-1992*, Cambridge Massachussets.

Tilly, Charles. (2004), *Social Movements, 1768-2004*, Boulder-Paradigm Publishers.

Tournefort, Joseph Pitton de (1717), *Relation d un voyage du Levant*, 2 vols, Paris.

Tourtoglou, M. (1991-1993), 'Φορολογικές διενέξεις "Φράγκων" και "Ρωμαίων" στη Νάξο κατά την Τουρκοκρατία', *EEKM* 14, p. 37-48.

Vallat, J.P. (2003), 'Le bail roman dans l' historiographie de la Méditerrannée occidentale', in Gerard Béaur, Mathieu Arnoux & Anne Varet-Vitu (eds), *Exploiter la terre. Les contrats agraires de l' Antiquité à nos jours, Rennes-Presses Universitaires de Rennes*, p. 13-34.

Yerasimos, Stéphane (ed.) (1982), *Joseph Pitton de Tournefort, Voyage d'un botaniste. 1. L'Archipel grec*, Fr. Maspero, Paris.

Zachariadou, Elizabeth A. (1992), 'The sanjak of Naxos in 1641', in Chr. Fragner-Kl. Schwartz (eds), *Festgabe an Josef Matuz: Osmanistik-Turkologie-Diplomatik*, Berlin-Klaus Schwarz, p. 329-342.

Zachariadou, Elizabeth A. (ed.) (2002), *The Kapudhan Pasha: his Office and his Domain, Halcyon Days in Crete IV, A Symposium held in Rethymnon, 7-9 January 2000*, Crete University Press, Rethymno.

Zachariadou, Elizabeth A. (2004), 'Changing Masters in the Aegean', in Julian Chrysostomides, Charalambos Dendrinos & Jonathan Harris (eds), *The Greek Islands and the Sea. Proceedings of the First International Colloquium held at the Hellenic Institute, Royal Holloway, University of London, 21-22 September 2001*, Porphyrogenitus-Great Britain, p. 199-212.

Zei, Eleftheria, (2001), *Paros dans l' Archipelago Grec, XVIIe-XVIIIe siècles: Les multiples visages de l'insularité*, unpublished doctorate thesis (University of Paris I-Paris 2001), 2 vols.

Zei, Eleftheria (2008), 'La terre et la taxe dans la Méditerrannée orientale latine (XIVe-XVIIIe siècles)', in Simonetta Cavaciocchi (ed.), *Atti della XXXIX Settimana di Studi, La fiscalità nell'economia europea. Secc. XIII-XVIII, 22-26 aprile 2007*, Istituto Internazionale di storia economica F. Datini, Prato-Le Monnier, p. 241-251.

Zei, Eleftheria (2017), *Visages et visions d'insularité: Paros dans l'Archipel grec pendant la première moitié du XVIIIe siècle*, Isis, Istanbul.

Zerlentis, P. (1887), 'Διαμάχαι Καστρινών και Νεοχωριτών', *Παρνασσός* 11, p. 408-427.

Zerlentis, P. (1925), *Φεουδαλική πολιτεία εν τη νήσω Νάξω*, Hermoupolis.

EFI ARGYROU, SEVASTI LAZARI

14. Agrarian Practices and their Social and Ideological Ramifications in the Ionian Islands during the Venetian Domination

It is quite fortunate that most of the Ionian islands have managed to salvage a considerable amount of archival material referring to the period of the Venetian domination, so that it is possible for us now to trace among this material a great number of documents dealing with land ownership issues and the subsequent relations of the landholders with the state as well as with the farmers[1]. Quite often the content of these documents points to various situations of the agrarian space, the origins of which can be detected in contracts, already valid from the medieval period. This fact has fired many discussions with regard to the transference of feudal phenomena in the Ionian space, most of which focused on Corfu, the island of the greatest importance for the sovereign State and the most representative case of the continuous Western dominance and of the adoption of feudal relations[2].

In this short report we intend to discuss the phenomena that interest us through the land tenure contracts in Lefkada, in order to discern the extent of dispersion of these events, the divergences they present, and in order to sketch out aspects of the social structure of the island, as these have been shaped under the impact of commercial capitalism[3]. Lefkada, an island with particularly rich archives, allows quantitative as well as qualitative surveys

1 Most of the material presented here is based on the notarial acts of the first twelve notaries of the island of Lefkada from the end of the seventeenth century up to the middle of the eighteenth century and on the Venetian cadastre of the beginning of the eighteenth century. All references given from the archival material of the General State Archives of Greece, department of Lefkada will be quoted by the name of the notary accompanied by the abbreviation Arch. (= archives); Reg. for register.

2 There is a rich bibliography concerning the feudal system of Corfu. Among them: Pantazopoulos (1969); Alvanas (1894); Polylas (1864, 1868); Typaldos (1864); Asdracha & Asdrachas (1985); Asdrachas (1985). In Anogiatis-Pele & Prontzas (2002) the discussion about the feudal characteristics of the economy of Corfu is thoroughly presented, taking into consideration the respective Greek and international bibliography. Thus we have kept the term feudal instead of seigneurial, since the term is constantly employed in the bibliography we have used.

3 Argyrou (2003). This article concerns a first presentation of the issue in the *International Congress* in Caen. An interesting bibliography is included in the corresponding volume.

Agrarian Change and Imperfect Property, ed. by Rosa Congost and Pablo F. Luna, Rural History in Europe, 15 (Turnhout, 2018), 297-311

DOI 10.1484/M.RURHE-EB.5.116129

of these phenomena, so that the historians can construct a case-study that, along with similar case studies of other Ionian islands, will help us form a picture of the overall economic reality of the region.

Our interest in the case of Lefkada derives from its different historical fortune that sets it apart from the rest of the Ionian islands. While the latter almost continuously remained under Western domination from the thirteenth century to 1797, Lefkada passed from Western domination (1296-1479) to Ottoman domination (1479-1684) and finally to the Venetian rule (1684-1797)[4]. The feudal structures developed under the Western domination were overthrown, when the Ottomans occupied the island in 1479. During their period of power, the land was categorized as public, private and *vakouf*. Although our knowledge on this period is generally restricted, during this time there emerged some big Muslim landowners and a limited number of local Christians[5].

Under the Venetian rule, the main categories are the same: public (in their case consisting of the former Ottoman lands, but also *soprapiu*[6] or confiscated land), private, and monastery land. Public land was bestowed to their army, diplomatic, and administrative cooperators, of Venetian descent but also refugees from former Venetians areas (cf. Chios, Crete, Prevesa), *armatols* from Ottoman areas (Ipiros, Roumeli) or from other Ionian islands, local notables, even Christianized Ottomans[7]. A great variety of terms accompanies the concession of land according to its origin, the type and the extent of the culture, the duration as well as the time of the concession, its obligations (land was given *gratis* (*graciosa concessione*), permanently in return for a certain sum of money per annum (*livello*) or as a lease (*affitto*) (Andreadis, 1914, I: 82-83, 209, 262-287; Rontoyiannis, 1980: 553-554, 605,13), but also according to the persons involved, their origin and their relation to the State (Machairas,1951; Chortis & Michailaris, 1996). We also have to take into consideration the fact that at this period, Venice is motivated by the need to reinforce the population of the island, decreased by 3,000 persons, who left together with the Ottomans, as well as the produce and revenues of the island (Chortis, 1992).

It is this late integration of the island into the Venetian state and its pre-existing economic and social situation that necessitate a different approach

---

4 Kouniakis (1928); Vlandis (1902); Machairas (1951); Rontoyiannis (1980) are local historians who have sketched in their works the history of the island over the centuries.

5 So far the best source for this period was Rontoyiannis (1980: 377-500). Cf. the recent study on the Ottoman past of the island, Kolovos (2013).

6 *Soprapiu* land consisted of former Ottoman estates that accidentally had not been measured or were intentionally hidden by the locals. When the State discovered them, at the beginning it leased them to the denunciator, while later on to the communities of villages, to whose district they belonged. Cf. Rontoyiannis (1980: 554, 613).

7 Machairas (1951: 21-25, 77, 86-87, 132-144); Andreadis (1914, I: 230-231) mentions that the revenues from the public land were much more important in Lefkada than in the rest of the Ionian islands.

to its land ownership issues. The feudal system is implemented on the island, yet the power resulting from it is limited to the land granted rather than over the cultivators, in contrast to what happened in Corfu, where the concession of land is coupled with power over the farmers, too[8]. This important difference shaped the formation of separate land *elites* on the two islands. In Lefkada during the eighteenth century next to the foreign elite a new local elite emerged, in which some big farmers from the villages disposing of a location in the city of the island were incorporated (Rontoyiannis, 1980: 507, 654) as their economic vigor permitted them to enter as *cittadini* the Council of the island (Rontoyiannis, 1980: 537, 551, 650-651; Machairas, 1951: 38-47, 123-124). This local elite sent their sons to study in Italian universities (Rontoyiannis, 1980: 506-507), although the titles of nobility remained out of reach[9] and they never approached the status of the corfiote elite, which had long before acquired titles of nobility (Karapidakis, 1985: 95-122). The emergence of this elite, as well as that of middle class strata that will profit from the opportunities presented in the land tenure system, is witnessed by the agrarian contracts.

It is well known that the agrarian contracts are concluded either orally or in writing, their registration being done either by means of a private action or an official notarial contract. The agrarian contracts mostly cover the need for legal transactions relevant to the consolidation of the titles of property and rights in rem (Argyrou, 1996: 301). However, we must point out that in these contracts from Lefkada we notice a fluidity concerning the legal terminology used in order to determine not only the contracts and the revenues, but also the relations between the landholders and their tenant farmers as well as the relation of the latter with the land (Argyrou & Katiforis, 2009: 438-439, 445, 447). This fluidity certainly reflects a legal stratification shaped in the passage of centuries, but also the decreased resistance of the local language towards the language of the Western sovereign, in comparison to Corfu[10]. This fluidity, although it gives the impression of the absence of an explicit legal code of communication, is offset by the insistent reference to the dimension of time in the contract (Argyrou, 2004: 595-607).

---

8 It is indicative that, contrary to Corfu, *angaria* exists only in one notarial act in Lefkada (an *affitto* for a definite period of time), even in the form of annulation. Arch. Carvella, reg.1, 61v (2 Aug. 1719). In Lefkada even in the cases of lands granted as fiefs, our documents make no reference to any relation between the beneficiaries and the farmers, or even the corresponding obligations of the latter. Mixhailaris (1996: 128) comments that this sort of information was probably kept by the representatives of the fiefs beneficiaries, who lived away from the island.

9 See Papadopoli-Stavrou (1992); Argyrou, under publication.

10 Rodolakis, (2004: 381-382) notices the strong resistance of the greek language in the agrarian contracts of Corfu as well as the consolidation of forms and terms as early as in the fifteenth century.

We have come across the following types of contracts: permanent lease – *livello* (and rarely *soliatiko*)[11], temporary lease (*affitto, affitanza, pachto*) and sharecropping farming.

Livello, the equivalent of *contractus emphyteucarius*, concerns the permanent concession of a property in return for an annual sum of money or produce (*kanon*), and is a feudal type revenue[12]. From the middle of the eighteenth century its permanent character is abolished and it is transformed into a long time lease. *Affitto, affitanza, pachto* is a lease of landed property for a definite period – mostly about four years – during which the tenant exploits and reaps the benefits of a plot of land in return for a rental.

In sharecropping contracts, *sembria*, the tenant undertakes the cultivation of a certain kind of crop (field, vine, trees) or planting in wasteland and thereafter the cultivation of a vineyard and quite rarely of an orchard or trees. On this last occasion the process of clearing is rarely distinguished from that of planting. When sharecropping concerns a vineyard, crops of annual rotation (dry vegetables or green ones, etc.) are also planted. The tenant provides the work force and the mobile capital and the landholder rarely participates in improvement work and farming expenses.

Some of these contracts are permanent, others of limited time, and the duration of some is defined on the basis of the life span of the crop, that is up to its uprooting or the life span of either the landholder or the tenant. Some of them are hereditary with the possibility of being transferred; others establish a right in rem or in property, thus interrupting the arrangement of co-ownership. This is the case in contracts of definite time concerning planting a vineyard that at the end of the contract anticipate sharing the planted land in two – between the landholder and the tenant – thus interrupting their arrangement of co-ownership. When sharing concerns only the vines, the tenant, cultivator who had been dependent thus far becomes independent,

---

11 As for *soliatiko* in Corfu (*censual* in the texts) cf. Asdrachas, 1983: 52-54.

12 This character of the convention *livello* is also confirmed by the fact that, whether the permanent concession concerns agrarian or urban holdings the documents use the same term, *livello*, as opposed to the concessions for a definite period of time, where, referring to the agrarian holdings the terms used are *pachto, affitto* and less common *gimoro*, while for the urban ones the term used is lease. We notice, thus, that *livello* whether it concerns the agrarian or the urban space, is bound to serve the same non economic logic, as opposed to the concessions and revenues serving a market logic. It is not at all accidental that what is mostly conceded as *livello* is land (quite often wild, waste, inappropriate for vineyard planting, buildable plots), land not connected with cash crops, as opposed to what happens with *affitto*, that does not necessitate the cultivators' participation and efforts to improve the soil or intervene in the farming process. To corroborate the above, it is worth mentioning the case of Corfiot *feudi* from the time of D'Anjou, the Venetian rule, and quite later, when the equivalent of *livello* is called *soliatiko* or *soldiatiko*, an impost implying bare ownership the ψιλή κυριότητα of the fief holder over the land, while in cases of long time or temporary tenures the terms used are *kaniski* and *syngrateia*, the former term one implying concession of the land while the latter one co ownership.

while when it concerns the vine as well as the land itself, the tenant becomes landowner. The tenant becomes landowner in certain cases of sharecropping contracts concerning wasteland.

The relationship between the landholder and the land-tenant is close and could be seen in terms of personal dependence, since at the time of the harvest, the most crucial moment of the farming period, the landlord is present. His presence indicates at symbolic level that, despite the arrangement of co-ownership, it is he that remains lord of the property and of the production. Moreover, he is the one that controls the whole process up to the sharing.

The majority of cases involve permanent or long time contracts, (*livello, permanent sharecropping cultivation and plantation*). Such logic is obviously dictated by an important part of landholders and reveals a certain perception of immobility, consistent with the economic and social situation of the island. This preference for permanent agrarian acts demonstrates a mentality in which any prospect for improvement of the yield of lands or any connection with the market is beyond reach. It is a mentality based not on any entrepreneurial dexterity but on divine providence, evident on the continuous invocations for divine help that we come across in the documents. '...They may do as they want and desire, though if ever this land is given away, God may not permit it, in this case of selling may s. Manolis (landowner) and his heirs be asked'[13].

The rent is paid either in kind or in money, fixed or proportional. The majority of our contracts from the end of the seventeenth century up to the middle of the eighteenth century show a preference for a rent in kind, whether it concerns contracts of *livello, affitto* or *sharecropping farming*. This preference strengthens our conclusion concerning the conservative mentality of most of the landholders, but also about the degree of growth of the local economy. The meager monetization of the economy keeps most of the landholders attached to the natural rent, since they try to exploit the inadequacy of the land tenants to respond to the limited existing market.

A stable, fixed rent is paid with *livello*, but also with *pachto* or *affitto*. A proportional rent is paid on occasions of sharecropping farming, *sembria*, consisting of a proportion of the produce that in most cases amounts to half, *misakariko*, but also to one quarter, two fifths, etc. In general terms, given the supremacy of sharecropping farming system of *misakariko* (in half), the proportional rent is much higher than the fixed one. This means that the proportional rent contracts mostly concern cultivators with little negotiating power, while the fixed rent ones concern leasers who are not necessarily farmers.

Besides these rents, we also come across certain types of feudal impost, such as *simio livello*, which may consist of the offer of one or two hens, as a sign of recognition of property. There exist various such imposts by different names (*kaniski, psoni of Sunday* etc.) and they concern certain products offered on different occasions. Their offer in kind is consistent with the preference

13 Arch. Zampelli G., reg.1, p. 153v (1738).

of certain landholders for a natural rent. It is evident that this feudal shell in which our contract acts take place is hard to break, because even the leasing of rural property for a definite period of time (*affitto, pachto, apokopi*), a process that is connected to the market laws, is accompanied by various imposts such as *bdomadiatiko gift, psoni of Sunday, regalo, kyriakatiko, kaniski,* or by various other products, such as pomegranates, eggs, flax, broad beans, etc., that have to be provided in different periods of the year in small quantities. These imposts, reminiscent of a feudal past, are deeply rooted in the agrarian practices of the wider geographical area, (*πίτα*, a pie, *κότα*, a hen etc. in Corfu or *kalathiatiko* in the Cyclades). We must also point out that in certain cases the quantity of products imposed in this way may rise considerably, as in the case with the payment of even twelve hens when land is leased for a definite period of time[14].

We think that in this way conservative landholders, applying non entrepreneurial methods, try to compensate for the loss of profits, but also for the increasing cost of living imposed by the superior social order they belong to. Besides these revenues, in certain contracts we meet *charisma*, an important pecuniary sum, paid once and for all in the strongest currency and presented in the documents as a voluntary offer to the landowner. *Charisma* conceals a specific kind of sale, since the legal and property status of the period does not view public land as a commodity subject to the laws of the market, but as a commodity acquired through administrative mechanisms (Argyrou, 1996: 303). *Charisma* facilitates the transfer of property and mostly the increased profit of the landholder, since the revenue *livello* is bound to remain fixed for ever. Another impost to the landholder is the interest-free loan. It appears that interest-free loans serve the same logic as *charisma*, so that we could conclude that they serve necessities of a market in a feudal administrative frame.

There are some interesting exceptions. On certain occasions of sharecropping vineyards, along with the proportional rent, fixed rent (*livello* or *pachto*) is paid for the same part of land, not only as a means of compensation for possible loss of profit but also as a feudal type revenue[15]. In the case of *charisma* in a sharecropping vineyard, this is paid when the contract comes into force, while thereafter a proportional rent is paid[16]. We have also come across instances of sharecropping plantations for a definite period of time in which *charisma* is paid in advance and *livello* thereafter[17]. On this last occasion for the first years of the co ownership agreement up to the sharing of the culture,

14 In Arc. Barbarigo Z., reg.2, p. 106 (August 29, 1710) in an act of leasing for a definite period of time each of the two tenants is obliged to give four hens; Ibid., p. 106v (August 31, 1710) each of the three tenants is bound to give four hens.

15 Permanent contract in Avast. Reg. 2, p. 43 (1724), Barb, reg. 8, p. 2. Contract up to the uprooting, Papacost., reg. 2, p. 22 (1729). To compare this system to the one existing in Corfu, *syngratia* in Polylas, 1868: 2-3.

16 Zamb. Reg. 2, p. 19 (1739), Zamb. Reg. 2, p. 136v (1741).

17 Barb. Reg. 7, p. 92 (1726).

a proportional rent is paid concerning crops resulting from sowing the land, but not as regards the grapes resulting from the vines planted.

We realize that in Lefkada the *livello* revenue comes to the same amount of money as *pachto* (*affitto, apokopi, gemoro*) for a plot of land of the same area. Sometimes it is the basic and obligatory revenue, some other times it is optional and complementary to the proportional rent and some other times it is accompanied by a nominal in kind *simio livello* or by an important sum of money *charisma*. In sharecropping plantations that end up in sharing of land, in reality *charisma* allows buying off the land's property right, while in the rest sharecropping plantations it allows co-ownership or in cases of permanent lease (*livello*) the right in rem. As we will see further down, most of the tenants that pay *charisma* and the interest free loans are not members of the upper social class; they simply strive to find their way through an economic environment bound to traditional practices and mechanisms outside the market. In this way, they become bearers of another logic that will undermine the prevailing mentality, not only in the sector of agrarian relations, but also in the entire economic social field.

The types of agrarian contracts and their respective revenues define the social and ideological framework in which the various social categories of the inhabitants of the island live and act. In order to approach this framework, we must take into consideration the litigations invoked and the social realignments. On the one hand, the juridical court cases, the frequent claims to the Venetian state and the clauses of contracts according to which the tenant undertakes to liberate the lands conceded from its transgressors reveal the extent of conflicts concerning the concessions of land and rights[18]. On the other the impact of the market triggers serious realignments not only at the top of social strata but also the middle ones. This middle class strata will make their way upwards by leasing and subleasing public land and by sharecropping farming[19].

A characteristic example of litigation and claim of public land is the case of the residents of the village of Saint Petros versus the DeTzortzi brothers. DeTzortzi, nobles from Crete with conservative agrarian practices, undertake as *livellatarii* the plain of Vasiliki. In 1701, the State of Venice grants 240 *stremmata* (acres) of uncultivated fields and pasture lands in Saint Petros to Michail DeTzortzi, resident of Italy, with the only obligation of the payment of the tithe. As landowners, they show a preference for permanent conventions, rents in kind and *simio livello*. They live in the capital city of the island, far from the area of their holdings, which are leased to Petros Tzankarolo and cultivated

18 From cadastrial data of Meganissi (1720) it appears that these conflicts concern an important part of lands of this islet, since 15% of the island's land is contested (*contezioso*). Cf. LAZARI (2011). For an ample bibliography on the conflicts due to land rights cf. ZEI' s here published chapter.

19 Land will be the basic source of income even in the nineteenth century when all the professionals of the island (doctors, notaries, etc.) will be involved in land tenure contracts (ARGYROU, 2005: 620).

by the villagers of the area (Chortis, 1992: 58). Later on, in 1747, the farmers in question, residents of the village of Saint Petros, contested DeTzortzis' rights and after a court trial against Tzouane DeTzortzi, the villagers acquired the tenure (*possesso*) of 120 *stremmata* under the obligation to pay to the state the sum of 906 *cecchini*[20]. Since these lands had not been granted in the form of a sharecropping vineyard for a definite period of time, a contract that would give them the right to claim the vineyard on the grounds of having planted the vines, but were planted with maize, the villagers' claims were obviously based on the right of usucaption.

A similar case concerns the claim of the inhabitants of Sfachiotes against Makola's fief.Makola was granted Ottoman land in the village of Sfachiotes after the conquest of the island by the Venetians, a similarly long-lasting court case, from 1750 up to 1791 (Rontoyiannis, 1980, I: 418). Among these frequent cases, we can mention that of Giuseppe Darmis: in 1741 the public land that he was granted is conceded to Spyros Melidoni and Yannis Lazari, on the grounds of the policy of the State to grant land to persons that live in the island (Chortis, 1992: 33).

Quite schematically, the behaviour of the landholders of this upper strata can be broken down into two categories: a conservative backward-looking group showing a preference for feudal type revenues such as *livello* and *sign of livello* and a more entrepreneurial preferring *charisma* and interest-free loans, choices that indicate their effort to secure mainly interest-free capital. The first one is represented for instance by DeTzorzi, the second one by Soumila.

Aspects of the attitude of the first group are illustrated in the case of *Signiori* Chiotes to whom the Senate granted the tax revenues and the public land of Meganissi, a small islet of eastern Lefkada. Chiotes were granted by the Senate in 1719, 1722, 1725 *in solidum* (*natione Schiotta*): a) the right to receive public lands (*beni livelati ai communi dell' isole*) and b) the right to rent the public revenues (tithes on fields, vineyards, etc.), with the exclusion of any other participant from this right, initially in return for 180 *reali*. From the very beginning they leased from their 'four parts one, whether it concerned *gimora* (land rent) or tithes or other rights', in return for a certain amount either in kind or in money together with the tithe paid to the State and any juridical expenses incurred (Svoronos, 1940; Lazari, 2011). In case of natural rent, this one was deposited in a shop in Vlycho (a port in the eastern part of Lefkada, opposite Meganissi), away from the city of Amaxichi (the capital of the island), in which they lived, so that the commercialization of the products was carried out by the sublease holders. They made no investments in the secondary and tertiary sector of the island economy and finally most of them left the island. Acting mainly as renters, who let their revenues, they were progressively led to indebtedness.

---

20 Chortis (1992: 34). The Community had the right of pre-emption in granting public land (*investiture*) against any other person, cf. Machairas (1951: 117-118).

Their huge debts to the public fund prove that their traditional logic of return was not effective. The dire need for money imposed from the monetized economy, the increasing commercialization of rural products and the market laws as well as their non-entrepreneurial logic account for it. Living a costly life due to their noble position, they left ample space to people willing to take more risk, the sublease holders (Lazari, 2011).

In the second category we can find members of the land owning elite, such as the colonel Anastasios Metaxas from Cephalonia, who was bestowed by the Senate the *conte* title or Angelis Soumilas knighted *kavaliere di San Marco*, etc. (Chortis, 1992: 17-18). In such an economic environment, determined on the one hand by the administrative mechanisms and on the other by the low technological level, these people demonstrate a more entrepreneurial logic. A very interesting example of the possibilities but also of the coercions they had to deal with, is the case of Metaxas, who was granted the public land and revenues of the small islet of Meganissi before the arrival of the group of Chiotes, mentioned before (Rondoyiannis, 1980, I: 553). Metaxas on one hand acts according to the status of the class he wants to belong to, claiming public revenues in compensation for his military obligations and participation in the fight against the Turks, etc. On the other hand, sensitive to the possibilities of profits made via the market economy he opts for rational investments concerning his property: he tries to unify his different estates so that they are profitably utilised; he adopts cash crops and even transfers *coloni* to work on them. At the same time, he tries to register all his belongings so that in those precarious times his fortune will be secured. However, while he tries to adopt a modern economic logic, the non-economic political decisions of the Venetian State nullify all his efforts. The State, wishing to solve the problem of survival and maintenance of the group of Chiotes that cost a lot to the public funds, decides to allocate the public revenues of Meganissi to them, so Metaxas is deprived of his revenues in Meganissi in favour of this new coming group, although he contributed with a considerably higher sum of money to the public fund.

Locals involved in leasing and subleasing revenues and public land will manage to improve their economic position, as is the case of locals in Meganissi mentioned before, vis-à-vis *signori* Chiotes. As *signori* Chiotes were absent from the islet and gradually even left Lefkada, local sublease holders managed to profit from the collection of the revenues and their advancement in the market, but also from the loans *a godis* that they imposed on their farmers-cultivators – unable to cope with the pressures of taxation and land rent[21]. This is also the case in Lefkada with Petro Tzankarolo and Ioannis Smyrnaio, successful leaseholders of public properties granted to DeTzorzi and Makola, that they granted to farmers (Chortis, 1992: 58).

---

21 According to *a godis* loans, the creditor, instead of taking interest for his loans, prefers to keep the land or its yield, as long as the loans exists.

Sharecropping grape growing, a cash crop, for a definite period of time, will allow enterprising cultivators to rise to the status of independent cultivator or owner. The fact that these land tenants participate in other sectors of the economy, such as trade, manufacture, but also leasing of taxes, makes us believe that, apart from their personal work, they employ salaried workers or dependent *sembri*. Due to their economic possibilities they are able to pay *charisma* as tenants and give interest-free loans to the landholders. It seems, therefore, that there exists a category of affluent land tenants, not belonging to the upper social strata, capable of undertaking entrepreneurial activity, investing in land, either subleasing public land or undertaking sharecropping vineyard planting for a definite period of time.

All the above account for the fact that feudal type logic is partly and with great difficulty imposed in the island. On the contrary, in Corfu, where the feudal system had been consolidated long before, the feudal character of land and as well as mechanisms outside the market that regulated its transfer not only prevent its transformation into a commodity, but also prevent the alternative of *charisma*. Therefore, it is not at all peculiar that the question of fiefs of Corfu was not easily regulated in the nineteenth century, when the Ionian islands were united with the Greek State, the fiefs being considered as 'the living monuments of the Middle Age'[22].

In our documentation we come across a lot of interesting examples of that middle social strata, active simultaneously in almost every sector of the economy. People like Ioannis Tzourakis, Zisimos Skiadaresis, Stamatis Smyrnaios, Yiannis Sourbis, Yannis Zoulinos, Mathios Katiforis, and Nikolas Malakasis manage to rival successfully the initially foreign beneficiaries of public lands and revenues (Chortis, 1992: 55-56).

Let's take, for instance, the case of Ioannis Tzourakis, who in 1720 acts as a land tenant in a sharecropping vineyard for a definite period of time, anticipating sharing of vineyards after plantation[23], on the 17th of May 1723 and on the 7th of January 1731 as a land tenant is obliged to pay *charisma* and rents in advance[24], while on the 26th of April 1726 he acts as a merchant[25].

Zisimos Skiadaresis between 1712 and 1726 is already a creditor in loans of land and sea[26], a buyer of land[27], but also a land tenant in a *livello* contract, obliged to pay *charisma* and to give an interest free loan to the landowner, an

---

22 V.Kremidas's report *The living monuments of the Middle Age and the 'sacred rights of property': the land issue in Corfu and the discussions in the Parliament*, is indicative of this issue (Kremidas, 2005: 623-633); As for the recent bibliography on the issue Aroni-Tsichli, I, 2005: 594; Karapidakis, 1992.

23 Arch.Montesanto D., reg.2, p. 36; Arch.Gavalla Z., reg.5, p. 45.

24 Arch.Montesanto D., reg.2; Arch.Karvela Z., reg.8.

25 Arch.Barbarigo Z., reg.6.

26 Arch.Barbarigo Z., reg.6 (September 10, March 11, May 5).

27 Arch.Barbarigo Z., reg.6 (Octobre 14).

act to be ratified on his return to the island[28], something possibly connected to his commercial activities (Argyrou, 2003: 164).

Dimitris Zoulinos is also frequently involved in land tenancy, participating in 1712 as a land tenant in a sharecropping vineyard for a definite period of time[29]. In 1718, as a tenant in a sharecropping vineyard for a definite period of time, he receives his share from the plantation, according to the decision of experts *praktikoi*, voted from both contractors[30]. In 1722, he participates as tenant in a lease of land for a definite period of time (*affitto*) that anticipates change of culture –the vineyard is to be converted into a field[31] – and in 1726 as a tenant in a permanent lease of land (*livello*)[32]. In 1724, acting as a tenant in a sharecropping vineyard, he participates in the ratification of the convention on the part of the widow of the dead landholder, since the land involved concerned her dowry and consequently her approval was necessary to continue the convention[33]. In 1737, he participates as tenant in a permanent sharecropping vineyard, but, at the same time, he concludes a partnership agreement with another tenant to plant it together, while later on he buys his partner's share[34]. Having a continuous presence in the transfers of land, he is eager to take over land in any kind of concession.

The fact that these members of middle social strata conclude partnership agreements between them springs from their need to increase their negotiating power and address the risks of the investment and is indicative of their efforts to enter the land transfers sector and of their entrepreneurial spirit. So, Dimitris Zoulinos and Dimoulas Malakasis conclude an agrarian partnership agreement in order to undertake jointly the permanent sharecropping grape planting in two pieces of fields. In 1737, Dimitris Malakasis, son of Dimoulas, is forced to sell his share of the planted vineyard to his companion Zoulinos, receiving five *cecchini*, on condition that, if he is able to pay off this sum, he can regain partner status in the sharecropping relation[35]. Two years later, a member of the same family, Dimitris Malakasis' first cousin, Georgakis, according to the pre-emption law, pays back the sum of five *cecchini* to Zoulinos, buying off the share of his relative, a fact recorded on the margin of the contract on March 14th, 1739.

In 1710, Nikolaos Malakasis, in a contract of sharecropping vineyard for a definite period of time, acts as representative of the tenant, his relative, paying *charisma* in two installments, a larger part on the occasion of the contract

---

28 Ibid., reg. 7 (May 10), reg.7 (May 10 and January 17) correspondingly.

29 Arch.Gaetani V., reg.2, p. 34v.

30 Arch.Barbarigo Z., reg.5, p. 34v.

31 Arch.Gavalla Z., reg.8, p. 44v (27 September 1722).

32 Arch.Gaetani V., reg.7, p. 42.

33 Arch.Barbarigo Z., reg.6, p. 195.

34 Arch.Zambelli Z., reg.1, p. 112 (he buys his partner's share on March 14, 1739, an act registered in the margin of the initial contract).

35 Ibid., p. 112.

and a smaller one later when sharing the vineyard[36]. In 1724, in a permanent lease of land, he acts not only as representative of the landholder, who is absent, but also as a guarantor of the tenant in case the landholder does not ratify the contract on his return[37]. In 1720, he prefers to compromise so as to avoid the expenses of a juridicial adventure resulting from the following difference: Malakasis' father had bought a field and had planted in it a vineyard in Frini (a village close to the city, in the north of island). However, the bride of the seller (his son's wife) buys it off, so that the buyer-undertaker of the plantation is obliged to accept the payment of ten *reali* that his deceased father had paid for this field and to accept the sharing with the family of the ex-seller, as if it were a sharecropping vineyard for a definite period of time and as if the tenant had given an interest free loan to the landholder[38]. In 1724, Nikolas Malakasis agreed to an agrarian partnership with Zoulinos on a sharecropping vineyard[39]. In an earlier contract in 1711, he participates as tenant in a convention of a sharecropping vineyard anticipating sharing at the end of seven years. However, in 1729, he is forced to appear in court, because the landholder refuses to ratify the sharing that had taken place in 1718. Despite the favourable for him decision of the court, he is obliged to reconcile when the landholder, *sior* Gallos, appealed in front of the *Provedditore da Mare*, by exchanging the shares that they had received at the expiration of the convention and the sharing of the vineyard, and by also undertaking also judicial expenses[40]. In this case, the sharing took place seven years after vine planting (1718), but the heir of the landholder contests the sharing ten years later (1729), after a period during which the tenant undertaking the plantation had obviously assiduously worked and improved his own share. It is clear that the tenants in question had to face a host of obstacles resulting from non economic mechanisms. However, driven by an entrepreneurial spirit, they expanded their activities in various sectors of the economy, they strove to enhance their financial position by taking part in land.

In 1723, another member of the Malakasis' family, Dimoulas the so-called protogeros from Frini contracts as tenant a sharecropping vineyard, anticipating sharing the soil together with the vines at the end of seven years, with the obligation to give as *charisma* a quantity of wheat (of seven *tetartia*). Interestingly, in 1730, as noted on the margin of the contract, he resigns from his rights in favour of the landholder, receiving from him 9.5 *reali* for the expenditure and work done during planting, accepting the opinion of two experts *praktikoi* elected by both the contractors in a private act[41].

---

36 Arch.Gaetani V., reg.1, p. 7v.
37 Arch.Barbarigo Z., reg.7, p. 9v.
38 Arch.Gavalla Z., reg. 5, p. 43v.
39 Arch. Barbarigo Z., reg. 6, p. 195.
40 Arch. Barbarigo Z., reg. 8, p. 47v.
41 Arch. Gavalla Z., reg. 9, p. 32v.

The social mobility of people like these is also reflected in the fluidity of titles by which they are called in the documents, *kyr*, *miser* or *sior*. This reinforcement of the middle class strata will also lead to the progressive enlargement of the City Council of the island, extending and at the same time differentiating the order of *cittadini* that participate in it[42].

In conclusion, the behaviour and mobility we have noticed not only relate to the tendencies prevalent in the middle social strata, but also to those observed in the upper ones. Part of the leukadian land owning elite tries to take advantage of the opportunities offered by the developing world market demonstrating entrepreneurial spirit, while members of the middle class manage to play a dynamic role and profit from the inertia of the conservative elite. It is them that activate various mechanisms, such as introducing extra workforce in the family (Argyrou, 2006; 2006-2007), creating brotherhoods (Argyrou, 2011) or engaging in partnerships[43]. Finally, it is worth noticing that though the foreigners initially played a leading part in all sectors of life, hereafter the locals took the initiative[44].

Bibliography

The titles of Greek bibliography have been translated in English and placed in brackets.

ALVANAS, Freiderikos (1894), *About the corfiote itles of nobility and the timars*, Corfu, 'Ermis', N. Petsali, 1894.

ANOYIATIS-PELE, Dimitris & PRONTZAS, Evangelos, (2002), *Corfu in 1830-1832: between feudality and colonization*, University Studio Press, Thessaloniki.

ANDREADIS, Andreas (1914), *The Financial Administration of Eptanese under the Venetians*, Athens.

ARGYROU, Eustathia (1995), *Les baux ruraux dans l' île ionienne de Leucade au XVIIIe siècle*, 1-2, doctoral thesis, University of Paris I.

ARGYROU, Eustathia (1996), 'Agrarian relations in Lefkada in the 18th c.', *Acts of the 4th Congress of the eptanisian civilization, (Sept. 8-12, 1993)*, Etairia Lefkadikon Meleton, Athens, p. 301-315.

ARGYROU, Eustathia (2003), 'Les baux ruraux dans une île ionienne. L' exemple de Leucade au XVIIIe siècle', in Gerard BÉAUR, Mathieu ARNOUX & Anne VARET-

42 The constitutional chartes *Privilegi della Comunita di Santa Maura* that led to the creation of the City Counsil were granted to the island after 1684, the date of its annexation to Venice. Cf. MACHAIRAS, 1951, p. 38-53, 117-126.

43 We must thank Mrs Dimitra Trikka for the information she gave us from her unfinished thesis concerning *The Companies of Lefcada in the 18th c.*

44 A notable example of this social evolution is Georgios Zambelis, a well established notary presented by ARGYROU, 2010.

Vitu (eds), *Exploiter la terre. Les contrats agraires de l'Antiquité à nos jours, Rennes-Presses Universitaires de Rennes*, p. 155-165.

Argyrou, Eustathia (2004), 'The time dimension in concept-linguistic categories in the Ionian Islands in the 18th c. during the Venetian domination: the case of Lefkada', *Acts of the 7th Panionion Congress (Lefkada, May 26-30, 2002)*, Etairia Lefkadikon Meleton, II, Athens, p. 595-607.

Argyrou, Eustathia (2005), 'The agrarian relations in Lefkada after the union of the Ionian islands with Greece', *Acts of scientific Congress: The union of the Ionian islands with Greece, 1864-2004*, I, Greek Parliament and Academy of Greece, Athens, p. 609-621.

Argyrou, Eustathia (2006), 'Family reinforcement mechanisms: Mechanisms of family reinforcement with male working force', *Istorika*, 23, Athens, Melissa, p. 281-314.

Argyrou, Eustathia (2006-2007), 'Systems of human workforce introduction in the families of Lefkada in the 18th c.', *Mnimon*, vol. 28, Athens, p. 49-90.

Argyrou, Eustathia (2010), 'Georgios Zambellis in the 18th c.; Nikos Katiforis in the 20th.The use of language and the ideological orientation of two Leukadians exercising legal professional activities', *Actes of the XIV Symposion The inconspicious people of Lefkada*, Athens.

Argyrou, Eustathia (2011), 'Fraternities in the notarial acts of temporary and renewing character', *Actes of the XVe Symposion Routes and sidewalks of the local history, 19th-20th of August 2010*, Athens.

Argyrou, Eustathia (2014), 'The land owning elite in Lefkada in the 18th c.', *Acts of the 9th Panionion Congress*, Paxi (May 26-30, 2010), Etairia Paxinon Meleton, p. 249-268.

Argyrou, Eustathia & Katiforis, Konstantinos (2009), 'The legal terminoly of the agrarian relations in the Ionian islands in the 18th c.: the case of Lefkada', *Acts of the 8th International Panionion Congress (Kythira, May 21-25, 2006)*, Etairia Kythiraikon Meleton, Kythira, p. 437-448.

Arnoux, Mathieu, Béaur, Gérard & Varet-Vitu, Anne (dir.) (2003), *Les contrats agraires de l'Antiquité à nos jours, Actes du colloque de Caen (10-13 septembre 1997)*, Presses Universitaires de Rennes Association d' Histoire des Sociétés Rurales, Rennes, p. 155-165.

Aroni-Tsichli, Kaiti (2005), 'The agrarian issue in Corfu after the union of the Ionian Islands with Greece through contemporary pamphlets', *Acts of scientific Congress: The union of the Ionian islands with Greece, 1864-2004*, I, Greek Parliament and Academy of Greece, Athens.

Asdracha, Aikaterini & Asdrachas, Spyros (1985), 'In feudal Corfu: from parrechi to vassalli angararii', *Istorika* 2 (May 1985), Melissa, Athens, p. 77-95.

Asdrachas, Spyros. (1983), *Historical issues*, Themelio, Athens.

Asdrachas, Spyros (1985), 'Feudal rent and land rent in Corfu under the venetian rule', *Istorika* 2 (Dec.1985), Melissa, Athens, p. 371-386.

Chortis, Angelos (1992), *A Contribution to the Economic History of Lefkada, 1684-1774*, (landproperty, agriculture, livestock farming, fishery, tax system, commerce and shipping), doctoral thesis, Athens.

KARAPIDAKIS, Nikos (1985), 'The corfiot nobility in the beginning of the 17th c.', *Istorika* 3 (May 1985), Melissa, Athens, p. 95-124.

KARAPIDAKIS, Nikos (1992), *Civis fidelis. L' avénement et l' affirmation de la cittoy-enneté corfiote (XVIe-XVIIe s.)*, Frankfurt.

KOLOVOS, Ilias. (ed.) (2013), *Ottoman sources concerning the history of contemporary Lefkas*, Crete University Press.

KREMMYDAS, Vassilis (2005), '"The living monuments of the Middle Age" and the "sacred rights of property": the land issue in Corfu and the discussions in the Parliament', *Acts of scientific Congress: The union of the Ionian islands with Greece, 1864-2004*, I, Greek Parliament and Academy of Greece, Athens, p. 623-633.

KOUNIAKIS, Panagiotis (1928), *The Island of Lefkas from Antiquity until Nowadays*, I.

LAZARI, Sevasti (2011), 'Meganissi: before and after Chiotes', *Actes of the XVe Symposion Routes and sidewalks of the local history, 19th-20th of August 2010*, Lefkada.

MACHAIRAS, K. (1951), *Lefcada under the Venitiens (1684-1797)*, Athens.

MICHAILARIS, Panagiotis (1996), 'Feudal registrations in Lefkada', *Acts of the 4th Congress of the Eptanisian civilization*, Lefkada (Sept. 8-12, 1993), Etairia Lefkadikon Meleton, Athens, p. 119-129.

PAPADOPOLI-STAVROU, Sprydon (1992), *The Ionian Nobility in Lefkas*, Athens.

PANTAZOPOULOS, Nikolaos (1969), 'The timariot system and sharecropping farming in the Ionian Islands during the venetian domination', *Acts of the 3rd Ionian Congress, 23-29 of September 1965*, II, Athens.

POLYLAS, Michail (1864), *About the timariot land in Corfu*, Corfu.

POLYLAS, Michail (1868), *Some remarks on the corfiot syngratia and Kaniskevsi*, Athina, Athens.

RODOLAKIS, Georgios (2004), 'The formation of legal terminology in the agrarian relations', *Acts of the 7th Panionion Congress (Lefkada, May 26-30, 2002)*, I, Etairia Lefkadikon Meleton, Athens, p. 379-393.

RONTOYIANNIS, Panos (1980), *History of the island Lefkas*, Athens, Etairia Lefkadikon Meleton.

SVORONOS, Nikos (1940), *Schiotti refugies in Lefkada*, K.I. Amanton Special Issue, Athens, 198-202.

TYPALDOS-ALFONSATOS, Ioannis (1864), *Feudal system and agriculture in the Ionian Islands*, Athens.

VLANDIS, Andreas (1902), *Lefkas under the Frankish, Ottoman and Venetian rule (1204-1797)*, Lefkada.